Recent Innovations in Information Systems Technology

Recent Innovations in Information Systems Technology

Edited by Max Jackson

CLANRYE
INTERNATIONAL
www.clanryeinternational.com

Clanrye International,
750 Third Avenue, 9th Floor,
New York, NY 10017, USA

ISBN: 978-1-63240-922-5

Cataloging-in-Publication Data

Recent innovations in information systems technology / edited by Max Jackson.
    p. cm.
Includes bibliographical references and index.
ISBN 978-1-63240-922-5
1. Information technology. 2. Information storage and retrieval systems. 3. Cybernetics.
4. Electronic data processing. I. Jackson, Max.
T58.5 .R43 2020
004--dc23

For information on all Clanrye International publications
visit our website at www.clanryeinternational.com

Contents

Preface

A sociotechnical, formal and organizational system that is designed to collect, process, distribute and store information is called an information system. It refers to the information and communication technology (ICT) that an organization uses. Information technologies enable the performance of complex tasks such as handling large data and information, controlling several simultaneous processes and performing complex calculations. An information system aims to manage operations and aid in decision-making. Data, software, hardware, people, procedures and feedback are the components that constitute an information system. Office information systems, decision support systems, learning management systems, transaction processing systems, knowledge management systems and database management systems are some of the different types of information systems. This book contains some path-breaking studies in the field of information systems technology. The ever-growing need of advanced technology is the reason that has fueled the research in this area in recent times. This book aims to equip students and experts with the advanced topics and upcoming concepts in this area.

Various studies have approached the subject by analyzing it with a single perspective, but the present book provides diverse methodologies and techniques to address this field. This book contains theories and applications needed for understanding the subject from different perspectives. The aim is to keep the readers informed about the progresses in the field; therefore, the contributions were carefully examined to compile novel researches by specialists from across the globe.

Indeed, the job of the editor is the most crucial and challenging in compiling all chapters into a single book. In the end, I would extend my sincere thanks to the chapter authors for their profound work. I am also thankful for the support provided by my family and colleagues during the compilation of this book.

Editor

Gait Speed Measurement for Elderly Patients with Risk of Frailty

Xavier Ferre,[1,2] **Elena Villalba-Mora,**[1] **Maria-Angeles Caballero-Mora,**[3] **Alberto Sanchez,**[1] **Williams Aguilera,**[1] **Nuria Garcia-Grossocordon,**[3] **Laura Nuñez-Jimenez,**[3] **Leocadio Rodríguez-Mañas,**[3] **Qin Liu,**[2] **and Francisco del Pozo-Guerrero**[1,4]

[1]*Center for Biomedical Technology, Universidad Politécnica de Madrid, Madrid, Spain*
[2]*School of Software Engineering, Tongji University, Shanghai, China*
[3]*Servicio de Geriatría, Hospital Universitario de Getafe, Getafe, Madrid, Spain*
[4]*Biomedical Research Networking Center in Bioengineering Biomaterials and Nanomedicine (CIBER-BBN), Madrid, Spain*

Correspondence should be addressed to Xavier Ferre; xavier.ferre@ctb.upm.es

Academic Editor: Pino Caballero-Gil

The ageing of the population poses a threat to both public and private health and social systems. In the last 50 years, life expectancy has increased by an average of 20 years, and by the year 2050, life expectancy will exceed 90 years of age. However, quality of life in the last years of life is not guaranteed due to conditions such as functional decline and frailty, ultimately progressing to disability. Thus, the detection of such a condition in time is of utmost importance. This paper presents an ultrasonic sensor-based gait speed measurement device controlled via a mobile interface, which permits patients to self-assess physical performance. The system was developed and validated in an iterative process involving a total of 28 subjects (21 in the first round and 7 in the second one). After first evaluation at Hospital Universitario de Getafe, some technical problems arose whereas usability testing was well evaluated. The second version addressing the identified issues was technically validated at university premises with good and promising results. Future work envisages deployment of the system developed at subjects' homes to be remotely and unobtrusively monitored.

1. Introduction

According to the WHO (World Health Organization), in the last 50 years, life expectancy has increased by an average of 20 years, and if it continues increasing, by the year 2050, life expectancy will surpass 90 years of age [1]. Thus, elderly associated conditions and illnesses are more common today than they were in the past. For these reasons, major efforts are being undertaken investigating and analyzing the effects of aging, in conditions such as frailty, their impact on the cognitive and physical functions, and how to prevent these to improve the quality and duration of life. Frailty is defined as a state of increased vulnerability to adverse outcomes due to a reduction in the ability to respond to stressors [2]. The trajectory of frailty is usually characterized by a progression of functional decline that culminates in dependency and disability [2, 3].

The early detection of impeding disease is complex, and a clear algorithm and clinical-friendly screening tools for detection of frailty and/or disability are lacking. Living longer does not necessarily equate to healthy living. Development of early detection tools will permit intervention to prevent or delay the onset of frailty, thus preventing further disability.

Small changes in various health-related metrics could indicate the existence of an underlying condition in the patient. Such a condition might not present with visible symptoms until much later, when it is too late to take preventive measures and very costly to intervene, resulting in lengthy hospital stays and a higher risk for permanent institutionalization. Metrics such as the gait speed are used to measure a person's frailty level [4–6].

Gait speed deterioration is one of the most important indicators of decay in functional ability, with the risk of developing frailty, and later disability [7]. Early detection of any functional decay is critical to improve the quality of life of elderly people and reduce their level of dependency.

Gait speed is typically measured by health professionals in hospital or daycare settings, by manually measuring the time the patient takes to walk between two stripes situated in the floor at different distances, depending on the tool used. In the case of the classical SPPB (short physical performance battery) test [8], the distance is 4 meters, but for Fried's criteria, this distance is 4.3 meters [2]. Healthcare professionals use a manual chronometer, which has a risk of inaccuracy and discrepancies between different professionals and different sets of measurements (inter- and intraobserver variability). Additionally, patients may spend several months without getting their gait speed measured, possibly worsening their functional condition to an irreversible state before any health professional can intervene.

This paper presents the design, construction, and validation of an ultrasonic sensor-based gait speed measurement device controlled via a mobile interface, which aims to empower patients in the unsupervised self-assessment of physical performance in both home and hospital settings and to make the measurement more reliable for health professionals.

Next section introduces related work in the subject. Section 3 presents the first version of the proposed device and its clinical evaluation in a hospital environment. Section 4 presents the modified version of the device and the technical validation of this second version. Finally, section 5 presents the conclusions gathered.

2. Related Work

Research on systems for gathering health-related metrics, and for measuring gait speed, can be divided into wearable- and non-wearable-based devices and sensor networks.

2.1. Wearable Devices. Most of the works related to monitoring and sensorization of medical analysis for elderly patients are based on the usage of wearable devices which gather the data and sometimes even perform simple measures. For example, Tirosh et al. proposed a sensorized sock equipped with pressure sensors to measure the variables for the gait test [9]. Adelsberger et al. proposed equipping a patient with inertial sensors to obtain measures for the gait analysis as well and send these data wirelessly via Bluetooth to a laptop computer for further analysis [10]. In the same line, there are many proposals that make use of different wearable sensors for data collection, such as the one from Morris and Paradiso [11] that advocates integrating the sensors to the patient's insoles and the one from Atallah et al. [12] that proposes to measure variables through a series of accelerometers placed on the patient's ear, among others.

Alternatively, Miura et al. proposed to use a mobile phone hung around the neck and fitted inside the user's jacket to measure walking characteristics, such as walking distance, time taken, speed, balance functions, body sways, and the number of steps taken. However, its accuracy for gait speed is too low for the SPPB test [13].

Finally, ultrasound sensors have been used to estimate the gait speed of subjects embedded with wearable devices; Weir and Childress proposed a device that combines ultrasound pulses and infrared technology to determine the real-time position of a user with respect to a base unit. Gait speed profile analysis provides parameters such as the cadence, step length, or step time variation [14].

The main shortcoming of the usage of these wearable devices that need to be attached to the patient in some way, is their intrusiveness. They may alter the conditions in which the analysis is performed, affecting users' behavior, and in some cases, they could be incompatible with some users' conditions. For example, some patients use orthopedic insoles on a daily basis, which makes it impossible to introduce a second insole to measure walking variables. The same issue can occur with socks or shoe-coupled devices as well as other nonwearable devices.

Some proposals use diverse ambient sensors for gathering vital variables. One of the most-used devices for this purpose is the Kinect®, developed by Microsoft, which groups a series of cameras and infrared sensors, allowing it to detect depth, record videos, and analyze movements and posture, among other features. Several research papers are based on this device, such as [15, 16], taking advantage of its resources to record the measures and then to model a series of significant parameters, such as longitude of the stride, walking speed, and walking direction, among other measures. These proposals are designed to work in the patient's home and collect all possible data for further analysis, obtaining extrainformation through modeling that could be important for the health professional. Kinect-based systems may raise privacy concerns, since it is composed of a camera recording users.

Other studies, like [17, 18], propose sensorized mats, based on a pressure sensor matrix, for obtaining these variables. These solutions are mostly restricted to use inside a health facility, operated by health professionals in a controlled environment. They are too costly and too difficult to calibrate for use in a home setting.

When considering in-house monitoring systems, there is an added difficulty in the analysis and evaluation of data because the measured events occur without monitoring, as opposed to the controlled environment of a medical office. When the patient is at home, there is no easy way of detecting when a walk begins and when it ends, if there are external factors affecting the speed and direction of the walk (e.g., if the patient is carrying something) or if there is some other variable affecting the measurement. Stone and Skubic minimize the "noise" introduced by these factors through the application of decision models, algorithms, and the gait variables to identify "valid" walks [16]. Van Den Broeck et al. proposed in their investigation a formula, using global coherence field (GCF), to estimate and remove the possible effects of the aforementioned noise [19].

2.2. Sensor Networks. Some research efforts have been focusing on behavioral monitoring, such as how to use sensor networks to help in the early detection of medical problems and to monitor adherence to doctors' recommendations regarding lifestyle and medication intake for chronic illness [20].

The University of Rochester built a smart medical home in their Center for Future Health, filled with different types of sensors, functioning as a laboratory, to test and develop various gadgets, sensors, and applications, that could be used as part of a health-integrated system [21]. Similarly, the Aware

Home in Georgia Tech, is a 3-storey, 5040 square feet facility designed to facilitate research in three main areas: health, entertainment, and sustainability, investigating how new technologies can impact the lives of people at home [22].

Implementing home sensors could give the elderly population the perfect balance between independence and proper monitoring. For example, Zouba et al. proposed the implementation of multiple sensors attached to furniture at home, combined with cameras for video analysis to monitor the behavior of elderly people performing everyday activities, such as cooking meals and eating [23]. Wood et al. took behavioral monitoring a step further by combining it with assisted living. They took data gathered from multiple heterogeneous sensors and fed them into a backend layer that analyzes and combines the data in order to produce decisions that could influence other devices, such as a power manager [24]. This system was thought to be extensible with the ability to add more sensors and user interfaces, which is a similar objective to the one proposed in this work. As with many other proposed solutions, it uses a proprietary query software language called SensQ, developed solely for this system which makes it harder for other consumers to adopt it. It also has a closed architecture which makes it complicated to integrate 3rd party external developments. These two limitations usually result in increased deployment costs and the risk of obsolescence.

3. UltraGaitSpeed System v1.0

For the measurement of the gait speed in a home setting, we have designed a lightweight and low-cost ultrasonic sensor-based system called UltraGaitSpeed. The sensor device connects via Bluetooth with an Android mobile phone that logs the measured data and allows the user to control the system. When an Internet connection is available, the data are sent to a Cloud server.

Our approach to gait speed measurement aims to offer a lightweight and unobtrusive solution that liberates the user from wearing any kind of gadgets and takes advantage of a very powerful device (modern smartphones) that has a tremendous processing power and good quality/price ratio.

A strip of light sensors with an Arduino board can be easily deployed in a house and can provide the necessary information to monitor decay in gait speed, possibly indicating more serious health problems that require immediate assistance. The gathered information is uploaded to a server and securely connected to the HIS (hospital information system), so physicians can monitor patient evolution, and alarms can be raised in a clinical setting when the condition of a patient rapidly deteriorates.

3.1. System Design. We chose HC-SR04 ultrasonic sensors for their lightweight and low-cost characteristics. This sensor uses sonar, sending a signal from one side and receiving it on the other, to measure the distance of an object in front of it by subtracting the time between both signals. This means that we can detect when an object moves in front of the sensor by tracking the distance variations between measures. Since these sensors emit an ultrasonic sound wave and

sound waves dissipate in a cone-shaped way, we need to perform some tests with the sensors to make a decision about the number of sensors and to establish a minimum distance between sensors to avoid interference (Figure 1).

After extensive testing, we determined that 35 centimeters is the minimum distance between sensors for them to work without interference and that 5 sensors provided enough accuracy since additional sensors did not improve the measurements (Figure 2).

The 5 sensors are connected to an Arduino UNO board and set up with 1-meter separation between them along a flexible EVA foam strip. The resulting 4-meter strip can serve to reproduce the SPPB gait speed test used by health professionals.

In order to cover the sensors and protect the cables, cases were printed in 3D for every sensor and its connections (Figure 3). This provides the required robustness for a solution to be installed in a home setting.

The device runs a simple software that loops through the connected sensors, sends a signal, and listens for the response, which is stored in a local variable. After looping through all the sensors, it sends via Bluetooth the data gathered from the sensors in JSON format, with the number of milliseconds relative to the system start as a timestamp.

The mobile application allows the user to calibrate the sensors, start the measurement, and get data results on the screen. It also stores measurements in an internal log, which is uploaded to a server when an Internet connection is available.

This first version of the UltraGaitSpeed system works according to the flowchart shown in Figure 4. The application guides the user in all the steps required for system operation, namely, Bluetooth enabling, sensor calibration, step measurement, and final result display.

Bluetooth connection is enabled in two steps. First, the application checks the activation of Bluetooth in the device and then connects with the Arduino Board. Next, the sensor calibration starts, using a series of iterations to make sure that stable distances are measured by each sensor. These distances are the baseline for the later measurements. If there is movement in front of any sensor, the calibration will fail. If there is a failure in any of these steps, the application displays an error message to the user.

When calibration finishes, the system starts measuring gait speed. Measurement is achieved by means of detection events. When a user is detected by a sensor, the distance measured deviates from the sensor baseline measure and a timestamp is logged. Finally, when every sensor has detected the patient, the passing time at each sensor and the overall time are calculated by subtraction.

By pressing the Restart button on the screen, the process can start again for a new measurement.

3.2. Evaluation. Even if our system is meant to be used by patients and informal caregivers in an extrahospital setting, we need to validate that the system gathers gait speed measurements as reliably as the manual measurement by health professionals in medical facilities.

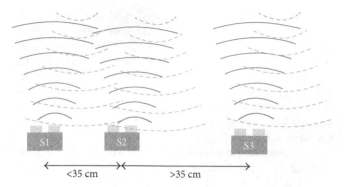

FIGURE 1: Minimum distance between sensors.

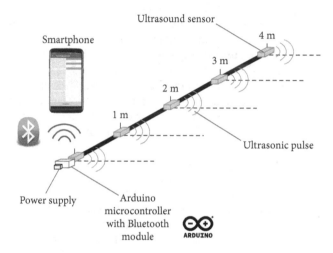

FIGURE 2: Equidistant sensor placement in the strip.

FIGURE 3: 3D printed case for covering sensors and connections.

For that purpose, we carried out an experiment with older patients attending the Day Hospital in the Geriatric Service at the Hospital Universitario de Getafe (HUG). The objective is to validate the accuracy and feasibility of the proposed measurement solution as compared to the current manual practice.

3.2.1. Experiment Design.

Our hypothesis is that the usage of the proposed ultrasound sensor-based solution allows the conduction, in a precise way, of the SPPB gait analysis, with a difference threshold of ±0.5 seconds compared to the manual measures, which is the current practice in Geriatric Service at HUG.

The inclusion criteria for the patients to take part in the experiment were as follows:

(i) Older than 70 years

(ii) Patient of the Geriatric Service at HUG.

The exclusion criteria were as follows:

(i) Cognitive impairment: minimental test result lower than 20

(ii) High degree of disability: Barthel index lower than 60.

The patients were randomly selected from those that come to the Day Hospital, with at least 2 patients selected in each one of the following groups:

(i) Patients that do not need any technical help for walking

(ii) Patients that need a cane for walking

(iii) Patients that need a walker for walking.

Two separate tests were conducted with each patient. First, the gait test as described in point 2 of the SPPB analysis was used to measure the speed of the walk, having the patient standing right on the start line of the 4-meter strip, including acceleration speed (static start). Second, an ordinary gait test was performed, having the patient start a meter before the starting line (dynamic start) in order to exclude acceleration from the measure.

The experiment was designed to simultaneously measure using both the current manual method and the proposed system. The manual method is done with the patient walking between two green lines while the health professionals measure with a stopwatch. For each of the tests, three measurements were taken in total: two separate manual measures and one with the proposed solution, all of them done by health professionals experienced in measuring gait speed. None of the health professionals involved in taking the measures could see the measures taken by the others.

Forms for the manual measure results were prepared as well as an SUS (System Usability Scale) [25] satisfaction questionnaire and an impressions questionnaire to gather information about the system usability from the health professional using our proposed system in the experiment.

The current protocol for gait speed measurement for the SPPB test was followed: measuring two walks for each patient and taking as valid the best of both measures.

The Ethical Committee of the University Hospital of Getafe approved the protocol.

3.2.2. Experiment Execution.

On the day of the experiment, we set up the data gathering device and the mobile application to conduct the tests. The setting up of the gathering device was a very simple procedure, taking less than 5 minutes.

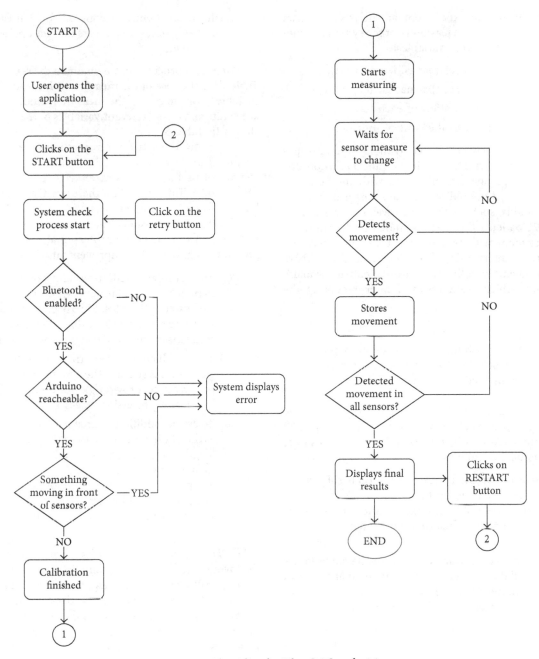

FIGURE 4: Algorithm for UltraGaitSpeed v1.0.

Three health professionals volunteered to participate in the experiment as data gatherers, among whom we randomly distributed the roles for manual collection and usage of the application. After selecting the professionals, we gave them a brief explanation of the experiment and their tasks and provided them with the individual data collection forms. A mobile device that had the application already installed was provided to the health professional for taking measurements. The experiment was conducted as follows:

(1) After selecting those patients that met the inclusion criteria and that expressed willingness to participate (by signing the informed consent), the health professional proceeded to explain what the test consisted of.

(2) The subjects were asked to carry out the two tests (the static and dynamic start). Their gait speed was measured by health professionals. One professional measured gait speed automatically with the proposed system, and the two other professionals performed the test manually using the current method (stopwatch). Manual results were collected in an ad hoc paper form.

(3) After finishing with all the patients of the study, we gathered the paper forms from the health professionals and asked the one that was using the application to complete the satisfaction and impressions questionnaires.

After carrying out the experiment, an analysis of the data was conducted to ensure the feasibility of the system through the analysis of the following variables:

(i) Number of measures that ended correctly

(ii) Number of measures that had to be repeated

(iii) Time for the preparation of each test

(iv) Deviation related to the control measure.

The experiment was conducted with 21 voluntary patients that complied with the inclusion and exclusion criteria. Their average age was 81 years, with the youngest patient being 71 and the oldest 90. The number of patients with technical aids, such as canes and walkers, was 7 from the total of 21 patients that were included in the study.

The experiment with patients went smoothly with no need for further intervention from the researchers. There were slight problems with the calibration in patients who use walking canes, which were resolved after rebooting the system.

3.2.3. Results.

After finishing the experiment, we proceeded with the extraction of data gathered from the forms and the questionnaires completed by the health professional using the application.

First, we merged the data gathered into one single spreadsheet, grouped by a type of measure (stopwatch 1 and 2 and application). After this, a series of data treatments were applied to the data as follows:

(1) We selected as final measure for each subject the lower measure between the two that were taken for each one of the tests (the dynamic and static start), as is usually done by health professionals when performing this test.

(2) With the final measure for each of the subjects, we calculated the average between the manual measures taken with the stopwatch to compare those measures with the ones obtained from the application.

(3) We then proceeded to calculate the difference module of the measures obtained with the manual procedure, and those from the application, and all the combinations between them:

(a) Between manual measure 1 and manual measure 2
(b) Between the average of the manual measures and the application
(c) Between manual measure 1 and the application
(d) Between manual measure 2 and the application.

(4) Having these measures, we proceeded to calculate statistical variables of the differences. These are relevant in order to measure the degree to which the application was able to get correct measures in the experiment. The variables obtained were the mean, the median, the mode, and the truncated mean.

(5) We decided to calculate the truncated mean of the differences with a threshold of 10%. This allowed us to remove 10% of outliers from the calculation of

the mean (which accounted for 2 measures), thus omitting occasional errors that the application might have had.

After data processing, we obtained the results detailed in Table 1 for the case of the measure with no acceleration and in Table 2 for the case of the measure including the patient's acceleration. Overall relevant variables of the experiment are shown in Table 3.

Regarding the satisfaction questionnaire, the responses produced an SUS score of 72.5, which is slightly over the average of usability scores taken as a reference for an SUS score of 68.5. This shows that there is satisfaction in the user but not to an exceptional level.

The open impressions questionnaire shows a favorable perception from the health professional, and it offers several relevant suggestions for improvement:

(i) To optimize calibration and to not require the patient to wait, standing without movement while the system calibrates. Elderly patients have difficulty standing for some time, since they get easily tired. In some cases, there is a risk that they lose their balance

(ii) To avoid having to perform a calibration every time, a measure is started. The system could calibrate only the first time, providing a button to recalibrate when the health professional sees fit

(iii) To extract additional variables from the sensors, such as direction of the walk, variability of the speed, stride length, step length, and others. For the implementation of this suggestion, we will need to review and perform a deeper analysis of the gathered data, in order to determine which of these proposed new variables can be obtained from the current sensors.

3.2.4. Discussion.

These results show the feasibility of deploying our proposed system in a clinical setting and having health professionals use it. But the reliability of the measures falls below the threshold established of a maximum difference of 0.50 seconds between the manual measure and the automatic measure. Considering that all the measures fall in the interval 2.15–9.47 seconds, average differences of 0.64 or 0.67 are too high.

Further detailed study of the results with health professionals at HUG unveiled that the algorithm used in UltraGaitSpeed v1.0 for measuring gait speed did not exactly comply with the measuring criteria used in classical gait speed tests, as routinely performed at HUG. Both for the static and dynamic start gait speed tests, the event triggering the start and finish of measuring is the moment when the last heel of the subject reaches the mark on the floor, while the algorithm implemented in v1.0 of our solution starts measuring when the sensor detects the first foot. This is why the presence of walking aids produced some errors.

Regarding calibration, the system failed several times for the static start gait speed tests. In this case, the subject stands right in front on the starting line, with the tip of his foot on it, and waits for the command to go. Even the smallest variation in the distance detected at the starting line, due to subjects'

TABLE 1: Experiment results for the dynamic start measure with UltraGaitSpeed v1.0.

	Differences (seconds)			
	Stopwatch 1 and stopwatch 2	Stopwatch avg. and UltraGaitSpeed v1.0	Stopwatch 1 and UltraGaitSpeed v1.0	Stopwatch 2 and UltraGaitSpeed v1.0
Mean	0.13	0.66	0.66	0.67
Median	0.06	0.71	0.70	0.63
Mode	0.03	No mode present	0.75	1.13
Truncated mean (10%)	0.10	0.62	0.62	0.62
Average relative error with respect to manual watch average time (%)	2.8%	13.6%	13.7%	14.0%
Standard deviation	0.13	0.45	0.42	0.50

TABLE 2: Experiment results for the static start measure with UltraGaitSpeed v1.0.

	Differences (seconds)			
	Stopwatch 1 and stopwatch 2	Stopwatch avg. and UltraGaitSpeed v1.0	Stopwatch 1 and UltraGaitSpeed v1.0	Stop watch 2 and UltraGaitSpeed v1.0
Mean	0.20	0.64	0.64	0.64
Median	0.13	0.45	0.38	0.49
Mode	0.28	No mode present	0.13	0.47
Truncated mean (10%)	0.16	0.55	0.53	0.56
Average relative error with respect to manual watch average time (%)	3.7%	11.9%	11,9%	11.9%
Standard deviation	0.20	0.57	0.63	0.53

or walking aids' movement, triggered the timing and produced irregular measurements.

Additionally, the system requires that the test is carried out only in one direction, while software could detect the walking direction and thus capture two measurements per patient without requiring him or her to walk back to the starting point. The patient could just turn around after the first measurement and walk in the other direction for the second measure.

4. UltraGaitSpeed v2.0

In order to overcome the main problems identified for v1.0, we designed a new algorithm (Figure 5) and a new version for the mobile app (Figure 6), the UltraGaitSpeed v2.0.

The new algorithm considers the last detection event in a sensor to be the moment to consider for user passing such a sensor (Figure 7). This better fits the moment when the patient's heel leaves the sensor detection field. This moment is used for both establishing the start and finish of the measure, mirroring the way the health professionals define the start and finish time when performing this test. Likewise, this criterion determines partial timing.

The distance between sensors is fixed and known, and the detection field angle is the same for all of them. Therefore, if we assume that the patient will walk straight, the point where the last foot abandons each detection field will be separated by the same distance as the sensors themselves.

So, with v2.0 of our device, we can measure the time spent moving from sensor A to sensor B.

TABLE 3: Variables obtained from the experiment with UltraGaitSpeed v1.0.

Variable	Result
Time for the preparation of each test	Mean of 4 minutes
Deviation related to the control measure	Mean of 0.58 seconds
Maximum time measured	9.47 seconds
Minimum time measured	2.15 seconds

Figure 5 depicts the new algorithm designed for v2.0 of our system. When one of the sensors detects the user, it is activated and waits for the field-of-view exit event, at which point the timestamp is registered. In order to make sure that the exit event was actually the last part of the body to pass (and not, e.g., just the first foot or a walking cane), the measurement for each segment of the gait speed test is not confirmed until the exit event is produced in the next sensor in the strip. (The last sensor has a timeout for confirmation, since it has no other sensor next to it.) In the case of a new detection event before confirmation in the following sensor, the sensor waits for the expected exit event and then the timestamp is reset.

This new algorithm entails the following advantages:

(1) It replicates the measuring criteria used in the classical gait speed tests carried out by professionals in clinical settings.

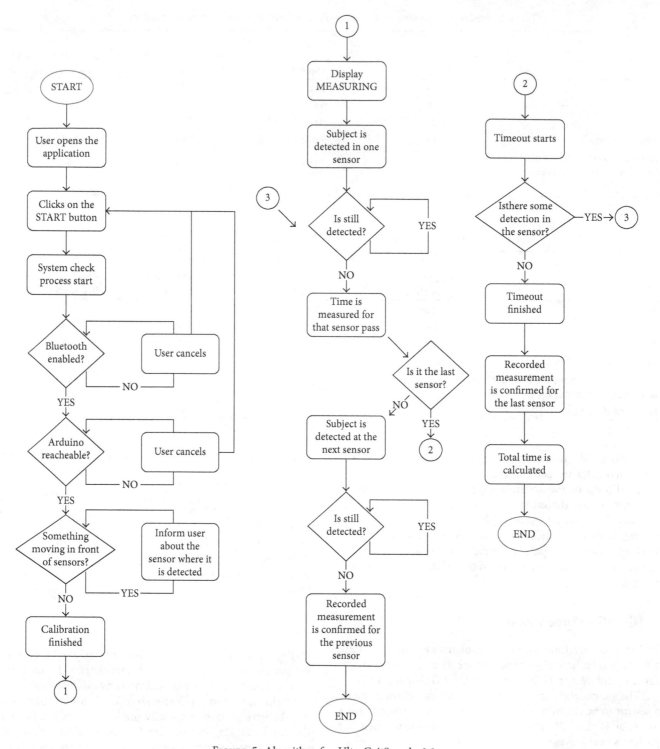

FIGURE 5: Algorithm for UltraGaitSpeed v2.0.

(2) Start time is automatically triggered when the patient leaves the first sensor, instead of requiring an action in the mobile app.

(3) Calibration does not require that the patient waits motionless just before the first sensor. It is carried out with the patient positioned behind or far away from the sensor strip, and the measuring will automatically start when the patient goes through the

first sensor. We will thus avoid errors arising from the small distance variations while patients wait for the calibration to end.

4.1. Evaluation. We have evaluated this new version of our proposal with seven users between 68 and 79 years of age, six of them with mobility problems and two requiring a cane.

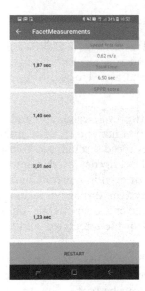

FIGURE 6: Screen capture of the mobile app for UltraGaitSpeed v2.0.

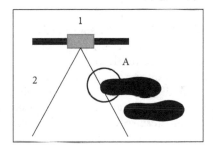

FIGURE 7: Detection moment for the user passing through a sensor.

We have deployed UltraGaitSpeed v2.0 at CTB with indications of the place for subjects to position themselves for both the dynamic and the static start tests. We have briefly explained how the system works, and how it is controlled from the mobile app to the subject, in the same way as we foresee system installers doing when the system is actually used in a home setting.

Each participant is asked to measure two walks with a static start and two more with a dynamic start, in total providing four measures to the system.

A biomedical engineer trained at HUG on the SPPB test measures manually with a stopwatch the time spent by the user between the two extremes of the sensor strip (4 meters). The measurer followed the criteria used in regular clinical practice. Timing must be recorded when the last heel of the patient passes over the line that marks the start and finish of the four-meter walk.

4.1.1. Results. The results obtained for timing were analyzed replicating the protocol of UltraGaitSpeed v1.0 evaluation but having only one stopwatch measurement as a reference for comparison.

The results obtained are presented in Tables 4 and 5.

TABLE 4: Experiment results for the static start measure with UltraGaitSpeed v2.0.

Differences (seconds) UltraGaitSpeed v2.0 and stopwatch	
Mean	0.35
Median	0.29
Mode	None
Truncated mean (10%)	0.35
Average relative error with respect to manual watch mean time (%)	7.39%
Standard deviation	0.22

TABLE 5: Experiment results for the dynamic start measure with UltraGaitSpeed v2.0.

Differences (seconds) UltraGaitSpeed v2.0 and stopwatch	
Mean	0.15
Median	0.19
Mode	None
Truncated mean (10%)	0.15
Average relative error with respect to manual watch mean time (%)	4.13%
Standard deviation	0.10

The new algorithm demonstrated a greater reliability for measurement than the one implemented in the previous version of the device. Both the absolute and relative errors between the stopwatch and UltraGaitSpeed v2.0 have been reduced. In fact, the average absolute error is smaller than the established accepted error of 0.5 seconds. Moreover, the standard deviation of the error is smaller compared with the first version, which suggests the error of this version falls in a smaller range, and therefore is more predictable.

The timing problem associated with the use of walking aids has been solved in this new version. The trials with two patients who use walking aids demonstrated the reliability of UltraGaitSpeed v2.0. The average relative error for their tests was smaller than the overall (3.95%), and the measurer did not report any incident related to this issue.

Observation of subjects while using the system and open conversation with them have provided insight about some usability problems that need to be addressed as follows:

(i) The word "measuring..." conveys the idea that the time watch is already ticking, while it actually means that the sensors have been calibrated and are already working to detect whatever passes by.

(ii) Error and warning messages, such as the one appearing when the timeout for the last sensor goes off, need to be reconsidered to speak the user's language, and some of them should not even be shown unless the app is in developer mode.

Despite the room for improvement, UltraGaitSpeed v2.0 was accepted by the users. They completed the

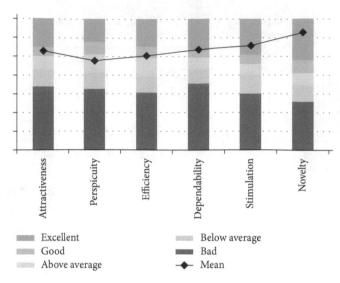

FIGURE 8: Results for UEQ.

System Usability Scale (SUS) and User Experience Questionnaire (UEQ) [26] after performing the gait speed tests, giving an average SUS score for UltraGaitSpeed v2.0 of 73.5.

Studies have demonstrated that the average SUS score is 68. Therefore, we have shown that our system is more usable than the benchmark and is in the second quartile [27].

In the case of the UEQ, we obtained excellent results in Novelty and Stimulation, good results in Attractiveness, Efficiency, and Dependability, and results above the average in Perspicuity (Figure 8).

4.1.2. Discussion. Despite the small size of the study population, results suggest that UltraGaitSpeed v2.0 may be used in unsupervised environments for evaluating the gait speed of patients, from a technical point of view.

Additionally, the new algorithm prevents one of the more recurrent errors of UltraGaitSpeed v1.0. The initial algorithm triggered incorrect start of timing when small movements of patients waiting to begin the static start test were detected as actual movement.

With these results, we confirm that the new design eliminates the error in the start of each measure, by having the measuring algorithm consider the moment when the user leaves each field of detection as the time of passing.

The validation of UltraGaitSpeed v2.0 has shown the system feasibility in its usage by the intended audience: elderly people. Participants in the validation have shown a favorable opinion of the usefulness and usability of the system, even though they suggested necessary improvements.

Further validation is necessary in the intended final environment: patients' homes. A longitudinal study is necessary to better understand how the system can be regularly used by its intended users.

5. Conclusions

We have presented two versions of UltraGaitSpeed (v1.0 and v2.0), a sensor-based system controlled through a mobile app for measuring gait speed, aimed to be used by patients themselves or their caregivers.

Through the two-cycle validation and redesign process, the proposed system has shown its usefulness to automatically measure gait speed through a low-cost and lightweight solution that can be easily deployed in any medical facility, in a daycare center, or even in a private home. As an Android app controls the system, this allows its usage in the patient's or informal caregiver's own mobile phone, thus further reducing the cost of the integrated solution.

Even if the validation has been carried out in a controlled environment with health professionals or researchers, the proposed system can be part of an ambient-assisted living network of sensors, that contributes to a better quality of life and earlier detection of deteriorating conditions that require professional medical help.

The usability level of the system needs to be improved with a new redesign-evaluation loop, where acceptability and usability issues are resolved.

The next step in our research is to validate the system in a hospital setting like the one used in the validation of the first version and a longitudinal study carried out in in-home settings. In these studies, we will inquire about the most appropriate amount of sensors and length of the strip. The aim is to reduce the strip to a length of 2 meters, facilitating its reliable usage in home environments with limited space.

The system will be extended to address other SPPB test parts and other elements from the comprehensive geriatric assessment like the chair stand test (measuring how long the patient takes to sit down in a chair and stand up again five times), involuntary loss of weight, and the items of the Linda Fried criteria of frailty. We will provide these elements either through sensor-based systems like the one presented in this paper or through an extension of the mobile app.

At a subsequent stage, the aim is to create a system based on UltraGaitSpeed that measures gait speed unobtrusively, without the need for the user to actively start the measuring. If the sensor strip can be inconspicuously installed in a corridor wall and measure gait speed every time the user passes by, it will provide much richer information without the added stress of following instructions and manipulating a mobile phone.

Acknowledgments

This research was funded by the EIT Health in the FACET (FrAilty Care and wEll funcTion) project and by funds from CIBERfes (FEDER). The authors would like to thank all the volunteers that helped them to validate their solution acting as test subjects and to thank the reviewers for their insightful comments.

References

[1] D. M. Ediev, "Life expectancy in developed countries is higher than conventionally estimated. Implications from improved measurement of human longevity," *Journal of Population Ageing*, vol. 4, no. 1–2, pp. 5–32, 2011.

[2] L. P. Fried, C. M. Tangen, J. Walston et al., "Frailty in older adults: evidence for a phenotype," *Journals of Gerontology Series A: Biological Sciences and Medical Sciences*, vol. 56, no. 3, pp. M146–M157, 2001.

[3] T. M. Gill, E. A. Gahbauer, L. Han, and H. G. Allore, "Trajectories of disability in the last year of life," *New England Journal of Medicine*, vol. 362, no. 13, pp. 1173–1180, 2010.

[4] M. Runge and G. Hunter, "Determinants of musculoskeletal frailty and the risk of falls in old age," *Journal of Musculoskeletal and Neuronal Interactions*, vol. 6, no. 2, pp. 167–173, 2006.

[5] J. M. Hausdorff, D. A. Rios, and H. K. Edelberg, "Gait variability and fall risk in community-living older adults: a 1-year prospective study," *Archives of Physical Medicine and Rehabilitation*, vol. 82, no. 8, pp. 1050–1056, 2001.

[6] J. M. Hausdorff, A. Schweiger, T. Herman, G. Yogev-Seligmann, and N. Giladi, "Dual-task decrements in gait: contributing factors among healthy older adults," *Journals of Gerontology Series A: Biological Sciences and Medical Sciences*, vol. 63, no. 12, pp. 1335–1343, 2008.

[7] E. Villalba Mora, R. Petidier-Torregrossa, C. Alonso-Bouzon, J. A. Carnicero-Carreño, and L. Rodríguez Mañas, "Early detection of Heart Failure exacerbation by telemonitoring in old people," *International Journal of Integrated Care*, vol. 15, no. 5, pp. 116972–116974, 2015.

[8] J. M. Guralnik, E. M. Simonsick, L. Ferrucci et al., "A short physical performance battery assessing lower extremity function: association with self-reported disability and prediction of mortality and nursing home admission," *Journal of Gerontology*, vol. 49, no. 2, pp. M85–M94, 1994.

[9] O. Tirosh, R. Begg, E. Passmore, and N. Knopp-Steinberg, "Wearable textile sensor sock for gait analysis," in *Proceedings of the 2013 Seventh International Conference on Sensing Technology (ICST)*, pp. 618–622, IEEE, Wellington, New Zealand, December 2013.

[10] R. Adelsberger, N. Theill, V. Schumacher, B. Arnrich, and G. Tröster, "One IMU is sufficient: a study evaluating effects of dual-tasks on gait in elderly people," in *Proceedings of the International Conference on Wireless Mobile Communication and Healthcare*, pp. 51–60, Springer, Paris, France, November 2012.

[11] S. J. Morris and J. A. Paradiso, "Shoe-integrated sensor system for wireless gait analysis and real-time feedback," in *Proceedings of the Second Joint 24th Annual Conference and the Annual Fall Meeting of the Biomedical Engineering Society EMBS/BMES Conference 2002 (Engineering in Medicine and Biology, 2002)*, vol. 3, pp. 2468–2469, IEEE, Houston, TX, USA, October 2002.

[12] L. Atallah, O. Aziz, B. Lo, and G. Z. Yang, "Detecting walking gait impairment with an ear-worn sensor," in *Sixth International Workshop on Wearable and Implantable Body Sensor Networks, 2009 (BSN 2009)*, pp. 175–180, IEEE, Berkeley, CA, USA, June 2009.

[13] T. Miura, K. I. Yabu, A. Hiyama, N. Inamura, M. Hirose, and T. Ifukube, "Smartphone-based gait measurement application for exercise and its effects on the lifestyle of senior citizens," in *Proceedings of the Human-Computer Interaction (INTERACT 2015)*, pp. 80–98, Springer, Bamberg, Germany, September 2015.

[14] R. F. Weir and D. S. Childress, "A portable, real-time, clinical gait velocity analysis system," *IEEE Transactions on Rehabilitation Engineering*, vol. 5, no. 4, pp. 310–321, 1997.

[15] M. Rantz, M. Skubic, C. Abbott, Y. Pak, E. E. Stone, and S. J. Miller, "Automated fall risk assessment and detection in the home: a preliminary investigation," in *Proceedings of the AAAI Fall Symposium: Artificial Intelligence for Gerontechnology*, Arlington, VA, USA, November 2012.

[16] E. E. Stone and M. Skubic, "Mapping Kinect-based in-home gait speed to TUG time: a methodology to facilitate clinical interpretation," in *Proceedings of the 2013 7th International Conference on Pervasive Computing Technologies for Healthcare (PervasiveHealth)*, pp. 57–64, IEEE, Venice, Italy, May 2013.

[17] A. L. McDonough, M. Batavia, F. C. Chen, S. Kwon, and J. Ziai, "The validity and reliability of the GAITRite system's measurements: a preliminary evaluation," *Archives of Physical Medicine and Rehabilitation*, vol. 82, no. 3, pp. 419–425, 2001.

[18] D. Gouwanda, N. Senanayake, M. Marasinghe et al., "Real time force sensing mat for human gait analysis," *International Journal of Mechanical and Mechatronics Engineering*, vol. 2, no. 3, pp. 349–354, 2008.

[19] B. Van Den Broeck, L. Vuegen, H. Van Hamme, M. Moonen, P. Karsmakers, and B. Vanrumste, "Footstep localization based on in-home microphone-array signals," in *Proceedings of the 12th Biennial European Conference of the Association for the Advancement of Assistive Technology in Europe (AAATE 2013)*, vol. 33, p. 90, IOS Press, Amsterdam, Netherlands, September 2013.

[20] A. Helal, D. J. Cook, and M. Schmalz, "Smart home-based health platform for behavioral monitoring and alteration of diabetes patients," *Journal of Diabetes Science and Technology*, vol. 3, no. 1, pp. 141–148, 2009.

[21] J. Marsh, "House calls," in *Rochester Review*, vol. 64, no. 3, pp. 22–26, University of Rochester, Rochester, NY, USA, 2002, https://www.rochester.edu/pr/Review/V64N3/feature2.html.

[22] Georgia Tech, *Aware Home Research Initiative*, Georgia Institute of Technology, Atlanta, Georgia, 2017, http://www.awarehome.gatech.edu.

[23] N. Zouba, F. Bremond, and M. Thonnat, "An activity monitoring system for real elderly at home: validation study," in *Proceedings of the 2010 Seventh IEEE International Conference on Advanced Video and Signal Based Surveillance (AVSS)*, pp. 278–285, IEEE, Boston, MA, USA, September 2010.

[24] A. Wood, J. Stankovic, G. Virone et al., "Context-aware wireless sensor networks for assisted living and residential monitoring," *IEEE Network*, vol. 22, no. 4, pp. 26–33, 2008.

[25] J. Brooke, "SUS-A quick and dirty usability scale," *Usability Evaluation in Industry*, vol. 189, no. 194, pp. 4–7, 1996.

[26] B. Laugwitz, T. Held, and M. Schrepp, "Construction and evaluation of a user experience questionnaire," in *Symposium of the Austrian HCI and Usability Engineering Group*, pp. 63–76, Springer, Graz, Austria, November 2008.

[27] A. Bangor, P. Kortum, and J. Miller, "Determining what individual SUS scores mean: adding an adjective rating scale," *Journal of Usability Studies*, vol. 4, no. 3, pp. 114–123, 2009.

2

Multistage Dynamic Packet Access Mechanism of Internet of Things

Yi Meng ⓘ,[1] Chen QingKui ⓘ,[1,2] and Zhang Gang[1]

[1]*School of Management, University of Shanghai for Science and Technology, Shanghai, China*
[2]*School of Optical Electrical and Computer Engineering, University of Shanghai for Science and Technology, Shanghai, China*

Correspondence should be addressed to Chen QingKui; chenqingkui@usst.edu.cn

Academic Editor: Paolo Bellavista

In the scenario of mass control commands requesting for network access, confined by the best-effort network service mode, it is easy to bring about resource competition and thus a phenomenon of access failure on major and urgent service request at the data access center for the Internet of Things. In this event, the dynamic diversification of control command is unable to access the necessary resources on a comparatively fair basis, causing low efficiency in heterogeneous resource utilization at the access center. This paper defines the problem of group request dynamic resource allocation and further converts it into the problem of 0-1 integer and linear programming and proposes a multistage dynamic packet access strategy. This strategy works first on dynamic group division on the users' mass control requests using the high ability of self-organizing feature maps and then searches for the optimized matching resources based on the frog-leaping algorithm which has a better capacity for global searching for the best resources. This paper analyzes the feasibility of this strategy and its astringency. The experimental results demonstrate that the strategy can effectively improve the success rate of access to the data center for the Internet of Things and reduce network blockage and response delay.

1. Introduction

The Data Access Center for the Internet of Things (DACIOT), serving as the core layer of Internet of Things (IoT), has already become a current research focus [1–3]. In the different applications of the smart city, such as smart healthcare [4, 5], smart home [6], intelligent transportation [7], smart logistics [8], and intelligent security [9], IoT firstly collects the mass sensing data in real time from hundreds of sensor devices in accordance with the corresponding communication protocols. Secondly, DACIOT carries out preprocessing of the sensing data by means of data cleaning, data integration, selection, and transformation. In order to support the upper application system for automatic identification, accurate positioning, intelligent tracking, and intelligent supervision of entities and processes, DACIOT integrates the perception information and coordinates communications between devices. Therefore, a universal and integrated network is generated by the fusion of human, machine, and things. In the process of such fusion of the upper IoT application system, a variety of value type and nonvalue type of data are continually transmitted by different types of sensors [10]. In this process, different kinds of control requests will be delivered to the masses of sensing devices by a great quantity of end users. From the perspective of the application architecture of IoT [11, 12], DACIOT is mainly located at the application level, which is the top level of IoT architecture [13], as shown in Figure 1.

As shown in the above figure, a large number of static or mobile sensing equipments constitute the sensing net in the form of self-organizing or multi-hop. After optimization, the data collected by sensing equipments are transmitted to information processing center via radio waves and then converged to sending net (network layer in Figure 1). The major role of DACIOT is to provide services of network access for end users (including mobiles and PCs) and coordinate that the service requests of a large number of end users can be transmitted onto the corrective sensing equipments [14] via Internet. Relatively speaking, the topology of sensing net is more vulnerable to the external environment than the topology of sending net. In terms of processing capacity of network, sending net has a stronger data processing and control ability,

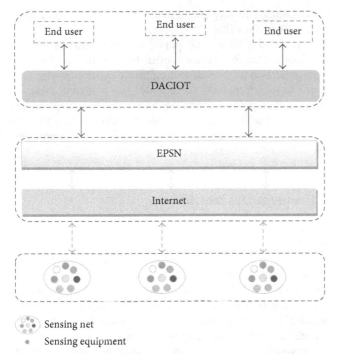

FIGURE 1: Structure of "man-machine-thing" integration of the IoT application system.

while the sensing net is only responsible for perception data collecting without the ability of intelligent data processing. Moreover, as the channel of information transmission of DACIOT, the sending net based on Internet exchanges the data from end users and sensors in real time accurately with the convergence of various wired and wireless networks. In respect of transmission of control demand, due to the features of Internet network of complicated and flexible structure and fast resource consumption when a large number of users request for access, EPSN (effective path statistic network) is constructed and deployed on the basis of the network coverage theory [15]. EPSN is a logic and virtual subnet of the Internet, and it is composed of a set of communication service agents, which contains a couple of simple functions, including packet sending, packet receiving, packet storage, and interaction. Using statistical theory, EPSN network explores the effective "gap" path which means the resources on the Internet [16]. Moreover, the primary function of EPSN lies in measuring and collecting the statistics of routing metrics on the logical link among communication service agents and constructing effective paths in real time based on the measurement and statistics result. In this significance, the network that end users request for access is transformed from an Internet network with uncontrollable parameters to a transparent EPSN network with controllable parameters. However, as the network features best-effort service [17], when mass requests from end users are accessed into the EPSN network via DACIOT, resource competition will take place and lead to the following problems: (1) the best-quality resources are taken and occupied by nonurgent requests so that urgent requests are inaccessible and cannot be transmitted onto the sensing device via the EPSN network transmission; for example, the switch control access command is blocked by ordinary access requests on the sensing device; (2) as users'

requests are dynamic and diversified, the heterogeneous resources of DACIOT may not meet the demand for high service quality; for example, when users' request commands which are used to query sensed data come to access, they require a very strict response delay and packet loss rate; and (3) when allocating resources, it is hard for DACIOT to treat the various types of service requests fairly, causing service overleaning; for example, DACIOT may allocate more resources to users who request access to humidity and temperature sensing devices while allocating less resources to users who request access to carbon dioxide sensing devices. Therefore, it is critical and urgent for DACIOT to efficiently coordinate the mass access requests from users for quality resources.

2. Related Work

In relation to the current research on DACIOT, the work in [18] provides a summary of the system structure and characteristics of the M2M communication network in a 3GPP environment; analyses the potential problems existing during the access process in terms of the physical-layer transmission, random access procedure, and wireless resource allocation; and further proposes a solution with a QoS guarantee. A method of effective user authentication and access control at a perceptive layer is proposed in [19]. This method establishes a session key based on an elliptic curve encryption mechanism and further enhances the mutual authentication process between the user and sensor node. The work in [20] provides a cloud manufacturing service method based on the smart perception and resource visit control of IoT, which includes a five-level IoT resource framework, that is, levels of resources, perception, network, service, and application. The research in [21] proposes an IoT-based urgent medical service system on the basis of heterogeneous resource instant visits, which combines ambulance, nurse, doctor, and medical records into a huge resource repository to be the resource level of the system. The literature in [22] discusses a service-oriented QoS optimization scheduling algorithm based on the Markov decision process for the IoT application level. The work in [23] discusses an IoT congestion control mechanism based on improved random early detection, and the mechanism is analyzed using the Queueing Theory. The research in [24] provides a cost-efficient analytic model which can predict device performance according to a limited capacity queueing system with prioritized services and is specific to heterogeneous IoT devices with the feature of postponing sensitive information. The literature in [25, 26] discusses a kind of resource allocation algorithm which concentrates on searching for the Nash equilibrium. The literature [27] discusses the request access control mechanism for limited resources based on the Zero-sum Game, which makes a decision as to whether a request is to be accessed or not based on the request's utility function. The work in [28] analyses the behavioral characteristics of individual and group users of mobile, providing resource allocation models for wireless communication between devices. However, in the above proposed methods, the methods in [18, 21, 23] do not take the differences of access resources into consideration. The proposed method in [19] only solves the problem of resource limitation of IoT at the perceptive layer. The work in [20, 24] is only applicable to small-size access requests. The research in [22, 25–28] does not have answers to address competition when core request services match high-quality resources. Generally, these models are not able to solve the problem of competition between important and urgent service requests in the process of IoT mass access.

In regard to DACIOT, a large amount of real-time data collected by thousands of sensors arrive continuously every day, and end user requests are always under the constraints of the "Things-Contact" features in IoT: (1) the scale of sensor data is large; (2) every end user's service request has a high constraint of reliability and quality of service [29, 30], such as it requires a shorter response time for intelligent terminal equipment, and the service request should be transmitted to the intelligent terminal successfully through the data access center; and (3) the group service requests require all requests in the same group to be able to access DACIOT under the condition of the group constraint set; moreover, the group requests as a whole have a strict limit of response delay for DACIOT. For instance, in a service group with 20 commands, each service group command needs to complete the task within a specific time and resource constraint, and the service group is regarded as having successful access if only these 20 commands have been given access within the limited response time and resources. Currently, the types of end user request commands tend to be relatively small; moreover, the network infrastructure and resource distribution are relatively concentrated [31]. Hence, under the condition of sharing a particular service resource, a large number of end users' service request commands in IoT require DACIOT to provide group access services at the same time with very high service constraints.

Based on this background, to address the problem of competition among important and urgent service request in the process of IoT access, all the users' access requests should be seen as obtaining the best-matched resources under the condition of meeting more than one limit. When similar service requests are separated from those that are different, based on the type and response domain of access requests, the similar service requests tend to share a close resource distribution area, and these similar access requests can thus been seen as a bionic group. Each group's access request searches for the optimal-matching resources at that moment under the current network environment. As access requests change, so will DACIOT's resource distribution, requiring DACIOT to allocate the optimal resources at the moment for all the groups' service requests. This further converts IoT's mass access into the dynamic grouping resource allocation problem (GRAP) [32]. In GRAP, each of the access requests represents a compete process, which means that the access will fail if all the necessary resources cannot be obtained, and there will be an upper boundary constraint on the number of access service requests and a lower boundary constraint on resource measurement. With such a feature and for the purpose of finding a solution, GRAP can be converted into 0-1 integer and linear programming [33]. Moreover, this is NP Hard [34] that the general algorithm is difficult to solve due to the limitation of the special problem. Therefore, this paper proposes a multistage dynamic grouping access strategy (MSDGAS) based on

self-organizing feature maps neural network [35] and frog-leaping algorithm [36].

The third part of the paper describes this issue and provides the mathematical model; the fourth part first designs a self-adaptive scheduling mechanism for resource dynamic grouping and further designs a group dynamic resource allocation algorithm based on the frog-leaping algorithm; the fifth part presents the experiment process and analysis; and the sixth part gives the conclusion and suggestions for future research.

3. Problem Description

3.1. Analysis of the Dynamic Grouping Resource Allocation Problem. To solve the problem of mass data access of IoT, it needs to meet users' demand of access request with a limited network load. With the confinement of the network service model, when the data access center meets an urgent service request, GRAP will face optimal resource competition, causing failure of the access request. This requires searching for a group of optimal solutions based on the confined network conditions in a dynamic network condition so that mass users' requests can access DACIOT. In the process of requesting access, as lots of the control commands have certain common attributes, such as being in the same geographic area, taking control of the intelligent equipments with the same type, and so on, these commands can be clustered into different command groups by similar attributes and these groups are sent at the same time in order to save network bandwidth and improve the efficiency of access. Suppose there are k-command groups in a single access process, and each command group G contains N control commands. Moreover, each command C in the command group G denotes that one end user can take control of L intelligent equipments simultaneously. For the sake of presentation, if the control command C does not intend to control an intelligent device, the corresponding value in the command is set to 0. Furthermore, these k command groups can be regarded as k two-dimensional matrices with N rows and L columns, and each control command C can be considered as a vector with L dimensions after regularization. Since the high-quality resources are limited, different command groups will compete for resources in the process of access, and then each command group G will have a corresponding competition weight. Meanwhile, each smart device has a variety of control types, which take on different urgency in different scenarios. The urgency can be expressed by the weight value: the greater the value is, the more urgent the command group is. Choose the weight of the most urgent control type in control command C as the weight of this control command C, and then use the weight of all the control commands in the command group G to measure the urgency of this command group G, namely, the comprehensive competition λ. Therefore, to solve the group dynamic resource allocation problem under the condition of limited network resources is to find a set of optimal resource access path, coordinating these different command groups to be transmitted onto the corresponding intelligent equipments using the minimum resource load. Here is the detailed process of mathematical modeling of this problem.

3.2. Modeling Process of the Dynamic Grouping Resource Allocation Problem.

It is assumed that the command group set: $G_1, G_2, \ldots, G_k$, with a weight function $\lambda(\psi)$ ($\psi \in \{1, 2, \ldots, k\}$), which reflects the competitive ability of a command group in the process of service request access in terms of geometrical significance. Moreover, $\lambda(\psi)$ has a range of values from 0 to 1, and the closer the value of $\lambda(\psi)$ is to 1, the stronger the competitive ability of the corresponding command group. Conversely, the closer value of $\lambda(\psi)$ to 0, the weaker the competitive ability. The request type set CAT is comprised of r command request types and $\text{CAT} = \{\text{cat}_1, \text{cat}_2, \ldots, \text{cat}_r\}$. In the command group of G_ψ, $\psi \in \{1, 2, \ldots, k\}$, $\mathbf{C}_1, \mathbf{C}_2, \ldots, \mathbf{C}_m$ are service request commands of DACIOT, $\mathbf{C}_i$ refers to the ith service request command, and $\mathbf{C}_i = (c_{i1}, c_{i2}, \ldots, c_{in})^T$, cat_i^ψ refers to the request type of the most urgent subcommand in $\mathbf{C}_i$, and $\text{cat}_i^\psi \in \text{CAT}$. $\vartheta_{\text{cat}_i^\psi}$ is the weight value of the request type cat_i^ψ, which is generally set according to the emergency degree of the commands in this request type upon initialization. Then, the weight value of G_ψ can be represented as

$$\lambda(\psi) = \frac{\sum_{i=1}^{m} \vartheta_{\text{cat}_i^\psi}}{\sum_{\psi=1}^{k} \sum_{i=1}^{m} \vartheta_{\text{cat}_i^\psi}}. \tag{1}$$

$R_1, R_2, \ldots, R_n$ represent the resource of DACIOT, R_j is the jth resource, LM_i is the load metrics function consumed by the command $\mathbf{C}_i$ in resource access, and E_i is the load value consumed by the command $\mathbf{C}_i$ to acquire all the resources it needs and

$$E_i = \sum_{d=1}^{n} \text{LM}_i(c_{id}). \tag{2}$$

Φ_i is the resource confinement for $\mathbf{C}_i$, Q_ψ is the resource confinement for command group G_ψ, and F_{G_ψ} is the objective function of command group G_ψ at the current load confinement; Q means the system resource confinement and

$$Q \geq \sum_{\psi=1}^{k} Q_\psi. \tag{3}$$

Table 1 presents the parameter list for the GRAP modeling, and a mathematically formalized description is given as follows.

GRAP: when the load function meets the measurement confining condition, the GRAP objective function will reach the optimal value (the minimum means the optimal):

$$\min F = \sum_{\psi=1}^{k} \lambda(\psi) F_{G_\psi}, \tag{4}$$

$$F_{G_\psi} = \sum_{i=1}^{m} \sum_{d=1}^{n} \text{LM}_i(c_{id}),$$

subject to: $E_i \leq \Phi_i$,

$$0 \leq \lambda(\psi) \leq 1, \tag{5}$$

$$\sum_{i=1}^{m} E_i \leq Q_\psi.$$

In light of the GRAP characteristics, to obtain a convenient solution, GRAP can be converted into 0-1 integer and linear programming. Suppose δ_{ij} refers to the load value in

TABLE 1: Parameters of the GRAP modeling.

Parameters	Descriptions
k	The number of command groups
G_ψ	The ψth command group
CAT	The set of command request types
$\lambda(\psi)$	The weight function of command groups
m	The number of service request commands
C_i	The ith service request command
cat_i^ψ	The request type of the most urgent subcommand in C_i
$\vartheta_{\text{cat}_i^\psi}$	The weight value of cat_i^ψ
n	The number of effective resources
R_j	The jth resource
LM_i	The load metrics function consumed by the command C_i in resource access
E_i	The load value consumed by C_i to acquire all the resources it needs
Φ_i	The resource confinement for C_i
Q_ψ	The resource confinement for G_ψ
F_{G_ψ}	Objective function of G_ψ at the current load confinement
Q	System total resource confinement
δ_{ij}	The load value of C_i acquiring resource R_j
F	Objective function of GRAP

the process of command $C_i (C_i = (c_{i1}, c_{i2}, \ldots, c_{in})^T)$ acquiring resource $R_j (R_j = (r_{j1}, r_{j2}, \ldots, r_{jn})^T)$, and

$$\delta_{ij} = \sum_{d=1}^{n} \text{LM}_i(R_{jd}), \quad d \in \{1, 2, \ldots, n\}. \tag{6}$$

Suppose $\lambda_1, \lambda_2, \ldots, \lambda_k$ are, respectively, the weight factors of command group $G_1, G_2, \ldots, G_k$, then the mathematical model for the minimum load function of DACIOT is described as follows:

$$\min F = \lambda_1 F_{G_1} + \lambda_2 F_{G_2} + \ldots + \lambda_\psi F_{G_\psi} + \ldots + \lambda_k F_{G_k}, \tag{7}$$

$$F_{G_\psi} = \sum_{i=1}^{m} \sum_{j=1}^{n} \delta_{ij} X_{ij},$$

$$\text{s.t.} \sum_{i=1}^{m} X_{ij} = 1, \quad j = 1, 2, 3, \ldots, n$$

$$\sum_{j=1}^{n} X_{ij} = 1, \quad i = 1, 2, 3, \ldots, m$$

$$X_{ij} \in \{0, 1\}, \quad \forall i, j \tag{8}$$

$$\delta_{ij} \leq \phi_{ij},$$

$$0 \leq \lambda_\psi \leq 1,$$

$$\sum_{i=1}^{m} E_i \leq Q_\psi.$$

In (7), F represents the objective function, which reflects the total load value consumed by all the group commands acquiring all the computing resources in the practical scene; $\min F$ means the minimum objective function; and λ_ψ refers the weight value of the command group G_ψ, which reflects the competitive ability of the command group G_ψ. In (8), F_{G_ψ}

means the load value consumed by the ψth command group acquiring the resource it needs in the real applications; δ_{ij} refers to the load value of command C_i acquiring resource R_j; s.t. refers to the limited conditions of the objective function F; $X_{ij} = 0$ means command C_i does not acquire the resource R_j; $X_{ij} = 1$ means C_i acquires R_j successfully; and ϕ_{ij} means the confinement when the service request command C_i matches the optimal resource R_j. In such a scenario, GRAP can be further defined as the problem to search for a set of optimal solutions so that the current objective function (7) is optimal (the minimum means optimal as a definition), when each of the request commands meets the condition of the load confinement.

To make it easier to follow the above formulas, a real application of Smart Home described in reference [37] is taken, for example. As mentioned in the reference, Smart Home is a classic example of IoT, wherein smart appliances connected via home gateways constitute a local home network to assist people in activities of daily life, and the remote DACIOT controls the home gateways to build a wider network. Smart Home involves IoT-based automation (such as smart lighting, heating, window, power plug, and surveillance), remote monitoring, and control of smart appliances. In a scene, it starts to rain suddenly, and then twenty employees of the same company in a Central Business District will want to take control of smart appliances inside their own homes in the meantime. For example, the company employee Jack wants to query the screen of smart monitor device, turn off the smart window, and turn on heating and lighting appliance inside the home for his mother who is coming home. In general, the type of shutdown command has a higher priority than that of the query command, and the command of "turn off smart window" is the most urgent in this scene. As a supplement, each command of company employees has the properties of atomicity; in other words, Jack's control command is effective as a whole only if all the subcommands (query the screen, turn off smart window, turn on heating, and lighting appliance) run successfully. For this scenario, because of the same properties of the geographic region, the twenty employees' commands are classified as a same command group, and G_ψ is used to represent the group of the twenty employees' commands. Moreover, there are many companies in the Central Business District; that is, lots of command groups will be generated at the same time. The command type set CAT contains "turn off" which is coded as 1, "turn on" which is coded as 2, and "query" which is coded as 3; Jack's command can be represented by C_i, and the command has many subcommands; the control command of Jack can be represented as $C_i = (3, 1, 2, 2, 0, 0, 0, 0, 0, 0)$, where $C_{ij} = 0$ means that Jack does not take control of the jth appliance; the value of cat_i^ψ is "turn off" for Jack; $\lambda(\psi)$ refers to the weight value of the command group composed of twenty employees' commands; E_i means the network bandwidth consumed by Jack's control command when the command is transmitted to the smart devices inside home; Q_ψ means the network bandwidth consumed by the twenty employees' control command. Based on this, formula (1) is used to calculate the weight value of the company's control

command group on smart appliances at DACIOT. Furthermore, the weight value reflects the priority of the command group since DACIOT needs to handle a large number of service requests from different companies at the same time. Formula (2) is used to calculate the value of network bandwidth consumed by the device control command; formula (3) is used to convey the system resource constraints of formula (2); formula (5) is to calculate the minimum value of network bandwidth consumed by all the group commands at the current time.

Regarding 0-1 integer and linear programming, this paper proposes a multistage dynamic grouping access strategy (MSDGAS). The following paragraphs provide a detailed description on MSDGAS.

4. Multistage Dynamic Grouping Access Strategy

The central idea of the MSDGAS is that when the amount of requests has become huge, the requests will be grouped based on certain properties at the users' request side, and requests with similar properties are included into the same user group, which refers to the service request collection divided by the request type and attributes. A user group can be distinguished by the type of request or scene area, and each of the groups has more or less the same request amount. At the resource side of IoT, similar resources are divided into groups and each group's resource volume varies. Their structure is shown in Figure 2.

MSDGAS is composed of three main parts: ReqEthnic, ResGrp, and Dev. ReqEthnic means the user group, and each group has many requests; Req refers to the user's request; for instance, the first request grouping includes the requests Req_1, Req_2, and so on; ResGrp refers to resource grouping, and each grouping has a number of relevant resources; Res refers to the resources of DACIOT; for instance, the first resource grouping includes resource Res_1, Res_2, Res_3, and Res_4; Dev refers to the responding device, including Dev_1, Dev_2, ..., Dev_n. In DACIOT, a large amount of service request at the ReqEthnic side will be grouped automatically, and then they will seek a group of optimal resources based on the constraint conditions of the request grouping from the ResGrp side. Finally, these service requests are transmitted to devices in the Dev side. MSDGAS first introduces optimized dynamic self-organizing feature maps (DSOM) to work on the dynamic grouping of the users' access request. It then applies improved frog-leaping algorithms to search for the optimal path for the grouped access requests.

4.1. Optimized Dynamic Self-Organizing Feature Maps

4.1.1. DSOM Introduction. Finnish scholar Kohonen first proposed an algorithm called self-organizing feature maps neural network (SOM) [38], which has been widely used in many fields of information processing based on the feature of distributed information storage, topographical structure maintenance, good self-organizing and self-learning ability,

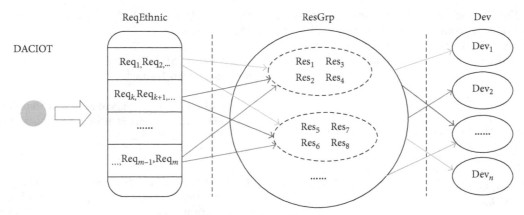

FIGURE 2: Structure of MSDGAS.

information visualization, nonsupervision clustering, and massive parallel processing. SOM not only includes an input layer but also contains a competitive layer, and the input layer is the status of full mesh with the competitive layer through each neuron which refers to one category [39]. According to the rules of learning, the objective of capturing the feature of each of the input models can be attained by repeated learning, and the self-organizing clustering will be carried out in these features. In the end, the cluster analysis results will be generated at the competitive layer. Figure 3 illustrates the topographical graph of SOM. The figure shows that the input layer is composed of N input neurons, and the competitive layer is composed of M output neurons. In the input layer, $X_1, X_2, \ldots, X_n$ denote the N input neurons and are mapped into the competitive output layer through clustering analysis. Dotted lines completely connect neurons between the input layer and the competitive layer. In order to acquire an accurate enough grouping result in the competitive layer, the repeated self-organizing clustering needs to be carried out. When making use of a SOM model, the number of neurons M is preset at the competitive layer, so the convergence speed will be astricted to a large extent. Therefore, under the environment of the Internet of things large-scale access requests, in order to meet the users' access requests to realize self-organizing clustering based on their measurement nature, the method of SOM needs to be improved. In this sense, an optimized method of DSOM is proposed, which combines a disturbance factor and growing threshold. Here, variable ξ is used to represent the disturbance factor, and variable φ means the growing threshold. φ will affect the network structure growth dynamically among the training process, while ξ can regulate the growth direction of network and restrain it falling into local optimization. Consequently, the goal of hierarchy clustering is achieved.

The calculation method of growing threshold φ is defined as follows:

$$\varphi = \begin{cases} (d \times f(\xi) \times n(t))/(1 + n(t)), & \text{init} = 0 \\ d \times f(\xi), & \text{otherwise,} \end{cases} \quad (9)$$

where $n(t)$ refers to the current network node number at the tth time iteration; d represents input vector dimension;

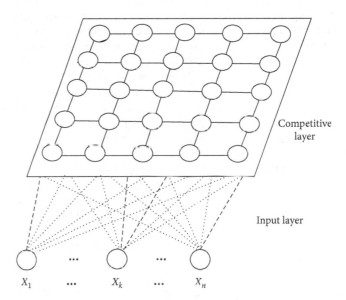

FIGURE 3: Topology of SOM neural network.

init = 0 stands for the initial status; and $f(\xi)$ is called the hierarchical classification function.

$$f(\xi) = \sqrt{1 - \xi},$$
$$\xi = \text{rand}(t); \quad (10)$$

where $\text{rand}(t)$ is the random number, and the value of which ranges from 0 to 1 at the tth time of iteration.

Definition 1. For $\mathbf{v}$, the network's input dimension vector, the nearest node is viewed as the best matching node at the competitive layer, and the abbreviation of the best matching node is bmn. Therefore, the formula is defined as

$$\left\| \mathbf{v} - \boldsymbol{\omega}_{\text{bmn}} \right\| \leq \left\| \mathbf{v} - \boldsymbol{\omega}_{n_i} \right\|, \quad \forall n_i \in N, \quad (11)$$

where $\boldsymbol{\omega}$ is regarded as the weight dimension vector of the node, n_i is the ith network node, N stands for the total of n_i, and $\|\bullet\|$ is called the Euclidean distance. $\|\mathbf{v} - \boldsymbol{\omega}_{\text{bmn}}\|$ means the Euclidean distance between vector $\mathbf{v}$ and vector $\boldsymbol{\omega}_{\text{bmn}}$, which is the weight dimension vector of bmn.

Definition 2. The distance between the input dimension vector **v** and its best matching node bmn is regarded as the standard deviation value between them, which is represented by E. Therefore, the formula is defined as

$$E = \sum_{k=1}^{d} \left(v_k - \omega_{\mathrm{bmn},k} \right)^2. \tag{12}$$

In the above formula, d is the dimension of **v**.

Definition 3. The node of the competitive layer n_i and its direct subnode are referred to as the neighborhood of n_i, which is called $\sigma(n_i)$.

4.1.2. Description of Optimized Dynamic SOM. $N = \{n_0, n_1, n_2, \ldots, n_m\}$ is the node set of the competitive layer, and $V = \{\mathbf{v}_1, \mathbf{v}_2, \ldots, \mathbf{v}_m\}$ stands for the input dimension vector set; $v_i = (v_{i1}, v_{i2}, \ldots, v_{id})$ is the ith input dimension vector; d represents the dimension of the input vector; n_0 is called the initial node; $\sigma_k(n_i)$ denotes the neighborhoods of the node n_i at the kth time of iteration, and $\sigma_k(n_i) = \sigma_0 \exp(-(k/\tau))$ where σ_0 represents the initial value of σ_{n_i} which is a bigger value in general and τ is called the exponential decay constant. The process of DSOM algorithm is determined by the following steps.

Step 1. Initiate the node n_0, neighbourhoods $\sigma(n_0)$, weight dimension vector ω_{n_0}, and growth threshold φ; ω_{n_0} is a random value ranging from 0 to 1, at the initial period $t = 1$; φ is calculated according to formulas (9) and (10), and then each vector of the input vector set V is standardized between 0 and 1. When it is $\overline{\mathbf{v}}_i = \left(\sum_{j=1}^{d} v_{ij}^2 \right)^{1/2}$, the standardized $\mathbf{v}_i$ is $\dot{\mathbf{v}}_i = (v_{i1}/\overline{v}_i, v_{i2}/\overline{v}_i, \ldots, v_{id}/\overline{v}_i)$.

Step 2. Select the input dimension vector sequentially from V, and search for the best matching node (bmn) of the vector **v** from the current network node collection N, calculated by formula (11).

Step 3. Calculate the deviation between bmn and v as E according to formula (12). If $E \leq \varphi$, skip to Step 4 for weight value updating operation; if not, go to Step 5 for the node growth operation.

Step 4. Adjust bmn neighborhood's weight value via formula (13).

$$\omega_{n_j}(k+1) = \begin{cases} \omega_{n_j}(k), & j \notin \sigma_{k+1}(\mathrm{bmn}) \\ \omega_{n_j}(k) + \mathrm{LR}(k) \times \left(\dot{v} - \omega_{n_j}(k) \right), & j \in \sigma_{k+1}(\mathrm{bmn}), \end{cases} \tag{13}$$

In the above formula, $\mathrm{LR}(k)$ is the learning rate, when $k \to \infty$, $\mathrm{LR}(k) \to 0$, and $\omega_{n_j}(k)$ and $\omega_{n_j}(k+1)$ are the weight values of n_j prior and post adjustment, respectively. $\sigma_{k+1}(\mathrm{bmn})$ is the neighborhood when bmn is at $k+1$ times of iteration.

Step 5. Generate a new node n_p of bmn, and make $\omega_{n_p} = \dot{v}$.

Step 6. $\mathrm{LR}(t+1) = \mathrm{LR}(t) \times \alpha$, α is the regulating factor of LR, $0 < \alpha < 1$.

Step 7. Repeat Step 2 to Step 6 till all input dimension vectors in V have been trained completely.

Step 8. Make $t = t + 1$, repeat Step 2 to Step 7, and enter into the next iteration period till no more new nodes are generated in the network.

4.2. Dynamic Niche-Based Shuffled Frog-Leaping Algorithm. The shuffled frog-leaping algorithm (SFLA), a new-type bionic group intelligent optimized algorithm, was proposed first by Eusuff and Lansey in 2003 for the purpose of combinatorial optimization [40]. The algorithm combines the merits of the two intelligent algorithms, namely, the meme algorithm based on meme evolution, and particle swarm optimization based on group behavior. It integrates the overall information exchange and local depth search with an aim to realize a balance between the overall search for the best and local solutions. This algorithm has advantages [41] such as its simple concept, fewer parameters to adjust, fast calculation, powerful overall searching for the best solution, and robustness. However, SFLA is not fast in convergence when it is working on a local search within a group, and it is easy to converge to the local best solution, which will further impact the algorithm's overall convergence. In this regard, niche technology [42] is able to maintain the group diversity and constrain the overmature phenomenon effectively. Inspired by the niche technology, this paper proposes a dynamic niche shuffled frog-leaping algorithm (DNSFLA). The proposed DNSFLA absorbs the advantages of SFLA and niche technology, and it can find the global optimal solution with a faster and easier way. Furthermore, the essence of the proposed algorithm is to search the resource sequence for each group command from end users in the global resource space using parallel computing.

4.2.1. Idea behind DNSFLA. In the traditional shuffled frog-leaping algorithm, group $P = \{X_1, X_2, \ldots, X_F\}$ is comprised of many frogs of the same structure, and each of the frogs represents a viable solution for the problem of optimization. $f(X_i)$ means the adaptability value of the individual frog X_i; individuals in Group P are arranged in order based on their adaptability values, and then the individual frogs in order are allocated into m groups; that is, the first frog is allocated into Group 1, the second into Group 2, the m into Group m, and $m + 1$ into the Group 1, and so forth, till F frogs are evenly allocated into Group P and in each of the groups, there are the same number (n) of frogs. In this sense, $F = m \times n$. Different groups can be regarded as frog collections with different thoughts. Each of the subgroups has its best adaptability X_b and the worst adaptability X_w. In the process of searching for the best solution among subgroups, it only needs to update the location of the worst solution X_w, and the formula for updating this is

$$\Delta = \text{rand}() \times (X_b - X_w), \qquad (14)$$

$$X_w = X_w + \Delta, \quad -\Delta_{\max} \le \Delta \le \Delta_{\max}. \qquad (15)$$

In the above formula, Δ is the length of movement, rand() is the random number between 0 and 1, and $\Delta_{\max}$ is the maximum length of movement.

After updating X_w, if a better solution is found, it will be applied to replace the worst solution X_w, otherwise the overall best solution X_g is used to replace X_b in formula (14), and the new solution is recalculated; if a better solution is not found, then a randomly generated new solution will be used to replace the worst solution X_w. This process is repeated till N, the predetermined evolutionary algebra, finishes the partial search amidst the subgroups. For the next step, all individuals in the subgroups are shuffled to form a new group P including F individual frogs, and their order is arranged from best to worst again, based on their adaptability for subgroup division and for next round of local search. Such an iteration is repeated till the termination condition is met.

In the process of local search according to the above algorithm, as updating the worst solution relies on the best solution, the algorithm is inclined to fall into searching for the local best, and the coefficient of the length of movement is a random function, which can make the algorithm premature and converge after several iterations. The DNSFLA algorithm, which is based on SFLA algorithm, applies the advantages of niche technology to maintain the solutions' diversity and has a better capacity in the overall search for an optimal solution and convergence and speeds up the elimination of the worst solution and increases the accuracy of the best solution. The idea behind the DNSFLA algorithm is that after dividing the subgroups by the SFLA algorithm, Chebyshev distance [43] is compared in pairs between X_{ib} and X_{jb} of the subgroups:

$$D(X_{ib}, X_{jb}) = \max_d \left(\left| X_{ib}^d - X_{jb}^d \right| \right). \qquad (16)$$

If $D(X_{ib}, X_{jb})$ is smaller than niche distance L, the individual with the smaller value of adaptability in X_{ib} and X_{jb} is allocated with a punishment function $g(X_b)$ with the aim to change the adaptability value and place this individual into the subgroup which was initially to replace the original partially best individual and carry out the new local search till the iteration ends.

4.2.2. Realization of DNSFLA.
In light of the aforementioned, the steps to realize the DNSFLA algorithm are detailed as follows:

(1) Initiate parameters including F, the total number of group solutions (frog); m, the number of the subgroups; n, the number of solutions in each of the subgroups; d, the number of problem dimension; G, times of shuffled iteration; N, times of partially updating each of the subgroups; $D_{\max}$, the maximum length of movement of solutions; L, the niche radius; $f(X)$, the function calculating adaptability; and $\Delta_{\min}$,

the minimum change value of adaptability function. In the area of viable solutions, they will randomly generate F solutions, which form a group $P = \{X_1, X_2, \ldots, X_F\}$, and $f(X_i)$ the adaptability values of each of solutions are calculated, of which the ith solution is described as $X_i = \{X_i^1, X_i^2, X_i^3, \ldots, X_i^d\}$.

(2) All viable solutions in P are arranged in an A–Z order, and X_g, the highest adaptability, is recorded as the best solution in the entire collection of the viable solutions, that is, the overall best solution. Then, divide group P into m groups and form subgroups and place the first solution into the first group, the second solution into the second group, No. m solution into the No. m group, and the No. $m + 1$ into the first group. Each of the subgroup has n solutions. Separately record the solution of the maximum adaptability of each of the groups as X_b, and the solution of the minimum adaptability of each of the groups as X_w.

(3) Place the best solution of each of the subgroup into the niche group DN, that is, DN $= \{X_{1b}, X_{2b}, \ldots, X_{mb}\}$; No. i and No. j best solutions are X_{ib} and X_{jb}, respectively; set $i = 1$ and $j = 1$.

(4) If $i \neq m - 1$, then compare the Chebyshev distance between the best solution of No. i ($1 \le i \le m - 1$) and the best solution of No. j ($i + 1 \le j \le m$) in DN; otherwise, turn to step (6).

(5) If $D(X_{ib}, X_{jb}) < L$, in which L is the niche radius and $j \neq m$, set $j = j + 1$, otherwise set $i = i + 1$ and $j = j + 1$; return to step (4); If $D(X_{ib}, X_{jb}) > L$ and $f(X_{ib}) > f(X_{jb})$, use punishment coefficient $g(X_b)$ to update $f(X_{ib})$, randomly initiate X_{ib}, and place the best solution X_{ib} into the responding subgroup to recalculate the partial best solution; otherwise, update $f(X_{jb})$, randomly initiate X_{jb}, and return to step (4).

(6) If each of the subgroups has the best solution, then move to step (7); otherwise, return to step (3) and compare the best solutions of the subgroups again.

(7) For each of the subgroups, update the worst solution X_w via formulas (14) and (15), and the adaptability value of the worst solution after updating $f'(X_w)$ is compared to that of the original $f(X_w)$. If $f'(X_w) < f(X_w)$, replace the original solution with the updated worst solution; otherwise, calculate the length of movement of the worst solution:

$$\Delta_i = \text{rand}() \times \frac{i}{N} \times (X_g - X_w), \quad i = 1, 2, \ldots, N. \qquad (17)$$

Update the location of the worst solution X_w as per formula (15). In the formula, i is the number of iterations for the current local search. Then, the adaptability value of the worst solution after updating $f''(X_w)$ is compared to that of the original $f(X_w)$. If $f''(X_w) < f(X_w)$, replace the original solution with the updated worst solution; otherwise, it will randomly generate a new solution to replace the original worst solution.

```
(1) Initialize $m, D_{max}$, $L$, $f(X)$, $g(X)$, $P = \{X_1, X_2, \ldots, X_F\}$, and $i = 1$, $j = 1$
(2) for $i \neq m - 1$ do
(3)     Calculate $D(X_{ib}, X_{jb})$
(4)     if $D(X_{ib}, X_{jb}) < L$ then
(5)         if $j \neq m$ then
(6)             $j = j + 1$;
(7)         else
(8)             $i = i + 1, j = j + 1$
(9)         end if
(10)    end if
(11)    if $D(X_{ib}, X_{jb}) > L$ then
(12)        if $f(X_{ib}) > f(X_{jb})$ then
(13)            $f(X_{ib}) = g(X_b)$
(14)            Randomly generate $X_{ib}$
(15)        else
(16)            update $f(X_{jb})$, and initialize $X_{jb}$
(17)        end if
(18)    end if
(19) end for
```

ALGORITHM 1: Local search of DNSFLA.

```
(1) Initialize $f(X), g(X), P = \{X_1, X_2, \ldots, X_F\}$
(2) Update the worst solution $X_w$ via formulas (14) and (15), recorded as $f'(X_w)$
(3) if $f'(X_w) < f(X_w)$ then
(4)     $f(X_w) = f'(X_w)$
(5) else
(6)     $\Delta_i = \text{rand}() \times i/N \times (X_g - X_w), X_w = X_w + \Delta_i$
(7)     Record the adaptability value after updating as $f''(X_w)$
(8)     if $f''(X_w) < f(X_w)$ then
(9)         $f(X_w) = f''(X_w)$
(10)    else
(11)        randomly generate a new solution to replace the original worst solution
(12)    end if
(13) end if
```

ALGORITHM 2: Elimination mechanism of DNSFLA.

(8) Judge if the predecided local evolution algebra N has been reached. If yes, a round of local search in each of subgroups has finished; otherwise, return to step (7).

(9) After finishing the partial evolution, calculate the variation of the adaptability of the best solution of each of the subgroups. If the variation is smaller than a comparatively small value within the predecided continual algebra, then the relevant subgroup is eliminated and initiated randomly; otherwise, reshuffle the solutions of all subgroups and form them into a complete group including F solutions.

(10) Judge if it meets the predecided times of shuffled iteration or termination conditions. If yes, the algorithm is finished; otherwise, return to step (2), and continue to do the next round of local search.

The core of the DNSFLA algorithm is the local search and the elimination mechanism of the subgroups. In order to assist it to understand, DNSFLA is decomposed into two subalgorithms (Algorithm 1 and Algorithm 2), and both the pseudocodes are given below, respectively.

Algorithm 1 shows the pseudocode of the local search, and the elimination mechanism's pseudocode is shown in Algorithm 2.

Combine Algorithm 1 and Algorithm 2, then the pseudocode of the DNSFLA algorithm is as shown in Algorithm 3.

4.3. Steps for MSDGAS.
Depending on the previously mentioned DSOM and DNSFLA, the steps in detail that realize the MSDGAS strategy are given as follows.

Step 1. Initiate GRAP and its relevant functions and parameters, give GRAP's relevant measurement parameters and confinement condition, and move to Step 2.

Step 2. Simplify GRAP into 0-1 programming, convert the relevant functions and confinement conditions, and move to Step 3.

(1) Initialize $F, d, G, N, f(X), \Delta_{\min}, P = \{X_1, X_2, \ldots, X_F\}$ and $gt = 0, lt = 0$
(2) **for** $i = 1 : F$ **do**
(3)   Calculate $f(X_i)$, and $X_i = \{X_i^1, X_i^2, X_i^3, \ldots, X_i^d\}$
(4) **end for**
(5) **repeat**
(6)   Descending $f(X_i)$ and record the best solution X_g
(7)   **for** $j = 1 : m$ **do**
(8)   Calculate X_g and X_w, put X_b into niche group DN
(9)   Choose X_{ib} and X_{jb}
(10)   Search X_w using Algorithm 1
(11)   **repeat**
(12)   Update X_w using Algorithm 2
(13) $lt = lt + 1$
(14)   **until** $lt = N$
(15)   Calculate the variation of $f(X_b)$, recorded as $\Delta f(X_b)$
(16)   **if** $\Delta f(X_b) < \Delta_{\min}$ **then**
(17)   Initiated X_j randomly
(18)   **else**
(19)   Reshuffle the solutions of all subgroups
(20)   **end if**
(21)   **end for**
(22) $gt = gt + 1$
(23) **until** $gt = G$

ALGORITHM 3: Dynamic niche-based shuffled frog-leaping algorithm (DNSFLA).

Step 3. Specific to 0-1 programming, dynamic grouping is carried out based on the DSOM algorithm, and move to Step 4.

Step 4. Specific to the grouped request models, calculate the model result based fon the DNSFLA algorithm, and move to Step 5.

Step 5. Save the calculation result and exit.

4.4. Analysis of MSDGAS. MSDGAS is made up of two parts, the DSOM algorithm and the DNSFLA algorithm. In DSOM, the φ value determines the network growth size. When the value of φ is larger, the DSOM algorithm applies the weight value update operation more frequently; less nodes are generated in the objective network, but it generates a network at a faster speed and can only realize coarse-granularity clustering. On the other hand, when the value of φ is smaller, the DSOM algorithm applies more node growing operations, and more nodes are generated in the objective network, but it generates a network at a slower speed and can realize fine-granularity clustering.

After introducing disturbance factor (ξ), ξ tends to set a larger value when it is initiated. From formula (10), it can be seen that φ is comparatively small at this moment and can make a rough classification of the transmission command, which is able to have a holistic mastering of the group transmission command. As the number of iterations increase, the value of ξ will increase, and an accurate clustering result can be acquired and so can layered clustering. Further, from formula (9), it can be seen that an increasing number of iterations will lead to a weaker strength of φ in adjustment and higher

weight value updating. Select the properties playing a bigger role in the clustering result and ignore the properties playing a lesser role to decrease the number of dimensions of clustering as this will reduce the workload of the calculation and further enhance the algorithm's convergence speed and efficiency.

The work in [44] prudently demonstrates the convergence of SFLA algorithm by applying the Markov mathematical analysis model. The DNSFLA algorithm in this paper ensures that the SFLA algorithm has a higher capacity of overall searching for the best solution and convergence speed through introducing niche technology to maintain the solutions' diversity. It prevents the SFLA algorithm from becoming "premature" after the local search is done for a certain number of iterations. In the process of updating the worst solution, the calculation of the length of movement is improved by using formula (17). At the initial period of evolution, the length factor is made smaller to expand the search scope, forcing the algorithm to search for better space for viable solution at a faster pace. With the increase of the number of evolutions, the length factor will gradually grow and the overall search capacity of the solution will be enhanced, which is beneficial to a frog to leap out of the partial best, and hence speed up the algorithm's convergence speed. Both the proposed DSOM and DNSFLA have a wide range of real application scenarios. For reference, the rudiment example of formulas included in the DSOM algorithm can be found in [45, 46], and the rudiment example of formulas included in the DNSFLA algorithm can be found in [47, 48]. To make it easier to follow the formulas proposed in this section, we still take the application of Smart Home described in reference [37] as an example. Formula (9) is used to calculate the value of growing threshold, which reflects the precision of the control command clustering. In this practical scenario, there is diversity upon control commands on different smart appliances from different families. Formula (16) is used to calculate the distance metric of two objective resources in the scenario, which suppresses the convergence due to collaboration of control command groups, enhances the global optimization ability of the algorithm, and improves the convergence speed under current conditions. Besides, the role of formula (17) is to lead the control commands of company employees to move towards the direction of optimal resource in DACIOT.

In terms of MSDGAS execution complexity, the number of the SOM algorithm iterations is t, the number of input nodes is N, the maximum number at each iteration is $N \log N$, the maximum space occupied is N, the overall time complexity after t iterations is $O(t \times N \log N)$, and the space complexity is $O(N)$. For the DNSFLA algorithm, the mixed iteration number is G, the solution number is F, run time complexity is $O(G \times F^2)$, and space complexity is $O(F)$. Hence, MSDGAS' execution time complexity is $O(\text{Max}\{t \times N \log N, G \times F^2\})$. However, in the process of actual operation, $G \times F^2$ is greater than $t \times N \log N$ and N is greater than F; therefore, the time complexity of MSDGAS is $O(G \times F^2)$, and space complexity is $O(N)$.

5. Experiment and Analysis

The settings for the experiment environment are as follows: 12 sets of Inspur servers, each configured with a CPU of Intel (R) Xeon(R) E5-2603 v2 @ 1.80 GHz, 40 G memory, 1 T hard disk, CentOS-6.4; 4 sets of them are used for the access of cluster servers; and the remaining 8 sets are used for servers for mass requests at users end. The experiment involves placing 8 sets of Linux servers at different areas as the user's end to send requests. Each of the host machines imitates 500 users, respectively; the remaining 4 sets of Linux servers are placed in a computer lab in order to build up the DACIOT's server cluster. A long-distance control system is adopted to control the 8 host machines when they send service requests of different sizes and types, in order to imitate a mass access environment. In the following, the experiment parameters settings for MSDGAS and the results of the performance tests are discussed.

5.1. Discussion of Experiment Parameters. In MSDGAS, some experiment parameters are optimized based on the work in [49, 50]. The user requests in the experiment are simulated data generated by a developed computer program. Generally, the dimension for a request command in an actual situation ranges from 3 to 6, and the larger the request command dimension, the more difficult it is for the algorithm to implement and the easier to test the bottleneck of the algorithm. Here, we take the maximum dimension value of 6. Further, calculate the growth threshold φ and disturbance factor ξ according to formulas (9) and (10). As to the initial neighborhood radius, it reflects the clustering range of the request commands, and also the command classification is often very vague at the beginning, so the value σ_0 is bigger, but the value has little influence on the clustering result because a different initial neighborhood can obtain the same result after a different number of iterations. Here, take the value σ_0 as 12. The regulator α of learning rate LR reflects the ease of request command clustering because as the number of iterations increases, the size of α increases and the easier it is for the request command to find its category. In this regard, according to the characteristics of the simulated service request of users, α varies between 0.6 and 0.9, and further experiments are needed to test the α sensitivity influence on the MSDGAS strategy. Based on the work in [40, 50], the DNSFLA algorithm can obtain the global optimal solution before 500 hybrid iterations. Here, set the maximum number of hybrid iterations as $G = 500$ and the maximum number of local iterations as $N = 20$. The niche distance L and the largest movement step length $D_{\max}$ reflect the scope of the service request command to avoid invalid service resources, indicating the rate of obtaining the optimal-matching resource to a certain extent. Further experiments are needed to test their sensitivity influence on the MSDGAS strategy. In the experiments of choosing parameters, we use 8 clients impersonating different scales of users to generate the test data sets. Limited by the number of data center servers in the test experiment, data center network architecture is fixed, while the request commands are generated randomly. In order to avoid the influence of the initial solutions on the test results, we randomly generate initial solutions for MSGDAS in each test, and to reduce the randomness of the parameters settings, the MSDGAS strategy is independently executed 10 times in each experiment, recording the maximum, minimum, and average.

Table 2 presents the test results of parameter variation among regulator α, niche distance L, and largest movement step length $D_{\max}$. In Table 2, T is the trial number, F_{best} represents the optimal solution tested out in the experiments, F_{mean} represents the average solution, and F_{worst} represents the worst solution. It can be seen, respectively, from the experiments $T1$–$T4$, $T5$–$T9$, and $T12$–$T15$ that the three parameters, α, L, and $D_{\max}$, do not have a linear influence on the performance of the proposed algorithm, which also indicates that the experimental factors (the regulator, the niche distance, and the largest movement step length) have a certain comparative independence. The experiments $T1$–$T4$ are used to test the sensitivity of MSDGAS when the value of α varies. The result indicates that the average solution does not become better with the increasing value of niche distance, while the best value of which is obtained when the value of niche distance is 5. Similarly, the experiments $T5$–$T9$ are used to evaluate the impact of regulator α on MSDGAS sensitivity, and the result shows that the average solution reaches the best when the value of α is set to 0.75. Moreover, the result of experiments $T7$, $T10$, and $T11$ further demonstrates it and obtains a better performance in the condition that niche distance is set to 5 and regulator is set to 0.75. The effect of the parameter $D_{\max}$ (the largest moving step) on MSDGAS performance is evaluated by experiments $T12$–$T15$, and the result shows that it reaches a better solution when the $D_{\max}$ is set to 10 under the condition that the value of α is set to 0.75 and the value of L is set to 5. As a supplementary, when the

TABLE 2: The sensitivity analysis for MSDGAS.

T	α	L	$D_{\max}$	F_{best}	F_{mean}	F_{worst}
1	0.6	4	8	3.8312	3.9126	3.9513
2	0.6	5	8	3.4243	3.6831	3.8257
3	0.6	6	8	3.6581	3.8105	3.9018
4	0.6	7	8	3.7917	3.8372	3.8924
5	0.65	5	8	3.2536	3.5918	3.8049
6	0.7	5	8	2.8313	3.9395	3.0782
7	0.75	5	8	2.8109	2.8192	2.8201
8	0.8	5	8	2.8981	2.9203	2.9316
9	0.85	5	8	3.2546	3.3189	2.3247
10	0.75	4	8	2.9385	3.0138	3.1412
11	0.75	6	8	3.2821	3.3231	3.3397
12	0.75	5	9	2.5597	2.5735	2.5783
13	0.75	5	10	2.2386	2.2387	2.2390
14	0.75	5	11	2.6105	2.6732	2.7218
15	0.75	5	12	2.9133	2.9779	3.1023
16	0.75	6	9	2.8849	2.8905	2.9021
17	0.75	6	10	2.6312	2.6329	2.6376
18	0.75	6	11	2.8914	2.9143	2.9198
19	0.7	5	10	2.6219	2.7346	2.7912
20	0.8	5	10	2.6831	2.7128	2.7254

value of α is set to 0.75 and L is set to 6 in the experiments $T11$ and $T16$–$T18$, it also shows that the proposed algorithm gets the optimal solution with the value of $D_{\max}$ being set to 10. However, the average optimal solution is inferior to that when L is assigned a value of 5. For experiments $T13$, $T19$, and $T20$, in the given conditions that parameter L and parameter $D_{\max}$ are all set to the best value, it tries to test the change of MSDGAS' optimal solution as the value of parameter α increases. The result indicates that the proposed algorithm reaches a better optimal solution when parameter α is set to 0.75, which is consistent with the results of experiments $T7$, $T10$, and $T11$. Based on the above analysis, the MSDGAS is able to obtain better performance when experiment parameters take $\alpha = 0.75$, $L = 5$, and $D_{\max} = 10$.

5.2. Performance Tests of MSDGAS. Depending on the above experiment parameter settings, we start the performance tests. The next experiments are carried out using the following methods. In addition, without loss of generality, both algorithms are executed ten times independently to obtain the average statistical results in each experiment.

(1) Under the situation of increasing IoT access, compare the access success rate (ASR) of the users' service requests between MSDGAS and the other algorithm (WQoS [51]) and define ASR = number of access success/total number of access requests.

(2) Under the situation of increasing IoT access, compare the response delay rate (RDR) between MSDGAS and the current other algorithm and define RDR = time of response delay/time of normal response.

(3) Under the situation of increasing IoT access, compare the access blocking rate (ABR) between MSDGAS and the other algorithm and define ABR = blocked number of service requests of the

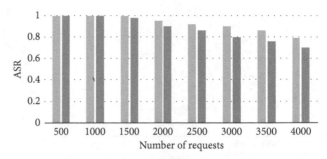

FIGURE 4: ASR with different access scales.

same type/total number of service requests of the same type.

(4) Under the situation of increasing IoT access, compare the resource utilization rate (RUR) between MSDGAS and the other algorithm. The number of online access machines is set as κ, the time consumed by Number j access server when requesting access is AT_j, the real occupation time of Number j access server is OT_j, and then RUR is defined as $\text{RUR} = (1/\kappa) \sum_{j=1}^{\kappa} (\text{AT}_j / \text{OT}_j)$.

Experiment 1. Test ASR performance with the maximum number of requests being 4,000 and the minimum 500.

As shown in Figure 4, the horizontal coordinate represents the number of requests at DACIOT ranging from 500 to 4000 while the vertical coordinate represents the access success rate. It can be seen from the figure that when the access scale is within 1,500, both MSDGAS and WQoS can maintain smooth access. When the scale of command requests is between 500 and 1000, due to the smaller size of the requests, the access cluster computing ability and resource service ability are not under any pressure, and both algorithms show good service performance, without the occurrence of requests loss as a result. When requests number reaches 1500, the ASR of MSDGAS is 100% and the ASR of WQoS algorithm is 98.6%. However, when the access scale is over 1,500, WQoS starts to show partial access failure while MSDGAS can still maintain full access. When the request scale is 2000, the access success rate of MSDGAS is 95.8%, while WQoS only has a access success rate of 90.4%, it shows the phenomenon of competition gradually, particularly, over high-quality system resources and ASR becomes lower and lower for both algorithms. With a rising service request, the network bears a larger load and network links start being blocked and requests loss begins at the data access center for Internet of things. Generally speaking, however, MSDGAS is more advantageous. Moreover, the ASR of the MSDGAS changes quite gently, which shows that MSDGAS has a good robustness.

Experiment 2. Test RDR performance with the maximum number of requests being 4,000 and the minimum 500.

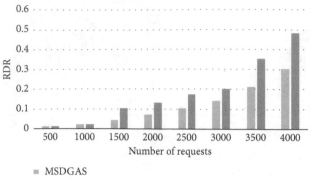

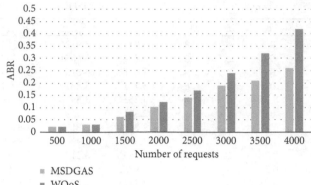

FIGURE 5: RDR with different access scales.

FIGURE 6: ABR with different access scales.

As shown in Figure 5, the vertical coordinate represents the response delay rate of requests at DACIOT while the horizontal coordinate represents the amount of access requests. It can be seen from the figure that when the access scale is within 1,000, both MSDGAS and WQoS only have a very low delay rate ranging from 1% to 2%. In the process of the request number gradually increasing from 500 to 1000, the figure shows that the pressure on each access server remains low and network link congestion does not appear as the access cluster enjoys ample network resources when the access service request number is low. Network response delay mainly refers to the transmission time at this stage. In this sense, the response delay of the two algorithms is all low and at similar levels. As the request scale grows and more resources are consumed, urgent requests have a more rigid demand for the response speed of DACIOT. In such scenarios, both algorithms show an increasing response delay rate. When the access service request number surpasses 1500, the two algorithms clearly start to differ from each other. With the ever-growing pressure from the access servers, the time to process the service request and network transmission gradually starts to increase, and the two algorithms start to differ from each other clearly in the response delay rate. Furthermore, when the number of access requests grows to 2,000, the RDR of MSDGAS is 7% while that of WQoS is 13%, nearly double that of MSDGAS, indicating that the MSDGAS algorithm is more stable in the condition of mass access requests.

Experiment 3. Test ABR performance with the maximum number of requests being 4,000 and the minimum 500.

As shown in Figure 6, the vertical coordinate represents the access blocking rate of requests at DACIOT while the horizontal coordinate represents the amount of access requests. When the service request number is below 1500, the access cluster server at the DACIOT can deal efficiently with the service requests and the DACIOT does not have pressure from network communication and resource consumption. It can be seen from Figure 6 that when the access scale is within 1,500, both MSDGAS and WQoS have a very low blocking rate, at around 3%, and overall, DACIOT does not appear to be under pressure. When access requests grow to 1,500, both algorithms perform differently—the former has a blocking

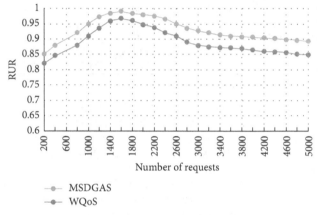

FIGURE 7: RUR with different access scales.

rate of 6% and the latter 8%. With ever-growing service requests concurrency, the MSDGAS needs more network bandwidth and computing resource to cluster service requests into groups. When access requests surpass 1,500, the two algorithms show an obvious difference—the former has a lower blocking rate than the latter strictly. As the MSDGAS algorithm considers grouping the users' requests, it shows an advantage in the aspect of average network load. Furthermore, this advantage is increasingly apparent as the request scale grows.

Experiment 4. Test RUR performance with an increasing number of access requests at DACIOT.

As shown in Figure 7, the vertical coordinate represents the DACIOT's resource utilization rate for MSDGAS while the horizontal coordinate represents the number of access requests. At the beginning, the effective resources at DACIOT are not the bottleneck of the current service requests, network bandwidth resource is sufficient for both MSDGAS and WQoS algorithms. In other words, each server at the DACIOT has the ability to process service requests quickly. As the experimental results shows, the resource utilization rate of system is growing along with the increasing number of requests. When the access scale is around 1,600, both algorithms reach the highest RUR, and the MSDGAS algorithm is able to ensure that the DACIOT maintains full utilization status. With the growth in the request scales and resource consumption, urgent requests have more rigid demands on the DACIOT's response speed and the real occupation time of each server becomes longer, causing partial access failure and a decline in RUR. However, from the decreasing curve trend, it can be seen that the MSDGAS algorithm can ensure that the DACIOT maintains a higher RUR than WQoS and the system can maintain reasonably good stability, and with the growing request scale, the system load can be effectively controlled. When the scale of access requests exceeds 4,000, RUR is inclined to be stable, indicating that the MSDGAS algorithm has better convergence.

However, when facing a more realistic workload where the number of requests varies over time, the MSDGAS will show little difference compared to the simulation experiments. This paper uses the increasing request scale to identify the performance limit of the algorithms under the condition of resource constraints. In a real scenario, the number of requests is disorderly and cannot be controlled accurately, making it difficult to measure the bottleneck of algorithms in this way [52]. Namely, it shows a bigger value at a point in time but a smaller value at the next time. Thus, the results shown in Figure 7 will be alternately high and low, but on some level, this situation is included in the above simulated experiments when the number of requests varies over time with a specific trend. In conclusion, it can be understood from the above analysis that, compared with the other algorithms, MSDGAS is able to maintain better service quality under the scenario of mass access requests. It works to dynamically group the users' requests and comprehensively weigh the performance of DACIOT in order to search for the best matching resources and maintain the maximum request load that the current network can bear. Finally, it shows an advantage over other algorithms in terms of access success rate, response rate, blocking rate, and resource utilization rate.

6. Conclusions and Future Work

In this paper, we formally defined a dynamic grouping resource allocation problem based on the background of mass control commands requesting for network access. In order to solve this problem, a novel resource access model was designed and a multistage dynamic packet access strategy was proposed along with it. The proposed strategy first adopted an optimized dynamic self-organizing feature map to cluster users' service requests into different command groups and then applied the dynamic niche-based shuffled frog-leaping algorithm to quickly and accurately acquire the best matching resources for these command groups. The experiments show that the proposed strategy can enhance the access success rate and resource utilization of service requests and reduce the network blocking and response delay. In conclusion, it can effectively solve the mass requests access problem of Internet of Things.

As further work, there are a number of directions that can enhance access capabilities of the proposed strategy in the context of IoT:

(i) *Support for delay access.* The strategy proposed in this paper does not consider the delay access mechanism when users' requests fail. Hence, considering network congestion, the delay access of DACIOT after failure will be the focus of further research.

(ii) *Pretreatment mechanism with Fog and Edge computing.* As the increasing computing and storing capacity of mobile devices or sensors, Fog and Edge computing are emerging as attractive solutions to the problem of data processing in IoT. In the future, we would like to preprocess the massive service requests using Edge computing, at the stage of request commands clustering in MSDGAS.

(iii) *Dynamic resource scheduling and virtualization techniques.* In DACIOT, heterogeneous network and sensing resources have to be often shared with multiple applications or services with different and dynamic quality of service requirements. Therefore, in order to allow more flexible scheduling, future research studies can also consider and compare the performance of resource virtualization (as instances of network virtualization) and operating system level virtualization such as containers.

Acknowledgments

The authors gratefully acknowledge the support of the National Natural Science Foundation of China (61572325 and 60970012), Ministry of Education Doctoral Fund of Ph.D. Supervisor of China (Grant no. 20113120110008), Shanghai Key Science and Technology Project in Information Technology Field (14511107902 and 16DZ1203603), Shanghai Leading Academic Discipline Project (no. XTKX2012), and Shanghai Engineering Research Center Project (GCZX14014 and C14001).

References

[1] J. Gubbi, R. Buyya, S. Marusic, and M. Palaniswami, "Internet of things (IoT): a vision, architectural elements, and future directions," *Future Generation Computer Systems*, vol. 29, no. 7, pp. 1645–1660, 2013.

[2] L. Atzori, A. Iera, G. Morabito, and M. Nitti, "The social internet of things (SIoT)–when social networks meet the internet of things: concept, architecture and network characterization," *Computer Networks*, vol. 56, no. 16, pp. 3594–3608, 2012.

[3] R. Bonetto, N. Bui, V. Lakkundi, A. Olivereau, A. Serbanati, and M. Rossi, "Secure communication for smart IoT objects: protocol stacks, use cases and practical examples," in *Proceedings of the IEEE International Symposium on World of Wireless, Mobile and Multimedia Networks (WoWMoM)*, pp. 1–7, San Francisco, CA, USA, June 2012.

[4] C. Luca, D. D. Danilo, and M. Luca, "An IoT-aware architecture for smart healthcare systems," *IEEE Internet of Things Journal*, vol. 2, no. 6, pp. 515–526, 2015.

[5] F. Firouzi, A. M. Rahmani, and K. Mankodiya, "Internet-of-Things and big data for smarter healthcare: from device to architecture, applications and analytics," *Future Generation Computer Systems*, vol. 2018, pp. 583–586, 2018.

[6] B. L. R. Stojkoska and K. V. Trivodaliev, "A review of internet of things for smart home: challenges and solutions," *Journal of Cleaner Production*, vol. 140, pp. 1454–1464, 2017.

[7] A. Al-Dweik, R. Muresan, M. Mayhew, and M. Lieberman, "IoT-based multifunctional scalable real-time enhanced road side unit for intelligent transportation systems," in *Proceedings of the IEEE 30th Canadian Conference on Electrical and Computer Engineering*, pp. 1–6, Windsor, ON, Canada, April-May 2017.

[8] T. Qu, S. P. Lei, Z. Z. Wang, D. X. Nie, X. Chen, and G. Q. Huang, "IoT-based real-time production logistics synchronization system under smart cloud manufacturing," *International Journal of Advanced Manufacturing Technology*, vol. 84, no. 1–4, pp. 147–164, 2016.

[9] K. M. Cheng, C. E. Tseng, and C. H. Tseng, "Maker and Internet of Things application in the intelligent security by example of power extension cord," in *Proceedings of the IEEE International Conference on Applied System Innovation (ICASI)*, pp. 239–241, Sapporo, Japan, May 2017.

[10] D.-Y. Kim and M. Jung, "Data transmission and network architecture in long range low power sensor networks for IoT," *Wireless Personal Communications*, vol. 93, no. 1, pp. 119–129, 2017.

[11] R. Khan, S. U. Khan, R. Zaheer, and S. Khan, "Future internet: the internet of things architecture, possible applications and key challenges," in *Proceedings of the 10th International Conference on Frontiers of Information Technology (FIT)*, p. 257C260, Islamabad, Pakistan, December 2012.

[12] S. Andreev and Y. Koucheryavy, Internet of Things, Smart Spaces, and Next Generation Networking, in Lecture Notes in Computer Science, vol. 7469, Springer, Berlin, Germany, 2012.

[13] D. Singh, G. Tripathi, and A. J. Jara, "A survey of internet-of-things: future vision, architecture, challenges and services," in *Proceedings of the IEEE World Forum on Internet of Things (WF-IoT)*, pp. 287–292, Seoul, Korea, March 2014.

[14] Y. Meng and C. QingKui, "DCSACA: distributed constraint service-aware collaborative access algorithm based on large-scale access to the Internet of Things," *Journal of Super-computing*, vol. 2018, pp. 1–20, 2018.

[15] G. Zhang and Q. K. Chen, "Group command transmission model based on effective path statistics network," *Chinese Journal of Electronics*, vol. 43, no. 9, pp. 1826–1832, 2015.

[16] G. Zhang and Q. K. Chen, "Construction and application of effective path statistics network," *International Journal of Hybrid Information Technology*, vol. 8, no. 9, pp. 369–380, 2015.

[17] M. Wollschlaeger, T. Sauter, and J. Jasperneite, "The future of industrial communication: automation networks in the era of the internet of things and industry," *IEEE Industrial Electronics Magazine*, vol. 11, no. 1, pp. 17–27, 2017.

[18] S. Y. Lien, K. C. Chen, and Y. Lin, "Toward ubiquitous massive accesses in 3GPP machine-to-machine communications," *IEEE Communications Magazine*, vol. 49, no. 4, pp. 66–74, 2011.

[19] N. Ye, Y. Zhu, R. C. Wang, R. Malekian, and L. Min, "An efficient authentication and access control scheme for perception layer of internet of things," *Applied Mathematics and Information Sciences*, vol. 8, no. 4, pp. 1617–1624, 2014.

[20] F. Tao, Y. Zuo, X. L. Da, and L. Zhang, "IoT-based intelligent perception and access of manufacturing resource toward cloud manufacturing," *IEEE Transactions on Industrial Informatics*, vol. 10, no. 2, pp. 1547–1557, 2014.

[21] B. Xu, X. L. Da, H. Cai, C. Xie, J. Hu, and F. Bu, "Ubiquitous data accessing method in IoT-based information system for emergency medical services," *IEEE Transactions on Industrial Informatics*, vol. 10, no. 2, pp. 1578–1586, 2014.

[22] L. Li, S. Li, and S. Zhao, "QoS-aware scheduling of services-oriented internet of things," *IEEE Transactions on Industrial Informatics*, vol. 10, no. 2, pp. 1497–1505, 2014.

[23] J. Huang, D. Du, Q. Duan et al., "Modeling and analysis on congestion control in the internet of things," in *Proceedings of the IEEE International Conference on Communications (ICC)*, pp. 434–439, Sydney, NSW, Australia, June 2014.

[24] I. Awan and M. Younas, "Towards QoS in internet of things for delay sensitive information," in *Proceedings of the International Conference on Mobile Web and Information Systems*, pp. 86–94, Paphos, Cyprus, August 2013.

[25] G. Zhang, L. Cong, E. Ding, K. Yang, and X. Yang, "Fair and efficient resource sharing for selfish cooperative communication networks using cooperative game theory," in *Proceedings of the IEEE International Conference on Communications (ICC)*, pp. 1–5, Kyoto, Japan, June 2011.

[26] G. Wei, A. V. Vasilakos, and Y. Zheng, "A game-theoretic method of fair resource allocation for cloud computing services," *Journal of Supercomputing*, vol. 54, no. 2, pp. 252–269, 2010.

[27] D. E. Charilas and A. D. Panagopoulos, "A survey on game theory applications in wireless networks," *Computer Networks*, vol. 54, no. 18, pp. 3421–3430, 2010.

[28] L. Song, D. Niyato, Z. Han, and E. Hossain, "Game-theoretic resource allocation methods for device-to-device communication," *IEEE Wireless Communications*, vol. 21, no. 3, pp. 136–144, 2014.

[29] J. Jin, J. Gubbi, and T. Luo, "Network architecture and QoS issues in the internet of things for a smart city," in *Proceedings of the IEEE International Symposium on Communications and Information Technologies*, vol. 2012, pp. 956–961, Gold Coast, QLD, Australia, October 2012.

[30] F. Al-Turjman, "QoS—aware data delivery framework for safety-inspired multimedia in integrated vehicular-IoT," *Computer Communications 2018*, vol. 121, 2018.

[31] D. Guinard, V. Trifa, and F. Mattern, "From the internet of things to the web of things: resource-oriented architecture and best practices," in *Architecting the Internet of Things*, , pp. 97–129, 2011.

[32] Z. Xiao, W. Song, and Q. Chen, "Dynamic resource allocation using virtual machines for cloud computing environment," *IEEE Transactions on Parallel and Distributed Systems*, vol. 24, no. 6, pp. 1107–1117, 2013.

[33] Y. Zhang, X. Sun, and B. Wang, "Efficient algorithm for k-barrier coverage based on integer linear programming," *China Communications*, vol. 13, no. 7, pp. 16–23, 2016.

[34] G. J. Woeginger, *Exact Algorithms for NP-Hard Problems: A Survey*, Optimization Eureka, You Shrink!, Springer, Berlin, Heidelberg, Germany, 2003.

[35] T. Kohonen, "Essentials of the self-organizing map," *Neural Networks*, vol. 37, pp. 52–65, 2013.

[36] X. Li, J. Luo, M. R. Chen, and N. Wang, "An improved shuffled frog-leaping algorithm with extremal optimisation for continuous optimisation," *Information Sciences*, vol. 192, pp. 143–151, 2012.

[37] M. Bansal, I. Chana, and S. Clarke, "Enablement of IoT based context-aware smart home with fog computing," *Journal of Cases on Information Technology*, vol. 19, no. 4, pp. 1–12, 2017.

[38] K. Tasdemir and E. Merenyi, "Exploiting data topology in visualization and clustering of self-organizing maps," *IEEE Transactions on Neural Networks*, vol. 20, no. 4, pp. 549–562, 2009.

[39] D. Sacha, M. Kraus, and J. Bernard, "SOMFlow: guided exploratory cluster analysis with self-organizing maps and analytic provenance," *IEEE Transactions on Visualization and Computer Graphics*, vol. 24, no. 1, pp. 120–130, 2018.

[40] M. M. Eusuff and K. E. Lansey, "Optimization of water distribution network design using the shuffled frog leaping algorithm," *Journal of Water Resources Planning and Management*, vol. 129, no. 3, pp. 210–225, 2003.

[41] L. Wang and C. Fang, "An effective shuffled frog-leaping algorithm for multi-mode resource-constrained project scheduling problem," *Inform Sciences*, vol. 181, no. 20, pp. 4804–4822, 2011.

[42] X. Liu, H. Liu, and H. Duan, "Particle swarm optimization based on dynamic niche technology with applications to conceptual design," *Advances in Engineering Software*, vol. 38, no. 10, pp. 668–676, 2007.

[43] H. Esmaeili-Najafabadi, M. Ataei, and M. F. Sabahi, "Designing sequence with minimum PSL using Chebyshev distance and its application for chaotic MIMO radar waveform design," *IEEE Transactions on Signal Processing*, vol. 65, no. 3, pp. 690–704, 2017.

[44] J. P. Luo, X. Li, and M. R. Chen, "The markov model of shuffled frog leaping algorithm and its convergence analysis," *Dianzi Xuebao (Acta Electronica Sinica)*, vol. 38, no. 12, pp. 2875–2880, 2010.

[45] J. L. Wu, P. C. Chang, and C. C. Tsao, "A patent quality analysis and classification system using self-organizing maps with support vector machine," *Applied Soft Computing*, vol. 41, pp. 305–316, 2016.

[46] V. Caquilpan, D. Sáez, and R. Hernández, "Load estimation based on self-organizing maps and Bayesian networks for microgrids design in rural zones," in *Proceedings of the IEEE PES Innovative Smart Grid Technologies Conference-Latin America (ISGT Latin America)*, pp. 1–6, Quito, Ecuador, September 2017.

[47] S. Kayalvili and M. Selvam, "Hybrid SFLA-GA algorithm for an optimal resource allocation in cloud," in *Proceedings of the Cluster Computing*, pp. 1–9, Belfast UK, September 2018.

[48] Y. Miao, F. Rao, and L. Yu, "Research on the resource scheduling of the improved SFLA in cloud computing," *International Journal of Grid Distribution Computing*, vol. 8, no. 1, pp. 101–108, 2018.

[49] J. Faigl, M. Kulich, and V. Vonasek, "An application of the self-organizing map in the non-Euclidean Traveling Salesman Problem," *Neurocomputing*, vol. 74, no. 5, pp. 671–679, 2011.

[50] B. Amiri, M. Fathian, and A. Maroosi, "Application of shuffled frog-leaping algorithm on clustering," *International Journal of Advanced Manufacturing Technology*, vol. 45, no. 1-2, pp. 199–209, 2009.

[51] C. H. Wu, M. L. Chiang, and T. L. Lu, "Kernel mechanisms for supporting differentiated services and content-aware request distribution in web clusters providing multiple services," in *Proceedings of the IEEE 24th International Conference on Advanced Information Networking and Applications Workshops (WAINA)*, pp. 473–478, Biopolis, Singapore, March 2010.

[52] S. Verma, Y. Kawamoto, and Z. M. Fadlullah, "A survey on network methodologies for real-time analytics of massive IoT data and open research issues," *IEEE Communications Surveys & Tutorials*, vol. 19, no. 3, pp. 1457–1477, 2017.

3

Decision Tree-Based Contextual Location Prediction from Mobile Device Logs

Linyuan Xia, Qiumei Huang ⓘ, and Dongjin Wu

School of Geography and Planning, Sun Yat-Sen University, Guangzhou, China

Correspondence should be addressed to Qiumei Huang; hqium@mail2.sysu.edu.cn

Academic Editor: Dik Lun Lee

Contextual location prediction is an important topic in the field of personalized location recommendation in LBS (location-based services). With the advancement of mobile positioning techniques and various sensors embedded in smartphones, it is convenient to obtain massive human mobile trajectories and to derive a large amount of valuable information from geospatial big data. Extracting and recognizing personally interesting places and predicting next semantic location become a research hot spot in LBS. In this paper, we proposed an approach to predict next personally semantic place with historical visiting patterns derived from mobile device logs. To address the problems of location imprecision and lack of semantic information, a modified trip-identify method is employed to extract key visit points from GPS trajectories to a more accurate extent while semantic information are added through stay point detection and semantic places recognition. At last, a decision tree model is adopted to explore the spatial, temporal, and sequential features in contextual location prediction. To validate the effectiveness of our approach, experiments were conducted based on a trajectory collection in Guangzhou downtown area. The results verified the feasibility of our approach on contextual location prediction from continuous mobile devices logs.

1. Introduction

With the rapid development of mobile computing and positioning technology, it has made great progress in the ability and quality of location data acquisition. And nowadays, mobile phone becomes a necessity for everyone everywhere and every time which makes it convenient to capture people's daily activity trajectories. Given this, human mobility and behavior pattern analysis have become hot topics. Location-based services (LBS) has gained a great development in this few years, such as navigation services, social networking services, and personalized recommendation services. In order to provide a better service for people, it is significant to discover valuable knowledge, such as interesting locations of individuals from historical trajectories. Therefore, extracting and recognizing interesting locations and predicting next location have been an essential task for remarkable LBS. For now, despite many years of research on location prediction issue, there are still some problems: (1) using raw location data without semantic information makes it hard to study personal

purpose of daily route; (2) uncleaned check-in data from social platforms increase the cost of data process and analysis despite dispersed semantic information. To deal with these problems, a contextual location prediction framework is put forward in this paper. We demonstrate the feasibility of predicting contextual location from continuous mobile devices logs by machine learning techniques. The approach proposed in this paper includes three main modules: stay point detection, semantic places recognition, and decision tree-based prediction. The first module is applied to discover individuals' behavioral sequence by extracting spatial feature from cluttered mobile device logs. Next, in order to enrich location information, the visited points extracted by the first module are attached significance in the second module through several matching methods. Based on the temporal, sequential, and semantic features of historical trajectories, a decision tree-based algorithm is applied to predict contextual location in the third module.

Regarding the prediction of people's movements, this paper attempted to predict the location type a person would visit given his last visiting location. To our best knowledge, this has rarely been explored in the former literatures. It could be the first work to focus on contextual location prediction based on mobile device logs covering a couple of months. On the whole, this paper offers the following contributions:

(1) A modified trip-identify method is proposed to deal with consecutive mobile phone data addressing the cold-start problem for attaching location information to a more accurate extent.

(2) A semantic matching model is designed to attach place type information to the extracted stay points based on several matching rules and a self-designed POI dictionary.

(3) A decision tree-based contextual location prediction method is designed for predicting individuals' contextual location with spatial, temporal, and sequential features.

The rest of this paper is organized as follows: Section 2 introduces the related works of main procedures. Section 3 shows architecture of our approach on contextual location prediction and illustrates three processes in detail, respectively, including the modified trip-identify algorithm, semantic places recognition, and decision tree-based contextual location prediction. In Section 4, experiments are conducted to evaluate our approach. The conclusion and future work are described in Section 5.

2. Related Works

Location prediction usually refers to predicting the user's location at the next moment. Generally, two steps of stay point detection and location prediction are needed to predict locations from mobile device logs in the former researches [1–3]. In the following, previous works are reviewed with respect to the two steps.

2.1. Stay Point Detection. Pervasive location acquisition technologies produce a large amount of spatial-temporal data. Among them, GSM, WiFi, and GPS become the main sources which used in identifying people's mobility patterns [1, 2]. Call detail records (CDRs), which contains mass mobile information on call manager, is an indirect GSM-based data and allows us to reveal characteristics about the city dynamics and human behaviors [4, 5]. However, the coarse granularity, low location accuracy, and a tremendous periodic uncertainty lead to an issue of ubiquitous and continuous user-tracking capability [6]. As WiFi becomes increasingly popular in general surroundings, researchers began to discover interesting places from WiFi information by using the fingerprint-based approach [7–9]. However, the huge work on database construction makes the fingerprint-based approach unsuitable for positioning in a large-scale region. Furthermore, the outside location is hard to be obtained under the limited conditions of radio signal [10].

GPS outputs are the most common data for discovering people's visits. To find out locations where a person stays for significant time periods based on a history of successive positions, different kind of algorithms have been proposed in previous works. Clustering algorithms are popular in detecting stay points, such as K-Means clustering [11] and DJ-Cluster [12] algorithms. Besides, Palma et al. proposed a spatiotemporal clustering method, named CB-SMOT, which considers the notion of minimal time for finding clusters in single trajectories [13]. Li et al. proposed a stay point detection algorithm based on distance and pace times [14]. Zhang et al. proposed a trip-identify method in which candidate stay positions are merged in a loop until it meets a certain condition [15]. It is observed that there are different approaches aiming at different data sources and accuracy requirements. In this paper, stay points are detected following the idea of trip-identify method which can provide a fine granularity to discover individual's precise behaviors.

2.2. Location Prediction. Many researchers have paid a lot of attention on location prediction with historical human trajectories since users' mobility pattern shows a high degree of temporal and spatial regularity and hides a high degree of potential predictability despite the fact that there is individual's randomness involved [16, 17]. Based on the sequential characteristic of moving locations, studies have realized location prediction by extending the Markov model [11, 18–22]. For example, Gambs et al. proposed Mobility Markov Chain model (n-MMC) [19], and Mathew et al. trained Hidden Markov Models (HMMs) [23] for each clustered location to predict the future locations of mobile individuals. In addition to the idea based on the Markov model, machine learning is another common method in dealing with location prediction problem. It usually takes two steps in the process including pattern mining and matching. For example, Morzy proposed Traj-PrefixSpan algorithm [24], and Lei proposed a probabilistic suffix tree [25] to discover movement behaviors and predict future locations.

For better understanding human trajectories, scholars have introduced information related to location properties into trajectory analysis and put forward a concept of semantic trajectory [26]. Semantic trajectories are the track records enriched with related contextual data which give significance to meaningless raw GPS data. Considering the users' semantic-triggered intentions, Ying et al. proposed a mining-based location prediction called Geographic-Temporal-Semantic-Based Location Prediction (GTS-LP) to estimate the probability of the user in visiting a location. The main ideas of this method are to describe GTS patterns using a prefix tree and to calculate the similarity between current movements and GTS patterns by matching rules [27].

However, these previous works mainly focused on the issue of predicting users' next locations where they had been before. But, actually the predictive ability of new future location for users is more important in many cases, such as location recommendations [28]. Therefore, check-in data from social networks such as Facebook become another research data for location prediction [29, 30]. For example, Gao et al. put forward a prediction model blending social networks and the relationship of historical check-in records

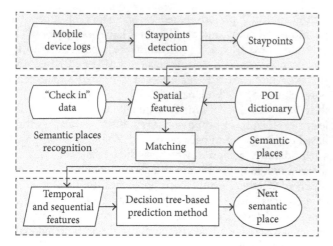

FIGURE 1: The workflow of the personally contextual location prediction approach.

```
Input: GPS, δ_time, δ_distance, δ_v
Output: Staypoints
 (1)  n=GPS.Count;changecount = 0;
 (2)  for i=1 ... n−1 do
 (3)    SegmentList=PointToSegment (p_i, p_{i+1});
 (4)  end for
 (5)  while changecount!=0 do
 (6)    changecount=0;
 (7)    SegmentList=ConcatenateSegments (SegmentList, δ_v)
 (8)    for segment in SegmentList do
 (9)    if SegmentTypeChange (segment, δ_time, δ_distance) then
 (10)   changecount+=1;
 (11)  end while
 (12)  for segment in SegmentList do
 (13)  if Segment.Type=='stay' then
 (14)  Staypoint=SegmentToStayPoint (Segment);
 (15)  end for
```

ALGORITHM 1: The modified trip-identify method.

of users' friends [31]. Although check-in data contain semantic information-included location properties and social relations, problems of temporal continuity and human dependency exist with this kind of data. In order to handle these problems and to achieve semantic location prediction, we propose to fuse mobile device logs, check-in data, and POIs.

3. Contextual Location Prediction

In this section, the proposed approach for predicting next contextual location is illustrated in detail. Figure 1 gives an overview of the workflow of our approach. Given the uniqueness of each individual, the GPS trajectories are manipulated and analyzed separately. In the first step, a stay point detection method is adopted to extract interesting locations from irregular and high-sampling-rate mobile device logs based on time and velocity parameters. Next, a semantic places recognition process is proposed to discover semantic information by fusing POI and check-in data. Finally, a decision tree-based method is adopted to predict next semantic place according to the extracted spatiotemporal features.

3.1. Stay Point Detection. The stay points (see Definition 1), denoting the locations where people have stayed for a while, are the most significant points in trajectories, such as restaurants for lunch and tourist attractions. To find out the stay points from mobile devices logs and improve the location accuracy, we modified the trip-identify method [15] for high-sampling-rate GPS data. The main idea of our algorithm is to determine whether the segment's type (see Definition 2) is "stay" or "move" and concatenate adjacent segments with the same state until all the neighboring segments' type are different. Algorithm of the modified trip-identify method is shown in Algorithm 1.

Definition 1. Stay point: a stay point ($sp_i = (Lng_i, Lat_i, T_{arv}, T_{lev}, POI_{name})$) stands for a location where people have stayed in a certain area for a while. T_{arv} and T_{lev} represent the timestamps that the user arrive and leave the location,

respectively, and POI_{name} represents the nearest POI according to real map database.

Definition 2. Segment: a segment ($segment_i = (P_{arv}, P_{lev}, V_i, type_i)$) consists of neighboring points in time and location series with the same type. P_{arv} and P_{lev} represent two endpoints of a segment, V_i describes the velocity, and $Type_i$ describes the state ("stay" or "move") which is determined by the corresponding velocity.

In the Algorithm 1, GPS data are turned into segments according to time series (line 2–4). For each segment in segment list, the distance and duration can be described through two endpoints as follows.

$$\text{Distance}(p_{arv}, p_{lev}) = R * \arccos(\sin(p_{arv} \cdot lat) * \sin(p_{lev} \cdot lat)$$
$$+ \cos(p_{arv} \cdot lat) * \cos(p_{lev} \cdot lat)$$
$$* \cos(p_{arv} \cdot lng - p_{lev} \cdot lng)) * \frac{Pi}{180}, \quad (1)$$

where R represents the Earth radius (R = 6371.004 km), lat and lng represent the latitude and longitude of endpoints, respectively, and Pi is a mathematical constant and approximated as 3.14159.

$$\text{Duration}(p_{arv}, p_{lev}) = p_{lev} \cdot time - p_{arv} \cdot time, \quad (2)$$

where time attribute is the timestamp of GPS record.

The velocity and type of segments are calculated and determined based on a walking speed threshold δ_v [32] in line 7. Also, adjacent segments with the same type will be combined. If the duration of new stay segment is shorter than time threshold δ_{time}, it is considered as a move, while if the distance of move segment is less than distance threshold $\delta_{distance}$, it is considered as a stop (line 8–10). Repeat these judgments until the segments' type wouldn't change anymore. At last, the results of stay segments are converted into stay points (line 12–15).

When dealing with GPS data, a cold-start problem should be considered to prevent missing extraction. For example, the

GPS signal would be lost immediately when people enter interior of a building, but to the contrary, GPS result would not be calculated at once when people leave the building after staying for a certain time (as shown in Figure 2). To improve location accuracy which is important in semantic place recognition process, we chose the location of arriving point as the location of stay segment instead of the center of endpoints in this case. Besides, a similar problem exists when people enter and leave from different gates of the same large building. The distance between two endpoints from different gates is greater than that from the same gate. Therefore, the distance threshold δ_{distance} should be reasonably set under the consideration of the average of building length in the experimental area.

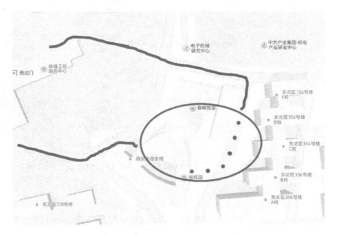

FIGURE 2: An example of the effect of GPS cold-start problem.

3.2. Semantic Places Recognition.

Stay points, represented in exact location with longitude and latitude, are almost meaningless in personal location description. Therefore, it is crucial to annotate stay points with location types and turn them into semantic places when taking destination as the predictive object. To endow stay points with individuals' information, we put forward a semantic places recognition process using "check in" points (see Definition 3) and POI dictionary (see Table 1).

Definition 3. "Check in" points: a "check in" point ($cp_i = (\text{Lng}_i, \text{Lat}_i, T_i, \text{type}_i)$) is similar to GPS point in expression, but the numerical values are totally dependent on the user themselves. Lng_i and Lat_i are picked up from a digital map. T_i represents the timestamp that the user checks in, and Type_i denotes the trip purpose.

To better recognize places, three steps are needed including the "check in" data matching process, clustering process, and POI dictionary matching process.

TABLE 1: A POI dictionary to recognize stay points without labeled information.

Type	Dictionary
Home	Dormitory, housing estate, apartment
Work	Laboratory, school, teaching building, company, office building
Restaurant	Canteen, dining room, restaurant, grogshop, hotel, pub
Shopping	Supermarket, mall, bazaar, market, department store, pedestrian street
Entertainment	Playground, cinema, KTV, swimming pool, square
Business	Hospital, administration, bank, bureau, police station, health center
Attractions	Park, museum, scenic spot, memorial hall, exhibition, temple, parkland, ruins
Others	Primary school, wharf, industrial zone, motor station, etc.

3.2.1. "Check in" Data Matching.

"Check in" data are given priority compared with POI dictionary since the same physical location may imply differently for different individuals. Besides, the location types which are totally dependent on personal information can only be classified based on "check in" data such as "home" and "work." For example, a shopping mall is a place for shopping for most people, and then it falls into "shop" type. But, on the other side, it may be a place for work to salesmen, and then it should be classified as "work" type places.

As illustrated in Figure 3, the "check in" data matching rule must consider time and distance thresholds at the same time. In general, the extracted stay point matches "check in" point if the timestamp of "check in" point falls between the arriving time and leaving time of the stay point. Besides, the distance between two points is smaller than an appropriate threshold at the same time (see Definition 4).

Definition 4. Match: the matched "check in" point (cp) for a certain stay point (sp) meets the following criteria: $\text{sp}.T_{\text{arv}} < \text{cp}.T < \text{sp}.T_{\text{lev}}$ and $\text{distance}(\text{sp}, \text{cp}) < \delta_{\text{match\_distance}}$.

3.2.2. Clusters Matching.

It is normal that there are some deficiencies in "check in" data because of people's forgetfulness. For most of the unmatched detected stay points, we can attach semantics to them with their address names labeled by Baidu Maps according to a self-designed POI dictionary. But in this case, it is difficult to recognize home, work, and some other places which mainly depend on individual information rather than the detailed address names. Given this, a clustering algorithm is applied to classify unmatched stay points according to the cluster type based on matched stay points. The type of each cluster is determined by the maximum probability of the corresponding stay points. The DBSCAN algorithm [33] (line 8) groups together points that are closely packed together (points with many nearby neighbors). The two required parameters, Eps and MinPts, represent the neighborhood radius and the minimum number of points to consider a point as core point, respectively. Here, it is used to gather the surrounding stay points in order to recognize places with high frequency and attach semantic type to the unmatched stay points.

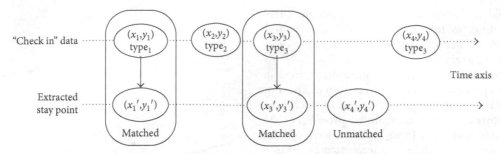

FIGURE 3: An example of "check in" data matching for semantic recognition.

3.2.3. POI Dictionary Matching. After matching with "check in" data, a POI dictionary matching process is applied for the still unmatched stay points. According to user survey and place category, we selected and defined several places where people stay with high frequency in daily life and designed a POI dictionary for each place type according to address name (see Table 1). The unmatched stay points will be attached with location type based on their key words of POI_{name}.

3.3. Decision Tree-Based Location Prediction. Sequential semantic trajectories of each individual are constructed after the semantic place recognition process. According to the historical movement paths, we could find the individual's activity routines and behavior patterns by decision tree method, a popular machine learning method. Usually, it takes two steps to build a decision tree, including growing a decision tree and pruning it.

3.3.1. Grow a Tree. In this paper, the ID3 decision tree algorithm [34, 35] was adopted as the main tool for executing a decision tree for our experiment. This algorithm creates a multiway tree, where there are root nodes, child nodes, branches, and leaf nodes, finding for each node the categorical feature that will yield the largest information gain for categorical targets. The formulas of information entropy and information gain are shown as follows:

$$\text{entropy}(D) = -\sum_{i=1}^{n} p_i \log_2 p_i,$$

$$\text{gain} = \text{entropy}(D) - \sum_{j=1}^{k} \frac{|D^j|}{|D|} \times \text{entropy}(D_j),$$

$$(3)$$

where p_i is the probability of appearance of class i in dataset D, j represents each branch node in the tree, and $|D^j|/|D|$ describes the weight of the jth partition. The attribute with highest information gain is selected to be the best extended branch for the corresponding node.

Given the people's behavior pattern in daily life, we took corresponding contextual information including temporal and sequential features into consideration in the decision tree construction (see Table 2). Temporal features include the day of week and the time of day, which represent the specific leaving time from one place to another. Sequential feature refers

TABLE 2: The contextual information used in decision tree construction.

Feature	Description
Day of week	Mon, Tue, Wen, Thu, Fri, Sat, Sun
Time of day	1, 2, ... , 23, 24
Present location	Home, Work, Restaurant, Shopping, Entertainment, Business, Attractions, Others

to the moving sequence. There is high correlation between two successive locations. For this reason, we took the present location as a sequential feature in the next place prediction. Since we assumed that all the input features are discrete values, the time attribute was divided into 24 sections. For example, "12" domain ranges from 11:30 am to 12:30 am, which is lunch time for most people. Besides, location types were predefined according to the specific places with high frequency and purpose. These specific places include the following types: Home (cover dormitory for students), Work (cover laboratory building for students), Restaurant (cover canteen for workers or students), Shopping (cover all the shopping area, from small supermarket to large shopping mall), Entertainment (cover playground, cinema, KTV, etc.), Business (cover communal services, e.g., hospital, administration, etc.), Attractions (cover park, museum, scenic spot, etc.), and Others (cover places except for the above). In this way, the temporal and spatial characteristics are easier to be utilized in feature analysis.

3.3.2. Prun the Tree. Decision trees are created for individuals in location type prediction according to the feature selection above. When a decision tree is built, some branches might reflect noises from the training data. Then a pruning process is carried out to solve the data over-fitting problem. ID3 uses pessimistic pruning, which makes use of error rates estimated from the training set, to replace subtree with a leaf node. This leaf is labelled with the most frequent class among the subtree being replaced [36]. An example of a decision tree structure for location prediction is shown in Figure 4. It follows a top-down approach, which starts with a training set of tuples and their associated feature labels. Based on the personalized decision tree, next location type can be calculated by providing the user's present spatial-temporal-semantic feature. For example, we can predict that the user will go for shopping when at noon at Tuesday after work. In this case, it would be incredibly helpful in places

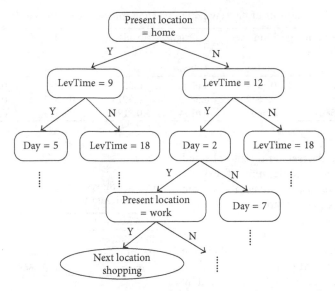

FIGURE 4: An example of a decision tree structure for location prediction.

TABLE 3: Some information of collected examples.

Items	User 1	User 2	User 3	User 4	User 5
GPS points	435822	456682	1354073	1335542	2351170
"Check in" points	468	279	322	448	147
Valid days	88	82	81	84	83
Size of data (MB)	48.1	49.2	146	133	239

recommendation system to realize location type prediction according to current geographic position.

4. Experiments and Results

In this section, we will introduce the evaluation method and give the comparative experimental analysis of the proposed contextual location prediction method.

4.1. Data Description. In this paper, we performed our experiments with two datasets: Geolife dataset [37] which is collected by Microsoft Research Asia and our own collected dataset. In the Geolife dataset, GPS trajectories are represented by a sequence of time-stamped coordinates collected by 178 users in a period of over three years from 2007 to 2011 in Beijing, China. Our own dataset is real mobility data (GPS, BDS) which are collected by 14 participants for three months (from 2016-10-15 to 2017-01-15) through their GPS-enabled smartphones. All the participants live in Guangzhou, China, and basically lead a regular life. Seven of them are office workers, and the others are students. A self-made program was running in participants' smartphones all day long for recording their daily mobility data continuously. In addition to GPS data (date, time, and coordinates), location description and POIs are also recorded through Baidu Maps API. As for "check in" data, participants are asked to check in by clicking on a digital map when they visit a place and stay more than 10 minutes. In the meantime, they should choose a place type from a predefined list based on the

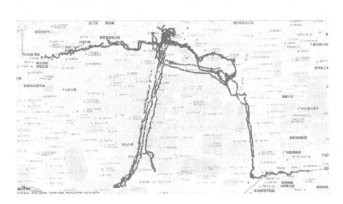

FIGURE 5: An example of user trajectories in one day.

purpose (going for work, going for dinner, etc.) which used to improve the accuracy of places recognition in semantic places recognition process.

We finally collected 15568306 GPS points (13561 points per person a day at average) and 5064 "check in" records (4.4 records per person a day at average). Some information of collected examples are shown in Table 3. Figure 5 shows an example of a participant's trajectories in one day.

4.2. Stay Point Detection. In order to verify the feasibility of the modified trip-identify method (MTI), we compared our method with the classical stay point detection algorithm (SPD) [14] and the original trip-identify method (OTI) [15]

TABLE 4: Comparisons of the stay point detection methods with the Geolife dataset.

	Stay point detection algorithm (SPD) [14]			Original trip-identify method (OTI) [15]			Modified trip-identify method (MTI)		
	100 m	200 m	500 m	100 m	200 m	500 m	100 m	200 m	500 m
Precision	0.5931	0.6192	0.6914	0.6726	0.6850	0.6927	0.6822	0.6983	0.6964
Recall	0.4947	0.5756	0.6642	0.5850	0.5914	0.6563	0.5926	0.6073	0.6616
F-measure	0.5103	0.5801	0.6644	0.6154	0.6190	0.6524	0.6239	0.6339	0.6670

using two datasets, the public dataset, and self-collected dataset. F-measure [38], which is a measure of experiment accuracy in statistical analysis, is considered as the evaluation criteria to evaluate the performances of stay point detection. The formulas of the statistics are as follows:

To investigate the performances on accuracy of different area sizes among three algorithms (SPD, OTI, and MTI), we conducted experiments with different distance values while time threshold was set as 10 minutes. The labels recorded by volunteers are used to judge the results. The experimental results are shown in Table 4. We find that these three algorithms are comparable when the distance value is 500 meters. However, when the distance value is smaller than 500 meters, that is 200 or 100 meters, it is obvious that two trip-identify methods perform better than the SPD algorithm. The F-measures of them exceed by 8.0% and 21.4% at average, respectively. It demonstrates that trip-identify methods work better in extracting stay points on a larger spatial scale.

Our own dataset is used to test the effectiveness of the MTI method focusing on a small distance again. The parameters are set as follows, as the distance value is 100 m, time threshold is 10 minutes, and the walking speed threshold is 0.5 m/s [32]. "Check in" points are treated as the true values and used to determine whether the detected stay points are correct. Table 5 presents the comparisons of performances between the proposed MTI method and the other ones. As can be seen from the table, two trip-identify methods are obviously superior to the SPD algorithm with high-sampling-rate-mobile device logs, and the MTI method is slightly better than the OTI method by solving the cold-start problem.

$$\text{precision} = \frac{\text{the correct detected stay points}}{\text{all the detected stay points}},$$

$$\text{recall} = \frac{\text{the correct detected stay points}}{\text{all the real stay points}}, \quad (4)$$

$$\text{F} - \text{measure} = \frac{2 \times \text{precison} \times \text{recall}}{\text{precison} + \text{recall}}.$$

Extensive experiments were conducted to find out a suitable distance value for the MTI method considering different types of users. Figures 6(a) and 6(b) present the recall rates and precisions with respect to different distance values. In this case, the recall rate is opposite to the distance value, the distance value is larger, and the recall rate is smaller. However, the changing law of the precision is different from the recall rate. The precision first goes up and

TABLE 5: Staypoints extraction results of three methods on our own collected data (100 m).

	SPD	OTI	MTI
Precision	0.4918	0.7685	0.7933
Recall	0.6861	0.7028	0.7208
F-measure	0.5664	0.7236	0.7445

then stays around 80% when the distance value is larger than 100 m. The number of the detected stay points is correlated with the distance value. It is known that the distance value is smaller and more stay points are detected. In the meantime, the more stay points ensure the recall rate to some degree. But, the precision is relatively low for the reason that an excess of stay points are judged as errors when the time-stamps have not matched to corresponding "check in" points.

As for the comparison between office workers and college students, both the recall rate and precision are slightly different on two types of people. For example, living in school campus, students mainly move among teaching buildings, canteens, and dormitories. Most stay points are located in a small area; thus, the recall of college students decreases more quickly than that of workers. To determine the best distance value, F-measure rate, which synthesizes the recall and precision, is taken as the main consideration. Although there is different impact on the F-measure with the same distance value between office workers and college students, the changing law of F-measure is coincident. Besides, there is no significant impact on parameter selection with two types of people. In order to simplify and unify the experiment, we chose a proper distance parameter value (80 m) for the next process for the reason that the values of F-measure (Figure 6(c)) are basically consistent when the distance parameter is set to 60 m or 80 m for both workers and students.

4.3. Semantic Place Recognition. After stay point detection, we tried to turn the coordinate positions into semantic places by using "check in" data and POI dictionary. To better obtain people's destinations of their trips, especially home and work places, the labels ("check in" data) should be given prior consideration in the matching process. To recognize special unmatched stay points, DBSCAN algorithm is adopted to find out individuals' frequent regions for the second step. At last, key word matching process with POI dictionary is also applied for the still unmatched stay points.

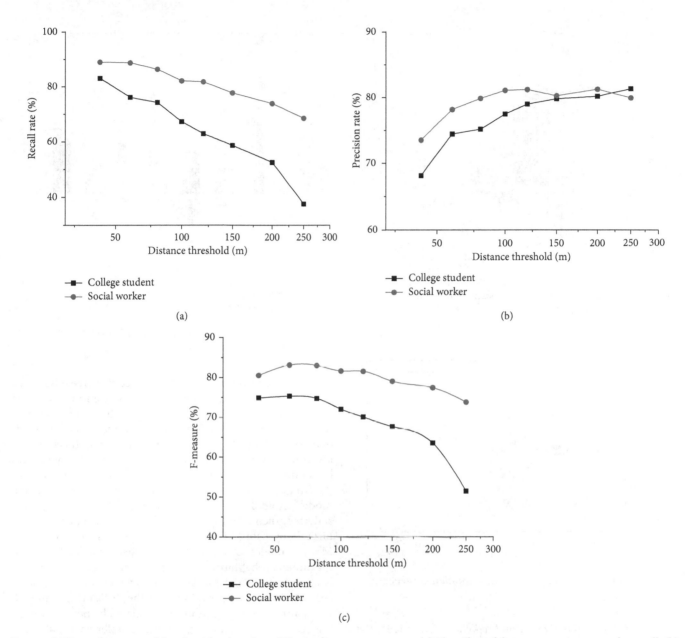

FIGURE 6: The performance of the algorithm based on different distance parameters. (a) The effect of distance parameters on the recall. (b) The effect of distance parameters on the precision. (c) The effect of distance parameters on the F-measure.

For the first step, a traversal method is applied to match a corresponding check-in point for each single stay point according to timestamp and position attributes. The related matching rule has been mentioned in Section 3; then we will not go into all the details of "check in" data matching processes here. During the second step, as mentioned above, the value of Eps and MinPts in DBSCAN algorithm have a great impact on individuals' frequent locations extraction and place type estimation. Thus, an experiment was conducted to find out the proper parameter values for discovering people's locations of interest.

Figure 7 shows the number of extracted clusters with different parameter values and indicates that the number of the extracted frequent locations is opposite to both parameters. The Eps and MinPts values are smaller; the

number of extracted frequent locations is larger. But frequent locations approach to constant around two to three as the values of Eps and MinPts increase. Figure 8 gives an example of frequent location clusters. Considering the performance of clustering, we compared the result with the truths from participants and chose number three as the clustering number of frequent locations taking the common daily lives into consideration. According to the clustering result, the stationary point of the figure appears at (6, 40). Thus, we chose 6 and 40 as the proper MinPts and Eps values during the clusters matching process. After that, the unmatched stay points away from the frequent locations clusters are attached with semantic information based on self-designed POI dictionary as mentioned in Section 3.

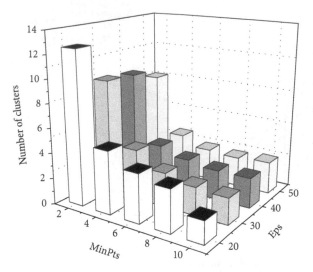

FIGURE 7: Performance of frequent locations extraction with different Eps and MinPts value.

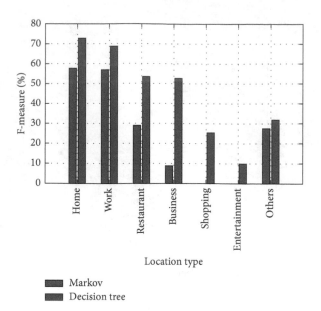

Markov
Decision tree

FIGURE 9: Performance of location type prediction based on the Markov model and the decision tree model.

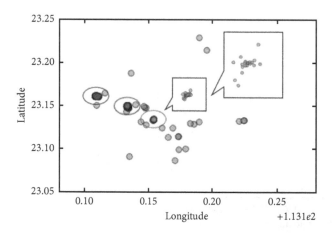

FIGURE 8: An example of frequent location clusters.

4.4. Decision Tree-Based Location Prediction.

To validate the suitability of the decision tree model in location type prediction, the classical Markov model [19] was used for comparison. The Markov model is a stochastic model used to model randomly changing systems. It assumes that future states depend only on the current state. As for the contextual location prediction here, a set of states corresponds to the locations types extracted from spatial and semantic features. The Markov transferring matrix consists of the probabilities extracted from temporal and sequential features. They are calculated based on the number of times of each historical route. A higher Markov probability in the transferring matrix indicates that the corresponding transferring route is a more frequent route in user's daily life.

In the experiment, mobile devices logs collected in the two former months were used as training data, while the data of the last month were used as testing data. Likewise, precision, recall rate, and F-measure are used again to evaluate the performances of the prediction models. Figure 9 shows the F-measure comparisons of the contextual location type

prediction performance between the decision tree model and the Markov model. It is obvious that home and work places are considered as the most frequently visited locations for all the participants. This pattern is one of the main characteristics of human's daily life. As for the restaurant type, it is tested as a medium frequency visited place since people sometimes have dinner at home or company. In this case, F-measure of the Markov model is lower than that of the decision tree model. In addition to these periodic activities, occasional activities, such as business and shopping, also become predictable by using historical mobile devices logs. Since the Markov model is a probability statistic model based on maximum probability theory. Only the maximum probability is considered in the Markov model while spatial-temporal characteristics are all exploited in the decision tree model. Here, attraction type cannot be predicted by both methods. The reason is that younger generations prefer staying at home to relax rather than going outside for entertainment these years. And it can be inferred that data of three months are not so sufficient as to fail to build a perfect tree and predict attraction type. However, the above results indicate that the decision tree model achieves better contextual location prediction performance for individuals.

Figure 10 shows the experimental result of one participant. We can see from the figure that he may be an office worker who basically follows a daily routine between home and work place. Both the Markov and decision tree models perform pretty well (about 70%) on type prediction of "Home" and "Work." However, it turns out to be a problem that small probability events have usually been ignored in the Markov model. By contrast, the decision tree model is able to predict restaurants, business, and the others in spite of low recall (lower than 40%). It proves that the decision tree model has better performances especially on prediction of types with low frequency by making full use of spatial-temporal features. Overall, the prediction of commercial

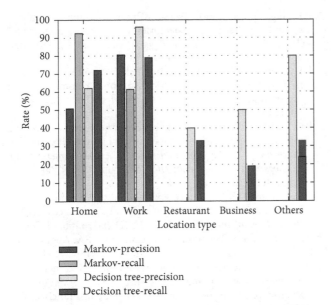

FIGURE 10: An example about location type prediction of one participant based on Markov and decision tee.

location type like restaurants, shopping, and entertainment can be predicted better by using the decision tree model.

5. Conclusions and Future Work

In this paper, we proposed a contextual location prediction framework for better personalized location recommendation in LBS by predicting next personally semantic place from mobile devices logs. It consists of three main modules: stay point detection, semantic places recognition, and decision tree-based prediction. The performances of each module have been evaluated with collected real-world dataset. The stay point detection results show that the modified trip-identify method extracts more precise locations with the challenge of cold-start problem compared with classical stay point detection and the original trip-identify method. A clustering algorithm and a designed POI dictionary have proven to be effective in semantic places recognition for dealing with the problem of the lack of semantic information on mobile data. The decision tree-based method, which has better performance in prediction compared with classical Markov model especially in location with low frequency, is applied for individuals' intention prediction. On the whole, the feasibility of the proposed contextual location prediction framework has been proved.

To the best of our knowledge, our work is the first to explore contextual location prediction based on the mobile devices logs collected by participants last for a couple of months. So, the proposed approach may inevitably have several limitations. For example, the prediction rate is easy to be affected by the quality of the real-world dataset. Besides, the specific value parameters in algorithms mentioned above depend on life experiences and repetitive testing. And in case office worker change their jobs or student change the schedules in a new term which has impact on personal activity prediction in real-time situation, the more recent historical

trajectories can be endowed with a larger weight in training process. Based on the above considerations, we will focus on the improvement of the adaptability of this approach including parameters self-adjusting and real-time capability in the future.

Acknowledgments

This work was supported by the Key Science and Technology Planning Project of Guangdong Province (No. 2015B010104003), the Key Science and Technology Planning Projects of Guangzhou (No. 201604046007), the National Key Research and Development Program of China (No. 2017YFB0504103), National Natural Science Foundation of China (No. 41704020), and the Fundamental Research Funds for the Central Universities (No. 17lgpy43).

References

[1] Y. Lu and Y. Liu, "Pervasive location acquisition technologies: opportunities and challenges for geospatial studies," *Computers, Environment and Urban Systems*, vol. 36, no. 2, pp. 105–108, 2012.

[2] Y. Ye, Y. Zheng, Y. Chen, J. Feng, and X. Xie, "Mining individual life pattern based on location history," in *Proceedings of the 10th International Conference on Mobile Data Management: Systems, Services and Middleware (MDM'09)*, pp. 1–10, Taipei, Taiwan, May 2009.

[3] A. Monreale, F. Pinelli, R. Trasarti, and F. Giannotti, "WhereNext: a location predictor on trajectory pattern mining," in *Proceedings of the 15th ACM SIGKDD International Conference on Knowledge Discovery and Data Mining*, pp. 637–646, Paris, France, June 2009.

[4] S. Isaacman, R. Becker, R. Caceres et al., "Identifying important places in people's lives from cellular network data," in *Lecture Notes in Computer Science*, vol. 6696, pp. 133–151, Springer, Berlin, Germany, 2011.

[5] M. Mamei, M. Colonna, and M. Galassi, "Automatic identification of relevant places from cellular network data," *Pervasive and Mobile Computing*, vol. 31, pp. 147–158, 2016.

[6] S. Hoteit, S. Secci, S. Sobolevsky, C. Ratti, and G. Pujolle, "Estimating human trajectories and hotspots through mobile phone data," *Computer Networks*, vol. 64, pp. 296–307, 2014.

[7] M. Brunato and R. Battiti, "Statistical learning theory for location fingerprinting in wireless LANs," *Computer Networks*, vol. 47, no. 6, pp. 825–845, 2005.

[8] J. Hightower, S. Consolvo, A. Lamarca, I. Smith, and J. Hughes, "Learning and recognizing the places we go," in *Proceedings of the 7th International Conference on Ubiquitous Computing (UbiComp'05)*, pp. 159–176, Tokyo, Japan, September 2005.

[9] D. Kim, J. Hightower, R. Govindan, and D. Estrin, "Discovering semantically meaningful places from pervasive RF-beacons," in *Proceedings of the 11th International Conference on Ubiquitous Computing(UbiComp'09)*, pp. 21–30, Orlando, FL, USA, September 2009.

[10] M. Lv, L. Chen, Z. Xu, Y. Li, and G. Chen, "The discovery of personally semantic places based on trajectory data mining," *Neurocomputing*, vol. 173, pp. 1142–1153, 2016.

[11] D. Ashbrook and T. Starner, "Using GPS to learn significant locations and predict movement across multiple users," *Personal and Ubiquitous Computing*, vol. 7, no. 5, pp. 275–286, 2003.

[12] C. Zhou, D. Frankowski, P. Ludford, S. Shekhar, and L. Terveen, "Discovering personally meaningful places: an interactive clustering approach," *ACM Transactions on Information Systems*, vol. 25, no. 3, p. 12, 2007.

[13] A. Palma, V. Bogorny, B. Kuijpers, and L. O. Alvares, "A clustering-based approach for discovering interesting places in trajectories," in *Proceedings of the 2008 ACM Symposium on Applied Computing (SAC)*, pp. 863–868, Fortaleza, Ceara, Brazil, March 2008.

[14] Q. Li, Y. Zheng, X. Xie, Y. Chen, W. Liu, and W.-Y. Ma, "Mining user similarity based on location history," in *Proceedings of the 16th ACM SIGSPATIAL International Symposium on Advances in Geographic Information Systems*, pp. 34:1–34:10, Irvine, CA, USA, November 2008.

[15] J. Zhang, P. Qiu, Z. Xu, and M. Du, "A method to identify trip based on the mobile phone positioning data," *Journal of Wuhan University of Technology*, vol. 37, no. 5, pp. 934–938, 2013.

[16] M. Gonzalez, C. Hidalgo, and A. Barabasi, "Understanding individual human mobility patterns," *Nature*, vol. 453, no. 7196, pp. 779–782, 2008.

[17] C. Song, Z. Qu, N. Blumm, and A. Barabasi, "Limits of predictability in human mobility," *Science*, vol. 327, no. 5968, pp. 1018–1021, 2010.

[18] M. Chen, X. Yu, and Y. Liu, "Mining moving patterns for predicting next location," *Information Systems*, vol. 54, pp. 156–168, 2015.

[19] S. Gambs, M. Killijian, and M. Cortez, "Next place prediction using mobility Markov chains," in *Proceedings of EuroSys 2012 Workshop on Measurement, Privacy, and Mobility (MPM)*, pp. 1–6, Bern, Switzerland, April 2012.

[20] A. Asahara, K. Maruyama, A. Sato, and K. Seto, "Pedestrian-movement prediction based on mixed Markov-chain model," in *Proceedings of the 19th ACM SIGSPATIAL International Symposium on Advances in Geographic Information Systems (ACM-GIS)*, pp. 25–33, Chicago, IL, USA, November 2011.

[21] W. Huang, S. Li, X. Liu, and Y. Ban, "Predicting human mobility with activity changes," *International Journal of Geographical Information Science*, vol. 29, no. 9, pp. 1569–1587, 2015.

[22] S. Cho, "Exploiting machine learning techniques for location recognition and prediction with smartphone logs," *Neurocomputing*, vol. 176, pp. 98–106, 2016.

[23] W. Mathew, R. Raposo, and B. Martins, "Predicting future locations with hidden Markov models," in *Proceedings of the 2012 ACM Conference on Ubiquitous Computing*, pp. 911–918, Pittsburg, PA, USA, September 2012.

[24] M. Morzy, "Mining frequent trajectories of moving objects for location prediction," in *Proceedings of the 5th International Conference on Machine Learning and Data Mining in Pattern Recognition (MLDM)*, pp. 667–680, Leipzig, Germany, July 2007.

[25] P. Lei, T. Shen, W. Peng, and I.-J. Su, "Exploring spatial-temporal trajectory model for location prediction," in *Proceedings of the 12th IEEE International Conference on Mobile Data Management (MDM)*, pp. 58–67, Luleå, Sweden, June 2011.

[26] C. Parent, S. Spaccapietra, C. Renso et al., "Semantic trajectories modeling and analysis," *ACM Computing Surveys*, vol. 45, no. 4, pp. 1–32, 2013.

[27] J. Ying, W. Lee, and V. Tseng, "Mining geographic-temporal-semantic patterns in trajectories for location prediction," *ACM Transactions on Intelligent Systems and Technology*, vol. 5, no. 1, pp. 1–33, 2013.

[28] J. Zhang, C. Chowmember, and Y. Li, "iGeoRec: a personalized and efficient geographical location recommendation framework," *IEEE Transactions on Services Computing*, vol. 8, no. 5, pp. 701–714, 2015.

[29] C. Jonathan and S. Eric, "Location 3: how users share and respond to location-based data on social networking sites," in *Proceedings of the 5th International AAAI Conference on Weblogs and Social Media (ICWSM)*, pp. 74–80, Barcelona, Spain, July 2011.

[30] A. Tarasov, F. Kling, and A. Pozdnoukhov, "Prediction of user location using the radiation model and social check-ins," in *Proceedings of the 2nd ACM SIGKDD International Conference on Urban Computing*, p. 7, Chicago, USA, August 2013.

[31] H. Gao, J. Tang, X. Hu et al., "Modeling temporal effects of human mobile behavior on location-based social networks," in *Proceedings of the Conference on Information and Knowledge Management*, pp. 1673–1678, San Francisco, CA, USA, August 2013.

[32] J. Du and L. Aultmanhall, "Increasing the accuracy of trip rate information from passive multi-day GPS travel datasets: automatic trip end identification issues," *Transportation Research Part A-Policy and Practice*, vol. 41, no. 3, pp. 220–232, 2007.

[33] M. Ester, H. Kriegel, J. Sander, and X. Xiaowei, "A density-based algorithm for discovering clusters in large spatial databases with noise," *Knowledge Discovery and Data Mining*, vol. 96, no. 34, pp. 226–231, 1996.

[34] J. R. Quinlan, "Induction of decision trees," *Machine Learning*, vol. 1, no. 1, pp. 81–106, 1986.

[35] J. S. Lee and E. S. Lee, "Exploring the usefulness of a decision tree in predicting people's locations," *Procedia-Social and Behavioral Sciences*, vol. 140, no. 4, pp. 447–451, 2014.

[36] B. B. Nair, V. P. Mohandas, and N. R. Sakthivel, "A decision tree- rough set hybrid system for stock market trend prediction," *International Journal of Computer Applications*, vol. 6, no. 9, pp. 1–6, 2010.

[37] Y. Zheng, X. Xie, and W. Ma, "Geolife: a collaborative social networking service among user, location and trajectory," *IEEE Data Engineering Bulletin*, vol. 33, no. 2, pp. 32–40, 2010.

[38] D. M. Powers, "Evaluation: from precision, recall and F-measure to ROC, informedness, markedness and correlation," *Journal of Machine Learning Technologies*, vol. 2, no. 1, pp. 37–63, 2011.

4

Immersive Gesture Interfaces for Navigation of 3D Maps in HMD-Based Mobile Virtual Environments

Yea Som Lee ⓘD and Bong-Soo Sohn ⓘD

School of Computer Science and Engineering, Chung-Ang University, Seoul, Republic of Korea

Correspondence should be addressed to Bong-Soo Sohn; bongbong@cau.ac.kr

Academic Editor: Marcos A. Vieira

3D maps such as Google Earth and Apple Maps (3D mode), in which users can see and navigate in 3D models of real worlds, are widely available in current mobile and desktop environments. Users usually use a monitor for display and a keyboard/mouse for interaction. Head-mounted displays (HMDs) are currently attracting great attention from industry and consumers because they can provide an immersive virtual reality (VR) experience at an affordable cost. However, conventional keyboard and mouse interfaces decrease the level of immersion because the manipulation method does not resemble actual actions in reality, which often makes the traditional interface method inappropriate for the navigation of 3D maps in virtual environments. From this motivation, we design immersive gesture interfaces for the navigation of 3D maps which are suitable for HMD-based virtual environments. We also describe a simple algorithm to capture and recognize the gestures in real-time using a Kinect depth camera. We evaluated the usability of the proposed gesture interfaces and compared them with conventional keyboard and mouse-based interfaces. Results of the user study indicate that our gesture interfaces are preferable for obtaining a high level of immersion and fun in HMD-based virtual environments.

1. Introduction

Virtual reality (VR) is a technology which provides users with software-created virtual 3D environments that simulate physical presence of users to provide immersion [1]. A great deal of research has been performed to enhance the realism of VR by making the user's actual motion match the real-time interaction with virtual space [2, 3]. In 1968, Sutherland invented a head-mounted display (HMD), and other VR devices have since been developed to stimulate a user's vision and movement. The HMD, which is now a commonly used VR device, is a glasses-type monitor worn on the head. HMDs are currently attracting a huge amount of attention from industries and users since they provide the VR experience at an affordable cost. HMDs provide a high level of immersion through (i) a stereoscopic display, (ii) wide viewing angles, and (iii) head orientation tracking. Because of the above advantages, HMDs can be utilized in various fields such as education [4, 5], medical treatment [5–7], and entertainment.

3D maps [8] such as Google Earth [9] and Apple Maps (3D mode) allow users to see and navigate 3D models of real worlds in a map. With the recent development of automatic 3D reconstruction algorithm applied to satellite images and mobile environments, high-quality 3D maps of places have become accessible in a wide and ubiquitous way, such that any remote user can explore any place with great realism. However, in most of these cases, the 3D maps can be experienced on a two-dimensional flat screen. Research on virtual maps can also be used to visualize statistics regarding climate change and population density, or to display topographical maps, building drawings, and information in augmented reality. This means that methods that utilize HMDs, rather than conventional monitors, for 3D map navigation are valuable.

However, since there is a limit to the sense of reality imparted by the HMD device, it is necessary for the user to adopt a technique to explore and perceive a virtual space just like a real space. Virtual reality programs running on a PC usually use traditional input devices such as a keyboard or a mouse, but this has the disadvantage that it does not match the behavior of the user in a virtual environment. Because computational speeds are limited, there is a time difference between a user's movements in physical space and movement in the virtual environment. In a VR environment, the time difference between the movement of the user and movement in the virtual space interferes with the immersion and causes dizziness [6, 10, 11], consequently reducing interest. For this reason, research has been needed to increase the immersion and interest in VR by adjusting the input methods to directly match body movements. Also, in order to maximize the satisfaction of the user, an intuitive interface method for the user in the virtual space is required.

Accordingly, development of devices related to the operation interface has been actively carried out in order to compensate for the disadvantage caused by the relative inability to use conventional input/output devices in the VR environment. A device that recognizes the user's motion is a haptic-type device [12], which is generally held in the hand, and the avatar in the virtual space has the ability to guide the user's desired motion naturally and without delay. For these reasons, joysticks or Nintendo Wiimote [13–16] controllers have been developed as control devices that replace the keyboard. As a result, there are more and more cases where appliances that recognize the movement of the user and improve the accuracy of the operation are utilized in the game or the virtual space. However, there is a limitation in maximizing the gesture recognition and immersion using the whole body of the user based on the position sensor of the haptic device in the virtual space. From this motivation, we designed and implemented various realistic gesture interfaces that can recognize user's gestures in real-time using Kinect to reflect the user's movements in an HMD-based virtual environment. In addition, we measured the usability of the proposed gesture interface and the conventional control interface based on the keyboard and mouse, and compared the advantages and disadvantages of each interface through a user study. Figure 1 shows a user wearing an HMD using customized motion recognition system, while experiencing a given virtual environment.

In this paper, we design and implement immersive gesture interfaces that are recognized in real-time using the Kinect depth camera. The position of each joint is identified and analyzed to allow the gesture of the user in the virtual environment to reflect the actual physical gestures. The degree of user satisfaction, including the degree of interest and ease of use, was checked according to the manipulation method. The main contributions of our paper are as follows.

(i) We designed and implemented immersive gesture interfaces with integration of flyover (bird, superman, and hand) and exploratory (zoom, rotation, and translation) navigation, which is recognized in real-time through the Kinect camera for HMD-based VR environments.

(ii) We evaluated the usability of the proposed gesture interfaces and conventional keyboard/mouse-based interfaces with a user study. Various usability factors

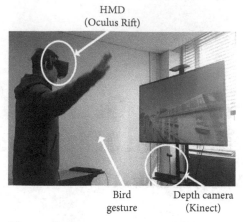

FIGURE 1: The virtual environment system implementation used in this paper. The user wearing the HMD (Oculus Rift CV1) performs an action similar to that of a bird, which the Kinect recognizes. In a virtual environment (Paris Town), the user feels immersed like a bird.

(e.g., immersion, accuracy, comfort, fun, nonfatigue, nondizziness, and overall satisfaction) were measured.

(iii) We analyzed the advantages and disadvantages of each interface from the results of the user study.

As a result of the user study, it can be demonstrated that the users prefer the gesture interface to the keyboard and mouse interface in terms of immersion and fun. The keyboard interface received high marks for accuracy, convenience, and unobtrusiveness. These results confirm that the method of manipulating a virtual environment affects the usability and satisfaction regarding the experience of the virtual environment.

The remainder of this paper is organized as follows. We discuss related papers in Section 2. The design and method of the proposed gesture interfaces are described in Section 3 and Section 4, respectively. Section 5 describes the user study design and the results of the user study. Section 6 discusses our conclusions.

2. Related Work

One of the main goals in VR research is to increase the sense of immersion. Mass-market HMDs are becoming popular because they can provide a high level of immersion at an affordable cost. With the emergence of a need for immersive movement control [17], companies that produce HMD devices have recently been introducing game controllers with auxiliary functions (e.g., Oculus Touch) [18]. The HMD was initially invented by Ivan Sutherland in 1968 [19], but it was initially difficult to commercialize for many reasons, including the high cost, heavy weight, space limitations for installation, and a poor display. The biggest problem was the limitation of the display technology [20]. HMDs are divided into two types, a desktop and a mobile VR, depending on the size of the image that can be processed and the complexity of the structure. Mobile VR is hosted and ultimately displayed on a mobile phone, and there is no real restriction on the range of movement because it is wireless.

Recently, IT companies have been developing a variety of products by studying and developing interfaces for HMDs that provide high immersion and allow for smooth and seamless user interaction. Desktop VR is widely used for research purposes. As the computational power and display resolution of smartphones increase, companies have developed diverse content using Mobile VR, rather than Desktop VR platforms. As HMD technology has progressed, HMDs have been used in various fields such as education [5], medical care [5–7], and architecture. Kihara et al. [21] conducted a study and experiment on laparoscopic surgery using an HMD and verified the feasibility of using HMDs in the medical field. It is now possible to use an HMD to minimize laparotomy incisions, instead of using abdominal laparotomy or high-cost robotic surgery systems, in which a large scar may remain, with an increased risk of infection. The surgeon wears an HMD, and the system provides a 3D image, depth map, and tactile feedback associated with the affected area, and performs a safe operation. In addition, varied research is being conducted to recognize the facial expressions of users using an HMD and to simulate these expressions in a virtual environment [22].

Research on the interaction between humans and computers has been studied in earnest as soon as personal computers became available. The HCI (human-computer interaction) [23] aims to allow people to use and communicate with a computer in a human-friendly manner. As the use of computers increases, HCI is carefully considered in the development of computer-user interfaces (UI) [24, 25]. For this purpose, a study has been conducted on an interface using body gestures rather than the conventional input devices [26]. The main difference from previous HCI-related researches is that our approach focuses on improving the level of immersion in an HMD-based virtual environment for designing navigation interfaces in addition to other important usability factors such as the level of accuracy, fun, and comfort.

Humans have the ability to make emotional expressions using the body and to allow meaningful behaviors to take the place of language [24, 25]. Gesture recognition can be applied to various fields, such as sign language [6, 12], rehabilitation [13, 15, 27], and virtual reality, and is easy to utilize in computer applications. In particular, a meaningful gesture using the body refers to expressible behavior related to the physical movement of a finger, hand, arm, leg, head, face, or body. The main purpose of human gestures is to communicate meaningful information or to interact with the surrounding environment. However, since the various operations used for this purpose may overlap or have different meanings, it is necessary to sufficiently study the development of interface technology based on gesture recognition. Unlike existing keyboard and mouse input devices, it is necessary to search the body part using sensors and to recognize the operation after tracking the position [24, 25, 28].

In particular, a device such as a joystick, which can be used as a substitute for a keyboard and a mouse, can be used to increase the user's sense of immersion. Since the effectiveness of the hand manipulation method has since been verified, controllers such as the Kinect [23, 26, 28, 29] and Leap motion [28, 30] have been released. As games and applications that can be experienced in a VR environment have been developed, it has been confirmed that the act of controlling the virtual space through the movement of the body plays an important role in making VR realistic and immersive. In addition, various methods for recognizing user's movements have been studied [31–33].

As mentioned, the haptic-type device has been developed, held in the user's hand, in order to reflect the user's gestures in such a manner that the user can easily forget the difference between the virtual reality and the real world [12]. The keyboard, mouse, joystick, and similar traditional input devices can be used to move around in virtual space by holding the device with a hand or by wearing it. However, these conventional devices have limitations. The haptic device increases the probability of accurately recognizing the user's motion, but it can limit the range of motion, and consistently wearing the haptic device can be troublesome [12]. In addition, it requires time to learn a formal haptic device operation method [34], and it is insufficient to realize the virtual reality realistically because it is manipulated while holding it in the hand or wearing it directly.

For these reasons, in this paper we have developed immersive and intuitive gesture interfaces to control the navigation in a virtual environment for HMD users. In particular, we deployed simple algorithms to recognize natural gestures in real time. Preliminary results of this paper have appeared in [35, 36]. The main differences are the integration of gestures for flyover and exploratory (e.g., zoom/rotation/translation) navigation and a detailed description of the formal user study results.

3. Design of Immersive Gesture Interfaces

As the need for immersive interfaces to replace traditional input/output devices for HMD-based VR navigation increases, related research has been actively conducted. For this purpose, Microsoft Kinect, which contains a low-cost depth camera, can be used to track and recognize the user's body gestures in real-time and control navigation in the VR environment while wearing an HMD. We developed a VR software system, in which a user can experience a virtual reality through the Unity3D Engine that supports the simultaneous utilization of the Kinect and Oculus Rift. We also defined two types of immersive gesture interfaces, as well as conventional keyboard and mouse-based interfaces. There are six types of gesture interface methods that are proposed in this study. The proposed gesture interfaces that are recognized using the Kinect can be seen in detail in Figures 2 and 3. The location of each joint and body skeleton segment that connects the joints are extracted using Kinect SDK, as shown in Figure 4. These are then used for the real-time recognition of gesture types and intensities.

Most people use their hands when accurately controlling objects, such as when driving a car or playing a PC game [25]. We considered a natural gesture interface that tracks the location and movement of hands since the keyboard and mouse are also hand-based input devices. Because the ratio of right-handed people is high in general, we defined gesture interfaces that primarily use a right hand [37, 38]. The

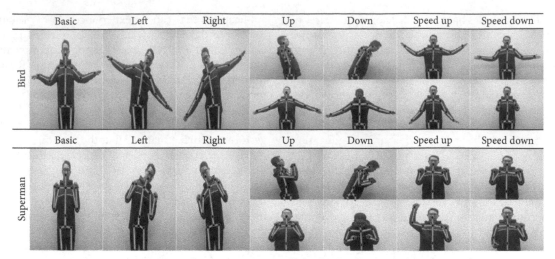

FIGURE 2: Flyover gesture interfaces (bird and superman).

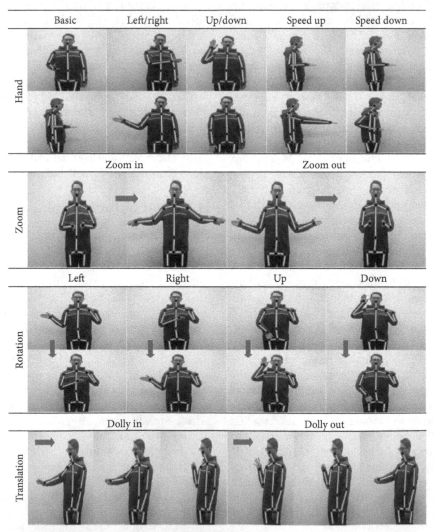

FIGURE 3: Exploration gesture interfaces (hand, zoom, rotation, and translation).

navigation interface implemented in this paper defines bird, superman, and hand gestures as flight mode operations [39] through the tracking of the user's movement with the Kinect. Our gesture interface also supports exploratory navigation features that are provided in Google Earth, such as zoom, rotation, and translation.

For thousands of years, humans have dreamed of being able to fly like a bird. Rheiner developed a VR simulator,

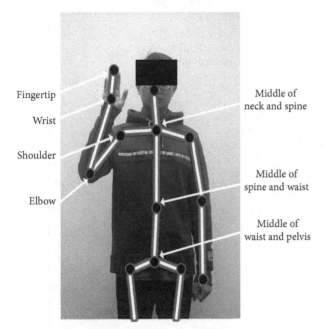

FIGURE 4: Location of joints and body skeleton segments that are recognized through the Kinect.

Fingertip
Wrist
Shoulder
Elbow

Middle of neck and spine
Middle of spine and waist
Middle of waist and pelvis

called *Birdly*, in which a user can experience flying through the 3D space with the Oculus Rift [40]. The user can navigate the Birdly simulator using hands and arms making a waving action that pantomimes the movement of bird wings in 3D. However, since this simulator is bulky and requires significant production costs, it is burdensome for a general user to possess it at home. Also, flying in the sky like a superman-like hero is hard to achieve. Therefore, we implemented a new and superman-like motion interface to implement a gesture interface that is difficult to otherwise experience, giving users a surrogate satisfaction.

3.1. Flyover Navigation.
We aim to make certain that our gesture interfaces: (i) allow a simple and natural action for flyover control that is similar to actual flying behavior, (ii) are recognized in real-time by a low-cost motion sensor, such as the Kinect depth camera, and (iii) enhance the degree of immersion, which is unique to the HMD-based virtual environment. For this purpose, we designed three gesture interfaces (i.e., bird, superman, and hand) for the flyover navigation. The scales of these three gesture interfaces are different (i.e., bird > superman > hand) such that we can understand implicit relationship between usability properties and the scales. The detailed gestures for each interface are shown in Figures 2 and 3, and can be described as follows.

3.1.1. Bird.
The user can adjust the direction by moving the body up, down, left, and right keeping the waist in the basic posture with both arms open, similar to bird wings. In the basic posture, both arms move up and down simultaneously to accelerate, and both arms can be stretched forward at the same time.

3.1.2. Superman.
As shown in Figure 2, hold both hands on both sides of the face at the level of the shoulder line. Move the upper body in the direction to move. Move the body back and forth to go up and down, respectively. When a user wants to adjust the speed, the user can accelerate or decelerate by moving his or her right hand up or down, respectively.

3.1.3. Hand.
Initially, the right hand is set as the reference point and the right hand is placed in the front of the body in a comfortable position, and then held at the initial reference position for 2-3 seconds. The user can manipulate the direction by moving his or her hands vertically or horizontally and can decelerate or accelerate the speed by moving the hand back or forth, respectively, as shown in Figure 3.

3.2. Exploratory Navigation.
Figure 3 shows the proposed gesture interface for 3D map navigation. The defined gesture interface is based on Kinect recognition instead of using a keyboard and a mouse. It implements the operation of moving left/right/up/down, speeding up/down, zoom-in/out, rotation, and translation, which are typical features of the interface provided by Google Earth. The hand interface can be manipulated vertically and horizontally with the right-hand position as the reference point at the first execution, and the hand is moved back and forth to adjust the speed.

3.2.1. Zoom.
The user can control zoom-in or zoom-out, which allows seeing objects either closer or farther away. For the zoom in motion, both arms are stretched straight ahead and then the arms are opened outward. This action gives the feeling of enlarging the space while maintaining symmetry about the body. In an opposite manner, for the zoom out motion, both arms start out to both sides, and are brought together in front of the body, keeping the symmetry as both arms are collected in front of the body.

3.2.2. Rotation.
The user can rotate the screen in four directions. The user can think of the left hand as a globe and use the right hand to rotate it in the desired direction while holding the fist with the left hand.

3.2.3. Translation.
This is an interface that allows one to move quickly to the desired location in the current VR environment and operates with the right hand only. The user has to move the right hand to the location to which he or she wishes to move and hold the fist at that position. The 3D map is enlarged or reduced as the user pulls or pushes the hand in the direction he or she wants to move, using the position of the right hand holding the fist as a reference point. The corresponding action of translating away from a location ends when the right hand with a fist is fully extended, and the fist is released.

The zoom and translation interfaces are similar but operate on different principles and differ from the actual moving subjects. Zoom is a function to zoom in or out of the current VR environment, and the translation interface moves the map such that the user is closer to or farther from the user's starting point in the map.

TABLE 1: Left/right and up/down angles of gestures.

Gesture interface	Left/right angle	Up/down angle
Bird	Angle between x-axis and the line connecting the left/right hands	Angle between y-axis and the line connecting the head and spine
Superman	Angle between y-axis and the line connecting the head and waist	Angle between y-axis and the line connecting the head and spine
Hand	Angle between the x-axis and the line connecting the right hand and right elbow	Angle between the z-axis and the line that connects the right hand and elbow

4. Recognition of Immersive Gesture Interfaces

In order to accurately recognize the meaningful behavior of the user, it is necessary to be able to track the position of the body features. Generally, there exist methods of learning to recognize body parts such as the face or hand in a photo, through Big Data Machine Learning [41]. However, it is difficult to recognize body parts in real-time because even using state-of-the-art algorithms optimized through machine learning, the classification of 3D body parts involves a nontrivial, potentially sickness-causing delay. The Kinect is a device that provides the ability to track a human joint using a depth camera. Skeleton points that are primarily used in this study include the human body parts of the hand, wrist, elbow, and shoulder. We also used a method to calculate the position of the center of the palm to accurately track the state of the hand (fist, palm, etc.) [42].

We utilized the depth map captured by the Kinect infrared projector sensor and Kinect SDK modules to track the location of feature points and extract a skeleton from the human body that was captured in a depth map. For the recognition of gesture types and intensity in bird, superman, and hand interfaces, we define the left/right and up/down angles as shown in Table 1.

We also utilized the Kinect to implement functions that Google Earth supports to navigate 3D maps. With Google Earth, one can perform zoom, rotate, and translate operations using the mouse and keyboard interface to navigate to the desired location in 3D models of buildings and terrain. While building a virtual environment for experiments, we implemented navigation functions that replace the traditional input devices, the mouse and keyboard functions.

Algorithm 1 describes the recognition of gesture interfaces and their magnitude defined in Figure 2.

In order to change the user's left and right direction, the angle between the x-axis (line 1) and the straight line between both hands is compared (line 2), such that the left and right movement is possible (line 3-4). To move up and down, it is necessary to calculate the angle between the line connecting the y-axis and the body part (line 5), and compare the angle (line 6), such that the line can be moved up and down (line 7-8). If the result obtained by calculating the difference from the previously measured distance from the current reference point distance is greater than the

```
A: left/right angle
D: up/down angle
HL: horizontal threshold
R: right hand
L: left hand
CA: left/right magnitude
VL: vertical threshold
CD: up/down magnitude
MD: distance threshold
(1)     if A > HL
(2)         if R > L
(3)             CA = −A;
(4)         else CA = A;
(5)     if D > VL
(6)         if R > L
(7)             CD = −D;
(8)         else CD = D;
(9)     else CD = 0;
(10) if Distance - MD > SpeedUp
(11)        accelerate;
(12) else if Distance - MD < SpeedDown
(13)        break;
```

ALGORITHM 1: Recognition of navigation gestures and their magnitude.

acceleration threshold (line 10), then the speed is increased (line 11), and otherwise the speed decreases (line 12). We experimentally found that it was the best choice for setting horizontal and distance threshold to 0.4–0.7.

Algorithm 2 describes the rotation interface, defined in Figure 3 alongside the samples of zoom and translation interfaces. These operations basically consist of only the values of x and y subtracted by the z value, when the difference between the right hand and the right shoulder is smaller than a predefined threshold (line 1), and the z coordinate should be 0. When rotation or translation occurs (line 3), the degree of the change is shifted by the difference of the right hand, which is changed from the position of the right hand (line 4). When moving in the virtual space, the position of the current right hand becomes the position of the reference hand (line 6-7). When we rotate based on the horizontal and vertical lines (line 9), the values of the horizontal line and the vertical line are added respectively (lines 9-11). The current rotation position is 0 (line 12); only the x-value and y-value are converted at that position (line 13).

Figures 5–7 show details of the zoom, rotate, and translate interface algorithms for tracing joints of depth cameras. The red circle represents the state of the fisted hand, and the green circle represents the palm of the hand. The gray circle implies that some parts of the body may overlap, making it difficult to represent the exact position value.

5. User Study and Results

5.1. User Study Design. For evaluation of our proposed interfaces and for a comparison, we developed VR software based on a 3D map and investigated user responses. We used two 3D datasets, a Grand Canyon model and a French Town

```
R: right
L: left
H: hand
Rot: rotation
c: current
Ho: horizontal line
Ver: vertical line
 (1)  if (LH == Fist and | LH.y–LSh.y | < 0.1f)
 (2)      RH.vector = RH.(x, y, 0);
 (3)      if Rotation
 (4)          add.Rot = RH.vector–cRH.vector;
 (5)          RotHV (add.Rot.x ∗ 100, add.Rot.y ∗ 100);
 (6)      else Rotation = true;
 (7)      cRH = RH;
 (8)  else Rotation = false;
 (9)      RotHV (Ho, Ver)
(10)          cRotH += Ho;
(11)          cRotV += Ver;
(12)          Rot.(cRotV, 0, 0);
(13)          Rot.(0, –cRotH, 0);
```

ALGORITHM 2: Rotation interface.

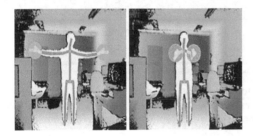

FIGURE 5: Kinect depth image with body skeleton representing zoom gesture interfaces.

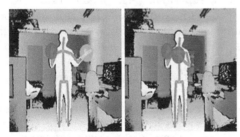

FIGURE 6: Kinect depth image with body skeleton representing rotation gesture interface.

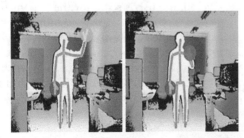

FIGURE 7: Kinect depth image with body skeleton representing translation gesture interface.

model as our test virtual environments (Figure 8). We chose the Oculus Rift (Consumer Version 1) and Microsoft Kinect (Version 2) as the test HMD device and motion sensor, which are relatively affordable for the general public. The VR environment was tested on a desktop PC equipped with an Intel i7 3.6 GHz CPU and 16 GB main memory.

The HMD-based VR software system for navigation was developed with Unity3D [43]. Our method for gesture recognition was developed using the Kinect SDK and Toolkit, distributed by Oculus and Microsoft. As a way to experience the environment for this user study, users could fly in the test virtual environments like birds and superman, and navigate using the right hand. We also made a scenario consisting of zoom, rotation, and translation navigations in the test.

The subjects were 23- to 31-year-old, 12 college students (10 males and 2 females) in the computer engineering department of our university. In order to confirm the clear difference between the existing interface and the proposed interfaces, we conducted a questionnaire to evaluate and quantify an experience index and usability score of each method. Experiments with HMDs were applied to the Grand Canyon model and French Town model, and experiments were conducted with six gesture interfaces and two interfaces based on the keyboard and mouse. For each participant who had never worn the HMD before or who complained of dizziness, we gave a rest period of 1 to 10 minutes between each experience depending on the degree of dizziness [11, 44].

The purpose of this study is to identify the necessity of the gesture interfaces that are needed to replace the existing keyboard manipulation method, through studying the development of technology that can enhance the satisfaction of experiencing a virtual space. We designed the user study to analyze advantages and disadvantages of the proposed interface compared to traditional interface and to verify the significance of the results.

5.2. Experimental Results. From the experiments, each of the 8 usability properties experienced in the two scenarios of the Grand Canyon and the French Town model (e.g., overall satisfaction, accuracy, ease of operation, comfort, immersion, and fun) were quantified in the questionnaire results. In Figure 9, we can see a picture of the average scores for the user's overall satisfaction with the above-mentioned 8 properties evaluated with scores ranging from 1 to 5. The graph starts from the middle (i.e., score 3) because it can better show whether it belongs to good (i.e., to the right from middle) or bad (i.e., to the left from middle) scores. Overall, the degree of fun was the highest, and the scores of other properties were generally good but subjects experienced significant dizziness when using the gesture interfaces.

The results obtained from the Grand Canyon and the Village model differed slightly. The bird interface scored high in the overall satisfaction, and the hand interface scored relatively high in the accuracy. The keyboard and mouse are the easiest to operate and can be redirected with fewer movements, resulting in greater convenience, nonfatigue, and nondizziness. The bird and hand interface is difficult to

FIGURE 8: Test virtual environments. (a) Grand Canyon model. (b) French Town model.

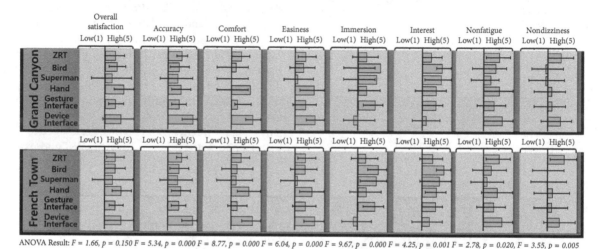

ANOVA Result: $F = 1.66, p = 0.150$ $F = 5.34, p = 0.000$ $F = 8.77, p = 0.000$ $F = 6.04, p = 0.000$ $F = 9.67, p = 0.000$ $F = 4.25, p = 0.001$ $F = 2.78, p = 0.020$, $F = 3.55, p = 0.005$

FIGURE 9: Survey results of our proposed and conventional device interfaces for test virtual environments, (a) Grand Canyon and (b) French Town. The green bars represent the average scores and horizontal whiskers represent standard deviations. The middle vertical line means mid-score (3). The result of the statistical test (ANOVA) is marked below the graphs. Significant difference exists when $P(Sig.) < 0.05$.

manipulate, but has a high score on the degree of fun and immersion. Fifty-eight percent of students prefer to use gesture interfaces that use both hands at the same time, rather than to use one hand. Sixty-seven percent of students responded that it was better to use gesture interface rather than the keyboard and mouse interface. In addition to this, 92% of students liked to wear and experience the HMD instead of the monitor when asked what kind of screen offers better realism.

In order to verify the significance of the experiments conducted in this paper, a one-way ANOVA and Scheffé tests were performed, and the significance was verified in Figure 9. The significance level between each interface and the evaluation items was less than 0.05 for the remaining seven items except satisfaction. At the significance level of 5% (Sig. < 0.05), the null hypothesis was rejected and the alternative hypothesis was adopted. Thus, it is justifiable that the difference of usability between the proposed and existing interfaces is significant. As a result, there was a significant difference in accuracy between the device interface and superman (Sig. = 0.002), gesture interface (Sig. = 0.006), bird (Sig. = 0.017), difference between hand (Sig. = 0.007) and device interface (Sig. = 0.000). In the easiness factor, there was a difference between superman interface and hand (Sig. = 0.011) and device interface (Sig. = 0.000). The immersion factor showed significant

differences between device interface and gesture interface (Sig. = 0.001), superman (Sig. = 0.000), bird (Sig. = 0.000) and between ZRT (zoom, rotation, and translation) interface and bird interface (Sig. = 0.035). In the interest, there was a difference between device and bird interface (Sig. = 0.006).

We observed that the keyboard interface has a higher score in terms of accuracy, comfort, and easiness, compared to gesture interfaces. On the contrary, the difference in the gap of scores between the gesture and keyboard interfaces is very large in the factors of immersion and interest.

In Figure 10, we can see that the two virtual map environments, Grand Canyon and French Town, affect user preference. Overall, the user's score for the two virtual map environments did not appear to be significant, but the overall satisfaction of the hand interface was very high in the Grand Canyon, while the overall satisfaction of the Superman interface was the lowest. However, in the French Town, the overall satisfaction with the hand interface and the interface using the keyboard and mouse was the highest, and the overall satisfaction scores of the rest of the interfaces were similar.

Since the sample size (i.e., 12 participants) is relatively small and test scenarios are rather simple, further research

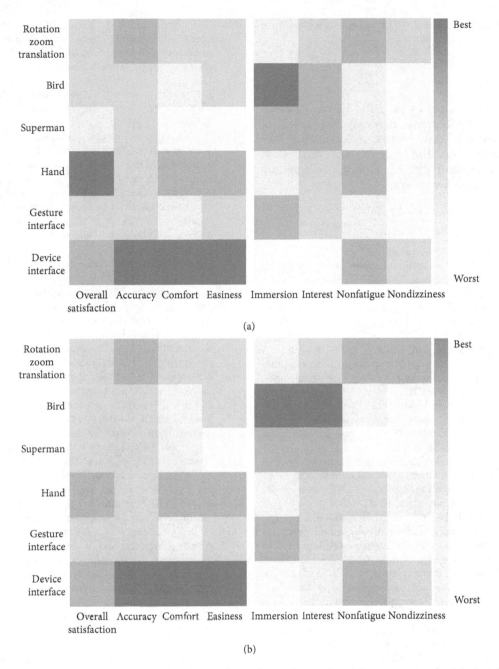

FIGURE 10: Visualization results of usability score distribution for each interface and usability properties for (a) Grand Canyon and (b) French Town model.

can be necessary to generalize and verify the usability of our method.

6. Conclusion

The results of this study indicate that the method of gesture recognition through body motion can provide a higher level of immersion than the conventional keyboard/mouse method. Since users experience an interface with which they are not familiar, it is necessary to learn the operation method and have time to adapt before the first execution. However, after a very short learning period, users were able to experience virtual reality more effectively. It is desirable to use the Kinect-based gesture interface for a higher level of immersion and fun. However, with long periods of VR use, users tend to become easily tired, and further research must be conducted to overcome this drawback. The results of this study show that it is more interesting and fun for the user to use his or her body to manipulate 3D space and navigate 3D environments, but the interface method can be different according to the type of scenario space. Considering the level of immersion and interest, it is necessary to research intuitive methods to perform operations that can easily make future human/computer VR interactions more easy and natural. Combination of gestures and speech recognition techniques can improve the usability of control interfaces.

Hence, we also consider the hybrid approach as a future research topic.

Acknowledgments

This research was supported by the Basic Science Research Program through the National Research Foundation of Korea (NRF) funded by the Ministry of Education (NRF-2017R1D1A1B03036291). The authors are grateful to Wonjae Choi for partial implementation of Kinect gesture recognition and related discussion.

References

[1] F. Biocca and M. R. Levy, *Communication in the Age of Virtual Reality*, Routledge, Abingdon, UK, 2013.

[2] D. A. Bowman and R. P. McMahan, "Virtual reality: how much immersion is enough?," *Computer*, vol. 40, no. 7, pp. 36–43, 2007.

[3] J. Gregory, *Virtual Reality*, Cherry Lake Publishing, North Mankato, MN, USA, 2017.

[4] J. C. P. Chan, H. Leung, J. K. T. Tang, and T. Komura, "A virtual reality dance training system using motion capture technology," *IEEE Transactions on Learning Technologies*, vol. 4, no. 2, pp. 187–195, 2011.

[5] H. H. Sin and G. C. Lee, "Additional virtual reality training using Xbox Kinect in stroke survivors with hemiplegia," *American Journal of Physical Medicine and Rehabilitation*, vol. 92, no. 10, pp. 871–880, 2013.

[6] A. Henderson, N. Korner-Bitensky, and M. Levin, "Virtual reality in stroke rehabilitation: a systematic review of its effectiveness for upper limb motor recovery," *Topics in Stroke Rehabilitation*, vol. 14, no. 2, pp. 52–61, 2007.

[7] C. Pietro, S. Silvia, P. Federica, G. Andrea, and R. Giuseppe, "NeuroVirtual 3D: a multiplatform 3D simulation system for application in psychology and neuro-rehabilitation," in *Virtual, Augmented Reality and Serious Games for Healthcare*, pp. 275–286, Springer, Berlin, Germany, 2014.

[8] S. Houlding, *3D Geoscience Modeling: Computer Techniques for Geological Characterization*, Springer Science & Business Media, Berlin, Germany, 2012.

[9] L. Yu and P. Gong, "Google Earth as a virtual globe tool for Earth science applications at the global scale: progress and perspectives," *International Journal of Remote Sensing*, vol. 33, no. 12, pp. 3966–3986, 2012.

[10] M. H. Draper, E. S. Viirre, T. A. Furness, and V. J. Gawron, "Effects of image scale and system time delay on simulator sickness within head-coupled virtual environments," *Human Factors*, vol. 43, no. 1, pp. 129–146, 2001.

[11] J. J. W. Lin, H. B. L. Duh, D. E. Parker, H. Abi-Rached, and T. A. Furness, "Effects of field of view on presence, enjoyment, memory, and simulator sickness in a virtual environment," in *Proceedings of the IEEE Virtual Reality*, Orlando, FL, USA, March 2002.

[12] T. R. Coles, D. Meglan, and N. W. John, "The role of haptics in medical training simulators: a survey of the state of the art," *IEEE Transactions on Haptics*, vol. 4, no. 1, pp. 51–66, 2011.

[13] F. Anderson, M. Annett, and W. F. Bischof, "Lean on Wii: physical rehabilitation with virtual reality Wii peripherals," *Studies in Health Technology and Informatics*, vol. 154, pp. 229–234, 2010.

[14] T. P. Pham and Y.-L. Theng, "Game controllers for older adults: experimental study on gameplay experiences and preferences," in *Proceedings of the International Conference on the Foundations of Digital Games*, Raleigh, NC, USA, May–June 2012.

[15] J. P. Wachs, M. Kölsch, H. Stern, and Y. Edan, "Vision-based hand-gesture applications," *Communications of the ACM*, vol. 54, no. 2, pp. 60–71, 2011.

[16] B. Williams, S. Bailey, G. Narasimham, M. Li, and B. Bodenheimer, "Evaluation of walking in place on a Wii balance board to explore a virtual environment," *ACM Transactions on Applied Perception*, vol. 8, no. 3, pp. 1–14, 2011.

[17] X. Zhang, X. Chen, Y. Li, V. Lantz, K. Wang, and J. Yang, "A framework for hand gesture recognition based on accelerometer and EMG sensors," *IEEE Transactions on Systems, Man, and Cybernetics: Systems and Humans*, vol. 41, no. 6, pp. 1064–1076, 2011.

[18] Oculus VR, LLC, *Oculus Touch*, Oculus VR, Irvine, CA, USA, 2016, https://www.oculus.com/rift/.

[19] I. E. Sutherland, "A head-mounted three dimensional display," in *Proceedings of the American Federation of Information Processing Societies Conference (AFIPS 1968)*, vol. 33, p. 1, San Francisco, CA, USA, December 1968.

[20] R. P. McMahan, D. A. Bowman, D. J. Zielinski, and R. B. Brady, "Evaluating display fidelity and interaction fidelity in a virtual reality game," *IEEE Transactions on Visualization and Computer Graphics*, vol. 18, no. 4, pp. 626–633, 2012.

[21] K. Kihara, Y. Fujii, H. Masuda et al., "New three-dimensional head-mounted display system, TMDU-S-3D system, for minimally invasive surgery application: procedures for gasless single-port radical nephrectomy," *International Journal of Urology*, vol. 19, no. 9, pp. 886–889, 2012.

[22] H. Li, L. Trutoiu, K. Olszewski et al., "Facial performance sensing head-mounted display," in *Proceedings of the 42nd ACM SIGGRAPH Conference and Exhibition ACM Transactions on Graphics*, Kobe, Japan, August 2015.

[23] Z. Ren, J. Meng, and J. Yuan, "Depth camera based hand gesture recognition and its applications in human-computer-interaction," in *Proceedings of the 8th International Conference on Information, Communications and Signal Processing (ICICS 2011)*, Singapore, December 2011.

[24] S. Mitra and T. Acharya, "Gesture recognition: a survey," *IEEE Transactions on Systems, Man, and Cybernetics, Part C (Applications and Reviews)*, vol. 37, no. 3, pp. 311–324, 2007.

[25] S. S. Rautaray and A. Agrawal, "Vision based hand gesture recognition for human computer interaction: a survey," *Artificial Intelligence Review*, vol. 43, no. 1, pp. 1–54, 2015.

[26] K. K. Biswas and S. K. Basu, "Gesture recognition using Microsoft Kinect®," in *Proceedings of the 5th International Conference on Automation, Robotics and Applications (ICARA 2011)*, Wellington, New Zealand, December 2011.

[27] D. Meldrum, A. Glennon, S. Herdman, D. Murray, and R. McConn-Walsh, "Virtual reality rehabilitation of balance: assessment of the usability of the Nintendo Wii® Fit Plus," *Disability and Rehabilitation: Assistive Technology*, vol. 7, no. 3, pp. 205–210, 2012.

[28] H. Cheng, L. Yang, and Z. Liu, "Survey on 3D hand gesture recognition," *IEEE Transactions on Circuits and Systems for Video Technology*, vol. 26, no. 9, pp. 1659–1673, 2016.

[29] M. N. Kamel Boulos, B. J. Blanchard, C. Walker, J. Montero, A. Tripathy, and R. Gutierrez-Osuna, "Web GIS in practice X: a Microsoft Kinect natural user interface for Google Earth

navigation," *International Journal of Health Geographics*, vol. 10, p. 45, 2011.

[30] G. Marin, F. Dominio, and P. Zanuttigh, "Hand gesture recognition with leap motion and Kinect devices," in *Proceedings of the 2014 IEEE International Conference on Image Processing (ICIP 2014)*, Paris, France, October 2014.

[31] Q. Chen, N. D. Georganas, and E. M. Petriu, "Real-time vision-based hand gesture recognition using Haar-like features," in *Proceedings of the Instrumentation and Measurement Technology Conference IMTC IEEE*, Warsaw, Poland, May 2007.

[32] C. Keskin, F. Kıraç, Y. E. Kara, and L. Akarun, "Real time hand pose estimation using depth sensors," in *Consumer Depth Cameras for Computer Vision*, pp. 119–137, Springer, London, UK, 2013.

[33] M. Van den Bergh and L. Van Gool, "Combining RGB and ToF cameras for real-time 3D hand gesture interaction," in *Proceedings of the IEEE Workshop on Applications of Computer Vision (WACV)*, Kona, HI, USA, January 2011.

[34] A. Shahroudy, J. Liu, T. T. Ng, and G. Wang, "NTU RGB+ D: a large scale dataset for 3D human activity analysis," in *Proceedings of the IEEE Conference on Computer Vision and Pattern Recognition*, Caesars Palace, NV, USA, June–July 2016.

[35] B.-S. Sohn, "Design and comparison of immersive gesture interfaces for HMD based virtual world navigation," *IEICE Transactions on Information and Systems*, vol. E99-D, no. 7, pp. 1957–1960, 2016.

[36] Y. Lee, W. Choi, and B.-S. Sohn, "Immersive gesture interfaces for 3D map navigation in HMD-based virtual environments," in *Proceedings of the 32nd International Conference on Information Networking (ICOIN)*, Chiang Mai, Thailand, 2018.

[37] M. C. Corballis, "From mouth to hand: gesture, speech, and the evolution of right-handedness," *Behavioral and Brain Sciences*, vol. 26, no. 2, pp. 199–208, 2003.

[38] J. R. Skoyles, "Gesture, language origins, and right handedness," *Psycoloquy*, vol. 11, p. 24, 2000.

[39] I. Yavrucuk, E. Kubali, and O. Tarimci, "A low cost flight simulator using virtual reality tools," *IEEE Aerospace and Electronic Systems Magazine*, vol. 26, no. 4, pp. 10–14, 2011.

[40] M. Rheiner, "Birdly an attempt to fly," in *Proceedings of the ACM SIGGRAPH 2014 Emerging Technologies*, Shenzhen, China, December 2014.

[41] J. Shotton, T. Sharp, A. Kipman et al., "Real-time human pose recognition in parts from single depth images," *Communications of the ACM*, vol. 56, no. 1, pp. 116–124, 2013.

[42] J. L. Raheja, A. Chaudhary, and K. Singal, "Tracking of fingertips and centers of palm using Kinect," in *Proceedings of the Third International Conference on Computational Intelligence, Modelling and Simulation (CIMSiM)*, Langkawi, Malaysia, September 2011.

[43] S. Wang, Z. Mao, C. Zeng, H. Gong, S. Li, and B. Chen, "A new method of virtual reality based on Unity3D," in *Proceedings of the 18th International Conference on Geoinformatics, 2010*, Beijing, China, June 2010.

[44] J. Häkkinen, M. Pölönen, J. Takatalo, and G. Nyman, "Simulator sickness in virtual display gaming: a comparison of stereoscopic and non-stereoscopic situations," in *Proceedings of the 8th Conference on Human-Computer Interaction with Mobile Devices and Services*, Espoo, Finland, September 2006.

5

Developing a Contextually Personalized Hybrid Recommender System

Aysun Bozanta ⓘ **and Birgul Kutlu** ⓘ

Department of Management Information Systems, Bogazici University, Istanbul 34342, Turkey

Correspondence should be addressed to Aysun Bozanta; aysun.bozanta@boun.edu.tr

Academic Editor: Ramon Aguero

It is hard to choose places to go from an endless number of options for some specific circumstances. Recommender systems are supposed to help us deal with these issues and make decisions that are more appropriate. The aim of this study is to recommend new venues to users according to their preferences. For this purpose, a hybrid recommendation model is proposed to integrate user-based and item-based collaborative filtering, content-based filtering together with contextual information in order to get rid of the disadvantages of each approach. Besides that, in which specific circumstances the user will like a specific venue is predicted for each user-venue pair. Moreover, threshold values determining the user's liking toward a venue are determined separately for each user. Results are evaluated with both offline experiments (precision, recall, F-1 score) and a user study. Both the experimental evaluation with a real-world dataset and a user study of the proposed system showed improvement upon the baseline approaches.

1. Introduction

Social media platforms are very rich data resources for researchers to mine and gain insight into user preferences. The increasing use of location-related technologies enables the development of location-based-services. Therefore, location-based social networks (LBSNs), which have become the host of new possibilities for user interaction, have emerged. These systems, which facilitate users to share their visits and explore other locations, have accumulated huge amount of data about users with extensive use over time. Location Recommendation Systems (LRSs) have been developed by discovering embedded information from these data to provide location suggestion for the users.

There are three main recommendation techniques, which are also applied for location recommendation, content-based filtering (CBF), collaborative filtering (CF), and hybrid recommendation. Content-based filtering utilizes the information about an item itself for recommendations and tries to find the most similar item with the user's previous preferences. Collaborative filtering recommends an item according to the similarity between one user's preferences and the preferences of other individuals. Hybrid approaches, which are the composition of at least two existing approaches, have recently been awarded for their ability to improve prediction. Contextual information (weather, time, date, etc.) is more important in travel and tourism domains. Therefore, context-aware recommender systems should be widely used for location recommendation rather than other types of recommendations (product, movie, music, etc.). However, most of the recommendation engines fail to consider contextual information for location recommendation.

Personalization, which should be handled from different angles, is another issue for recommendation systems. The effect of each variable used in the recommendation may vary among different users. For instance, two people may like the same places but in different contextual circumstances. Therefore, it is important to consider the changing effects of contextual variables on different users.

In this study, a contextually personalized hybrid location recommender system is developed. For this purpose, users' check-in history, visited location properties (distance, category, popularity, and price), and contextual data (weather, season, date, and time of visits) were collected from Twitter, Foursquare, and Weather Underground. A hybrid approach (user-based collaborative filtering, item-based collaborative filtering, content-based filtering, and context-aware recommendation) was applied, and results were evaluated with both offline experiments (precision, recall, F-1 score) and a user study. This study is an expanded version of the previous study [1]. The scientific value of this study can be listed as below:

(i) Three different types of variables (user-related, venue-related (content), and contextual) that have not been used together in existing recommender systems were used in one algorithm to develop a novel recommender system

(ii) Artificial neural network algorithm was applied to determine the weight of each algorithm (user-based collaborative filtering, item-based collaborative filtering, content-based filtering, and context-aware recommendation) that was used when developing the hybrid recommendation system

(iii) Threshold values determining the user's liking toward a venue were determined separately for each user

(iv) A contextually personalized recommendation was generated by determining which contextual circumstances were more appropriate for each specific user-venue pair

(v) Data sparsity problem was alleviated

(vi) Overspecialization was lessened

(vii) Cold start problem was partially solved.

2. Related Work

Developing a location recommender system is very attractive for researchers because of its importance in both academia and business. Therefore, although its history is based on less than a decade, there are many studies on this subject.

Content-based algorithms utilize the content information of a location in order to handle data sparsity problem that may occur in CF algorithms. Table 1 presents mostly used content information variables. The category variable specifies the category of a venue (restaurant, shopping center, theater, etc.). The distance variable specifies the distance from the user (GPS location, center of visited venues, etc.) to the venue. The tag variable specifies tags that are given by the users (can be visited with friends, romantic, etc.). Tips and comments are specified by the user about the venue. The popularity variable denotes the value of a location specified by ratings, number of visits, etc. The tags and tips/comments variables are used for sentiment analysis, which is not in the context of this study. For this reason, only the category, distance, and popularity variables were selected.

Collaborative filtering algorithms can be categorized as memory-based and model-based. In addition, memory-based CF is divided into two categories; user-based CF, which considers user similarity for recommendation [35–37] and item-based CF, which considers the item similarity

TABLE 1: Mostly used content-based variables for location recommendation.

Content-based variables	References
Distance	[2–12]
Category	[7, 9, 11, 13–22]
Tag	[19, 23–27]
Tips/comments	[19, 28–31]
Popularity	[7, 11, 32–34]

for recommendation [38, 39]. Data mining techniques such as neural networks [40], Naïve Bayesian modeling [13, 23], association rule mining [41], and SVD [2] are used for model-based CF.

The contextual approach emerged after traditional approaches, which simply focus on the past preferences of customers. Context represents a set of surrounding conditions of a user-item pair and affects the relation between them. A context-aware recommender system may consider either user context (income, profession, age, current user location, mood, and status, etc.) or environmental context (current time, weather, traffic conditions, events, etc.) [14, 42]. Contextual information is very crucial, especially for location recommendation. The decisions of the users for venue visits are generally based on environmental factors rather than on their decisions about other things (buying a product, listening to music, etc.). Even though contextual information is critical rather than additional for location recommendation systems, it is not used in existing systems commonly and effectively. In the literature, it is emphasized that context-based algorithms are demanding for effective recommender systems [43–46].

Contextual information for location recommendation can be specified with many variables. Mostly used variables are presented in Table 2.

As can be seen from Table 2, time and weather condition (e.g., sunny, rainy, and snowy) variables have been used for location recommendation more frequently than other variables. Therefore, time and weather conditions are selected as the contextual variables for this study.

Each filtering approach has different drawbacks. For example, the disadvantages of CF are the cold start problem, data sparsity, and scalability [57]. On the other hand, information need about an item and overspecialization are the drawbacks of the CBF [58]. Hybrid approaches combine at least two of the existing approaches and aim to minimize or remove the drawbacks of existing approaches, which may occur when they are used individually. Therefore, hybrid systems, which are the combination of some of these approaches, can be the solution for a better recommendation system [43, 44]. Even though some hybrid systems are presented in the literature, there are still untouched points for performance improvement of location recommender systems. There are studies considering different hybrid algorithms for location recommendation [2, 7, 19, 48, 50, 51, 59]. Seven different types of hybridization techniques are mentioned in the literature, namely, weighted, switching, mixed, feature combination, cascade, feature augmentation, and metalevel [60].

TABLE 2: Mostly used contextual variables.

Context-related variables	References
Time	[9–12, 19, 21, 47–52]
Weather conditions	[48, 51, 53]
Temperature	[48]
Trip type	[54]
Origin city/destination city	[54]
Speed and travel direction	[55]
Transportation type	[56]

This study aims to develop a personalized hybrid recommendation system using both user and location similarity, location-related properties (distance, category, popularity, and price classification), and varying effects of contextual data (weather, season, date, and time of visits) among different users. Weighted hybridization method is used to achieve better performance and to have drawbacks of any individual recommendation system.

3. Methodology

3.1. Data Collection. The aim of this study is to recommend new venues to the users according to their preferences. Therefore, a location-based social network should be chosen to collect the necessary data. For this purpose, two popular social networks, Twitter and Foursquare, were chosen. In order to crawl users' check-in history, Twitter is used since Foursquare does not allow direct streaming of user check-ins. Foursquare was chosen to collect the characteristics of various venues since it is one of the most popular location-based social networks and provides the characteristics of various venues with its API.

The REST API of Twitter, which is popularly used for designing web APIs to use pull strategy for data retrieval, was used for this study. The REST API–"GET search/tweets," which returns a collection of relevant tweets matching a specified query, was used. When a user who linked his/her account with Twitter check-ins using Swarm, a related tweet including all check-in data appears on the Twitter timeline. Firstly, Twitter user ids' of users who "checked-in" on the Swarm application and shared their check-ins over the Twitter application were collected for a two-month period. After that, all geocoded tweet history of collected users, which goes back to 2011, was retrieved and stored. The Twitter APIs (for Twitter API version 1.1) were used to collect dataset by embedding them into the PHP code, and dataset was stored in MySQL database.

When a user checks in using Swarm and shares this check-in on Twitter, the related tweet includes a URL starting with "https://www.swarmapp.com/," which contains a venue id at the end. Those venue ids were sent to the Foursquare API (https://api.foursquare.com/v2/venues/VENUE_ID) and venue name, category, latitude, longitude, check-in count, visitor count, tip count, and price classification of venues were collected as venue attributes.

Weather history data are collected from the "Weather Underground" website. Each check-in date is matched with the date in weather history for related weather condition (sunny, rainy, snowy, etc.).

3.2. Data Preprocessing. Data preprocessing helps to transform raw data into an understandable format. Real-world datasets are mostly incomplete, inconsistent, and lack certain behaviors. Data preprocessing is necessary for preparing these raw datasets for further processing. Data reduction, which is one of the data preprocessing steps, was applied to the raw dataset in order to obtain results that are more accurate.

The raw dataset consisted of 6738 users, 60202 venues, and 226227 visits. Data reduction was performed according to the following criteria:

(i) Only Istanbul check-ins were retrieved in order to increase visit frequencies.

(ii) There are various main categories of venues in Foursquare. For this study, "restaurant" was chosen as main category and all related subcategories of restaurant were used because of intensive check-in frequency in restaurants.

(iii) Users who visited only one venue were extracted.

(iv) Venues, which were visited by only one user, were extracted.

After that, 1101 users, 711 venues, and 4694 visits remained in the dataset.

The terms used in this study can be found in Table 3.

3.3. Rating. Foursquare does not provide the direct ratings for venues from each individual user. Therefore, rating was calculated from linear normalization of the frequencies in a range of 1 to 5 for each user-venue pair. If a user's maximum and minimum number of visits are equal, then the rating was determined as 1.

$$\text{Rating}\left(u_n, v_n\right) = \left(\left(\frac{\text{freq}\left(u_n, v_n\right) - \text{minfreq}\left(u_n\right)}{\text{maxfreq}\left(u_n\right) - \text{minfreq}\left(u_n\right)}\right) * 4\right) + 1. \tag{1}$$

3.4. Distance. The latitude and longitude values of venues, which were collected from Foursquare, were converted into the x, y, z coordinates (Equations (2)–(4)):

$$x = \cos\left(\text{longitude}\right) * \cos\left(\text{latitude}\right), \tag{2}$$

$$y = \sin\left(\text{longitude}\right) * \cos\left(\text{latitude}\right), \tag{3}$$

$$z = \sin\left(\text{latitude}\right). \tag{4}$$

User centers were calculated by taking the weighted average of x, y, z coordinates of all visits for each user in order to understand his/her active area. Euclidean distance from each venue to the user center was calculated and named as distance variable (Equation (5)):

TABLE 3: Terms used for the study.

Terms	Definition
$\text{freq}(u_n, v_n)$	Number of visits from nth user to the nth venue
$\text{minfreq}(u_n)$	Minimum number of visits of nth user
$\text{maxfreq}(u_n)$	Maximum number of visits of nth user
$\text{user\_sim}(\vec{u}_n, \vec{u}_m)$	Similarity between nth and mth users
$\vec{u}_n$	Vector consisting of ratings of nth user
$\vec{u}_m$	Vector consisting of ratings of mth user
$\text{Rating}(u_n, v_n)$	Rating of nth user to nth venue
$\text{venue\_sim}(\vec{v}_n, \vec{v}_m)$	Similarity between nth and mth venues
$\vec{v}_n$	Vector consisting of ratings of nth venue
$\vec{v}_m$	Vector consisting of ratings of mth venue
Check-in count	Total number of check-ins in a specific venue
Like count	Total number of people who liked the specific venue
User count	Total number of unique people who check in specific venue
Tip count	Total number of comments for specific venue
Rating	Score of each venue, which is provided by FS API and calculated from the scoring of all people who check in that specific venue out of 10

$$\text{distance} = \sqrt{(x - \text{center } x)^2 + (y - \text{center } y)^2 + (z - \text{center } z)^2}. \tag{5}$$

3.5. Popularity. Foursquare provides four variables about a venue; check-in count, like count, user count, and tip count. In this study, these variables were considered as reference to the popularity of a venue. Therefore, the popularity variable was formed from these four properties of venues by applying Principal Component Analysis (PCA), which aims at dimension reduction. Before applying PCA, sampling adequacy for PCA should be checked. For this purpose, KMO and Barlett's tests were used. Sampling adequacy can be observed in Table 4, which presents KMO value as 0.821 and significance of Barlett's test of sphericity as 0.001. The acceptable level of KMO is generally 0.6, and Barlett's test of sphericity is significant at the 1% alpha level. The results showed that the sample is adequate for PCA.

Ninety-three percent of the total variance was explained by only one component (Table 5). Therefore, it can be concluded that one variable, which was named "popularity," can be used instead of four variables.

The component matrix shows the correlation between variables and component. Since the correlation values range from −1 to +1, it can be concluded that there is a strong positive correlation between a component and each of the variables (Table 6).

3.6. Category. All subcategories of food, which were collected by the FS API, were included in this study. There are 34 restaurant categories including different countries' cuisine in the dataset. User-category matrix, which presents the

TABLE 4: KMO and Barlett's test results.

KMO measure of sampling adequacy		0.821
Barlett's test of sphericity	Approximate chi-square	13951.963
	Degrees of freedom	6
	Significance	0.001

TABLE 5: Total variance explained.

Component	% of variance	% Cumulative variance
1	93.69	93.69
2	4.46	98.15
3	1.08	99.19
4	0.80	100

TABLE 6: Component matrix for popularity.

Check-in count	0.965
Like count	0.985
User count	0.981
Tip count	0.941

number of visits of each user in each subcategory, was prepared.

3.7. Price. There is a four-price classification in Foursquare: 1-cheap, 2-average, 3-expensive, and 4-very expensive. The user-price matrix presenting the number of visits of each user in each price class was prepared by using the data coming from FS API.

3.8. Time. Twitter provides UNIX time format for each tweet, in order to understand date and time, it is converted to date and time stamp. For this study, season, day, and the different periods of the day were used as contextual variables. It was observed that some of the values of some contextual variables showed similar characteristics, such as users have the same pattern of check-in behaviors for weekdays. Therefore, discretization was applied to the contextual variables, which displayed a better performance. Days were discretized as "weekday" and "weekend" [51, 61]. The check-ins that were made in spring or summer were categorized as "hot season" check-ins while the check-ins that were made in autumn and winter were categorized as "cold season" check-ins [61]. In the studies of Majid et al. [48] and Wang et al. [62], time is discretized as morning, afternoon, evening, and night. In the study [61], a day is discretized as morning and evening only. However, after exploring the check-in behaviors in the dataset, it is found that discretization as morning, noon, and evening would be more suitable. The time range 07:00 to 11:59 was defined as "morning," 12:00 to 16:59 as "noon," and 17:00 to 06:59 as "evening." Thus, it is aimed to make a more accurate recommendation.

3.9. Weather. The data of weather condition, which is also a contextual variable, were collected from the Weather Underground API that provides more than 10 different weather conditions (sunny, rainy, snowy, rainy and stormy, snowy and stormy, etc.). It was observed that some weather categories showed the same patterns of user behavior. Therefore, they were discretized under three main categories: "sunny," "rainy" (all categories including rainy), and "snowy" (all categories including snowy). The percentage of which contextual circumstances the venue is preferred was calculated by the proportion of visits in the specific category over the total visits.

$$user\_sim\left(\vec{u}_n, \vec{u}_m\right) = \cos\left(\vec{u}_n, \vec{u}_m\right) = \frac{\vec{u}_n \vec{u}_m}{\|\vec{u}_n\| \|\vec{u}_m\|}, \tag{6}$$

$$rating_{ucf} = \frac{\sum user\_sim\left(u_n, u_m\right) \times rating\left(u_m, v_n\right)}{\sum user\_sim\left(u_n, u_m\right)}. \tag{7}$$

User similarity values were calculated from the user-category matrix (Table 7), which presents the number of venues that a specific user visited for each category with Cosine similarity in a similar manner as in Equation (2).

Popularity values were discretized into three categories, namely, high, medium, and low, according to their normalized popularity values, which were attained from PCA. Then, the user-popularity preference matrix (Table 8) was generated, which keeps the number of venues that a specific user visited in each popularity category.

User similarity values were calculated from the user-popularity matrix, which presents the number of venues that a specific user visited in each popularity class with

3.10. Development of Recommendation System.

3.10. Development of Recommendation System. Development steps of this recommendation system are explained in detail below.

User similarity values were calculated from the user-venue matrix, which presents the ratings of users to the venues with cosine similarity (Equation (6)). Ratings (rating$_{ucf}$) of the user to the other venues were predicted by using user similarity values (Equation (7)):

cosine similarity in the similar manner as in Equation (2).

The user-price preference matrix (Table 9) was also constructed, which keeps the number of venues that a specific user visited in each price category. User similarity according to price preferences was also calculated in the similar manner as in Equation (2).

Equation (3) was also used to calculate predicted ratings using user similarity, which depend on the category (rating$_{category}$), popularity (rating$_{popularity}$), and price (rating$_{price}$) preferences of users.

Venue similarity values were calculated from the user-venue matrix with cosine distance (Equation (8)). Ratings (rating$_{icf}$) of the user to the other venues were also predicted by using venue similarity values (Equation (9)):

$$venue\_sim\left(\vec{v}_n, \vec{v}_m\right) = \cos\left(\vec{v}_n, \vec{v}_m\right) = \frac{\vec{v}_n \vec{v}_m}{\|\vec{v}_n\| \|\vec{v}_m\|}, \tag{8}$$

$$rating_{icf} = \frac{\sum venue\_sim\left(v_n, v_m\right) \times rating\left(u_n, v_m\right)}{\sum venue\_sim\left(v_n, v_m\right)}. \tag{9}$$

The venue-context matrix (Table 10), which keeps track of the contextual features of the venues, was prepared. The percentages showing the venue preferences in different contextual circumstances were presented in this matrix. With the help of this matrix, venue similarities were also calculated using Equation (4). Predicted ratings (rating$_{context}$) are also calculated as in Equation (5) using the contextual similarity of venues.

The calculation of ratings (rating$_{distance}$) according to the distance between a venue to the user depends on the assumption that if this distance is short, then the user will visit that venue more frequently [63–66]. Although the users are

more willing to check in at nearby venues to their centers, distance perception of each user is different. Optimal coefficients (A, B, and n) for power law distribution [49, 64, 65] were determined to model the willingness of a user to go and check in at a place

$$rating_{distance} = A + B * distance^n. \tag{10}$$

In this study, a weighted hybridization technique was used to compute the score of recommended items using all available recommendation algorithms. Artificial neural network (ANN) analysis was applied in order to find the optimal weights for each technique instead of using equal weights for them. Inputs to the ANN were the results of

TABLE 7: Sample of user-category matrix.

User id	Turkish_rest	American_rest	Chinese_rest
11949	10	0	0
10147822	0	6	2
10437542	0	2	0

TABLE 8: Sample of user-popularity matrix.

User id	Low_popularity	Medium_popularity	High_popularity
11949	7	3	0
10147822	0	5	3
10437542	2	0	0

TABLE 9: Sample of user-price matrix.

User id	1	2	3	4
11949	6	3	1	0
10147822	0	0	3	5
10437542	2	0	0	0

all available recommendation algorithms, and the output to be predicted was the actual rating. Final ratings were calculated by multiplying the ANN weights and ratings:

$$\text{Rating} = w_1 * \text{rating}_{ucf} + w_2 * \text{rating}_{icf} + w_3 * \text{rating}_{distance}$$
$$+ w_4 * \text{rating}_{popularity} + w_5 * \text{rating}_{category}$$
$$+ w_6 * \text{rating}_{price} + w_7 * \text{rating}_{context}.$$
(11)

In order to decide whether to recommend a venue to the user or not, different threshold values were used for each user. The threshold value for each user was determined by taking the average ratings of that user. After that, if the calculated rating (Equation (11)) was greater than his/her threshold, then it was considered that the user will like that venue. This is the first version of the algorithm, and it is named as "HybRecSys."

Existing recommender systems do not consider that the preferences of the users are affected by different contextual circumstances. For instance, a user may prefer a venue on a rainy weekday at noon, while another user may prefer the same venue in another context. In order to handle this issue, our system calculates the probability of visiting a venue in a specific contextual category. For instance, the following equation calculates the probability of visit of user i to the venue j in the mornings:

$$P\left(\text{time} = \text{morning} \middle| \text{visit}_{ij}\right) = \frac{\sum_k \text{contextual similarity}_{jk} * \text{probablity of morning}_{ik}}{\sum_k \text{contextual similarity}_{jk}}.$$
(12)

For each user-venue pair, there are 36 different contextual circumstances (day = weekday, weekend; time = morning, noon, evening; season = hot, cold; weather = sunny, rainy, snowy). For each situation, probabilities were calculated, and the resulting table was constructed (Table 11).

Table 11, respectively, presents user id, venue id, average rating of related user, the percentage that the user will visit that venue in that time category, the percentage that the user will visit that venue in that day category, the percentage that the user will visit that venue in that season category, the percentage that the user will visit that venue in that weather category, total point from all contextual variables (sum of all percentages), predicted rating, and the final decision (Like).

The sum of all categories of each contextual variable should add up to one. For instance, since the day variable has two categories, weekdays and weekend, if a user's probability of visiting a specific venue on a weekday is 0.6, then the probability that user will visit the same venue on a weekend has to be 0.4. Therefore, the sum of the values of all contextual variables (Context$_{total}$) may have a maximum value of 4. The final decision of whether a user will like a venue or not depends on two things; the predicted rating having a greater value than the average rating of the user and the total context having a value of at least 2 out of 4. The final version of the algorithm was called "contextually personalized HybRecSys" and the whole development process is depicted in Figure 1.

4. Evaluation of Recommendation System

The performance evaluation of the proposed system will be explained in detail in this section. For the evaluation of recommender systems, there are three types of experimental settings [67]:

(1) Offline experiments, in which a precollected dataset of users is used to validate the results

(2) User studies, in which a small sample of users are asked to perform several tasks requiring an interaction with the recommendation system

(3) Online evaluation trying to evaluate different algorithms over online recommender system with a small percentage of the traffic.

4.1. Offline Experiments. The Contextually personalized HybRecSys was compared with five algorithms: user-based K-nearest neighborhood (KNN) [68], item-based KNN [69], biased matrix factorization [70], SVD++ [71], and HybRecSys [1]. First four algorithms were available in the LibRec, a Java library for recommender systems. For each

TABLE 10: Sample of venue-context matrix.

Venue id	Hot_season	Cold_season	W_day	W_end	Morning	Noon	Evening	Sunny	Rainy	Snowy
Venue1	0.75	0.25	0.68	0.32	0.08	0.17	0.75	0.67	0.25	0.08
Venue2	0.5	0.5	0.5	0.5	0	1	0	1	0	0
Venue3	0.83	0.17	0.96	0.04	0.13	0.52	0.35	0.65	0.35	0

TABLE 11: The final decision table.

Uid	Vid	Av_rating	Time	Day	Season	Weather	Context$_{total}$	Rating	Like
u1	v1	2.5	Morning = 0.5	Wdays = 0	Hot = 1	Sunny = 1	2.5	3	True
u1	v1	2.5	Morning = 0.5	Wdays = 0	Hot = 1	Rainy = 0	1.5	3	False
u1	v1	2.5	Morning = 0.5	Wdays = 0	Hot = 1	Snowy = 0	1.5	3	False
u1	v1	2.5	Morning = 0.5	Wdays = 0	Cold = 0	Sunny = 1	1.5	3	False

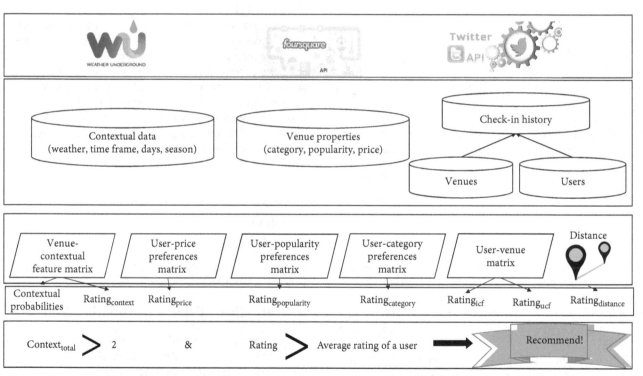

FIGURE 1: Framework of contextually personalized HybRecSys.

algorithm, the default settings of LibRec were used. Fifth algorithm, HybRecSys, is the earlier version of Contextually Personalized HybRecSys. Other hybrid algorithms defined in the literature could not be included in this study since the source codes were not available.

Precision, recall, and F-1 measures were used as evaluation metrics in this study. Precision specifies the percentage of correctly recommended items over total recommended items. Recall indicates the percentage of recommended items over the total number of liked items by the user. The F1 score measures the accuracy of the system by using both precision and recall.

In order to split the data into training and test sets, K-fold ($K = 10$) cross-validation technique was used. The dataset was divided into 10 disjoint sets making sure that

each set contains about 10% of the visits of each user. One set was used as the test set and nine sets were used as the training set for each fold.

Figure 2 shows precision, recall, and F1 measure of each algorithm and it is obvious that Contextually Personalized HybRecSys outperforms all other algorithms.

According to precision metric, HybRecSys, user-based KNN, item-based KNN, biased matrix factorization, and SVD++ follow contextually personalized HybRecSys, respectively. According to recall metric, HybRecSys, biased matrix factorization, item-based KNN, SVD++, and user-based KNN follow contextually personalized HybRecSys. According to F-1 measure, HybRecSys, item-based KNN, biased matrix factorization, user-based KNN, and SVD++ follow contextually personalized HybRecSys, respectively.

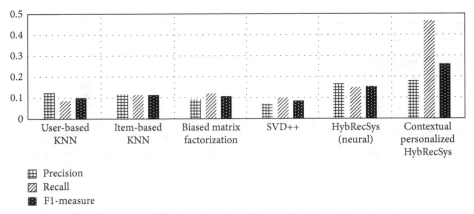

FIGURE 2: Graph of precision, recall, and F-1 measures of the algorithms.

4.2. User Study for Contextually Personalized HybRecSys.
As was indicated in the literature, user studies are very helpful to understand whether the recommendations are liked by the users and to collect more detailed data about the recommendation system [45, 57, 67]. Although conducting a user study is difficult, time-consuming, and costly, it is suggested to apply them after the offline experiments in order to validate the results of the offline experiments [67].

4.3. Steps of the User Study.
For this study, a user study was conducted on the users in our dataset. For this purpose, the Twitter account of each user in our dataset was checked to learn whether their profiles allow to receive direct messages. Out of 1101 users, 195 accounts were open for direct message. Those users were invited to attend our user study by direct message, and a small incentive (a movie ticket) was promised if they attend this evaluation.

Twenty-four users replied to the message and accepted to attend the study. After that, the user evaluation occurred in the following steps:

(1) The algorithm predicted the ratings of that user to all venues except the venues they visited.

(2) Among the results, the algorithm recommended three top-rated venues for each 24 users. These users were asked via Twitter message whether any of the recommended items attracted their attention.

(3) Twenty-one users replied to the recommendations. Only one of them said that none of the venues was suitable for them. Others were interested in at least one venue among the recommended ones.

(4) A survey, which also includes the Foursquare links of recommended venues, was prepared according to the participants' choices and sent to them.

(5) The users were asked to fill out the survey after they visit that recommended venue, or after examining the Foursquare page of the venues.

4.4. Survey Questions of the User Study.
There are 12 questions in the survey. The first question was asked to understand the appreciation of the participants to the recommended venues. It was asked in 5-point Likert scale (1-Not Like At All, 2-Not Like, 3-Not Sure, 4-Like, 5-Like Very Much).

The following four questions were asked to measure the appropriateness of the category, price, popularity, and the location of the recommended venue for the participant. They were also asked using a 5-point Likert scale (1-Not Appropriate At All, 2-Not Appropriate, 3-Not Sure, 4-Appropriate, 5-Very Appropriate).

The following four questions were asked to understand in which contextual circumstances the user would prefer the recommended venue. These questions were asked as fixed sum scale questions. The participants were asked to distribute a hundred points to the categories of a contextual variable according to the tendency of the user to visit that venue in these categories.

The last two questions were demographic questions. They were asked to learn the age, gender, and the education level of the participants.

4.5. Results of the User Study.
Participants' average age is 30 and the age range varies from 19 to 38. There are eight women and 12 men in the dataset. 12 of the participants graduated from high school, six of them have a bachelor's degree, and two of them have a master's degree. Table 12 presents the answers of the participants to the first five questions of the survey.

Ninety percent of the participants liked the recommended venues. Ten percent of them were indecisive about whether they like the recommended venue. Ninety percent of the participants thought that the price class of the recommended venue was suitable for them. Forty percent of the participants thought that the category of recommended venues were very appropriate for them while 20% of them thought that the categories were appropriate, and the remaining are indecisive. Seventy percent of the participants thought that the popularity class of recommended venues was appropriate for them, and 10% of them thought that the popularity classes of the venues were very appropriate. On the other hand, 10% were indecisive while another 10% thought that the popularity classes of the venues were not appropriate. Moreover, the address of the recommended

TABLE 12: Survey answers (Q1–Q5).

	1 (%)	2 (%)	3 (%)	4 (%)	5 (%)
1. Rate your liking			10	80	10
2. Rate the appropriateness of the price range		10		90	
3. Rate the appropriateness of the category of the restaurant			40	20	40
4. Rate the appropriateness of the popularity class of the restaurant		10	10	70	10
5. Rate the appropriateness of the location of the restaurant		30		30	40

TABLE 13: Answers of questions 6-7-8-9 and prediction of the answers.

	Answers of questions 6-7-8-9										Prediction of the answers									
	M	N	E	Wdays	Wend	Hot	Cold	Sunny	Rainy	Snowy	M	N	E	Wdays	Wend	Hot	Cold	Sunny	Rainy	Snowy
1	0.0	0.0	1.00	0.25	0.75	0.50	0.50	0.70	0.25	0.05	0.00	0.00	1.00	1.00	0.00	1.00	0.00	1.00	0.00	0.00
2	0.0	0.0	1.00	0.50	0.50	0.40	0.60	0.0	0.50	0.50	0.00	0.00	1.00	1.00	0.00	1.00	0.00	0.00	1.00	0.00
3	0.0	0.35	0.65	0.65	0.35	0.70	0.30	0.70	0.30	0.0	0.00	0.00	1.00	1.00	0.00	0.00	1.00	0.32	0.68	0.00
4	0.0	0.20	0.80	0.0	0.100	0.60	0.40	0.90	0.10	0.0	0.00	0.54	0.46	0.82	0.18	0.37	0.63	0.61	0.39	0.00
5	0.40	0.25	0.35	0.30	0.70	0.50	0.50	0.70	0.10	0.20	0.00	0.00	1.00	1.00	0.00	0.50	0.50	0.50	0.50	0.00
6	0.30	0.10	0.60	0.40	0.60	0.60	0.40	0.80	0.15	0.05	0.00	0.50	0.50	0.00	1.00	0.00	1.00	1.00	0.00	0.00
7	0.0	0.50	0.50	0.80	0.20	0.80	0.20	0.60	0.20	0.20	0.00	0.00	1.00	0.48	0.52	0.52	0.48	0.52	0.48	0.00
8	0.0	0.80	0.20	0.75	0.25	0.75	0.25	0.60	0.20	0.20	0.00	0.00	1.00	0.48	0.52	0.52	0.48	0.52	0.48	0.00
9	0.0	0.40	0.60	0.30	0.70	0.60	0.40	0.20	0.50	0.30	0.00	0.69	0.31	0.43	0.57	0.50	0.50	0.56	0.19	0.25
10	0.0	0.40	0.60	0.20	0.80	0.85	0.15	0.50	0.25	0.25	0.00	0.00	1.00	1.00	0.00	0.00	1.00	0.00	1.00	0.00
11	0.0	0.0	1.00	0.25	0.75	0.50	0.50	0.70	0.25	0.05	0.00	0.00	1.00	1.00	0.00	1.00	0.00	1.00	0.00	0.00
12	0.0	0.0	1.00	0.50	0.50	0.40	0.60	0.0	0.50	0.50	0.00	0.00	1.00	1.00	0.00	1.00	0.00	0.00	1.00	0.00
13	0.0	0.35	0.65	0.65	0.35	0.70	0.30	0.70	0.30	0.0	0.00	0.00	1.00	1.00	0.00	0.00	1.00	0.32	0.68	0.00
14	0.0	0.20	0.80	0.0	0.100	0.60	0.40	0.90	0.10	0.0	0.00	0.54	0.46	0.82	0.18	0.37	0.63	0.61	0.39	0.00
15	0.40	0.25	0.35	0.30	0.70	0.50	0.50	0.70	0.10	0.20	0.00	0.00	1.00	1.00	0.00	0.50	0.50	0.50	0.50	0.00
16	0.30	0.10	0.60	0.40	0.60	0.60	0.40	0.80	0.15	0.05	0.00	0.50	0.50	0.00	1.00	0.00	1.00	1.00	0.00	0.00
17	0.0	0.50	0.50	0.80	0.20	0.80	0.20	0.60	0.20	0.20	0.00	0.00	1.00	0.48	0.52	0.52	0.48	0.52	0.48	0.00
18	0.0	0.80	0.20	0.75	0.25	0.75	0.25	0.60	0.20	0.20	0.00	0.00	1.00	0.48	0.52	0.52	0.48	0.52	0.48	0.00
19	0.0	0.40	0.60	0.30	0.70	0.60	0.40	0.20	0.50	0.30	0.00	0.69	0.31	0.43	0.57	0.50	0.50	0.56	0.19	0.25
20	0.0	0.40	0.60	0.20	0.80	0.85	0.15	0.50	0.25	0.25	0.00	0.00	1.00	1.00	0.00	0.00	1.00	0.00	1.00	0.00

TABLE 14: Precision, recall, and F-1 measure for user study.

Approaches	Precision	Recall	F-1 score
User-based KNN	0.1220	0.0823	0.0983
Item-based KNN	0.1154	0.1107	0.1130
Biased matrix factorization	0.0893	0.1200	0.1031
SVD++	0.0702	0.0976	0.0816
HybRecSys	0.1667	0.1460	0.1493
Contextually personalized HybRecSys	0.18	0.45	0.25
User study results of contextually personalized HybRecSys	0.282	0.276	0.279

venue was given to the participants, and they were asked whether the location was appropriate or not. 40% of the participants said very appropriate and 30% of them said appropriate while the other 30% said not appropriate.

The following four questions were asked to understand in which contextual circumstances participants will prefer to visit the recommended venues. Table 13 presents the answers of each participant to these questions and the predictions, which are calculated from the algorithms for each user.

The predicted results were compared with the actual answers of the participants. The evaluation of the recommendation was measured with precision, recall, and F-1 measures. Table 14 presents the precision, recall, and F-1 scores for 20 participants. Precision value is 0.282, recall value is 0.276, and F1-score is 0.279.

The participants made some comments about the venues via Twitter messages. Some of the participants had been to some of the restaurants and supported the given recommendation with the following expressions:

(i) Participant 1 (Gender: Male, Age: 37, Education: High School)

    (a) "I always prefer going these two restaurants that you have recommended."

(ii) Participant 2 (Gender: Male, Age: 38, Education: High School)

    (a) "I have already been to one of the restaurants."

(iii) Participant 3 (Gender: Female, Age: 19, Education: High School)

    (a) "I have visited one of the restaurants before."

(iv) Participant 4 (Gender: Female, Age: 38, Education: Bachelor's Degree)

    (a) "I have already visited venue1 and venue2."

These statements demonstrate the ability of the recommender system's accurate prediction. Even participants that had not visited the recommended venues before stated that they like the recommended venues. This result reveals that the developed system has the diversity, novelty, and serendipity dimensions.

5. Conclusion

In this study, a contextually personalized hybrid recommendation model was proposed. This model integrates user-based and item-based collaborative filtering, content-based filtering together with contextual information in order to get rid of the drawbacks of each approach. Different data sources were used to collect the data: Visiting history of users was collected from Twitter. Venue characteristics (distance, category, popularity, and price classification) were collected from Foursquare, and contextual information (weather, season, date, and time of visits) related to each visit were collected from Weather Underground website. For content-based filtering, the variables distance, category, popularity, and price classification that have not been used before in one algorithm were used in order to determine content-based user similarity. Weather conditions, season, date, and time of each visit were used cumulatively as the properties of venues, and contextual similarities of venues were utilized. The artificial neural network algorithm was applied to determine the weights of each algorithm. Ratings coming from different algorithms (user-based CF, item-based CF, content-based filtering, and rating calculated from the contextual similarities of venues) were used as the predictors of the actual rating. Final ratings were calculated by multiplying the weights retrieved from neural network and the ratings from different algorithms. In addition, in order to make a more accurate recommendation and make the recommender system contextually personalized, our system calculates the probability of visiting a venue in a specific contextual category for each user-venue pair. The decision of recommendation of a venue to the specific user is made according to two rules. If the calculated rating is greater than the average rating of the user and the total contextual score is greater than two then that venue will be recommended to that user under the specific contextual circumstances. The Hybrid system prunes the disadvantages of each approach that may occur when they are used separately.

Contextually Personalized HybRecSys was compared to user-based and item-based KNN, biased matrix factorization, and SVD++. These algorithms are evaluated according to the metrics, which are used for ranking prediction (precision, recall, and F-1 measure). Training and test datasets were created using K-fold cross-validation ($K = 10$) technique. Results show that contextually personalized HybRecSys outperforms existing four algorithms according to each evaluation metric. Contextually Personalized HybRecSys effectively overcomes the data sparsity problem using venue category, popularity, and price to model user preferences.

In addition, recommending very similar venues to previous visits causes overspecialization. This problem is also reduced by considering the user preferences with different aspects and not just being stuck on only the venue characteristics. Hence, the quality of the recommendation is improved and the recommender system gained diversity, novelty, and serendipity dimensions.

The algorithm partially solves the cold start issue, which can be caused by both a new user and a new item. Even if a new user rates only one venue, the algorithm understands the user preferences from the characteristics of the venue (category, price, and popularity). Moreover, the algorithm figures out the contextual circumstances under which the user prefers that the specific venue. Therefore, by looking at these characteristics, the algorithm may recommend a venue to a new user.

The most important feature that distinguishes the developed algorithm from others is the contextual personalization. Contextually personalized HybRecSys solves this issue and recommends a right venue under the right conditions.

At the beginning, the collected data size was large, but after the filtration, it became moderately small. On the other hand, this small dataset generated significant results that may be improved with larger datasets. As a future study, it is planned to apply contextually personalized HybRecSys on larger datasets. Venue opening and closing hours can be checked for better results. In order to solve the cold start problem entirely, the system may recommend a venue to a new user by looking at the contextual circumstances and recommend the most preferred venue based on these contextual circumstances. In addition, even if a new venue is added to the system, it can be recommended by looking at the content-related characteristics. The online evaluation was conducted with only 20 people, which is a relatively small sample for obtaining statistically precise and coherent results. Therefore, more users should be reached for future studies. Finally, this algorithm can be embedded into a mobile application and this mobile application can be marketed in mobile application stores. Therefore, its performance can be measured via online experiments. As users download and use the application, they will score the recommendation, so that online feedback can be taken and the algorithm can be improved.

Acknowledgments

This study was funded by Bogazici University Scientific Research Fund (grant no. 11463).

References

[1] A. Bozanta and B. Kutlu, "HybRecSys: content-based contextual hybrid venue recommender system," *Journal of Information Science*, pp. 1–15, 2018.

[2] M. Sattari, I. H. Toroslu, P. Karagoz, P. Symeonidis, and Y. Manolopoulos, "Extended feature combination model for recommendations in location-based mobile services," *Knowledge and Information Systems*, vol. 44, no. 3, pp. 629–661, 2015.

[3] H. Wang, G. Li, and J. Feng, "Group-based personalized location recommendation on social networks," in *Web Technologies and Applications*, pp. 68–80, Springer, Berlin, Germany, 2014.

[4] H. Yin, B. Cui, Y. Sun, Z. Hu, and L. Chen, "LCARS: a spatial item recommender system," *ACM Transactions on Information Systems (TOIS)*, vol. 32, no. 3, pp. 1–37, 2014.

[5] M. H. Park, J. H. Hong, and S. B. Cho, "Location-based recommendation system using bayesian user's preference model in mobile devices," in *Ubiquitous Intelligence and Computing*, pp. 1130–1139, Springer, Berlin, Heidelberg, Germany, 2007.

[6] K. Aihara, H. Koshiba, and H. Takeda, "Behavioral cost-based recommendation model for wanderers in town," in *Human-Computer Interaction. Towards Mobile and Intelligent Interaction Environments*, pp. 271–279, Springer, Berlin, Heidelberg, Germany, 2011.

[7] Z. Yu, Y. Feng, H. Xu, and X. Zhou, "Recommending travel packages based on mobile crowdsourced data," *IEEE Communications Magazine*, vol. 52, no. 8, pp. 56–62, 2014.

[8] H. Yin, B. Cui, L. Chen, Z. Hu, and C. Zhang, "Modeling location-based user rating profiles for personalized recommendation," *ACM Transactions on Knowledge Discovery from Data*, vol. 9, no. 3, pp. 1–41, 2015.

[9] D. Zhou, S. M. Rahimi, and X. Wang, "Similarity-based probabilistic category-based location recommendation utilizing temporal and geographical influence," *International Journal of Data Science and Analytics*, vol. 1, no. 2, pp. 111–121, 2016.

[10] H. Zhu, E. Chen, H. Xiong, K. Yu, H. Cao, and J. Tian, "Mining mobile user preferences for personalized context-aware recommendation," *ACM Transactions on Intelligent Systems and Technology*, vol. 5, no. 4, pp. 1–27, 2015.

[11] Q. Fang, C. Xu, M. S. Hossain, and M. G. Stcaplrs, "A spatial-temporal context-aware personalized location recommendation system," *ACM Transactions on Intelligent systems and Technology*, vol. 7, no. 4, pp. 1–30, 2016.

[12] Q. Yuan, G. Cong, K. Zhao, Z. Ma, and A. Sun, "Who, where, when, and what: a nonparametric bayesian approach to context-aware recommendation and search for twitter users," *ACM Transactions on Information Systems*, vol. 33, no. 1, pp. 1–31, 2015.

[13] A. Gupta and K. Singh, "Location based personalized restaurant recommendation system for mobile environments," in *Proceedings of International Conference on Advances in Computing, Communications and Informatics (ICACCI)*, pp. 507–511, IEEE, Mysore, India, August 2013.

[14] J. Bao, Y. Zheng, and M. F. Mokbel, "Location-based and preference-aware recommendation using sparse geo-social networking data," in *Proceedings of 20th International Conference on Advances in Geographic Information Systems*, pp. 199–208, Redondo Beach, CA, USA, November 2012.

[15] H. Yin, Y. Sun, B. Cui, Z. Hu, and L. Chen, "Lcars: a location-content-aware recommender system," in *Proceedings of 19th ACM SIGKDD International Conference on Knowledge Discovery and Data Mining*, pp. 221–229, Chicago, IL, USA, August 2013.

[16] M. H. Kuo, L. C. Chen, and C. W. Liang, "Building and evaluating a location-based service recommendation system with a preference adjustment mechanism," *Expert Systems with Applications*, vol. 36, no. 2, pp. 3543–3554, 2009.

[17] K. Shimada, H. Uehara, and T. Endo, "A comparative study of potential-of-interest days on a sightseeing spot recommender," in *Proceedings of IIAI 3rd International Conference on Advanced Applied Informatics (IIAIAAI)*, pp. 555–560, Kitakyushu, Japan, August 2014.

[18] L. Ahmedi, K. Rrmoku, K. Sylejmani, and D. Shabani, "A bimodal social network analysis to recommend points of interest to tourists," *Social Network Analysis and Mining*, vol. 7, no. 1, p. 14, 2017.

[19] H. Gao, J. Tang, X. Hu, and H. Liu, "Content-aware point of interest recommendation on location-based social networks," in *Proceedings of the AAAI*, pp. 1721–1727, Austin, Texas, USA, January 2015.

[20] Z. Zheng, Y. Chen, S. Chen, L. Sun, and D. Chen, "Location-aware POI recommendation for indoor space by exploiting WiFi logs," *Mobile Information Systems*, vol. 2017, Article ID 9601404, 16 pages, 2017.

[21] W. X. Zhao, N. Zhou, A. Sun, J. R. Wen, J. Han, and E. Y. Chang, "A time-aware trajectory embedding model for next-location recommendation," *Knowledge and Information Systems*, vol. 56, no. 3, pp. 559–579, 2017.

[22] R. Srivastava, S. Hingmire, G. K. Palshikar, S. Chaurasia, and D. A. Csrs, "A context and sequence aware recommendation system," in *Proceedings of 8th Annual Meeting of the Forum on Information Retrieval Evaluation*, pp. 8–15, Kolkata, India, December 2016.

[23] V. Subramaniyaswamy, V. Vijayakumar, R. Logesh, and V. Indragandhi, "Intelligent travel recommendation system by mining attributes from community contributed photos," *Procedia Computer Science*, vol. 50, pp. 447–455, 2015.

[24] L. Cao, J. Luo, A. C. Gallagher, X. Jin, J. Han, and T. S. Huang, "A worldwide tourism recommendation system based on geotaggedweb photos," in *Proceedings of ICASSP*, pp. 2274–2277, Dallas, Texas, USA, March 2010.

[25] L. Guo, J. Shao, K. L. Tan, and Y. Y. Wheretogo, "Personalized travel recommendation for individuals and groups," in *Proceedings of IEEE 15th International Conference on Mobile Data Management*, vol. 1, pp. 49–58, Brisbane, Australia, July 2014.

[26] I. Memon, L. Chen, A. Majid, M. Lv, I. Hussain, and G. Chen, "Travel recommendation using geo-tagged photos in social media for tourist," *Wireless Personal Communications*, vol. 80, no. 4, pp. 1347–1362, 2015.

[27] Z. Xu, L. Chen, and G. Chen, "Topic based context-aware travel recommendation method exploiting geotagged photos," *Neurocomputing*, vol. 155, pp. 99–107, 2015.

[28] B. Dhake, S. S. Lomte, R. A. Auti, Y. R. Nagargoje, and B. Patil, "LARS: an efficient and scalable location-aware," *International Journal of Scientific Research And Education*, vol. 2, p. 11, 2014.

[29] M. Sarwat, J. J. Levandoski, A. Eldawy, and M. F. Mokbel, "LARS*: an efficient and scalable location-aware recommender system," *IEEE Transactions on Knowledge and Data Engineering*, vol. 26, no. 6, pp. 1384–1399, 2014.

[30] P. V. Krishna, S. Misra, D. Joshi, and M. S. Obaidat, "Learning automata based sentiment analysis for recommender system on cloud," in *Proceedings of International Conference on Computer, Information and Telecommunication Systems (CITS)*, pp. 1–5, IEEE, Athens, Greece, May 2013.

[31] M. Mordacchini, A. Passarella, M. Conti et al., "Crowdsourcing through cognitive opportunistic networks," *ACM Transactions on Autonomous and Adaptive Systems*, vol. 10, no. 2, pp. 1–29, 2015.

[32] Y. Zheng, L. Zhang, Z. Ma, X. Xie, and W. Y. Ma, "Recommending friends and locations based on individual location history," *ACM Transactions on the Web*, vol. 5, no. 1, pp. 1–44, 2011.

[33] V. W. Zheng, Y. Zheng, X. Xie, and Q. Yang, "Towards mobile intelligence: learning from GPS history data for collaborative recommendation," *Artificial Intelligence*, vol. 184–185, pp. 17–37, 2012.

[34] M. Korakakis, E. Spyrou, P. Mylonas, and S. J. Perantonis, "Exploiting social media information toward a context-aware recommendation system," *Social Network Analysis and Mining*, vol. 7, no. 1, p. 42, 2017.

[35] Q. Li, Y. Zheng, X. Xie, Y. Chen, W. Liu, and W. Y. Ma, "Mining user similarity based on location history," in *Proceedings of 16th ACM SIGSPATIAL International Conference on Advances in Geographic Information Systems*, p. 34, ACM, New York, NY, USA, November 2008.

[36] M. Ye, P. Yin, and W. C. Lee, "Location recommendation for location-based social networks," in *Proceedings of 18th SIGSPATIAL International Conference on Advances in Geographic Information Systems*, pp. 458–461, ACM, San Jose, CA, USA, November 2010.

[37] T. Hasegawa and T. Hayashi, "Collaborative filtering based spot recommendation seamlessly available in home and away areas," in *Proceedings of the IEEE/ACIS 12th International Conference on Computer and Information Science (ICIS)*, pp. 547-548, IEEE, Niigata, Japan, June 2013.

[38] J. J. Levandoski, M. Sarwat, A. Eldawy, and M. F. Mokbel, "Lars: a location-aware recommender system," in *Proceedings of IEEE 28th International Conference on Data Engineering (ICDE)*, pp. 450–461, IEEE, Arlington, VA, USA, April 2012.

[39] Y. Takeuchi and M. Sugimoto, "Cityvoyager: an outdoor recommendation system based on user location history," in *Ubiquitous Intelligence and Computing*, pp. 625–636, Springer-Verlag, Berlin, Germany, 2006.

[40] S. Knoch, A. Chapko, A. Emrich, D. Werth, and P. Loos, "A context-aware running route recommender learning from user histories using artificial neural networks," in *Proceedings of 23rd International Workshop on Database and Expert Systems Applications (DEXA)*, pp. 106–110, IEEE, Vienna, Austria, September 2012.

[41] M. Saraee, S. Khan, and S. Yamaner, "Data mining approach to implement a recommendation system for electronic tour guides," in *Proceedings of 2005 International Conference on E-Business, Enterprise Information Systems, E-Government, and Outsourcing, EEE 2005*, pp. 215–218, CSREA Press, Las Vegas, NV, USA, June 2005.

[42] R. Katarya and O. P. Verma, "Restaurant recommender system based on psychographic and demographic factors in mobile environment," in *Proceedings of International Conference on Green Computing and Internet of Things (ICG-CIoT)*, pp. 907–912, Uttar Pradesh, India, October 2015.

[43] R. Katarya and O. P. Verma, "Recent developments in affective recommender systems," *Physica A: Statistical Mechanics and its Applications*, vol. 461, pp. 182–190, 2016.

[44] R. Katarya, "A systematic review of group recommender systems techniques," in *Proceedings of International Conference on Intelligent Sustainable Systems (ICISS)*, pp. 425–428, Tirupur, India, December 2017.

[45] R. Katarya, O. P. Verma, and I. Jain, "User behaviour analysis in context-aware recommender system using hybrid filtering approach," in *Proceedings of 4th International Conference on Computer and Communication Technology (ICCCT)*, pp. 222–227, Allahabad, India, September 2013.

[46] R. Katarya, M. Ranjan, and O. P. Verma, "Location based recommender system using enhanced random walk model," in *Proceedings of Fourth International Conference on Parallel, Distributed and Grid Computing (PDGC)*, pp. 33–37, Waknaghat, India, December 2016.

[47] K. Waga, A. Tabarcea, and P. Fränti, "Context aware recommendation of location-based data," in *Proceedings of 15th International Conference on System Theory, Control, and Computing (ICSTCC)*, pp. 1–6, IEEE, Sinaia, Romania, October 2011.

[48] A. Majid, L. Chen, G. Chen, H. T. Mirza, I. Hussain, and J. Woodward, "A context-aware personalized travel recommendation system based on geotagged social media data mining," *International Journal of Geographical Information Science*, vol. 27, no. 4, pp. 662–684, 2013.

[49] Q. Yuan, G. Cong, Z. Ma, A. Sun, and N. M. Thalmann, "Time-aware point-of-interest recommendation," in *Proceedings of 36th International ACM SIGIR Conference on Research and Development in Information Retrieval*, pp. 363–372, ACM, Dublin, Ireland, July 2013.

[50] R. Baral and T. Li, "Maps: a multi aspect personalized poi recommender system," in *Proceedings of 10th ACM Conference on Recommender Systems*, pp. 281–284, ACM, Boston, MA, USA, September 2016.

[51] P. Hiesel, M. Braunhofer, and W. Wörndl, "Learning the popularity of items for mobile tourist guides," in *Proceedings of RecTour*, Cambridge, MA, USA, September 2016.

[52] L. Yao, Q. Z. Sheng, X. Wang, W. E. Zhang, and Y. Qin, "Collaborative location recommendation by integrating multi-dimensional contextual information," *ACM Transactions on Internet Technology*, vol. 18, no. 3, pp. 1–24, 2018.

[53] C. Trattner, A. Oberegger, L. Eberhard, D. Parra, and L. Marinho, "Understanding the impact of weather for POI recommendations," in *Proceedings of RecTour*, Cambridge, MA, USA, September 2016.

[54] Y. Zheng, R. Burke, and B. Mobasher, "Differential context relaxation for context-aware travel recommendation," in *Proceedings of International Conference on Electronic Commerce and Web Technologies*, pp. 88–99, Springer, Vienna, Austria, September 2012.

[55] M. J. Barranco, J. M. Noguera, J. Castro, and L. Martinez, "A context-aware mobile recommender system based on location and trajectory," in *Management Intelligent Systems*, pp. 153–162, Springer, Berlin, Heidelberg, Germany, 2012.

[56] N. S. Savage, M. Baranski, N. E. Chavez, and T. Hollerer, "I'm feeling loco: a location based context aware recommendation system," in *Advances in Location-Based Services*, pp. 37–54, Springer, Berlin, Heidelberg, Germany, 2012.

[57] J. L. Herlocker, J. A. Konstan, L. G. Terveen, and J. T. Riedl,

"Evaluating collaborative filtering recommender systems," *ACM Transactions on Information Systems*, vol. 22, no. 1, pp. 5–53, 2004.

[58] P. Lops, M. De Gemmis, and G. Semeraro, "Content-based recommender systems: state of the art and trends," in *Recommender Systems Handbook*, pp. 73–105, Springer, Berlin, Heidelberg, Germany, 2011.

[59] Z. Lu, H. Wang, N. Mamoulis, W. Tu, and D. W. Cheung, "Personalized location recommendation by aggregating multiple recommenders in diversity," *GeoInformatica*, vol. 21, no. 3, pp. 459–484, 2017.

[60] R. Burke, "Hybrid recommender systems: survey and experiments," *User Modeling and User-Adapted Interaction*, vol. 12, no. 4, pp. 331–370, 2002.

[61] L. Baltrunas and X. Amatriain, "Towards time-dependent recommendation based on implicit feedback," in *Proceedings of Workshop on Context-Aware Recommender Systems (CARS'09)*, New York, NY, USA, October 2009.

[62] X. Wang, Y. L. Zhao, L. Nie et al., "Semantic-based location recommendation with multimodal venue semantics," *IEEE Transactions on Multimedia*, vol. 17, no. 3, pp. 409–419, 2015.

[63] Q. Yuan, G. Cong, and A. Sun, "Graph-based point-of-interest recommendation with geographical and temporal influences," in *Proceedings of 23rd ACM International Conference on Information and Knowledge Management*, pp. 659–668, Shanghai, China, November 2014.

[64] Y. Mao, P. Yin, W. Lee, and D. Lee, "Exploiting geographical influence for collaborative point-of-interest recommendation," in *Proceedings of 34th ACM SI- GIR International Conference on Research and Development in Information Retrieval*, pp. 325–334, Beijing, China, July 2011.

[65] S. K. Gorakala and M. Usuelli, *Building a Recommendation System with R*, Packt Publishing Ltd., Birmingham, UK, 2015.

[66] Y. Zheng, L. Zhang, X. Xie, and W. Y. Ma, "Mining interesting locations and travel sequences from GPS trajectories," in *Proceedings of 18th International Conference on World Wide Web*, pp. 791–800, Madrid, Spain, April 2009.

[67] G. Shani and A. Gunawardana, "Evaluating recommendation systems," in *Recommender Systems Handbook*, pp. 257–297, Springer, Berlin, Heidelberg, Germany, 2011.

[68] J. A. Konstan, B. N. Miller, D. Maltz, J. L. Herlocker, L. R. Gordon, and J. Riedl, "GroupLens: applying collaborative filtering to Usenet news," *Communications of the ACM*, vol. 40, no. 3, pp. 77–87, 1997.

[69] M. Deshpande and G. Karypis, "Item-based top-n recommendation algorithms," *ACM Transactions on Information Systems*, vol. 22, no. 1, pp. 143–177, 2004.

[70] Y. Koren, R. Bell, and C. Volinsky, "Matrix factorization techniques for recommender systems," *Computer*, vol. 42, no. 8, pp. 30–37, 2009.

[71] Y. Koren, "Factorization meets the neighborhood: a multifaceted collaborative filtering model," in *Proceedings of 14th ACM SIGKDD International Conference on Knowledge Discovery and Data Mining*, pp. 426–434, Las Vegas, NV, USA, August 2008.

6

Improving Children's Experience on a Mobile EdTech Platform through a Recommender System

Almudena Ruiz-Iniesta,[1] **Luis Melgar,**[2] **Alejandro Baldominos** (iD),[3,4] **and David Quintana** (iD)[4]

[1]*Universidad Internacional de La Rioja, Logroño, Spain*
[2]*Banco Bilbao Vizcaya Argentaria (BBVA), Bilbao, Spain*
[3]*Smile and Learn Digital Creations, Madrid 28043, Spain*
[4]*Department of Computer Science, Universidad Carlos III de Madrid, Av. de la Universidad 30, Leganés 28911, Spain*

Correspondence should be addressed to David Quintana; dquintan@inf.uc3m.es

Academic Editor: Mari C. Aguayo Torres

Smile and Learn is an EdTech digital publisher that offers a smart library of close to 100 educational stories and gaming apps for mobile devices aimed at children aged 2 to 10 and their families. Given the complexity of navigating the content, a recommender system was developed. The system consists of two major components: one that generates content recommendations and another that provides explanations and recommendations relevant to parents and educators. The former was implemented as a hybrid recommender system that combines three kinds of recommendations. Among these, we introduce a collaborative filtering adapted to overcome specific limitations associated with younger users. The approach described in this work was tested on real users of the platform. The experimental results suggest that this recommendation model is suitable to suggest apps to children and increase their engagement in terms of usage time and number of games played.

1. Introduction

Smile and Learn is an EdTech digital publisher that creates and distributes educational mobile apps for children aged 2 to 10 and their families. The company offers a smart library of around 100 stories and gaming apps to provide a complete educational experience.

In addition to the content offering, the library has a smart component that gathers user information and analyses the performance across applications to obtain a detailed snapshot. Over time, the information regarding the state and the progress can be used by parents and educators both as an early warning mechanism and to keep track of child development.

The idea of using technology to enhance learning is hardly new. However, the increasing adoption of electronic devices, both in educational settings and at home, has created new opportunities to study user behavior and performance. This has allowed the development of a wide range of applications that perform tasks like monitoring progress [1] and student fatigue [2], scaffolding learners [3], recommending open educational resources [4], modeling learners [5], or predicting future performance [6, 7], among many others. While some of these systems work in ways that are nonintrusive and transparent to the user, others provide direct feedback to the user or the educator [8].

Smile and Learn intends to progressively add that kind of functionality to the smart library, building on the metadata derived from the interaction of the increasing number of applications. Unlike other tools with a limited scope, focused on the search for progress in a limited area like programming [9] or even wider like a generic class [10], the smart library follows a more global approach. It is closer to the aim of the system described by Lopez-Fernandez et al. [11] for the domain of engineering students, as it covers a wide range of cognitive skills together with the learning of values.

Due to the large number of alternatives on offer, the company has felt the need to develop a recommender system to help the users navigate through the library, increasing their engagement and the diversity of apps that they use. In this paper, we will thoroughly describe the functioning of the implemented recommender system. Additionally, we will evaluate the performance of the system in terms of how recommendations suggested to users impact the number of games and playing time.

Recommender systems is a very active research field [12–14]. Among the areas of application that show more potential, we can mention Education. The research effort that is being devoted to this area is very important, and so is the output in terms of academic publications and presentations made at conferences [15, 16].

The implementation and utilization of recommender systems for educational purposes is full of challenges [17]. Their evaluation is also full of difficulties [18]. From an algorithmic point of view, there are a number of approaches that differ widely in their degree of complexity and suitability, depending on the context [19]. Among the most popular ones, we can mention a few discussed in a recent benchmarking exercise for learning environments by Kopeinik et al. [20]: Most Popular [21], Collaborative Filtering [22], Content-Based [23], Usage Context-Based Similarity [24], Base Level Learning Equation with Associative Component [25], or SUSTAIN [26].

As we will discuss in detail later, the recommender system implemented in the smart library relies on a combination of demographic and use data gathered by other elements of the platform. This is consistent with other educational systems described in the literature [27]. The system consists of two major components: one that generates user-oriented content recommendations and another that provides explanations and recommendations relevant to parents and educators. It is worth noting that the former was designed to overcome specific limitations associated with younger users, such as the difficulty to provide meaningful feedback.

The rest of the document is organized as follows: Section 2 provides a general description of the system, including an introduction to the applications contained in the smart library, and the way in which the data are acquired and processed. That will be followed by Section 3 that discusses the specifics of the recommender system implemented for the case at hand. In Section 4, we report results of the experimental analysis used to evaluate the performance of the algorithm. Finally, Section 5 will be devoted to summary and conclusions.

2. Smart Digital Library

In this section, we introduce the Smart Digital Library. To that end, we provide a brief description of the structure, contents, and interaction with the system, followed by details regarding the way data are captured and analyzed.

2.1. Structure and Use. The Smart Digital Library (SDL) is a single platform of interactive games and stories that also provides access to proprietary apps designed following the principles of the theory of multiple intelligences proposed by Howard Gardner [28]. According to it, intelligence can be differentiated into specific "modalities", rather than being dominated by a single general ability. Hence, each app is focused on one of the specific abilities described in the theory.

There are three types of apps in SDL: games, tales, and quizzes. They reinforce multiple intelligences and cognitive skills with memory, attention, coordination, and logic. They are inspired in educational content and include a range of difficulty levels adapted to children of different ages and development levels.

The SDL is multilanguage, can be used at home, on the go, or at school and provides recommendations to children, parents, and educators.

The smart library works in the following way: children access the library through an app, downloaded by their parents or educators via Google Play (Google Play is a digital distribution service operated and developed by Google, http://play. google.com) or the App Store (App Store is a digital distribution platform, developed and maintained by Apple Inc., for mobile apps on its iOS operating system), which works as a sole access point and storage space for all of the games and interactive stories. From this app, parents and educators can download content for the child to use, which will be saved in the device after playing.

Each child's progress is registered, and relevant details are made available to parents and educators through the Learning Analytics Dashboard (LAD). This component, accessible from the app itself or a website, provides information on a child's progress and playing time, as well as recommendations for improvement. Currently, SDL has more than 11 k monthly active users and more than 1.2 M total app records.

2.2. Data Acquisition and Processing. Child progress is monitored by the system. The platform keeps track of the areas where the user shows better performance and also those where the child faces more difficulties. Teachers and parents are able to access the data from the platform, using the LAD.

In order to extract correlations between apps played and learning, we use a feedback platform, which provides time-stamped output of app-related events (score, failures, bonus, game mode, type of app, level, etc.). The recorded fields depend on the type of app played. The information recorded by the different types of app is the following:

(i) Tales: time spent on reading the tale, together with the level and reading mode (type of letter, reading, listening, or pictograms).

(ii) Quiz: quiz level, time spent on completing the quiz, number of hits, failures, and total number of questions.

(iii) Game: hits, failures, total of possible hits, time spent on completing the game, score, bonus, and level.

These data are used to enrich the child's profile. With it, the system estimates the mastery level according to multiple intelligences. This information is then employed by the recommender system to personalize a suggestion list.

The LAD shows the progress of the child and the proportion of time that the user devotes to each application. As will be explained in Section 3.2, it has been conceived to communicate the learning stages of each player effectively and includes recommendations for parents and educators. Its design follows closely numerous insights that were provided in interviews with specialists.

The recommender system plays a key role in the platform. We describe the implemented solution in the section that follows.

3. Recommender System

Recommender systems (RS) in this context are used to personalize online experiences. They are based on the fact that people's tastes generally follow patterns. People tend to like things that are similar to other things they liked before, and they tend to have a similar taste to other people they are close with. Among the alternatives mentioned in the introduction, the two most popular are Content-Based (CB) and Collaborative Filtering (CF) [29]. CB employs the description of the item and a profile of the user's preferences to make recommendations. Meanwhile, CF generates recommendations based on the preferences of similar users. As stated before, research on recommender systems is a very active field. Education is one of the areas where applications show great potential.

We aim at providing personalized recommendations that enable children to interact better with the SDL. The first release of SDL showed the apps grouped by worlds (Figure 1(a)). These worlds corresponded to the seven intelligences proposed in Gardner's theory; however, this user interface design had a limitation: it was difficult for children to find the applications they wanted to play. As a consequence, they always used the same apps because they already knew where they were located.

Given the mentioned use pattern, one of the goals of the RS was to design a frictionless SDL. That is, we aim at providing interactions that control the elements that inhibit people from intuitively and painlessly achieving their goals within a digital interface. For this purpose, we proposed a new use experience design with a list of seven recommended apps at the bottom of the screen (Figure 1(b)). In Section 4, we present an analysis of the benefits of this new design.

The RS uses data collected by the feedback platform in order to estimate the preferences of the child. We have also included an explanation module in our recommender system which will provide explanations of the recommendations to parents and educators through the LAD. As we will see in Section 3.2, explanations provide confidence and trust in the RS.

In the SDL, the personalization focuses on estimating the interest that a user will have in an application. For this, we combine in a hybrid recommender system [30] several types of algorithms, each one focused on one relevant aspect of our apps and our users as it is explained below:

(i) Trending apps: recommends two apps from the most widely played in our SDL to new users. These recommendations often comprise apps that due to their nature are very enjoyable to play regardless of the user profile.

(ii) Surprise of the month: recommends two apps taken from the new monthly releases.

(iii) Collaborative filtering: recommends three apps (not yet played by the user) based on the preferences of similar users.

The results from each recommender are combined in a unique list of outcomes with no further processing, where the recommendations are listed in this order: first, the trending apps are shown. These are followed by the surprise of the month and, finally, the CF recommendation. Given that ordering might have an impact, and the fact that it has not been optimized yet, our results might understate the potential benefits of the CF recommender system.

We have limited the size of the list of recommendations to seven, since displaying a larger number could be difficult in certain screens, therefore worsening the user experience. From this list, the majority of recommendations (three out of seven) are generated by the CF recommender, whose strategy we explain in further detail in the following subsection.

3.1. Collaborative Filtering Recommendation Strategy. The main goal of our collaborative filtering recommender is to select the apps of greatest interest to the target child according to the preferences of other SDL users. CF is the process of evaluating items using opinions of others. In the SDL, CF techniques help to identify those apps which are more useful and of more interest to each child in particular.

We have explored the use of the well-known user-based nearest-neighbor algorithm [31] in our CF. This algorithm generates predictions for users based on ratings from similar users. First, the algorithm identifies the users that, in the past, exhibited a similar behavior. Next, it analyses their ratings to identify the items that the target user should like. These similar users are the neighbors.

We have adapted the general CF process to our domain. The neighbors are those children who have played at least one application in common with the target user. Overall, the adapted process runs as follows:

(i) Neighborhood formation. We form the neighborhood in order to find those children who are more similar to the target child by using the data collected by the feedback platform. This step requires a proximity measure to generate like-minded peers and to select the top-K neighbors.

(ii) Rating prediction and top-K selection. For each app played by the neighbors, we generate a prediction using neighbors' ratings. Finally, the top-K apps are selected.

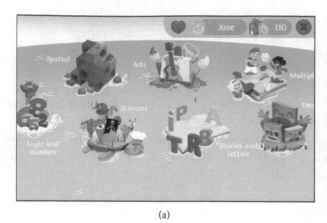

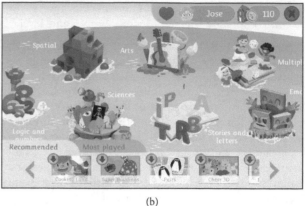

(a)   (b)

FIGURE 1: Screenshot of the smart library initial screen.

Next subsections describe each step of the process.

3.1.1. Neighborhood Formation.
The first step in the CF process is the selection of the children who are more similar to the target child, to form the neighborhood. Only children who played at least one application in common with the target child are candidates to form part of the neighborhood.

The child profile includes demographic information (e.g., age, gender, and education). Each app feedback also stores information about the IP connection, device information, and duration of the session. This information will be employed to measure the proximity of each user in order to form the neighborhood.

Traditionally, CF takes into account the ratings assigned by each user to each product to generate the neighborhood and the predictions. These RS have focused on users who are able to offer explicit feedback themselves. However, in our domain, users will be children. It is worth noting that children's patterns of attention and interaction are quite different from adults [32], and they are not capable of assigning ratings to the apps they play in a meaningful way. For this reason, the metric used to build the similarity matrix in our CF recommender system is designed to rely on implicit rather than explicit feedback.

We have chosen a similarity metric defined as the weighted sum up of two relevancies: the age similarity (*ageSim*) between the children and the number of common apps (*appSim*). In this equation, the common apps account for the fact of finding users with similar preferences, but the metric also receives feedback based on the user's age, which is relevant in the context of children, where preferences can change fast during growth. In order to calculate the age similarity, we have picked a distance-based metric using a threshold. To calculate the *appSim*, we employ the app usage records. We will take into account the applications most played by the child in relation to the total applications he has played. So, the more applications two children have in common, the more similar they are. Finally, the two indicators are combined as follows:

$$\text{similarity}(\text{Ch}_1, \text{Ch}_2) = \alpha \cdot appSim(\text{Ch}_1, \text{Ch}_2)$$
$$+ (1 - \alpha) \cdot ageSim(\text{Ch}_1, \text{Ch}_2),$$

$$(1)$$

where $\alpha \in [0, 1]$. This similarity measure reports a value in $[0, 1]$ that represents how similar two children are according to their profiles. Then, the top-K children with higher similarity values with the target child are selected as neighbors. We use the implicit feedback of these users to perform our recommendation.

3.1.2. Prediction Computation and Top-K Selection.
Finally, we have to generate predictions for the proposed apps. For each app, we analyze the records of children in the target child's neighborhood and we compute the weighted average of ratings. The value of each weight is directly related to the similarity of the target child and the corresponding neighbor, computed during the neighborhood formation. Once we have calculated the prediction for the candidate apps, we sort them according to this value. This way, the most interesting apps for the target child (the top-K apps) will be finally suggested.

3.2. Explanations and Recommendations for Parents and Educators.
The last component of our recommender system is the explanations module, which takes into account the characteristics of each app and the potential benefits that it could provide to the child. It attaches a message to the list of recommended apps and shows all this information in the LAD (Figure 2). Our goal is to provide feedback to educators and parents on how the use of certain apps can improve learning, based on the analysis of the child's use and progress observed. When generating the explanation for a recommended app, a phrase from among a set of predefined templates is selected and filled with information about the app and the child. This information will help parents and educators to better understand how the recommended app will influence the child's educational process. These templates differ based on the intelligence developed by the app and stage of learning, in order to provide a more customized

Figure 2: Explanations of the recommender system.

experience. A real example of this kind of explanations could be the following: "*By playing Bubbles, Alex could develop a variety of abilities such as spatial orientation, attention, visual memory and logic-spatial reasoning.*"

Displaying a plausible explanation along with a recommendation can do wonders at almost no cost, i.e., without making any changes to the underlying recommendation algorithms. The impact of explanations has been studied extensively by Tintarev and Masthoff [33]. Among the advantages, we could mention that it increases trust in the smart library, effectively helping parents and educators make good decisions in choosing the most suitable apps for their children.

4. Experimental Analysis

The main purpose of the implemented recommendation system is to facilitate the access to SDL, by limiting the amount of information that the user has to go through before starting to actually play, and the making the SDL more attractive to the user by implementing personalized suggestions.

The evaluation that we present here will let us know how the patterns of usage of the SDL are affected by the recommendation system. In order to do that, we will analyze whether it has any impact on the use of the applications in the aforementioned context. Specifically, we will study the impact of the recommender system on user engagement in terms of number of games played and time spent on the system, bearing in mind that we are in a scenario in which players might have limited access to their digital devices.

The dataset used in this analysis covers the six-month period between March and August 2018, both inclusive. The SDL is used both in educational settings, like schools, and domestic ones. Given that the interaction in the former is usually driven by teachers, and therefore, the recommender system is unlikely to have any impact, we disregarded those users. The resulting sample included 4,876 unique users and 78 applications. Finally, we filtered out the users for which there was incomplete information, leaving us with a final 4,712 users.

We only considered the applications available in the SDL that can be suitably described as interactive apps; this distinction is pertinent because the applications that were left out of the study have very different interaction dynamics (most of them can be considered tales, as the content is limited to a story).

We proceed to give a detailed description of the metrics, as well as the corresponding results. As we mentioned, we will focus on two aspects of engagement.

The formal definition of the average number of games per recommended app for user i, ANG_{Ri}, is defined by the following expression:

$$\text{ANG}_{Ri} = \frac{\text{Games}_{Ri}}{\text{NumApps}_{Ri}}, \tag{2}$$

where Games_{Ri} is the total number of games played by user i on apps recommended to her, and NumApps_{Ri} is the total number of apps recommended to i. For this sake, we define "game" as an event where the user has completed a level and obtained a score that is registered.

The complementary metric of ANG_{Ri} would be ANG_{NRi}. The only difference between them is the fact that the latter would consider the total number of nonrecommended apps, and the number of times that they were played by the user.

The second indicator of engagement is defined in terms of time, rather than the number of games. We therefore define the average game time per recommended app for user i, AGT_{Ri}, as

$$\text{AGT}_{Ri} = \frac{\text{GameTime}_{Ri}}{\text{NumApps}_{Ri}}, \tag{3}$$

where GameTime_{Ri} is the total accumulated time (in seconds) spent by user i playing apps recommended to her, and NumApps_{Ri} is the total number of apps recommended to i.

Once again, the complementary metric, GameTime_{NRi}, considers the total number of nonrecommended apps and the total time accumulated by user i playing them.

The experimental results are summarized in Table 1. There, we report the mean, median, and standard deviation by recommendation for the two indicators over the six-month period from the beginning of March 2018 to the end of August. As we can see, the evidence supports the positive impact of the recommendation system on engagement. There seems to be a strong positive connection between being recommended and both a higher number of games and more time spent using the SDL.

The statistical significance of the reported differences between the metrics for the recommended apps and the nonrecommended ones was formally tested. Once the null hypothesis of normality was rejected for the distribution of the four indicators using Lilliefors test ($p < 0.001$), we applied the Wilcoxon test to assess the differences. These were

TABLE 1: Engagement metrics for game apps by recommendation for the period 03/01/2018–08/31/2018.

Engagement metric	Mean	Median	Std. dev.
Games			
ANG_{NRi}	0.43	0.18	0.88
ANG_{Ri}	2.22	1.05	5.81
Time			
AGT_{NRi}	74.79	18.66	300.21
AGT_{Ri}	292.84	103.49	2005.45

TABLE 2: Engagement metrics for game apps by recommendation and for the period 1/03/2018–31/08/2018. Metrics grouped by quartile of usage intensity.

Quartile	Number		Time	
	ANG_{NRi}	ANG_{Ri}	AGT_{NRi}	AGT_{Ri}
Q4	0.07	0.58	4.57	41.05
Q3	0.18	1.46	15.09	101.53
Q2	0.37	2.21	37.79	199.85
Q1	1.11	4.61	241.19	746.34

found to be significant at the 1% conventional level ($p < 0.001$).

In order to provide a better understanding of the importance of the RS, we report the engagement metrics by usage intensity in Table 2.

We identified the total time spent playing games by the users of the SDL, regardless of whether the apps were recommended or not, and classified them by quartiles. As we can see, recommendations have more impact in absolute terms on the most active users. However, among the least active users, who sometimes limit their activity to opening one or two games for a little time and then proceed to uninstall the software, the effects in relative terms tends to be more important. These users, that do not know yet the library and have not had the chance to identify games that they like, often rely on the suggestions of the recommender to start the exploration of the SDL.

5. Summary and Conclusions

Smile and Learn's digital library includes around 100 educational stories and gaming apps aimed at children aged 2 to 10 and their families. Given the complexity of navigating the content, an RS was introduced to ease the process-improving engagement.

Recommender systems are often based on explicit user feedback. This, however, is a factor, as the approach requires users who are sophisticated enough to provide it. This imposes a major limitation in the children's educational technology space, for the patterns of attention and interaction with the apps are quite different from those of adults. In particular, children have a limited ability in terms of assigning ratings to the apps that they play. In order to overcome his problem, we introduce an approach that takes into account the above issues in order to enhance children's experience with the SDL.

The RS that we present combines three kinds of recommendations. Among these, we introduced one based on collaborative filtering aimed at inferring what can be of potential interest to users considering past user-item interactions. The approach, based on implicit feedback, adapts the standard algorithm to the children's educational app domain as a two-step process that starts with a neighborhood formation and ends with a rating prediction and top-K selection. The neighborhood formation is based on a similarity metric, tailored to this domain that considers both age and the number of apps in common among users. The RS also includes an explanations module for parents and educators.

In this context, we have studied in Section 4 to what extent has the RS achieved the goal of increasing engagement. The results support a direct connection between the use of the RS and two closely related aspects of this construct for gaming content: number of games and playing time. Recommended apps show a higher average number of games per recommended app than the nonrecommended ones, and the average game time per recommended app by user shows the same pattern. The positive impact of the RS is both substantial and statistically significant.

Even though we found different patterns depending on the intensity of use, the RS has a positive impact regardless of whether the users were among the most or the least active ones. The difference was that the impact in absolute terms was higher among the most frequent users, whereas the impact on the least frequent ones was higher in relative terms. More casual users rely more on the recommendations for their initial exploration.

This latter aspect is relevant, as it suggests that the first contact with the SDL can be managed effectively to favor positive experiences. Given that, according to the data, to an important extent, the first selections do not come from a rational analysis of the whole catalog of the SDL, but an impulsive choice based on the alternatives offered by the RS, the system could focus the selection presented to new users on trending apps. This possibility, yet to be tested, that would disregard the other two algorithms, could potentially bias the selection to increase the likelihood of a satisfying experience, hence improving engagement.

We are currently exploring new ways of personalization by aggregating information associated with the competency level of users in each of the cognitive areas. In the future, we will create a measure of profile-similarity based on the aforementioned capabilities in order to be able to provide recommendations that make the learning process more effective. This profile-similarity measure will be employed to recognize different learning styles and playing habits mining their feedback records. This approach can also be used in a clustering process that considers children habits and interests to obtain better personalized recommendations.

Finally, this longer-term vision will be complemented by near-term progress in two fronts: the optimization of the process in charge of combining and representing the output of the three subsystems of the described hybrid RS and benchmarking its performance against other state-of-the-art algorithms.

Acknowledgments

This research has received funding from the European Union's Horizon 2020 research and innovation programme under grant agreement no. 756826.

References

[1] S. Charleer, A. V. Moere, J. Klerkx, K. Verbert, and T. D. Laet, "Learning Analytics dashboards to support adviser-student dialogue," *IEEE Transactions on Learning Technologies*, vol. 11, no. 3, pp. 389–399, 2017.

[2] S. Gonçalves, M. Rodrigues, D. Carneiro, F. Fdez-Riverola, and P. Novais, "Boosting learning: non-intrusive monitoring of student's efficiency," *Advances in Intelligent Systems and Computing*, vol. 374, pp. 73–80, 2015, Conference of 1st International Conference on Methodologies and Intelligent Systems for Technology Enhanced Learning (MIS4TEL 2015), June 2015.

[3] M. Ueno and Y. Miyazawa, "IRT-based adaptive hints to scaffold learning in programming," *IEEE Transactions on Learning Technologies*, p. 1, 2017.

[4] A. Ruiz-Iniesta, G. Jiménez-Díaz, and M. Gómez-Albarrán, "A semantically enriched context-aware OER recommendation strategy and its application to a computer science OER repository," *IEEE Transactions on Education*, vol. 57, no. 4, pp. 255–260, 2014.

[5] T. Käser, S. Klingler, A. G. Schwing, and M. Gross, "Dynamic bayesian networks for student modeling," *IEEE Transactions on Learning Technologies*, vol. 10, no. 4, pp. 450–462, 2017.

[6] M. Al-Saleem, N. Al-Kathiry, S. Al-Osimi, and G. Badr, "Mining educational data to predict students' academic performance," *Lecture Notes in Computer Science*, vol. 9166, pp. 403–414, 2015, Conference of 11th International Conference on Machine Learning and Data Mining in Pattern Recognition (MLDM 2015), July 2015.

[7] H. Bydžovská, "Student performance prediction using collaborative filtering methods," *Lecture Notes in Computer Science*, vol. 9112, pp. 550–553, 2015, Conference of 17th International Conference on Artificial Intelligence in Education (AIED 2015), June 2015.

[8] R. Bodily and K. Verbert, "Review of research on student-facing learning Analytics dashboards and educational recommender systems," *IEEE Transactions on Learning Technologies*, vol. 10, no. 4, pp. 405–418, 2017.

[9] M. L. Barrón-Estrada, R. Zatarain-Cabada, F. G. Hernández, R. O. Bustillos, and C. A. Reyes-García, "An affective and cognitive tutoring system for learning programming," in *Advances in Artificial Intelligence and Its Applications: 14th Mexican International Conference on Artificial Intelligence, MICAI 2015*, O. Pichardo Lagunas, O. Herrera Alcántara, and G. Arroyo Figueroa, Eds., vol. 9414, pp. 171–182, Lecture notes in Computer Science, Springer International Publishing, Cuernavaca, Morelos, Mexico, October 2015.

[10] M. H. Dlab and N. Hoić-Božić, "Increasing Students' Academic Results in e-ourse Using Educational Recommendation Strategy," in *Proceedings of the 17th International Conference on Computer Systems and Technologies 2016 (CompSysTech '16)*, A. Smrikarov and B. Rachev, Ed., pp. 391–398, ACM, New York, NY, USA, 2016.

[11] D. Lopez-Fernandez, P. Alarcon, and E. Tovar, "Assessment and development of transversal competences based on student's autonomous learning," in *Proceeedings of 2016 IEEE Global Engineering Education Conference (EDUCON)*, pp. 482–487, IEEE Computer Society, Abu Dhabi, UAE, April 2016.

[12] G. Adomavicius and A. Tuzhilin, "Toward the next generation of recommender systems: a survey of the state-of-the-art and possible extensions," *IEEE Transactions on Knowledge and Data Engineering*, vol. 17, no. 6, pp. 734–749, 2005.

[13] J. Bobadilla, F. Ortega, A. Hernando, and A. GutiéRrez, "Recommender systems survey," *Knowledge-Based Systems*, vol. 46, pp. 109–132, 2013.

[14] J. Lu, D. Wu, M. Mao, W. Wang, and G. Zhang, "Recommender system application developments: a survey," *Decision Support Systems*, vol. 74, pp. 12–32, 2015.

[15] H. Drachsler, K. Verbert, O. C. Santos, and N. Manouselis, "Panorama of recommender systems to support learning," in *Recommender Systems Handbook*, F. Ricci, L. Rokach, and B. Shapira, Eds., pp. 421–451, Springer US, Boston, MA, USA, 2015.

[16] M. Erdt, A. Fernández, and C. Rensing, "Evaluating recommender systems for technology enhanced learning: a quantitative survey," *IEEE Transactions on Learning Technologies*, vol. 8, no. 4, pp. 326–344, 2015.

[17] J. Tarus and Z. Niu, "A survey of learner and researcher related challenges in e-learning recommender systems," *Communications in Computer and Information Science*, vol. 734, pp. 122–132, 2017, Conference of 6th International Workshop on Learning Technology for Education Challenges (LTEC 2017), August 2017.

[18] M. Lombardi and A. Marani, "A comparative framework to evaluate recommender systems in technology enhanced learning: a case study," *Lecture Notes in Computer Science*, vol. 9414, pp. 155–170, 2015, Conference of 14th Mexican International Conference on Artificial Intelligence (MICAI 2015), October 2015.

[19] I. Portugal, P. Alencar, and D. Cowan, "The use of machine learning algorithms in recommender systems: a systematic review," *Expert Systems with Applications*, vol. 97, pp. 205–227, 2018.

[20] S. Kopeinik, D. Kowald, and E. Lex, "Which algorithms suitwhich learning environments?," in *Proceedings of A Comparative Study of Recommender Systems in TEL. Adaptive and Adaptable Learning: 11th European Conference on Technology Enhanced Learning (EC-TEL 2016)*, K. Verbert, M. Sharples, and T. Klobučar, Eds., vol. 9891, pp. 124–138, Springer, Lecture Notes in Computer Science, Lyon, France, September 2016, 2016.

[21] R. Jäschke, L. Marinho, A. Hotho, L. Schmidt-Thieme, and G. Stumme, "Tag recommendations in folksonomies," in *Proceedings of Knowledge Discovery in Databases: PKDD 2007: 11th European Conference on Principles and Practice of Knowledge Discovery in Databases*, J. N. Kok, J. Koronacki, R. Lopez de Mantaras, S. Matwin, D. Mladenič, A. Skowron, Eds., vol. 4702, pp. 506–514, Lecture Notes in Computer Science, Springer Berlin Heidelberg, Warsaw, Poland, September 2007.

[22] J. B. Schafer, D. Frankowski, J. Herlocker, and S. Sen, "Collaborative filtering recommender systems," in *The Adaptive Web: Methods and Strategies of Web Personalization. Lecture Notes in Computer Science*, P. Brusilovsky, A. Kobsa, and W. Nejdl, Eds., vol. 4321Springer Berlin Heidelberg, Berlin, Heidelberg, , pp. 291–324, 2007.

[23] J. Basilico and T. Hofmann, "Unifying collaborative and

content-based filtering," in *Proceedings of Twenty-first International Conference on Machine Learning ICML '04*, p. 9, ACM, Banff, Alberta, Canada, July 2004.

[24] K. Niemann and M. Wolpers, "Usage context-boosted filteringfor recommender systems in TEL," in *Proceedings of Scaling up Learning for Sustained Impact: 8th European Conference, on Technology Enhanced Learning (EC-TEL 2013)*, D. Hernández-Leo, T. Ley, R. Klamma, and A. Harre Eds., vol. 8095, pp. 246–259, Lecture Notes in Computer Science, Springer Berlin Heidelberg. Paphos, Cyprus, September 2013.

[25] D. Kowald, S. Kopeinik, P. Seitlinger, T. Ley, D. Albert, and C. Trattner, "Refining frequency-based tag reuse predictions by means of time and semantic context," in *Proceedings of Mining, Modeling, and Recommending 'Things' in Social Media: 4th International Workshops, MUSE 2013 and MSM 2013*, M. Atzmueller, A. Chin, C. Scholz, and C. Trattner, Eds., Lecture Notes in Computer Science, Springer International Publishing, Cham, Vol. 8940, pp. 55–74, Prague, Czech Republic and Paris, France, September 2013 and May 2013.

[26] B. Love, D. Medin, and T. Gureckis, "Sustain: a network model of category learning," *Psychological Review*, vol. 111, no. 2, pp. 309–332, 2004.

[27] M. El Mabrouk, S. Gaou, and M. Rtili, "Towards an intelligent hybrid recommendation system for e-learning platforms using data mining," *International Journal of Emerging Technologies in Learning*, vol. 12, no. 6, pp. 52–76, 2017.

[28] H. E. Gardner, *Intelligence reframed: Multiple Intelligences for the 21st Century*, Basic Books, Hachette, UK, 2000.

[29] F. Ricci, L. Rokach, B. Shapira, and P. B. Kantor, *Recommender Systems Handbook*, Springer, Berlin, Germany, 2015.

[30] R. Burke, "Hybrid recommender systems: survey and experiments," *User modeling and user-adapted interaction*, vol. 12, pp. 331–370, 2002.

[31] P. Brusilovski, A. Kobsa, and W. Nejdl, *The Adaptive Web: Methods and Strategies of Web Personalization*, Springer Science & Business Media, Vol. 4321, Springer Science & Business Media, Berlin, Germany, 2007.

[32] Y. Deldjoo, C. Frà, M. Valla et al., "Enhancing Children's experience with recommendation systems," in *Proceedings of 11th ACM Conference of Workshop on Children and Recommender Systems (KidRec'17)*, Milan, Italy, August 2017.

[33] N. Tintarev and J. Masthoff, "A survey of explanations in recommender systems," in *Proceedings of 2007 IEEE 23rd International Conference on Data Engineering Workshop*, pp. 801–810, Istanbul, Turkey, April 2007.

7

The Effects of Consumer Innovativeness on Mobile App Download: Focusing on Comparison of Innovators and Noninnovators

Junseop Lee[1] and Jungmin Son[2]

[1]Department of School of Business, Yonsei University, 50 Yonsei-ro, Seodaemun-gu, Seoul, Republic of Korea
[2]College of Economics and Management, Chungnam National University, 99 Daehak-ro, Yuseong-gu, Daejeon, Republic of Korea

Correspondence should be addressed to Jungmin Son; sonjm81@gmail.com

Academic Editor: Xiapu Luo

In the new market for mobile apps, innovators, that is, early adopters of new products, have drawn attention from various researchers for their role in contributing to the success of a product. Due to the discrepancies between findings in these studies, a research framework and empirical model must be established to demonstrate how innovators affect the market for mobile apps in comparison to other types of users. To clarify the empirical basis on which innovators contribute to market development, we compare mobile app download patterns between innovators and noninnovators. Using the app download data of actual users in one of the largest app markets in Korea, we compare and analyze download behavior for a period of less than two years following their subscription to the market. The empirical analysis reveals that the download volume of innovators remains constant over a long period, while for noninnovators, volume is initially high, reflecting their interest in downloading, but it rapidly decreases thereafter. The results of this study have practical implications for companies seeking to assess the market value of innovators.

1. Introduction

How can we predict the process of developing the mobile app market? Do really innovators play an important role in the app market for the long term, such as in other new technology markets? Recent advances in mobile information technology have resulted in exponential diffusion of mobile devices among consumers of all ages. This feverish activity in the mobile environment has in turn triggered the rapid growth of the software market, including content for use on those devices. In the rapidly growing mobile content market, various mobile applications have become popular, including those that allow users to search for information on the Internet, watch videos, and play games. The IDC (2013) forecasted that the volume of the annual mobile application market would increase from $88 billion in 2013 to $187 billion in 2017 and that the sales revenue from mobile devices would increase from $10 billion in 2013 to $25 billion in 2017 [1]. This remarkable growth in the mobile application market will undoubtedly provide new opportunities for many companies; in light of this trend, consumers' application usage behaviors have a crucial meaning for these firms.

In this time of opportunity, practitioners launching new products such as mobile devices and applications for them must consider innovators, or early adopters of new products, and the relationship between the diffusion of new products and innovativeness, or users' willingness to be among the first to use them. In fact, research has found that understanding and prediction of innovators' behaviors is the key factor in the success of new, technology-intensive products [2, 3]. Innovators perceive themselves to be more active disseminators of new products than others [4–6]. Calculating the number of innovators has the advantage of enhancing the ability to predict the final market size [7]. Consequently, a scale to measure consumers' innovativeness has been developed [8] and analyzed using marketing models [6, 7, 9]. Several previous studies have expounded the significance of studying innovators' behaviors and applying the results to new product markets such as the mobile market.

The roles of innovators in the success of new products such as mobile apps may be summarized as follows. First, innovators are faster adopters of new products compared to followers [7], and, accordingly, they can facilitate companies' efforts to spread these products. To increase the initial market share of a new product, companies must mobilize a sizable consumer group, targeting those consumers who are inclined to adopt it in its early days. Innovators are motivated to adopt new products ahead of others in their social networks because acquiring knowledge of new products not yet experienced by others enhances their social status and puts them in the opinion leader position [6]. Second, innovators tend to purchase and explore new products voluntarily and actively recommend them to others. The motives of word-of-mouth activity may be related to the social activities and status of innovators. Researchers have also posited that innovators with greater knowledge tend to be heavy users of products who can affect others' purchasing of those products [10]. Third, early adoption and heavy usage often overlap [8]. Innovators frequently have a high level of product knowledge and expertise due to greater consumption. The more frequently a person uses new products, the more status and opinion leadership he or she will enjoy [6].

While the results of previous studies provide some guidelines for marketing managers, the roles of innovators versus noninnovators in the performance of new products have not been sufficiently clarified. Previous studies tend to expound the advantages of innovators because they purchase new products much more frequently than noninnovators [8, 11, 12]. In general, heavy users evaluate new products promptly and adopt them quickly [10]. Nonetheless, it may be that not all innovators are heavy users. In fact, one study reported that differences in usage volume between innovators and noninnovators were not significant [7]. In addition, many previous studies mainly engaged in (1) comparing the level of innovativeness between heavy users and general users [12], (2) examining the relationship between general consumer innovativeness and usage in a specific category [11], and (3) examining usage behaviors in the context of adopting new equipment [10]. Unfortunately, few researchers have compared product usage between innovators and noninnovators of new virtual goods directly.

The second limitation of previous studies is that they relied too much on cross-sectional methodology despite the value of using long-term data. In research on innovation and mobile content, actual usage data must be analyzed in the long term in order to provide valid results that are not possible to obtain using cross-sectional survey data. Previous studies posit that innovation of mobile services provides usefulness and ease of use to the consumer, thereby promoting adoption of new products. However, these studies focus on consumers' response to questionnaires rather than using actual mobile usage data [13]. Other limitations are related to measuring innovativeness. In previous studies, innate innovativeness was measured by referring to the level of abstraction [3]. This approach to measurement assumes that consumer innovativeness can be represented by numerous general characteristics in studies of wide scope. Accordingly, it is limited in its ability to predict consumer behaviors in specific categories. Furthermore, cross-sectional survey data are inappropriate for analysis of the long-term relationship between innovativeness and

heavy usage. Therefore, additional research is required in order to elucidate the exact dynamics of cross-temporal variations in innovative consumer behavior by measuring behavioral innovativeness in specific categories [6].

Based on the findings of various marketing, sociology, and information system studies, we present this study with the following research objectives. First, we compare consumption of mobile content between innovators and noninnovators in the expanding market for mobile apps. Then, based on the results of the first comparison, we conduct a second comparative analysis of the degree to which these two groups contribute to the success of the market for mobile apps and the importance of their contributions. Third, using an empirical model and long-term data, we measure consumer behaviors in the mobile market, comparing the behaviors of innovators and noninnovators.

We thereby contribute to the mobile marketing literature in various ways, which may be summarized as follows. First, the findings of this study enhance our understanding of the behavioral differences between innovators and noninnovators over a long period of time. As mentioned above, previous studies on consumer variations in innovativeness [10, 13] used cross-sectional data and focused on the psychological mechanisms underlying innovative behavior. In addition, we observe the actual behavior of consumers in the long term and interpret changes in behavior in the two groups in terms of actual market performance. Comparing the behavior of mobile app consumers against the backdrop of differentiation in the lower category of apps, we expand the findings of previous studies on innovativeness in a single category [6, 8]. Lastly, in measuring innovativeness, we utilize actual data accumulated from the date of launching of the mobile devices included in this study. This approach enables us to observe the behavior of consumers who are introduced for the first time to new products directly. These data are more appropriate for an accurate measurement of the behavior of innovators in the rapidly growing mobile market. Our systematic approach to collecting and analyzing these data for the study of innovators' consumption behavior is unique in research in this area.

In this study, we analyze the behavior of mobile application users in one of the largest app markets in Korea, by the pseudonym Goapps.com. The data collected include both records of consumer downloads on mobile devices following their subscriptions after the opening of the market and various variables related to consumer usage of mobile devices. The period of analysis was 1 year and 11 months, starting from the date of the first app download by each consumer new to the app market. These data are well suited to identification of the behavior of innovators, as they provide consumer records on downloads of various apps over a long period of time. We can therefore observe the time of selection and the type of apps downloaded at the consumer level and analyze how consumer characteristics affect the demand for apps. The data are also useful for measuring innovativeness because they are actual data rather than data self-reported from a questionnaire. To measure innovativeness on the basis of download behavior, we classify innovators and noninnovators at a particular point in time [7], observing download patterns from the date of market launch. The results provide statistical proof of what point in time is optimal to discern innovativeness specific to mobile apps. Finally, the app market data used in the analysis in this study represent the mobile app industry well, thereby increasing the possibility of generalizing the results. The Korean app market is regarded as highly significant in the global app market [14]. In this market, innovativeness and acceptance of information technology account for a large part of consumers' product selection. Accordingly, this market has been often studied for innovativeness in information and communication products [7, 9].

2. Preliminary Analysis and Conceptual Framework

2.1. Innovators in App Markets. Innovativeness is related to consumer-purchasing patterns at the early stage in a product life cycle [4], consumers' tendency to be interested in a variety of products [8], and voluntary searches for product information [6]. In previous studies, the most-often cited characteristic of innovativeness in early adopters of a product is the ability to be relatively quick in purchase decision-making. Innovators are eager to demonstrate their early acceptance of new products and technologies to other social groups. In this regard, innovators may be defined as first adopters of certain products and technologies in their social networks [7]. Also, in previous studies, innovators are defined as a minority group (less than 2% of all product adopters). Consumers in this group tend to find satisfaction in the fact that they are the first to experience and evaluate new technology in their social networks. This technological pioneering boosts their self-recognition and puts them in a superior social position relative to other groups in terms of knowledge and experience. Innovators prefer the freshness of a new product in itself and are willing to pay a higher price for it in order to be first. On the other hand, consumers in the noninnovator group place more emphasis on the practical utility deriving from the functions and economic value of the product. Accordingly, unlike innovators, noninnovators are more reluctant to pay a high price for newness [8].

Before comparing the behaviors of innovators and noninnovators, we herein define the metrics by which we distinguish the former from other types of consumers. In previous studies, innovators and noninnovators have been measured and classified according to various criteria. Purchase decision time (e.g., adoption time) is the most representative reference variable. In the study of Goldenberg et al. [7], the innovator group was defined by the standard of receiving content online, whereby innovators were significantly faster than noninnovators in terms of adoption time. In line with these earlier studies, we also utilize app adoption time for the mobile consumer as the criterion distinguishing innovators from other groups. That is, consumers who enter the mobile market at an earlier date are classified as innovators; those who enter it at a relatively later date are classified as noninnovators. For the purposes of statistical analysis, we also verify the exact adoption time through analysis of actual data.

To measure innovativeness in the app market, previous studies focused either on attitude [8, 10, 13] or on behavior [4, 6, 7]. This study focuses on behavior as the criterion measuring innovativeness, specifically, behavior-based innovativeness. For this purpose, we investigate consumer entry into the app market. The data reveal that nearly all consumers in this study had used old mobile devices but switched at some point to smart phones, enabling app usage. (Most apps can be downloaded and used only on smart phones.) Accordingly, these consumers entered the app market after their adoption of a new technology, the smart phone. Likewise, we posit that consumers in the app market will first adopt these devices prior to the adoption of the apps. Therefore, we also explore the differences in adoption patterns of both units (hardware) and apps (software).

In this study, consumers using Goapps.com are separated into innovators and followers. A preliminary analysis is performed to compare the characteristics of the two groups. The analytical data include records of consumers' behaviors on Goapps.com from January 2009 to January 2011. The consumer sample consists of 336 people randomly chosen from the pool of all subscribers. In total, they downloaded apps 5,395 times. For enhanced reliability of the analysis results, consumers with fewer than 5 downloads during the analysis period are excluded from the analysis. In consequence, the data for analysis are reduced to 258 consumers and 5,170 downloads in total. The time unit of analysis is the month, and three types of data are analyzed: (1) app download records, (2) mobile device usage records, and (3) demographic information. The app download records include relevant variables such as the type of app and download time. The mobile device usage records include relevant variables such as consumers' voice traffic fees, text and Internet traffic fees, and device prices. The demographic characteristics include age, gender, income, and residence. In general, since consumption behavior may be affected by both environmental factors and external characteristics, we examine the roles of various elements relevant to app downloading.

Figure 1 shows trends in the cumulative number of smart phone users and app users. Together, these numbers illustrate the patterns of diffusion of smart phone devices and the inflow of smart phone users into the app market. During the first one-year period, consumer inflow into the app market increased only sluggishly; however, a rapid increase occurred in October and November 2009 (i.e., the first tipping point). Subsequently, exponential growth is evident in May and June 2010 (i.e., the second tipping point). These two periods represent the cumulative inflow of followers. Hence, from Figure 1, we are able to identify the empirical criteria with which to divide app consumers into the innovator group and the follower group. Tipping points have been used as the criteria with which to distinguish between innovators and followers in previous research [4]. This approach is therefore adopted in this study. We take the average of the tipping points in the app market and utilize this as a way to classify innovators at the point in time by which 20% of consumers in the sample have entered into the app market from its inception date. Accordingly, those consumers who adopted

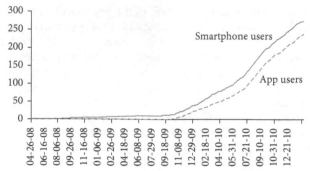

FIGURE 1: Patterns of consumer entry into Goapps.com.

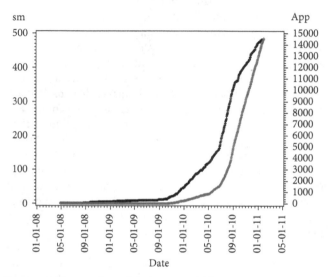

FIGURE 2: The number of the apps available to Goapps.com users and the total number of downloaded apps.

apps prior to May 2010 are classified as innovators and those who adopted them later as noninnovators.

Since several consumers may download one app over time, the total number of app downloads is always equal to or greater than the number of varieties of apps. The number of kinds of apps increases explosively over time in the data (Figure 2). This expansion of the market means that consumers enjoy more and more alternatives in the market, which tends to induce more consumption on average and provide greater utility to consumers, given the same conditions [15], because the larger number of alternatives increases the opportunity for consumers to choose the products they want most. In addition, increasing the number of alternative brands available to satisfy customers tends to increase the number of customers acquiring products from enhanced categories or induce the same customer to select more than one product within a certain time period (i.e., heavier usage) [10]. Accordingly, we deduce that a greater number of apps available in the market will increase the probability that consumers will download them. Based on this discussion, we posit that a change in the market (i.e., environmental factors such as the variety of apps) may have long-term positive effects on app usage. This fact needs to be taken into account during our analysis of long-term

data. Therefore, these market environmental factors are included in the analytical model outlined in the following sections.

2.2. Innovators and Noninnovators. The following question naturally arises: what intrinsic differences can be identified between the two groups, innovators and noninnovators, based on the information about app adoption time? In answering this question, we expect to demonstrate the validity of measuring innovativeness using adoption time as the determining factor. To find the answer, we examine the differences between the two groups in terms of demographics and mobile device usage behavior. Demographic characteristics are external features such as age, gender, and income. Usage patterns are the behavioral characteristics associated with app usage, such as voice traffic fees and text and mobile Internet traffic fees. Previous studies have suggested that innovators, on average, are more likely to be young and male [7]. It is also more likely that consumers in this demographic are heavy users in terms of product purchase volume and usage frequency [8]. In this study, we test these assertions by comparing the demographic characteristics and mobile device usage frequency between the two groups.

Table 1 shows this comparison. For the demographic characteristics, no significant differences in age, gender, income, or residence are evident between innovators and noninnovators. However, some nonsignificant trends are discernible. There may be a tendency for innovators to be young (innovators = 30.214, noninnovators = 32.389), male (0.464, 0.554), and have higher income (0.428, 0.359). These findings are consistent with the characteristics distinguishing innovators from noninnovators in other categories such as PC usage [16] and online content [7]. However, the lack of significance may have been due to the smaller size of the sample of innovators compared to that of noninnovators. In any case, these results indicate that the groups of innovators and noninnovators are heterogeneous by the adoption time criterion.

As for the characteristics of mobile device usage, the device purchase prices and voice traffic fees are not significantly different between innovators and noninnovators. While there seem to be significant differences in the fees for text traffic and data traffic, these differences are actually not significant due to the excessively wide dispersion of the variables. This result indicates heterogeneity within the whole innovator group and within the noninnovator group. Subject to these limitations, the results may be interpreted to signify the following points. First, innovators do not pay more (i.e., higher product purchase prices) than noninnovators. This result may cast doubt on the effectiveness of the skimming pricing strategy many managers used to target innovators in the app industry. In the skimming strategy, the initial price is set at a higher level based on the expectation that market innovators will be willing to pay a higher price in order to enjoy the benefits of being opinion leaders. This strategy has been widely adopted in marketing of innovative products such as apps and smart phones. This study has revealed, however, that the marginal effect of the difference

TABLE 1: Demographics and mobile device usage in the two groups.

	Innovators		Noninnovators		t-value
	Mean	SD	Mean	SD	
Demographic characteristics					
Age	30.214	12.256	32.584	11.823	1.29
Gender (female = 1)	0.464	0.503	0.553	0.498	1.19
Income (more than $100,000 per year = 1)	0.428	0.499	0.346	0.477	1.10
Residence (urban area = 1)	0.463	0.503	0.445	0.498	0.25
Features of mobile device usage					
Purchase price of mobile device ($)	126.786	88.134	121.165	100.014	0.50
Voice traffic fees per month ($)	30.874	19.823	32.782	17.737	0.65
Number of text messages per month	534.855	965.136	435.423	612.502	0.97
Mobile Internet traffic fees per month ($)	4.192	10.833	5.660	10.868	0.90
Observations	56		202		

in price is greater in innovators than in noninnovators. Hence, application of the skimming strategy should be carefully reviewed prior to undertaking. Second, innovators in the market for mobile apps are more easily inclined to utilize the latest means of communication (i.e., SMS, mobile Internet usage) rather than traditional voice communication. Since mobile apps combine both text and images, this may be one reason that innovators are more actively engaged in app usage and downloads than noninnovators. Accordingly, we now launch a comparison of patterns in app usage between the two groups in order to validate the findings of previous studies that innovators are heavy users.

For comprehensive understanding of the behaviors of innovators in the app market and to enhance the efficiency of marketing activities, we herein attempt to distinguish the behaviors of innovators and noninnovators. First, innovators can be "seeding targets," playing an important role in the initial distribution of a product. The significance of the initial distribution in new markets has been emphasized in numerous previous studies [2–4]. Innovators actively engage in word of mouth, providing valuable feedback and contributing directly to product diffusion. In the context of the app market, the more interest the innovators have in new apps, the greater awareness the followers will have of those products. Using the feedback of innovators, companies may improve the quality and functionality of their apps. Innovators have strategic potential to lay the groundwork for followers to enter the market; they play a decisive role in promoting new app products and pushing potential users to the tipping point.

Innovators also enter markets while they are still immature. In this regard, they help companies build their cost and revenue structures. In concrete terms, companies must make large investments as a necessary condition for market growth. As shown earlier, however, fewer apps of lesser variety are available in the initial stages of market development; rapid growth is evident at later stages. Thus, at the time of innovators' adoption of the technology, the market lacked sufficient product variety. It seems plausible, therefore, that the merit and utility of the app market was initially low. In this situation, innovators entered the market because they were motivated by the newness of the market itself [6]. In this initial market, during which app developers were keeping initial expenses low, innovators chose to adopt their products, thus providing direct assistance to these companies in terms of cost and revenue.

In addition, innovators have the potential to be heavy users of new products. As shown in the exploratory analysis, early adopters of mobile apps (innovators) have been identified as heavy users of text and imaging services provided by mobile carriers. We therefore infer that extensive use of mobile devices for Internet access, text messaging, and voice communication will enhance users' accessibility, familiarity, and knowledge of other software. Accordingly, when innovators encounter apps with multimedia capabilities, they are likely to become heavy users in the app market. One of the crucial objectives for enterprise marketing researchers is to explore the potential of innovators and make efforts to promote them to the status of heavy users who can directly benefit the companies' revenues.

2.3. App Downloads of Innovators. We now compare in detail the differences in app usage patterns between innovators and noninnovators. Certain descriptive differences in the characteristics of mobile device usage between the two groups have already been presented. We have shown that innovators spend more time with mobile devices, particularly engaging with apps that involve multimedia. These heavy users differ in many ways from noninnovators. Innovators may or may not use more apps than noninnovators. We now present a hypothesis regarding innovators' behaviors, conducting an exploratory analysis and presenting a detailed model.

2.3.1. Longitudinal Behavior of App Users. To determine if innovators in the mobile app market use more apps, we investigate users' behavior from the longitudinal perspective. Iyengar et al. [6] empirically analyzed the tendency of innovators to engage in more product consumption than followers over the long term. Innovators not only begin to use products earlier than others, but they also use them more frequently in the long term. In line with these previous findings, we explain the reasons for this greater usage as follows.

First, innovators embrace adoption of new products ahead of others and thus have longer periods of usage, during which they accumulate considerable knowledge about the products. In terms of cumulative purchase volume, therefore, innovators always purchase more than noninnovators overall, assuming that both groups purchase the products in almost the same volume on a periodic basis. Furthermore, innovators experience products for longer, thereby acquiring a higher level of understanding and evaluative ability [7]. This increases their chances of making additional purchases more frequently in the future. Their higher level of understanding often results in purchase-expanding behavior, in which they are likely to purchase other similar products. In a market replete with similar products (e.g., the app market), consumers are motivated to buy popular products according to their inclination in terms of risk recognition and avoidance [8]. In addition, consumers with cumulative experience have greater ability to evaluate products and more opportunities to evaluate and choose unpopular products. They gain competence to overcome the barriers involved in purchasing risky products by evaluating the products themselves based on accumulated knowledge.

Innovators must use many products to retain their expert status in their social networks. As experts, they play a central role in evaluating new products. To maintain this social position, they must demonstrate that they are actively acquiring and using new products, which is an effective means of appealing to others. Extensive usage allows them to learn about new products in the same category easily [6, 8]. They seek information on new products, thereby staying abreast of market trends. Through their personal experience with products, they aid in new product diffusion. Their ability to provide high-quality information to their neighbors in their social networks ensures their social status [7]. Accordingly, those consumers who demonstrate their innovativeness in order to retain their status in their social networks tend to be heavy users. Apps for mobile devices belong to the product category requiring personal experience for accurate product evaluation (i.e., they are experience goods). For dissemination of these products, word of mouth from opinion leaders is a crucial factor determining product performance in the market.

Innovators purchase and use products for a longer time; they tend to purchase products in larger volume more frequently in comparison with noninnovators. Iyengar et al. [6] conducted research on innovators in the medical field. They found that medical doctors differed in terms of the speed with which they adopted a new drug at the time of product launch. A particularly noticeable finding is that those who adopt new drugs ahead of other physicians tend to prescribe these new drugs more often and in larger doses than others. That is, innovators display the tendency to adopt new products more speedily and to use them more heavily than noninnovators. In addition, they demonstrate opinion leadership behaviors, introducing new products to noninnovators and taking the initiative in spreading their opinions in the market in order to demonstrate the benefits

of the products they have adopted. Therefore, they bring important direct and indirect benefits to companies.

To summarize, innovators in the app market are those who enter the app market earlier than noninnovators and indulge in the usage of apps for a longer time. They use a greater variety of apps by utilizing the knowledge accumulated during the usage period. In addition, innovators endeavor to maintain their social status by displaying to others their knowledge of the products. It is advantageous for them to accumulate usage experience and advanced knowledge of various products. Accordingly, we predict that innovators will have a higher degree of usage on average than noninnovators over the long term.

2.3.2. Exploratory Analysis. In order to examine the download behaviors of innovators and noninnovators, we focus on the average number of monthly downloads by users from the first market entry by members of the two groups to the final data observations in November 2011. We predict that innovators will have higher download counts on average than noninnovators during the study period. As shown in Figure 3, however, this prediction is hard to verify. In Figure 3(a), the horizontal axis corresponds to the calendar month, displaying in a time series the number of downloads by innovators and noninnovators. This figure reveals that both groups reach the highest number of downloads 3 to 4 months following initial product adoption. This may signify that these users need a long time to accumulate experience and knowledge of apps in order to be ready to engage in real usage. Figure 3(a) confirms that innovators do not download more apps than noninnovators on average.

By contrast, in Figure 3(b), the horizontal axis represents consumers' adoption time corresponding to the number of months (starting from number 1 for the month of initial product adoption). Here, the download patterns are somewhat different between innovators and noninnovators. In the case of innovators, the download pattern shows no discernible sign of decrease, whereas in the case of noninnovators, it shows a rapid decrease. From this observation, we may infer that noninnovators rapidly depart from the app market after a certain point in time. In Figure 3(b), however, no discernible sign is evident of more downloading by innovators in comparison with noninnovators. In October 2014, innovators' download counts begin to surpass those of noninnovators (i.e., lines for the two groups intersect).

To explain why innovators have lower download counts than noninnovators and why the two download patterns intersect, we may infer as follows. Over time, the number of available app alternatives increases along with the growth of the app market. Innovators entered the market in the early stages, whereas noninnovators did so after the market had already been established. Therefore, at the time of their entry into the market, the two groups were exposed to quite different situations in terms of the available kinds of apps in the market. In fact, the app market began to grow explosively in the period from September to December 2010 (Figure 2). For those users who subscribed to the market after this

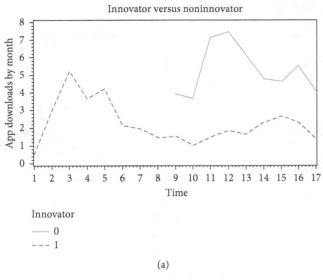

Innovator versus noninnovator

Innovator
—— 0
--- 1

(a)

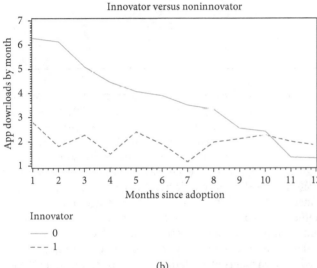

Innovator versus noninnovator

Innovator
—— 0
--- 1

(b)

Figure 3: App downloads of innovators versus noninnovators by month. (a) Calendar-date standard and (b) adoption-point-in-time standard.

tipping point, the number of attractive apps available to customers was considerable, providing ample opportunities for downloads. Another notable point is that the probability of downloading may have been actively facilitated by aggressive push marketing campaigns. For example, advertising and promotion of apps through mass media on a large scale and buzz marketing may have had an effect. Thus, consumer awareness may have increased, with the effect of inducing the downloading of more apps.

Despite the logic that innovators may download more apps than noninnovators, this exploratory investigation produced no evidence that innovators in the app market are heavy users. This result may have occurred due to the fact that noninnovators entered the market at the time of explosive growth. Accordingly, more in-depth and systematic investigation is necessary. Therefore, we now estimate and compare actual app download patterns of innovators and noninnovators using a regression test model.

3. Model and Measurements

This section presents a model of the differences in patterns and frequency of app usage between innovators and noninnovators. For a systematically accurate analysis, the model must satisfy the following conditions: first, it should allow us to analyze long-term usage patterns of various app consumers. Accordingly, the model should be panel-based for optimum data measurement and analysis. Second, it should have proper features with which to identify and compare the differences between innovators and noninnovators. For this purpose, it must be built in a specifically parsimonious manner, competently displaying the differences between the two groups. For example, Iyengar et al. [6] used dummy variables on the consumer level to measure the behaviors of innovators.

$AppDN_{it}$ is a dependent variable in this model corresponding to the app usage of mobile device users. It is measured by counting the number of app downloads by consumer i at time t. The sample includes only those consumers who have some experience downloading more than one app (i.e., an app adopter). Observations are monthly. The dependent variable, $AppDN_{it}$, is a continuous integer with a value of more than 0. Hence, to be consistent with the dependent variable, a linear regression model wherein the error terms of ε_{it} follow the normal distribution is suitable for this study.

$$AppDN_{it} = \beta_0 + \beta_1 \cdot NonInnovator_i + \beta_2 \cdot MonthsAdop_{it}$$
$$+ \beta_3 \cdot NonInnovator_i \cdot MonthsAdop_{it}$$
$$+ \beta_4 \cdot MonthCalendar_{it} + \beta_5 \cdot Age_i$$
$$+ \beta_6 \cdot Gender_i + \beta_7 \cdot Income_i + \beta_8 \cdot Voice_i$$
$$+ \beta_9 \cdot Sms_i + \beta_{10} \cdot Data_i + \beta_{11} \cdot Price_i + \varepsilon_{it}.$$

$$(1)$$

$AppDN_{it}$: the number of app downloads by consumer i at time t, $NonInnovator_i$: whether or not consumer i is a noninnovator (1 = noninnovator, 0 = innovator), $MonthsAdop_{it}$: months since entry into the app market by consumer i at time t, $MonthCalendar_{it}$: calendar month of downloads by consumer i at time t, Age_i: consumer i's physical age, $Gender_i$: consumer i's gender, $Income_i$: household income of consumer i, $Voice_i$: consumer i's voice traffic fees per month on average for the last 6 months, Sms_i: consumer i's number of text messages per month on average for the last 6 months, $Data_i$: consumer i's data traffic fees per month on average for the last 6 months, $Price_i$: price paid for consumer i's mobile device.

The number of app downloads is effectively determined by the innovativeness and experience of the consumer and market conditions. Accordingly, innovativeness, $NonInnovator_i$, which is the most crucial explanatory variable, refers to whether or not consumer i is an innovator. The criterion of innovators is time-based; consumers who subscribed to the market site prior to May 2010 are classified as innovators, whereas those who did so after May 2010 are classified as noninnovators. Next, the variable

TABLE 2: Summary statistics for variables included in the model.

Variables	Observation	Mean	SD
Dependent variables			
Number of app downloads in one month	2,492	3.638	6.862
Innovativeness			
Noninnovator dummy	258	0.783	0.413
Time control (user level)			
Months since adoption	2,492	5.759	3.504
Time control (market level)			
Calendar month of initial download	2,492	12.241	3.504
Demographic control variables			
Age	258	32.070	11.934
Gender (female = 1)	258	0.535	0.500
Income (more than $100,000 per year = 1)	258	0.364	0.482
Region (urban area = 1)	258	0.450	0.498
Device usage control variables			
Purchase price of mobile device ($)	258	12.139	9.751
Voice traffic fees per month ($)	258	32.368	18.187
Number of text messages per month	258	456.997	631.306
Mobile Internet traffic fees per month ($)	258	5.342	10.856

$MonthsAdop_{it}$ is measured by counting the number of months at time t from consumer i's entry into the app market. The application of these variables enables us to observe changes in app download patterns over time, which is a major objective of this study. β_0 indicates the baseline download by innovators, while $\beta_0 + \beta_1$ represents that of noninnovators. If innovators download more apps than noninnovators, as predicted herein, β_1 will tend to be negative. Furthermore, if the analysis reveals a decreasing trend in app downloads by consumers over time, β_2 will be negative.

The app market environment encompasses the number of available apps in the market and consumer awareness in the market. When the number of available apps is increasing and consumer awareness is being heightened by active company marketing, the probability of more apps being downloaded will progressively increase. While this premise is plausible, we utilize calendar dates as a proxy for measurement of the app market environment in this study [6]. Specifically, the variable $MonthCalendar_{it}$ is measured by the calendar month, time t, during which consumer i downloaded the app. As noted above, with the passage of time, the app market monotonically increases and corporate marketing activities began accordingly. This measurement method presupposes that the market's environmental factors also increased linearly. As the market matures, the probability of more apps being downloaded will correspondingly increase. Hence, it is predicted that β_4 will be positive.

A variety of demographics and behavioral control variables are included in this study to represent accurately the app download patterns reflecting the changes in experience of and differences between innovators and noninnovators over time. Thus, we consider external demographic variables such as Age_i and $Gender_i$ as well as other variables related to social class and consumption patterns, such as an income dummy variable, $Income_i$. To measure income, we consider any consumer earning more than USD $10,000 to be high-income earners (i.e., $Income_i = 1$). To characterize mobile device usage, we incorporate the variable $Price_i$ to represent the price of the mobile device purchased by consumer i. A higher-priced device may indicate that the consumer is more likely to use the mobile device frequently. Other variables considered in the study include the average monthly voice traffic fees, $Voice_i$, monthly text message traffic fees, Sms_i, and monthly mobile Internet traffic fees, $Data_i$. These variables are intended to control for changes in app download patterns caused by familiarity with the mobile device itself and usage experience.

Table 2 provides the summary statistics for all variables in the model. The independent variables (months since adoption, calendar month of first download) and the dependent variable (number of app downloads) are both measured at the level of consumer i and time t. On the other hand, the dummy variable measuring innovativeness is measured at the level of consumer i based on the assumption that it remains constant at the consumer level during the observation period. In addition, the demographic and device usage variables are also measured at the level of consumer i. These variables and their measurement have the advantage of versatility; they can be utilized in various online and mobile markets. For example, while Goapps.com is not yet exercising target-marketing strategies at the consumer level, it may enforce strategies differentiating consumers and download times using the variables included in this study.

4. Empirical Findings

In this study, we compare the app download patterns between innovators and noninnovators, presenting an

TABLE 3: Main results of the regression model 1: base model.

Variables	Base models	
	Model 1-1: no market control	Model 1-2: market control using calendar month
Intercept	2.146** (0.515)*	−0.139** (0.576)*
Noninnovator	4.578** (0.631)*	−0.230** (0.084)*
Months since adoption	0.008** (0.059)*	−0.336** (0.088)*
Noninnovator × months since adoption	−0.464** (0.088)*	−0.715** (0.103)*
Calendar month	—	0.761** (0.090)*
Demographic control variables		
Age	0.134 (0.137)	0.075 (0.135)
Gender (female, %)	−1.053** (0.271)	−1.261** (0.268)
Income (more than $100,000 per year, %)	1.190** (0.294)	1.062** (0.290)
Region (urban area, %)	−0.382 (0.279)	0.108 (0.281)
Device usage control variables		
Device purchase price ($)	−0.414** (0.134)	−0.440** (0.132)
Voice traffic fees ($)	−0.070 (0.134)	0.106 (0.134)
Instances of text usage	−0.125 (0.139)	−0.146 (0.137)
Online Internet traffic fees ($)	1.410 (0.133)	1.300** (0.132)
Observations	2,492	2,492
R^2	0.188	0.214

Note. ** $p < 1\%$, * $p < 5\%$, and ( ) is standard error.

empirical model and estimating it using actual app download records of a consumer panel. Table 3 presents the coefficients of the comparative model, which differ from those of the app download model presented earlier. Model 1-2 in the table shows the results of the proposed app download formula. To determine the necessity of controlling the market environmental factors described above, we present Model 1-1 without the market environment variables for comparison. If the market environment is not considered, the temporal flow pattern of downloads may simply be compared between innovators and noninnovators. Despite its simplicity, however, this approach has the intrinsic limitation that it does not consider the effects of external factors such as the number of available apps and improved app market awareness.

We now interpret the results of Model 1-1 wherein the market environment is not controlled. Model 1-1 in Table 3 presents baseline values that are positive for both innovators ($\beta_0 = 2.146$) and noninnovators ($\beta_0 + \beta_1 = 2.146 + 4.578$). It

is noticeable that the coefficient has a higher value in noninnovators than in innovators. This may be interpreted as a signal implying that, in the initial stages, noninnovators download more apps than innovators. However, innovators do not reduce their download behavior over time ($\beta_2 = 0.008$); on the other hand, a significant decrease in downloads is evident for noninnovators as they accumulate experience ($\beta_2 + \beta_3 = 0.008–0.464$). These results for Model 1-1 are almost the same as the download patterns for innovators and noninnovators in Figure 3. In the early days of adoption, noninnovators may download more apps; however, this gap is reduced as time passes. Overall, when we limit our focus to the results of Model 1-1, it seems that innovators may not be heavier app users than noninnovators. Nonetheless, this conclusion can be drawn from the analysis when we do not take into account external effects arising from changes in the market environment, such as increases in the number of attractive app products and market growth. Considering the restrictive nature of this model, we see that its results must be duly compared with those of Model 1-2, which incorporates control variables related to the market environment.

In Model 1-2, the market environment includes control variables. Model 1-2 is a practical model, useful for analyzing the download patterns of innovators and noninnovators. The estimation results of Model 1-2 may be summarized as follows. In Model 1-2, the coefficients corresponding to the baseline downloads of innovators and noninnovators are all nonsignificant (innovators $\beta_0 = -0.139$, noninnovators $\beta_0 + \beta_1 = -0.139–0.230$). In short, no significant differences in the number of monthly downloads are evident between innovators and noninnovators in the initial stage of market entry. By contrast, the results differ for download patterns after accumulated experience. Decreases in the number of downloads are evident for both kinds of consumers, but the proportional rate of decrease was far lower in innovators ($\beta_2 = -0.336$) in comparison with noninnovators ($\beta_2 + \beta_3 = -0.336–0.715$). That is, the number of downloads for both innovators and noninnovators is highest in the early days of app adoption, after which a gradual decrease occurs. In general, however, the decrease in the number of downloads is sharper for noninnovators (about 2.5 times that of innovators). From these results, we find evidence supporting the premise that innovators tend to download more apps than noninnovators over a long-time period. Accordingly, through the long-term analysis, it may be confirmed that innovators are heavier users than noninnovators in terms of the number of downloads.

The coefficient of calendar month is positive ($\beta_4 = 0.761$) in Model 1-2. This means that the number of downloads increased over time. A plausible cause may be found in Figure 2, which reveals an increase in the number of attractive apps available to consumers over time. Measurement of the effect of the market environment in Model 1-2 requires one condition: the changes in consumers' downloading behavior must be *linear*. However, the reality may be that changes in the market environment do not always occur in a regular pattern. It is necessary, therefore, to assume a *nonlinear* relationship between time and the number of downloads [6] in an effort to reflect reality in the model. Therefore, we introduce a dummy variable representing the time factor on a monthly basis, creating an additional model. This proposed time variable is based on a time-varying, semiparametric model [17]. The advantages associated with usage of a dummy variable include the following: (1) the new model embodies nonlinear causal relations, (2) it enables us to estimate the causal relations at each time point independently, and (3) it provides a robustness check for comparison with the estimation results of Model 1-2. In comparing the results of both models, we include the control effects of exogenous factors and then compare the app download patterns between innovators and noninnovators in a more sophisticated way. The results from estimation using this additional model are as follows: (1) they reveal an exponential increase in app downloads at the later stage rather than at the initial stage, and yet (2) the main effects are not significantly different from those of Model 1-2.

In conclusion, given that the main effect remains almost the same regardless of the linearity or nonlinearity of the market environment and the number of consumer downloads, we adopt Model 1-2 as the final model since it is more parsimonious in structure. We now undertake an additional analysis to focus on differences in the download patterns in subcategories of apps. Utilizing the results of Model 1-2, we investigate their implications for the app market as a whole. App developers or development firms, however, may be more interested in what types of consumers will download their apps and how long they will continue to do so. Then, the starting question is how we can classify the myriad different kinds of apps?

In the current app market, various kinds of apps have been released and are available to consumers, including games, information search engines, social network services, and business utilities. In this study, we classify these apps into three groups: (1) games, (2) hobbies, and (3) information. The following are the underlying reasons for this classification. First, this classification is similar to the categorization in the app market. This practical approach to app classification relies on the categorizer focusing on the similarity between apps in terms of function or usage purpose. Relevant to this practical guide is the fact that the categorical share in the market of apps related to games, hobbies, and information remains at similar levels: 34%, 31%, and 35%, respectively. Second, on the consumer behavior level, classifying apps into three types is justified on the grounds that they may differ in terms of the procedures used for processing consumer-related information. Games are inherently intended to be used for pleasure [18]. The essential features of game apps include their colorful graphics and sounds, which give pleasure to players. In addition, rewards for achieving goals provide motivation to continue usage [19, 20]. By contrast, for apps in the information category, consumers choose them for practical purposes such as efficiency and economy. For apps in the hobby category, both categorical and utilitarian features are important. While using game apps provides pleasure, consumers deal with information

through affective processes; when using information apps with utility traits, consumers engage cognitive processes. Likewise, apps must provide differentiated experiences to consumers. It is thus important to analyze consumer behavior with reference to categorical differences.

To analyze download patterns categorically, we extract three data sets, dividing all data according to the three categories described above. Next, using the same model structure as in Model 1-2, the three data sets may be analyzed. For example, we analyze only the records of downloaded games using the same variables as in Model 1-2. The results are represented by Models 2-1, 2-2, and 2-3 in Table 4. The interpretation of the estimation results may be summarized as follows. First, in the game category, innovators download more apps than noninnovators in the initial stage. No decrease in downloads between the two groups is found over time. That is, in the game category, innovators are always heavier users in comparison with noninnovators. Second, in the hobby and information categories, no difference in download behavior is evident between innovators and noninnovators at the initial stage; however, the degree of decrease for innovators is less than that for noninnovators over time. That is, in these categories, innovators are heavier users who download more and more apps over time. Thus, the analysis indicates that innovators are heavier users than noninnovators only in the two categories other than the game category.

As for the cause underlying these different patterns across the app categories, we postulate as follows. Innovativeness provokes the desire to explore new apps, and thus, innovators tend to download new apps periodically. The results of previous studies suggest that innovators acquire more professional knowledge about new products than their neighbors, thereby raising their social status [6, 10]. Accordingly, innovators have a greater desire to experience new apps in comparison with noninnovators. As a result, innovators download more apps on average than noninnovators in the long term. It is relevant that apps in the game category exhibit cyclical fluctuations, whereas those in the hobby and information categories are relatively free from such variation. Essentially, game apps provide the consumer with pleasure, and yet this pleasure lasts for a short time only, after which the app rapidly loses its effectiveness when usage reaches a certain level [18]. Inevitably, consumers pursue new pleasures through new game apps. As a result, download behavior in the game category is periodic, and the effect of innovativeness is minimal. On the other hand, in the case of hobby and information apps, consumers may continue using the same apps for a longer period if they provide utility. For example, in these two categories, consumers' needs are satisfied when they download apps with specific functions such as messaging, information searching, planning, and news. They have no need to download additional apps with the same functions. This characteristic of apps in the hobby and information categories results in a specific pattern whereby the number of downloads rapidly decreases over time. We therefore conclude that the number of downloads is less reduced for innovators than for

TABLE 4: Main results of the regression model 2: app category model.

Variables	Models by app categories		
	Model 2-1: game, apps	Model 2-2: hobby, apps	Model 2-3: information, apps
Intercept	0.289**	−0.137**	−0.097**
	(0.127)*	(0.179)*	(0.160)*
Noninnovator	−0.399**	0.068**	−0.174**
	(0.186)*	(0.263)*	(0.234)*
Months since adoption	−0.129**	−0.104**	−0.074**
	(0.022)*	(0.027)*	(0.024)*
Noninnovator × months since adoption	−0.013**	−0.173**	−0.179**
	(0.019)*	(0.032)*	(0.029)*
Calendar month	0.109**	0.190**	0.188**
	(0.020)*	(0.028)*	(0.025)*
Demographic control variables			
Age	−0.033	−0.188	0.087*
	(0.033)	(0.422)	(0.038)
Gender	−0.069	−0.276**	−0.463**
	(0.065)	(0.084)	(0.076)
Income	0.236**	0.297**	0.150
	(0.071)	(0.091)	(0.083)
Region (urban area)	0.033	−0.143	0.192*
	(0.069)	(0.088)	(0.080)
Device usage control variables			
Device purchase price ($)	0.007	−0.084*	−0.130**
	(0.032)	(0.041)	(0.038)
Voice traffic fees ($)	0.064	0.101**	−0.019
	(0.033)	(0.042)	(0.038)
Instances of text usage	0.027	0.043	−0.111**
	(0.033)	(0.043)	(0.039)
Online Internet traffic fees ($)	0.147**	0.434**	0.206**
	(0.032)	(0.041)	(0.038)
Observations	2,492	2,492	2,492
R^2	0.032	0.094	0.082

Note. $**p < 1\%$, $*p < 5\%$, and ( ) is standard error.

noninnovators since the former users are more actively searching for new apps.

5. Discussion

This study has some meaning for researchers. First, we targeted the app market, which has not yet been properly studied. While the recent exponential growth in this market has aroused widespread social interest, relatively few researchers have undertaken the task of directly observing and analyzing consumer behavior in this market. We collected actual download data at the consumer level in the app market, analyzed consumer download patterns, systematically considered consumer behavior in terms of mobile device usage, and examined the effects of demographic characteristics and the market environment. As a result, we found that various environmental factors should be considered for accurate understanding of consumer download patterns in this market.

In addition, this study provides useful parameters and models to measure variables pertinent to the app market and establishes helpful criteria to interpret the results. For

example, in terms of the market lifecycle, the app market is leaving the initial stage and entering into the expansion phase, in which downloading behavior varies considerably. Second, the results of this study have expanded those of previous research on the direct relationship between innovativeness and heavy usage of new products [8] and have further applied the findings of previous studies to the online content market. Based on previous studies in the field of innovativeness theory, we have extended the discussion of opinion leadership and social status to the consumption and diffusion of mobile apps [6, 10]. In this theoretical framework, innovators were predicted to look for new products periodically; efforts were made in the current study to confirm this prediction and to empirically demonstrate the validity of the finding that innovators lead market growth [4] and have a crucial impact on both initial product distribution and long-term market performance [7].

The results of the model estimation and interpretation presented herein provide some practical implications to marketers and manufacturers of apps, as summarized below. First, practitioners must utilize knowledge of the behavior of innovators in the app market in the longer term from a lifetime-value perspective. Due to their greater desire for new things, innovators tend to explore and download new apps periodically. They continue to download apps, and the cumulative number of apps downloaded increases over time. Hence, they tend to remain as customers for a longer period and have higher probability of downloading more apps on average than noninnovators. This behavior enhances their lifetime value for app companies [21]. Second, app companies should focus on the initial period of consumers' entry into the app market. The analysis results herein suggest that most downloading occurs in the early period, after which it gradually decreases. In the early period, consumers may do some basic research on their new mobile devices and explore the available apps. We also predict that consumers will continue using apps that were downloaded in the early period. Hence, the period during which the maximum revenue from downloading may be earned will be the initial period following consumers' entry into the market. Third, different target audiences can be identified according to different app categories. For game apps, companies should focus more intensively on innovators than on noninnovators both in the long and short term. For hobby and information apps, companies should target both innovators and noninnovators in the early stage but should focus on innovators in the long term. For game apps, the periodicity of downloading is similar in both groups; hence, companies should implement periodic recommendation programs targeted at both groups. Lastly, the number of app downloads must be generally increased in order to consolidate the maturity of the app market. The analysis results demonstrated that the average number of downloads tends to increase more rapidly as the market approaches maturity. Plenty of available alternatives in the market and improved convenience in searching for and selection of apps are critical factors in the efforts to increase the number of app downloads.

6. Conclusion

In this study, a comparative analysis was conducted to determine whether and how innovators are heavier users of apps in comparison with noninnovators. For this purpose, we classified the consumers in the pseudonym Goapps.com, a large app market, into innovators and noninnovators, collecting and analyzing data consisting of the number of apps downloaded at various points in time, information about mobile device usage, and demographic information. The results of the exploratory analysis provide no clear answer as to whether innovators do actually download more apps than noninnovators. On the contrary, noninnovators actually seem to download more apps than innovators in the early stages of app market development. In the analysis using a regression model capable of considering the market environment and other control factors, the results confirmed that innovators are significantly heavier users than noninnovators in the long term. The results have also demonstrated a basic trend wherein both groups do the most downloading in the early days of entry into the app market and then gradually reduce their downloading behaviors.

After the turning point, a sharper decrease in downloads was evident for noninnovators compared to innovators.

In a further analysis, we compared the patterns of innovators and noninnovators in three app categories: games, hobbies, and information. In the game category, there was no difference in the patterns of decreasing downloads between innovators and noninnovators. By contrast, in the hobby and information categories, noninnovators showed a sharper decrease than innovators. The reason for this difference lies in the periodic nature of game apps, which induces consumers to download new products regardless of their level of innovativeness, whereas the hobby and information apps may not affect consumers' downloading behavior in quite the same way once their initial functional goals for app usage are fulfilled. In this circumstance, developers take advantage of the fact that innovators have an inherent tendency to pursue new things and thus are likely to continue exploring new apps even if their functional needs have been satisfied. This characteristic is indeed reflected in their behavior in the data described herein, in which periodic downloads of hobby and information apps occur. The results imply the necessity to take into account the market environment and categorical differences in the comparison of innovators and noninnovators.

In this study, the findings of previous studies on the innovativeness in the app market in the initial stage have been applied and empirically analyzed to prove that innovators may contribute to app market performance more than noninnovators. Despite these contributions, this study has certain limitations. First, we measured consumers' choices and predicted market performance from the app download perspective. Downloads may be interpreted as adoption of individual apps. In this study, we did not collect and utilize observations on how long consumers actually used the products. In the real app market, companies earn revenues from advertisement fees based on usage time. Hence, additional studies must be conducted to measure performance based on multiple performance variables, such as app usage frequency and usage time. Furthermore, through the exploration of the various variables, we may analyze many models of the app usage process simultaneously by applying standards such as time of entry into the app market, app adoption, and app usage time. Second, classification in this study was conducted at the category level; apps were classified into three types (games, hobbies, and information). It is possible, however, that characteristics of apps may differ within each category; hence, more detailed criteria for observation must be introduced. A previous study on the categorical structure and categorizing criteria [22] can provide a basis to ascertain new categories and types suitable for observation of heterogeneous consumer behaviors. Third, while we were not able to observe the effect of differences in app prices, the price effect can be analyzed in future studies. In the app market, price is one criterion crucial to consumer choice [9], determining the degree of consumer engagement and attitude. Through using the additional variable, the differences in download patterns between paid and free apps may be examined. Lastly, in the previous studies, the innovativeness is measured by the internal and external [8, 11, 12] characteristics [3, 10, 13]. In this study, we divide the innovators and noninnovators using the purchase time. It would be useful to understand more comprehensive users' behavior in the multiple dimension of their characteristics.

Acknowledgments

This paper was supported by Chungnam National University in 2017.

References

[1] J. John, *Worldwide and U.S. Mobile Applications Download and Revenue 2013-2017 Forecast: The App as the Emerging Face of the Internet*, IDC Analyze the Future, 2013.

[2] S. Balasubramanian, R. A. Peterson, and S. L. Jarvenpaa, "Exploring the implications of M-commerce for markets and marketing," *Journal of the Academy of Marketing Science*, vol. 30, no. 4, pp. 348-361, 2002.

[3] D. F. Midgley and G. R. Dowling, "Innovativeness: the concept and its measurement," *Journal of Consumer Research*, vol. 4, no. 4, pp. 229-242, 1978.

[4] R. Agarwal and B. L. Bayus, "The market evolution and sales takeoff of product innovations," *Management Science*, vol. 48, no. 8, pp. 1024-1041, 2002.

[5] J. F. Engel, R. J. Kegerreis, and R. D. Blackwell, "Word-of-mouth communication by the innovator," *Journal of Marketing*, vol. 33, no. 3, pp. 15-19, 1969.

[6] R. Iyengar, C. Van den Bulte, and T. W. Valente, "Opinion leadership and social contagion in new product diffusion," *Marketing Science*, vol. 30, no. 2, pp. 195-212, 2011.

[7] J. Goldenberg, S. Han, D. R. Lehmann, and J. W. Hong, "The role of hubs in the adoption process," *Journal of Marketing*, vol. 73, no. 2, pp. 1-13, 2009.

[8] R. E. Goldsmith, L. R. Flynn, and E. B. Goldsmith, "Innovative consumers and market mavens," *Journal of Marketing Theory and Practice*, vol. 11, no. 4, pp. 54-65, 2003.

[9] A. Ghose and S. P. Han, "Estimating demand for mobile applications in the new economy," *Management Science*, vol. 60, no. 6, pp. 1470-1488, 2014.

[10] S. Hoffmann and K. Soyez, "A cognitive model to predict domain-specific consumer innovativeness," *Journal of Business Research*, vol. 63, no. 7, pp. 778-785, 2010.

[11] H. Gatignon and T. S. Robertson, "A propositional inventory for new diffusion research," *Journal of Consumer Research*, vol. 11, no. 4, pp. 849-867, 1985.

[12] J. W. Taylor, "A striking characteristic of innovators," *Journal of Marketing Research*, vol. 14, no. 1, pp. 104-107, 1977.

[13] S. Im, B. L. Bayus, and C. H. Mason, "An empirical study of innate consumer innovativeness, personal characteristics, and new-product adoption behavior," *Journal of the Academy of Marketing Science*, vol. 31, no. 1, pp. 61-73, 2003.

[14] Researchmoz, *Global Mobile Applications (free, paid & ad supported) Market by Stores, Category, Platform, Brands and Stakeholders (2012-2017)*, 2014.

[15] B. J. Kanninen, "Optimal design for multinomial choice experiments," *Journal of Marketing Research*, vol. 39, no. 2, pp. 214-227, 2002.

[16] M. D. Dickerson and J. W. Gentry, "Characteristics of adopters and non-adopters of home computers," *Journal of Consumer research*, vol. 10, no. 2, pp. 225-235, 1983.

[17] M. Wedel and J. Zhang, "Analyzing brand competition across subcategories," *Journal of Marketing Research*, vol. 41, no. 4, pp. 448-456, 2004.

[18] N. Yee, "Motivations for play in online games," *Cyber Psychology and Behavior*, vol. 9, no. 6, pp. 772-775, 2006.

[19] D. J. Kuss, J. Louws, and R. W. Wiers, "Online gaming addiction? Motives predict addictive play behavior in massively multiplayer online role-playing games," *Cyberpsychology, Behavior, and Social Networking*, vol. 15, no. 9, pp. 480-485, 2012.

[20] L. J. Shrum Jr., R. S. Wyer, and T. C. O'Guinn, "The effects of television consumption on social perceptions: the use of priming procedures to investigate psychological processes," *Journal of Consumer Research*, vol. 24, no. 4, pp. 447-458, 1998.

[21] P. Schmitt, B. Skiera, and C. Van den Bulte, "Referral programs and customer value," *Journal of Marketing*, vol. 75, no. 1, pp. 46-59, 2011.

[22] S. Ratneshwar and A. D. Shocker, "Substitution in use and the role of usage context in product category structures," *Journal of Marketing Research*, vol. 28, no. 3, pp. 281-295, 1991.

8

Analyzing Typical Mobile Gestures in mHealth Applications for Users with Down Syndrome

H. Luna-Garcia,[1] A. Mendoza-Gonzalez (iD),[2] R. Mendoza-Gonzalez,[3] H. Gamboa-Rosales,[1] J. I. Galván-Tejada,[1] J. M. Celaya-Padilla,[4] C. E. Galvan-Tejada (iD),[1] J. Arceo-Olague,[1] A. Moreno-Baez,[1] O. Alonso-González,[1] F. E. Lopez-Monteagudo,[1] R. Solis-Robles,[1] and J. Lopez-Veyna[5]

[1]Centro de Investigación e Innovación Automotriz de México (CIIAM), Universidad Autónoma de Zacatecas, Jardín Juárez 147, 98000 Centro Histórico, ZAC, Mexico
[2]Instituto de Investigación, Desarrollo e Innovación en Tecnologías Interactivas A.C. (IIDITI), Av. Moscatel 103, Aguascalientes, AGS, Mexico
[3]Depto. de Sistemas y Computación, Tecnologico Nacional de Mexico/Instituto Tecnologico de Aguascalientes, Av. Adolfo López Mateos 1801 Ote. Fracc. Bonagens, 20256 Aguascalientes, AGS, Mexico
[4]CONACyT, Centro de Investigación e Innovación Automotriz de México (CIIAM), Universidad Autónoma de Zacatecas, Jardín Juárez 147, 98000 Centro Histórico, ZAC, Mexico
[5]Depto. de Sistemas y Computación, Tecnologico Nacional de Mexico/Instituto Tecnologico de Zacatecas, Carretera Panamericana entronque a Guadalajara s/n, Zacatecas Centro, 98000 Zacatecas, ZAC, Mexico

Correspondence should be addressed to A. Mendoza-Gonzalez; mendoza.uaa@gmail.com

Academic Editor: Antonio Coronato

Mobile technology has provided many advantages for all members of the Information Society. Communication, Organization, Transportation, Health, and Entertainment are just a few areas of mobile technology application. Nevertheless, there are still some people who find difficulties using it. Although there are a lot of applications of mHealth available for almost any kind of mobile device, there is still a lack of understanding and attending users' needs, especially those of users with disabilities. People with Down syndrome have the potential to function as active members of our society, taking care of themselves and their own, having jobs, voting, and so on, but their physical limitations prevent them from handling correctly technological tools that could enhance their performance, including mobile technology. In this paper, we had analyzed how suitable the mHealth applications are for users with Down syndrome. We tested 24 users and analyzed their physical performance in fine-motor movements while developing a set of tasks over a mHealth application. Results showed that the design of a mHealth application for users with Down syndrome must center its interaction with simple gestures as *tap* and *swipe* avoiding more complex ones as *spread* and *rotate*. This research is a starting point to understand the fundamentals of people with Down syndrome interacting with mobile technology.

1. Introduction

The benefits of mobile technology can be found anywhere: communication, education, scientific research, healthcare, and entertainment, to name a few, but despite its multidisciplinary application, mobile technology and all its advantages are far away from being accessible to people with disabilities [1],

people with Down syndrome among them [2]. Researchers in Human-Computer Interaction (HCI) have recognized and analyzed several barriers that people with Down syndrome face when interacting with mobile technology [3–9].

Talking specifically about mobile Health (mHealth) software, it has various limitations, such as small screens, tiny graphical elements, tiny movements of the hand and fingers, and a very reduced interactive area [10, 11]. Due to their common problems in fine-motor skills, the potential of people with Down syndrome as mobile users might be perceived as limited. Nevertheless, the question is not if they are capable to manipulate the mHealth application, but if it is enough suitable for them.

People with Down syndrome can be benefited by many mHealth applications such as communication enhancers, treatment support tools, nutrition control tools, and so on. These tools in general will provide a more independent living. This is the main reason of why mHealth software designers and developers must know how these users learn, use, and enjoy their products.

The reminder of the paper is organized as follows: the main characteristics of people with Down syndrome and some relevant studies involving mobile technology are shown in Section 1. Section 2 presents the research methodology. The experimental work is presented in Section 3. Results are presented in Section 4. And, finally in Section 5, we present all concluding remarks.

1.1. Down Syndrome.

Down syndrome is a genetic anomaly that affects chromosome 21, making a full or partial extra copy of it; it brings limitations in the physical and cognitive profile of people who are born with it [12, 13]. Worldwide, the estimated incidence of Down syndrome is between 1 in 1,000 to 1 in 1,100 live births [14]. About 6,000 babies are born in the United States with Down syndrome each year [15]. The prevalence of this condition is in about 8 people with Down syndrome per each 10,000 people in the United States [15], 7 per 10,000 in England and Wales [16], and 8 per 10,000 in Spain [17], to quote some data. According to the National New York State Department of Health, the life expectancy for people with Down syndrome is around 60 years of plenty life, in which they attend school, work, participate in decisions that affect them, have meaningful relationships, vote, and contribute to society in many other ways [18].

According to the Diagnostic and Statistical Manual of Mental Disorders, almost 80 percent of the people with Down syndrome have moderate intellectual disability, which means that they can reach basic capabilities in reading, writing, mathematics, sports, computing, and other academic activities applicable further in jobs; people can be responsible of their personal needs such as feeding, dressing, and daily living. All these skills can be achieved after a long process of learning and training [19].

In addition to the intellectual disability, users with Down syndrome have physical disability that affects mainly their fine-motor skills (in the hand and fingers), visual and hearing perception, eye-hand coordination, and other psychomotor capabilities [12]; the most common limitations of Down syndrome people are as follows [20–22]:

(i) Short hands and broad fingers

(i) Difficulties in fine-motor skills

(ii) Low muscle tone

(iii) Poor eye-hand coordination

(iv) Vision problems

(v) Audition problems

(vi) Intelligence quotient average of 50

(vii) Low comprehension of abstract concepts

(viii) Delay in expressive language

(ix) Problems with short-term memory (verbal)

(x) Anxiety and stress propensity

(xi) Depression

(xii) Uncontrolled effusive behavior

(xiii) Lack of concentration in difficult problems.

1.2. Mobile Technology and Down Syndrome.

Most individuals with Down syndrome are able to live independently, but they commonly require assistance in financial, medical, and legal matters [12], which is a gap that mobile technology can close. This is the reason why some researchers have analyzed the particular and specific needs of these people as users of mobile technology.

In [7], the authors applied a usability test of mobile devices, to analyze the work-place related skills of adult expert users with Down syndrome. Among all the tasks made by users, some of them were very challenging. Testing sessions were quite long, lasting between 2 and 3 hours. The authors also denote the difficulty of users to work with tiny elements of the touch screen device. Finally, they also provide a set of suggestions to those who apply usability tests over users with Down syndrome: (1) applying pilot sessions to reveal potential challenges, using real examples; (2) to be flexible in tasks; (3) to present satisfaction scales visually; and (4) to reinforce instructions with visual clues.

An empirical study of three input techniques used by Down syndrome children and young adults was presented in [23]. The authors analyzed the use of the keyboard, word prediction, and speech recognition to a group of 10 users with Down syndrome between 10 and 24 years old. Besides the surprising results of performance in the keyboard and preference of speech recognition (see original paper for more details), the evaluation of the users implied the collection of demographic data. The authors also reported that some users were easily distracted during evaluation and have fatigue and lack of patience. The authors suggested that the computer experience (number of years using computers) can be a good predictor of users' performance. Also, they suggested that low performance shown by users in some activities was due to lack of motivation, training, and exposure to technology, rather than limitations in ability.

In [3], the authors presented a process for usability testing for users with Down syndrome, which consists in 9 phases: recruiting participants, establishing tasks, writing instructions, defining test plan, pilot testing, refining test plan, testing, analyzing collected data, and presenting the results. It was made from a previous literature review. Nevertheless, the literature review seems to be limited, the process considered only 5 papers from 2009 to 2013, and the process is not applied or validated. Still, the authors presented the need of a process when working with users with Down syndrome.

A mobile assistant for workers with Down syndrome was presented in [24]. The authors developed a full-functional mobile tool that guides workers step by step throughout a task sequence read from a QR tag, presenting information through different channels: video, audio, text, and static images. The steps sequence is delivered to users depending on the activity, in some cases the next step is shown automatically, and in other cases, the users are asked to continue. The interface design of the assistant was enhanced by the comments of experts in Down syndrome, resulting in a simpler and usable one. By using the assistant, errors in tasks decreased, supervisor activity was less required, and time expended in training activities was reduced. The authors described how difficult it was to deal with the great variability in user's capabilities, denoting that they could not generalize the evaluation method to all of them.

Feng and Lazar in [4] presented a summary of the difficulties experienced by users with Down syndrome using technology:

(i) Typing

(ii) Frustration in navigation

(iii) Frustration in trouble shooting

(iv) Lack of patience

(v) Low error tolerance

(vi) Frustration when excessive information was found

(vii) Frustration in inconsistencies in the interface design

(viii) Frustration when there are too many windows opened.

There is an active and growing engagement of people with Down syndrome and mobile technology, but there are some characteristics of them that limit and delay progress and achievement of all new technology advances and benefits. Now, there is a gap in the analysis of why people with Down syndrome have troubles using mobile technology; one question arises: is it because of their intellectual capabilities or because of their physical ones? By studying the performance of individuals with Down syndrome interacting with mobile gestures, we are looking for the most basic interaction issues in the simplest form of communication with these touchable devices.

2. Methodology

We divided our study in five stages. This methodology was proposed by our research team, and it has been enhanced through the years:

(1) Selection of target users to be evaluated

(2) Definition of test sessions and materials

(3) Definition of testing metrics

(4) Definition of users' tasks

(5) Definition of roles and functions.

3. Experimental Work

A task development test was applied in a group of 24 users with Down syndrome (further detailed) to assess physical challenge that implied the use of an mHealth application. In this section, we detail the stages of our experimental work.

3.1. Target Users. The study involved 24 subjects with Down syndrome, 14 men and 10 women between 12 and 20 years old ($\overline{X} = 16.1$, $S = 3.9$); all of them were enrolled in an institute of special education. This institute evaluated all students in six points: communication skills, physical development, self-direction, social behavior, literacy, and mathematics.

In these schools, students are categorized in three levels of psychoemotional development, by implementing a battery of tests, based on WISC-IV [25] and Valpar [26] tests. The objective of this categorization was to offer academic services according to student's needs. The next scale is used:

(1) Communication skills: grade for expressing ideas and emotions to others.

(a) High: the student has no problems in communication.

(b) Appropriated: the student need some help to put together and to express some ideas.

(c) Low: the student needs a lot of help to communicate.

(2) Physical skills: grade to develop gross movements such as walking, running, and crawling, among others.

(a) High: there are no difficulties in movement.

(b) Appropriated: the student has some troubles in coordination and precision.

(c) Low: the student has difficulties developing any movement.

(3) Self-direction: grade to be independent in daily living and self-care, to follow schedules, and to solve common problems.

(a) High: the student is independent in daily living tasks and has no trouble in learning new ones.

(b) Appropriated: the student needs help in some tasks, especially in the new ones.

(c) Low: the student cannot do any daily tasks by him/herself.

(4) Social behavior: capability to get integrated in social groups and to respect its rules.

(a) High: the individual can socialize easily and has no trouble with social behavior rules.

(b) Appropriated: the individual has some problems socializing and understanding the accepted social behavior.

(c) Low: it is very difficult for the student to get integrated in a social group.

(5) Literacy: ability to read and write.

TABLE 1: Participants skills.

Characteristic	Target users (%)
Communication skills	High: 37.5 Appropriated: 58.3 Low: 4.2
Physical skills	High: 41.7 Appropriated: 54.2 Low: 4.2
Self-direction	High: 37.5 Appropriated: 45.8 Low: 16.7
Social behavior	High: 12.5 Appropriated: 87.5 Low: 0
Literacy	High: 16.7 Appropriated: 70.8 Low: 12.5
Math	High: 0 Appropriated: 58.3 Low: 41.7

TABLE 2: Technology usage of participants.

Preferred device	PC: 25% Tablet: 29.2% Smartphone: 33.3% None: 12.5%
Frequency of use (hours/week)	0 (zero): 20.8% Less than 10: 25% Between 10 and 30: 33.3% More than 30: 20.8%
Purpose	Academic: 37.5% Leisure: 50% None: 12.5%
Computer classes	Yes: 45.8% No: 54.2%
Owns a device	Yes: 33.3% No: 66.7%
Device availability	None: 20.8% Borrowed: 20.8% Home/school: 37.5% Anywhere: 20.8%

(a) High: the student can read and write without troubles.

(b) Appropriated: the student can read and write simple sentences.

(c) Low: the student cannot read and write.

(6) Math: ability to solve problems involving numbers.

(a) High: the student can solve additions, subtractions, and multiplications.

(b) Appropriated: the student can read and write numbers, identifying tens and hundreds, but has some trouble in solving additions and subtractions.

(c) Low: the student at much can read and write numbers.

Table 1 presents the level of each skill for the test participants.

TABLE 3: Division of the participants.

Group	Number of participants
Isolated	5
Occasional	6
Regular	8
Unlimited	5

We asked parents and teachers about the use of technology by the kids: type of devices they use, software used, common activities, frequency of use, and so on. The results of how participants interact with technology are presented in Table 2.

This specific information of technological background shown clears the differences in their experience using technology (computers, video game, mobile, etc.).

Considering this, we opted to divide the population into four groups:

(1) Isolated: They have very little experience using technology and do not commonly interact with technology in their daily living. They had their first encounter with mobile technology in the first session of this study.

(2) Occasional: They can use basic features of computers (always with help), with which they interact 2 or 3 times per week at home or at the school. They use other devices such as video games consoles, music players, and mobile technology at home but twice a month as much.

(3) Regular: They can use basic features on computers, video games, and mobile technology without help. They interact frequently with them but for short periods of time every day.

(4) Unlimited: They can use several features of computers, video games, and mobile technology with independence. They use technology as video games, media players, computers, and mobile devices every day for more than 4 hours per day.

The number of participants by group is shown in Table 3.

Summarizing, around 50% of the test participants use mainly mobile devices (tablet, computers, and smartphones) over PC and other technological devices; nearly 60% of participants use them frequently at the basic level; 20% of participants are experts, and the last 20% has not used them at all.

3.2. Sessions and Materials. The study was extended throughout 6 months, having a total of 24 sessions per user. Each session lasted 20 minutes. Three different schools were involved, and each one provided a classroom to work in. There was not any characteristic of the classroom different from others: rectangular area, windows, a blackboard, several desks, and so on. We mounted three high-definition video cameras: one in front of the user (Figure 1), one in the right side (Figure 2), and one in the left side of the user (Figure 3).

All users worked with a 7.1″ screen Samsung® tablet computer and with a 5″ screen LG® smartphone, both with Android 4.4.

FIGURE 1: In front camera.

FIGURE 2: Right-side camera.

FIGURE 3: Left-side camera.

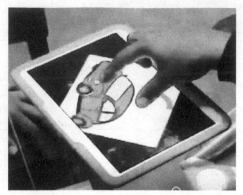

FIGURE 4: Rotate gesture app 7.1″ screen.

FIGURE 5: Rotate gesture app 5″ screen.

Searching in literature, users can apply between 12 and 15 different gestures to manipulate mobile applications of any device; but, in accordance with [27–29], there are 9 more commonly used gestures: tap, double tap, swipe, drag, hold, hold and drag, spread, pinch, and rotate. Among the less common gestures are those used only for some vendors like the 5 and 3 fingers pinch for iOS® and all their 3D taps [30]; for this reason, they were not taken into consideration for this study.

To assess these mobile gestures, we developed nine different applications, in order to clearly observe, analyze, and assess each one. As an example, Figure 4 shows a user interacting with the application of *rotate* gesture in the 7.1″ screen device, and Figure 5 shows in the 5″ screen device.

3.3. Definition of Test Metrics. Based on [31], the next performance metrics were used:

(i) Success in tasks: percentage of tasks completed successfully, arranged by gesture

(ii) Number of errors: number of trials that users took to complete a task

(iii) Time: time to complete successfully a task.

Based on [32] in the Durivage Test for physical performance [33], we defined the next metrics and divided into three groups: movement, metrics, and pressure:

(i) Movement:

   (a) Fluent: the gesture was made without hesitation, and its action is triggered.
   (b) Stepwise: user hesitated to develop the gesture, and its action was triggered.
   (c) Disrupted: user did not complete the gesture.

(ii) Position:

   (a) Looseness: the fingers and hands are relaxed.
   (b) Rigidity: the fingers and hands are tense.
   (c) Trembling: the hand or fingers are shaking while making the gesture.

(iii) Pressure:

   (a) High: the gesture was not detected because the user pressed too hard.
   (b) Low: the gesture was not detected because the user pressed weak.
   (c) Detectable: the pressure made in the screen allows the gesture to be detected.

TABLE 4: Users' tasks involving tap gesture.

Skill level	User task	Success state
Very easy	Single tap (7.1$'$ screen)	User touches only one time the indicated object, and the next slide is displayed.
Easy	Multiple tap in "X" (7.1$''$ screen)	User touches the four figures one time, making an X figure in the indicated order. When user touches the last figure, the next slide is shown.
Moderate	Single tap (5$''$ screen)	User touches only one time the indicated object (while holding the device), and the next slide is displayed.
Hard	Multiple tap in "X" (5$''$ screen)	User touches the four figures one time (while holding the device) making an X figure in the indicated order. When user touches the last figure, the next slide is shown.

3.4. Definition of User's Tasks. To analyze the physical challenge, the assessment was focused on the mobile gestures; considering this, we defined 36 user tasks, and each one implied the following:

(i) The use of only one gesture

(ii) A recognizable result

(iii) A skill level going from very easy to hard

(iv) A state of success.

To facilitate the application of all the sessions, we arranged users' tasks with the mobile gesture that implies. As an example, Table 4 presents a full description of the four tasks related to the tap gesture (a complete description of all activities can be requested by an e-mail to the main author of this paper). Instructions were given verbally to users, at the beginning of the task, and each time the user got confused, as a reminder, no other kind of help was provided to participants.

3.5. Definition of Roles and Functions. The next roles were involved during the evaluation:

(i) Test Applicator: an expert in user testing, researcher in HCI.

(ii) Applicator assistant: a college student specialized in computer science.

(iii) Physical therapist: a practitioner in physical therapy, with more than 10 years working in special education programs.

(iv) Observers: one psychology practitioner, specialized in intellectual disability and Gestalt therapy, working for more than 20 years in special education programs, one researcher in HCI, one teacher of special education, and two participants' parents.

Although the test applicator and the assistant are present in the testing room, only the applicator interacts with the users. Both, the physical therapist and the observers analyze the users through a video recording, to not interfere with the real user interaction. The applicator and the assistant socialized previously with users following the activities of the *user-background* phase.

4. Results

The resulting data of the study includes two axes: physical performance and tasks performance. To homogenize data analysis, results should be coded as *improvement rates*. The calculation can be made using the percentage increase formula:

$$\text{percentage change} = \frac{\text{amount of increase}}{\text{starting point}} \times 100. \quad (1)$$

Thus, the improvement rate is calculated as follows:

$$\text{improvement rate} = \frac{\text{final value} - \text{initial value}}{\text{initial value}} \times 100. \quad (2)$$

where the initial value is the data obtained in test 1 and the final value is the data obtained in the last test. At the end, the data analysis can be formed by a set of improvement rates that can be grouped as an average improvement in physical performance, tasks performance, or global performance (the global performance is the average of the other two rates).

The physical performance of each gesture was calculated by considering the improvement rate in the percentage of users who made each activity (of the corresponding gesture) with fluent movement, loose position, and detectable pressure, as the study progressed. In Figure 6, it is shown, for example, that users developing activities of *double tap*, improved their physical performance to almost 80%, in the six months the study lasted. Using *spread*, on the contrary, users only improved performance around 25%.

Task performance involved success in tasks, number of errors, and time. Figure 7 presents the improvement of success in tasks to each gesture. The greater improvement was observed in *swipe* gesture, having more than 70%. *Hold and drag* had lower improvement, almost 40% of improvement.

The error making rate improvement is shown in Figure 8. Big differences may be observed between *pinch* gesture, which had around 65% of improvement, and *rotate* gesture, which had only 20%. This means that, even after six months and 24 tests, users still made many errors using *rotate* gesture.

Figure 9 presents data about how users improved their time, making the activities to each gesture. The greater improvement was observed in gestures *tap* and *drag*, with

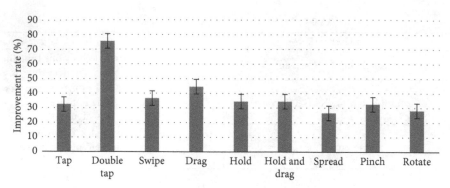

FIGURE 6: Physical success per gesture.

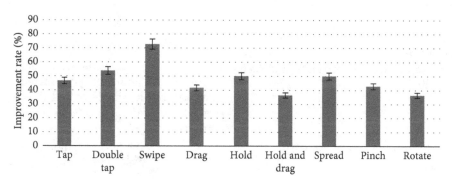

FIGURE 7: Success in tasks per gesture.

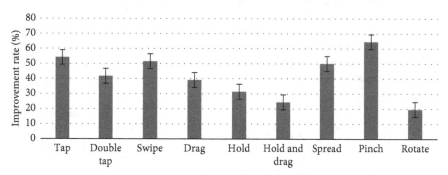

FIGURE 8: Error making results.

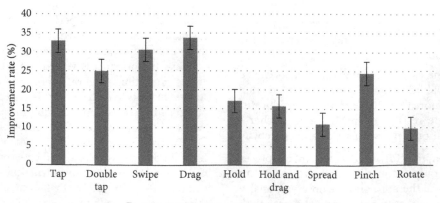

FIGURE 9: Time improvement results.

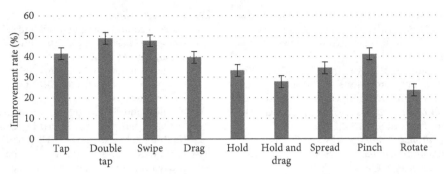

FIGURE 10: Global improvement level per gesture.

more than 30%; *spread* and *rotate*, had the smallest with just around 10% of improvement.

Finally, we present the global performance. It was calculated as the average improvement rate of users' performance, considering physical and tasks performance. Figure 10 shows, in general, how easy-to-learn the nine gestures were to participants. *Double tap* and *swipe* were the gestures in what users presented more improvement, having nearly 50%. Rotate, however, had only around 25% of improvement.

5. Concluding Remarks

mHealth applications require to attend the needs of users with Down syndrome in order to reach accessibility and provide to these group of users all health services. This paper presented an analysis of the physical challenge involved in the use of mHealth application, by the profile of people with Down syndrome. By analyzing the most basic form of communication with mobile devices, we found that the physical limitations of users with Down syndrome make quite hard to work in reduced areas, such as tablet computers and smartphones screens, developing the fine movements that mobile gestures require.

We had developed a study focused in the nine most common mobile gestures: tap, double tap, swipe, drag, hold, hold and drag, spread, pinch, and rotate. The analysis of 24 users with Down syndrome throughout the six months showed that gestures like *tap* and *swipe* are very easy to develop; double-tap and pinch gestures can be easily learned by users, even when they represent a challenge at the beginning. Spread and rotate gestures turn to be the hardest to learn, since when users deal with complex gestures they are more susceptible to making mistakes.

For mHeath software, it is very important to fit all users' needs and due to their own nature must fit the needs of users with disabilities. mHealth applications can provide the help, guidance, and knowledge that allow people with Down syndrome to be more independent, reach a better life, and realize as members of the information society. To do so, mHealth specialists must find the way to create more suitable products.

As future work, we have interest in applying a similar study to new gestures, such as the 3D tap of iOS, and to those gestures that do not involve the physical contact with devices. It is also important to extend this study, involving individuals with others disabilities (physical and intellectual)

and without any, in order to compare experiences and results. To continue working with people with Down syndrome, we have started a project to evaluate the usability of brain-computer interfaces with children with Down syndrome, applying the same methodology of the current work.

References

[1] V. G. Felix, L. J. Mena, R. Ostos, and G. E. Maestre, "A pilot study of the use of emerging computer technologies to improve the effectiveness of reading and writing therapies in children with Down syndrome," *British Journal of Educational Technology*, vol. 48, no. 2, pp. 611–624, 2017.

[2] C. González, A. Noda, and A. Bruno, "Learning subtraction and addition through digital boards: a Down syndrome case," *Universal Access in the Information Society*, vol. 14, no. 1, pp. 29–44, 2015.

[3] D. Caliz, L. Martinez, X. Alaman, C. Teran, and R. Caliz, "Usability testing process with people with Down syndrome interacting with mobile applications: a literature review," *International Journal of Computer Science and Information Technology*, vol. 8, no. 3, 2016.

[4] J. Feng and J. Lazar, "Computer usage by children with Down Syndrome: challenges and future research," *ACM Transactions on Accessible Computing*, vol. 2, no. 3, 2010.

[5] P. Williams, "Mobile technology use by people with learning disabilities: a qualitative study," *World Academy of Science Engineering and Technology*, vol. 12, no. 3, 2018.

[6] M. Khemaja and A. Taamallah, "Towards situation driven mobile tutoring system for learning languages and communication skills: application to users with specific needs," *Journal of Educational Technology and Society*, vol. 19, no. 1, pp. 113–128, 2016.

[7] J. Lazar, L. Kumin, and J. Feng, "Understanding the computer skills of adult expert users with Down syndrome: an exploratory study," in *International ACM SIGACCESS Conference on Computers and Accessibility*, New York, NY, USA, October 2011.

[8] A. Kirijian, M. Myers, and S. Charland, "Web Fun Central: online learning tools for individuals with Down syndrome," in *Universal Usability: Designing Information Systems for Diverse User Populations*, John Wiley & Sons, Chichester, UK, 2007.

[9] D. Lima, M. Sousa, R. Ara, J. Hannum, A. D. Rocha, and A. T. Barbosa, "Software with biofeedback to assist people with Down syndrome," *International Journal of Computer Applications*, vol. 158, no. 5, 2017.

[10] F. Ritter, G. Baxter, and E. Churchill, *Foundations for Designing User-Centered Systems: What System Designers Need to Know about People*, Springer Science and Business Media, London, UK, 2014.

[11] S. C. Simplican, C. Shivers, J. Chen, and G. Leader, "With a touch of a button: staff perceptions on integrating technology in an Irish service provider for people with intellectual disabilities," *Journal of Applied Research in Intellectual Disabilities*, vol. 31, no. 1, pp. e130–e139, 2018.

[12] P. Parker, *Down Syndrome: A Bibliography and Dictionary for Physicians, Patients, and Genome Researchers*, Icon Group International Inc., San Diego, CA, USA, 2004.

[13] K. Diamandopoulos and J. Green, "Down syndrome: an integrative review," *Journal of Neonatal Nursing*, vol. 24, no. 2, 2018.

[14] S. Jaruratanasirikul, O. Kor-anantakul, M. Chowvichian et al., "A population-based study of prevalence of Down syndrome in Southern Thailand," *World Journal of Pediatrics*, vol. 13, no. 1, pp. 63–69, 2017.

[15] S. Parker, C. T. Mai, M. A. Canfield et al., "National Birth Defects Prevention Network 2010: updated national birth prevalence estimates for selected birth defects in the United States, 2004-2006," *Birth Defects Research Part a Clinical and Molecular Teratology*, vol. 88, no. 12, pp. 1008–1016, 2007.

[16] J. Wu and J. Morris, "The population prevalence of Down's syndrome in England and Wales in 2011," *European Journal of Human Genetics*, vol. 21, no. 9, pp. 1016–1019, 2013.

[17] FESD (Federación Espaola de Sndrome de Down), *II Plan de Acción para Personas con Sindrome de Down, 2009–2013*, Down 21 España, Madrid, España, 2010.

[18] NYSDOH (New York State Department Of Health), *Report of the Recommendations: Down Syndrome*, Health Resources and Services Administration U.S. Department of Health and Human Services Parklawn Building, New York, NY, USA, 2006.

[19] APA (American Psychological Association), *Diagnostic and Statistical Manual of Mental Disorders (DSM) 5*, American Psychological Association, Arlington, VA, USA, 2014.

[20] R. Chapman and L. Hesketh, "Behavioral phenotype of individuals with Down syndrome," *Mental Retardation and Developmental Disabilities*, vol. 6, no. 2, pp. 84–95, 2000.

[21] S. Buckley, G. Bird, B. Sacks, and A. Tamsin, "A comparison of mainstream and special education for teenagers with Down syndrome: Implications for parents and teachers," *Down Syndrome Research and Practice*, vol. 9, no. 3, pp. 54–67, 2006.

[22] E. Ruiz, *Programación Educativa para Escolares con Síndrome de Down*, Fundación Iberoamericana Down 21, Madrid, España, 2012.

[23] R. Hu, J. Feng, J. Lazar, and L. Kumin, "Investigating input technologies for children and young adults with Down syndrome," *Universal Access in the Information Society*, vol. 12, no. 1, pp. 89–104, 2013.

[24] J. Gomez, J. Torrado, and G. Montoro, "Using smartphones to assist people with Down syndrome in their labour training and integration: a case study," *Wireless Communications and Mobile Computing*, vol. 2017, article 5062371, 15 pages, 2017.

[25] D. Weschler, *Weschler Intelligent Test for Children (WISC) IV*, Pearson, New York City, NY, USA, 2005.

[26] Valpar International, *Valpar Work Samples Test*, Valpar International Corporation, Tucson, AZ, USA, 2014.

[27] Apple Computers, *Touches, Presses, and Gestures*, 2017, https://developer.apple.com/documentation/uikit/touches_presses_and_gestures.

[28] Google, *Using Touch Gestures*, 2017, https://developer.android.com/training/gestures/index.html.

[29] Google, *Material Design*, 2017, https://material.io/guidelines/patterns/gestures.html#.

[30] Apple Computers, "Take Advantage of 3D Touch," *Apple Computers*, vol. 1, no. 1, 2018, https://developer.apple.com/ios/3d-touch/.

[31] T. Tullis and B. Albert, *Measuring the User Experience: Collecting, Analyzing, and Presenting Usability Metrics*, Morgan Kaufmann, Waltham, MA, USA, 2013.

[32] E. Camargos and R. Maciel, "The importance of psychomotricity in children education," *Multidisciplinary Core Scientific Journal of Knowledge*, vol. 9, pp. 254–275, 2016.

[33] J. Durivage, *Educación, y Psicomotricidad*, Trillas, Mexico, 2005.

9

Vertical Indexing for Moving Objects in Multifloor Environments

Sultan Alamri ⓘ,[1] David Taniar,[2] and Kinh Nguyen[3]

[1]*College of Computing and Informatics, SEU, Riyadh, Saudi Arabia*
[2]*Clayton School of Information Technology, Monash University, Melbourne, VIC, Australia*
[3]*Department of Computer Science and Computer Engineering, La Trobe University, Melbourne, VIC, Australia*

Correspondence should be addressed to Sultan Alamri; salamri@scu.edu.sa

Academic Editor: Laurence T. Yang

The indexing and tracking of objects moving in indoor spaces has increasingly become an important area of research, which presents a fundamentally different challenge. There are two main reasons for why indoor should be treated as cellular space. Firstly, an indoor space has entities, such as rooms and walls, that constrain the movement of the moving objects. Secondly, the relevant notion of locations of an object is cell based rather than an exact Euclidean coordinate. As a solution, in our earlier works, we proposed a cell-based indexing structure, called the C-tree, for indexing objects moving in indoor space. In this paper, we extend the C-tree to solve another interesting problem. It can be observed that many indoor spaces (such as shopping centers) contain wings/sections. For such a space, there are queries for which the wing/section location of an object, rather than the cellular location, is the relevant answer (e.g., "the object is in the east wing"). In this paper, we propose a new index structure, called the GMI-tree ("GMI" stands for "Graph based Multidimensional Index"). The GMI-tree is based on two notions of distance, or equivalently, two notions of adjacency: one represents horizontal adjacency and the other represents vertical adjacency.

1. Introduction

Indoor environments represent a promising area for the indexing and querying of mobile/moving objects in spatial databases [1–4]. People conduct most of their day-to-day activities in indoor environments, such as entertaining, living, working, and shopping. Studies have shown that people spend around 80% of their lives indoors [2, 5–9].

In addition, indoor environments are rapidly becoming larger and more complex. For example, the Beijing subway is a rapid transit rail networks with 227 stations and passengers numbering in excess of 7 million daily. Consequently, the positioning and monitoring of mobile objects indoors on different floors have become an essential research field with many applications for the location of mobile objects, indoor multifloor wayfinding, and security [10–14].

Until now, a great deal of research has been devoted to the indexing, querying, and tracking of objects moving in outdoor spaces. Unfortunately, such works often cannot be applied to objects moving in indoor spaces [15]. Indoor spaces contain entities such as walls and doors which play an important role

in controlling and restricting the movement of an object in the environment. Also, the cells (e.g., rooms) which can contain objects are entities of primary interest in indexing and querying. For example, a query may be performed to locate object O_5; in an indoor space, the logical answer is the room/cell in which O_5 is residing (e.g., room/cell 313). In this case, the exact locations of the moving objects, in terms of the numerical values of their coordinates, are not important. That is, indoor space is not to be treated as Euclidean space or as a spatial road network. It is also relevant to note that indoor spaces are not compatible with GPS tracking because of the inaccuracy of GPS systems in indoor environments [8, 16–18]. Given these factors, the notion of position to be used for indoors is based on the notion of cell-based space (or cellular space). Consequently, the current moving object researches that are based on metric distribution cannot be applied to an indoor situation [19–23].

In light of the starkly different nature of indoor space, compared to outdoor space, a fundamental challenge is how to build a cell-based index that can efficiently serve the purpose of querying and tracking of objects moving in

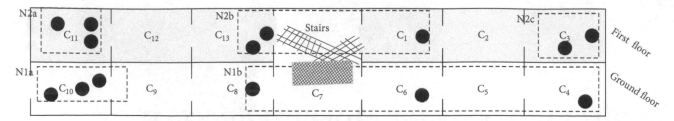

FIGURE 1: N2b and N1b are crossed-over nodes between the wings.

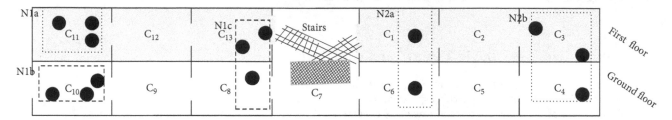

FIGURE 2: The moving objects are grouped in each wing.

indoor spaces. From a conceptual viewpoint, an indoor space can be regarded as a graph which consists of nodes (representing cells and rooms) and edges (representing connections between cells such as doors and stairways). Based on this model of indoor space, we propose a method for constructing the cell-based index, which is called the C-tree ("C" for "cell"). The work has been reported in [24]. The method for constructing the C-tree, together with associated concepts, will be described in Section 3.

In addition to our proposed solution to the fundamental problem described above, the C-tree can also be extended to provide a solution to another problem, which is the subject matter of this paper. Many queries can be raised in multifloor buildings which can be considered as multifloor queries regardless of the floor. Therefore, some queries can be raised such as "Where is object O_3?"; however, the exact location (in terms of cell) of the object may not be important at all, whereas the expected answer may be "north section/wing." Moreover, queries regarding the objects nearest to a certain lift can be considered as RNN queries in multifloor environments (detail with examples in Section 3). These types of queries raise the question whether grouping the moving objects vertically in addition to the traditional grouping (horizontally) can achieve efficiency of the indexing and querying processing. The challenge now is how to construct an index that is based on the primary location concept of cells while taking into account the secondary location concept of wing/section. Or, put simply, how can we build an index that can efficiently support queries regarding cells, but at the same time can support the wing queries and the multifloor RNN queries and pool queries?

As a solution, we proposed a mobile objects index structure called the GMI-tree ("GMI" stands for "Graph-based Multidimensional Index"), in which we extend the C-tree approach to account for more than one concept of adjacency (in the same or nearby cell and in the same wing/section). If the index structure is based solely on the cell-based distance (as treated in the previous

section), then it will require many verification steps in order to reach the targeted answer (in case of wing or multifloor RNN queries) (see Figure 1). This is obvious since, if the moving objects are grouped close to each other according to cell-based distance, then the index structures will need to check all the descending nodes on each floor individually, thereby incurring high access costs. In addition, it will cause many crossover nodes between the indoor areas of a building. That is, nodes might cross a wing to another in order to group the moving objects as in Figure 1, whereas in Figure 2 the objects are grouped in each wing without any crossover.

We call the new index "multidimensional" because, as will be seen in Section 4, our solution is based on two types of links: the usual "horizontal" links between the cells connected by doors (called the primary links) and the newly introduced "vertical" links which involve cells that are directly above or below one another (called the secondary links).

Our major contributions are as follows:

(i) We propose a model for representing indoor spaces.

(ii) Based on that model, we propose the C-tree as a fundamental indexing method for moving objects in indoor spaces.

(iii) We carry out experiments to thoroughly evaluate the C-tree approach.

(iv) We extend the basic indoor space model for multidimensional grouping (e.g., based on cells and wings) and identify typical situations where such a model can be usefully applied.

(v) We develop a mobile object index structure for multidimensional grouping, the GMI-tree.

(vi) Under a simulation environment, we conduct experiments in order to evaluate the proposed index structure of the GMI-tree by studying the costs of construction and insertion, and query performances.

The rest of the paper is organized as follows. Section 2 presents works related to the indexing of moving objects. Section 3 describes and illustrates the basic method for indexing objects moving in indoor spaces: the C-tree. Section 4 presents the structure and construction of the GMI-Tree, our proposed solution for indexing objects moving in indoor spaces which involves multidimensional grouping. Section 5 presents the results of a performance evaluation of the proposed GMI-tree. Section 6 concludes the paper and suggests possible directions for future work.

2. Related Work

As mentioned above, since the development of indoor positioning systems, the importance of indexing and querying mobile objects in indoor environments has become more significant. A number of works have been published in this area, although to the best of our knowledge, these are few in number.

The earliest paper on this topic is [7]. They proposed two types of index trees: RTR-tree and TP2R-tree. Both are based on *the positions of RFID readers* that are installed in the indoor environments. The RTR-tree is based on the R-tree method of node organization. The RTR-tree includes the form (MBR and recordID), where MBR is identified by recordID. However, the trajectories are treated as line segments in the indoor space (see Figure 3). The insertion of new index entries into an RTR-tree is carried out similar to the R-tree; however, the calculation of the MBR area will be based on the RFID readers, where the calculation of the area of an MBR in the RTR-tree is Area = (readerID$_{max}$–readerID$_{min}$) $*$ ($t<$ $t>$) [7]. In order to deal with a range query, the search will be conducted in the same way as for the R-tree; however, instead of searching on Euclidean space, the search will be done on a set of RFID readers.

On the other hand, the TP2R-tree changes the trajectories of data into a set of points in the indoor space which is different from the RTR-tree. The TP2R-tree can obtain fewer node accesses since it handles the case overflow nodes by the time extents. Here, the leaf node in the TP2R-tree includes the form (MBR, Δt, and recordID), where Δt is a time parameter that determines the duration of the continuous reading by the same reader. Note that the TP2R-tree has a better node organization than the RTR-tree does. A TP2R-tree is illustrated in Figure 4.

In [25], Lu et al. proposed a distance-aware indoor space structure which integrates indoor space distances. This structure provides an algorithm for *calculating the indoor space distances*. Indoor space rooms are connected by doors; therefore, a door connects two adjacent rooms (partitions). This distance-aware model proposed topology information mappings which basically map the indoor floor partitions and doors. Here, there are two concepts: first, D2P(D2Pdi) which can be unidirectional and bidirectional, if |D2P(di)| = 1 is considered as unidirectional, whereas |D2P(di)| = 2 is considered as bidirectional.

In our view, the three methods make some use of the characteristics of indoor space and associated tracking

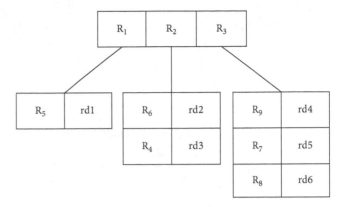

FIGURE 3: Example of the RTR-tree.

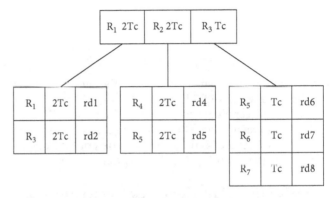

FIGURE 4: Example of the TP2R-tree.

technologies. However, there are important characteristics that are not taken into account. An indoor space has rooms, doors, walls, corridors, staircase, floors, etc. At least at a high level of abstraction, it consists of a set of cells (rooms, corridors, etc.) and connections between them (doors and staircases). Our idea is to build index trees that are based on these essential characteristics.

Therefore, we proposed the C-tree which is efficient for calculating the moving objects in 2D space [24]. The C-tree considers the uniqueness of the indoor space which contains partitions, walls, doors, and corridors. The C-tree represents indoor space as a connectivity graph. It also proposes an indexing method that is based on the concepts of cells and connections between cells. We call it a C-tree, "C" for "cell." The basic methodology for the C-tree is to construct the moving objects in the indoor floor as a horizontal grouping, whereby moving objects will be grouped with its adjacent moving objects in the same cell or in adjacent cells.

However, the methodology used for the C-tree can be efficient in some indoor queries such as positioning queries or Knn. However, in the case of some buildings, the importance of the position of mobile objects depends on the structure of the building. In some buildings (such as shopping centers), the positioning queries can be obtained by wings/sections of the building. In these cases, the locationing of any moving objects based on their wing location might be more useful to the user. Therefore, we proposed the GMI-tree in order to group moving objects both horizontally and vertically. Hence, we have a multidimensional

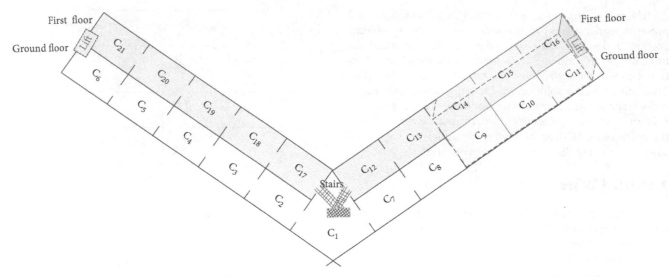

FIGURE 5: Example of an indoor space.

connectivity graph which considers the moving objects construction in a multidimensional way. Note that the concepts and techniques for C-Tree will be essential for the method/approach which is the subject of this work. Therefore, we devote Section 3 below to describe the method applied for the construction of the C-tree.

3. Basic Method for Indexing Object Moving in Indoor Space

In this section, we describe and illustrate our proposed method for indexing objects moving in indoor spaces. The outcome of the method is the C-tree, the indexing structure. Taking an example of an indoor space, we show

(i) how to convert the given indoor space into a connectivity graph;

(ii) how to derive the connectivity tree from the connectivity graph;

(iii) how to construct the C-tree.

3.1. Connectivity Graph. Consider the indoor space (a building) shown in Figure 5. An indoor space typically contains elements such as *rooms, doors, corridors, floors, stairs, elevators,* and *pathways* between buildings.

Our first step is to map the domain concepts (such as room, door, etc.) into the modeling concepts of cells and connections. The way to perform the mapping is summarized in Table 1. The result of the mapping is a *connectivity graph*, which represents the given indoor space (see Figure 6). More specifically, the graph is an *undirected graph* of *cells (nodes)* and *edges (connections)*, which, in addition, is a *connected graph* (i.e., there is a path between every pair of nodes).

3.2. Connectivity Tree. Given a connectivity graph representing an indoor space, the next step is to construct the connectivity tree, which is done as follows:

TABLE 1: Mapping domain concepts to modeling concepts.

Domain concepts	Modeling concepts
Room	A cell
Door	An edge
Corridor	One or more cells with one or more edges
Stair	One or more cells with one or more edges
Elevator	One cell with several edges
Pathway	One or more cells with several edges

(1) First we select one cell as the default cell of the connectivity graph. For our example, we choose cell C_1 in Figure 6.

(2) We then construct a spanning tree by performing a breadth-first search on the connectivity graph, starting from the default cell.

(3) We then order the siblings (nodes at the same level) of the spanning tree by the number of descendants. Those with more descendants are said to be higher. For siblings with the same number of descendants, we select an arbitrary order. In this way, all the nodes in the trees are ordered.

We refer to the tree, thus ordered, as the connectivity tree.

Example: for the indoor connectivity in Figure 6, we get the connectivity tree shown in Figure 7. C_1 is on level 1: it is the highest node according to our definition. On level 2, we have cells C_{12}, C_{17}, C_2, and C_7. The connectivity tree will be used as the major *input* for the construction of our C-tree.

Note that the connectivity tree not only represents the connections between the cells but also establishes an ordering of the cells. This ordering of cells is of fundamental importance to the construction of the C-tree. Formally, given a connectivity graph G and a default cell C, a connectivity tree T is a tree such that

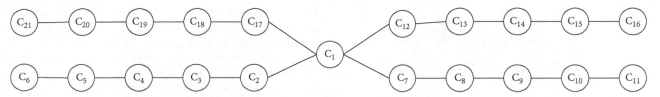

FIGURE 6: Connectivity graph for the indoor space of Figure 5.

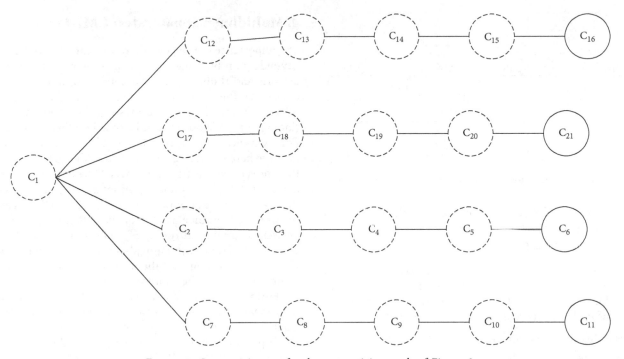

FIGURE 7: Connectivity tree for the connectivity graph of Figure 6.

(1) T is obtained as a spanning tree by performing a breadth-first search on G from default cell C;

(2) there is a function position that maps each cell (node) in the tree to a number such that

$$\forall C_i, C_j \in \text{Cells}, \tag{1}$$

$$\text{position}(C_i) > \text{position}(C_j) \Rightarrow \text{level}(C_i) < \text{level}(C_j) \lor, \tag{2}$$

$$\left(\text{level}(C_i) = \text{level}(C_j) \land \text{descendants}(C_i) \geq \text{descendants}(C_j)\right), \tag{3}$$

where level is the level of the cell on the tree and descendants is the number of descendants of the cell. Figure 7 shows an example of the connectivity tree.

Before describing the index construction algorithm, we define three terms that, though simple in their definitions, are very useful in showing how the index construction algorithm works.

3.2.1. Definition 1: Given a Connectivity Tree

(a) A node is an *expanding node* if it is a nonleaf node.

(b) A node is a *nonexpanding node* if it is a leaf node.

(c) The *expanding node of a node* C is C itself if C is an expansion node; otherwise, it is the parent of C.

Example: In Figure 7, all the expanding nodes are drawn as broken circles. The rest of the nodes are nonexpanding circles.

3.3. C-Tree.

The construction of the C-tree uses as inputs: (a) a connectivity tree and (b) a set of objects which are distributed into the cells. The output is a C-tree, which has nonleaf nodes and leaf nodes, whose structures are described below.

A *nonleaf node* has two parts: (a) PTRs, which are pointers to the children of the node, and (b) the range of expanding cells, denoted by RC. The RC of a nonleaf node are the highest and the lowest expanding cells in that nonleaf node. Consider, for example, the N2 nonleaf node of the C-tree in Figure 8. Its RC is determined as follows:

(1) This node, regarded as a subtree, contains four objects O_6, O_7, O_8, and O_9.

(2) They are in cells C_9 and C_{11}.

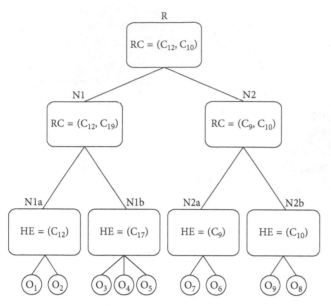

FIGURE 8: C-tree after inserting objects O_1, O_2, O_3, O_4,..., O_9.

(3) The expanding cells of those cells are C_9 (the highest) and C_{10} (the lowest).

(4) Hence, RC = (C_9, C_{10}).

A *leaf node* of the C-tree has two parts: (a) PTRs, which are pointers to the objects it contains, and (b) HE, which stands for "highest expanding cell." Consider, for example, the N1b leaf node in Figure 8. Its HE is determined as follows:

(1) This node contains objects O_3, O_4, and O_5.

(2) They are in cells C_{17} (the highest) and C_{19} (the lowest).

(3) Hence, HE = C_{17}.

We now illustrate how the C-tree is constructed. Consider, as an example, Figure 9, which shows a number of objects occupying the cells in the indoor space. We will be inserting the objects O_1, O_2, O_3, O_5, O_4, O_6, O_7, O_8, and O_9 into the C-tree in that listed order. We also assume that the C-tree is of order 3; that is, each node can have a maximum of three child nodes or objects.

Initially, the C-tree is empty. When inserting objects O_1 and O_2, the C-tree is as shown in Figure 10(a). It has one node, represented by a rectangle. The object, represented by a circle, is considered to be part of the node. The node has HE = (C_{12}).

The insertion of objects O_3 and O_5 requires splitting the node. The splitting is carried out as follows. First, we insert O_3 and O_5 into the root node (conceptually). This causes an overflow: there are more than the maximum of three objects. The node has to be split. The new objects are grouped together. Our strategy is to group the inserted object with the *nearest* object. In this case, O_3 and O_5 are the objects nearest to each other since they are in the same cell. With this grouping choice and using the splitting procedure of B+tree, we get the C-tree in Figure 10(b).

The insertion of object O_4, which is in cell C_{19}, requires us to move down the tree because the root has two children.

For this purpose, we examine the HEs of the children which are the expanding nodes C_{12} and C_{17}. The strategy is to go with the *nearest* expanding node. In this example, we chose C_{17} since it is the nearest (two hops away). Note that the RC of the root node is now updated to be C_{12} which is the highest and C_{19} which is the lowest (see Figure 10(c)). This procedure will continue to insert the remaining objects to produce the final C-tree as shown in Figure 8.

4. Multidimensional Index: GMI-Trees

The importance of the position of moving objects can differ depending on building structures. Some buildings (such as airports and shopping centers) contain wings/sections that determine the success or otherwise of the positioning queries. From observation, in some buildings, the positioning of mobile objects can be based on their section [13]. For example, "Where is object O_9?" The accuracy of the position here is not important, because the query can obtain the answer "east wing." Moreover, here we note that the accuracy of the floor is not important in this case. Not only is the exact room/cell not needed but it could also be useless to the user. For instance, for the query "Where is object O_9?", answers such as "cell/room 15" could not be useful to the user who has no information about where cell 15 is located. However, answering with the wing location (e.g., it is in the south wing) might be more useful to the user.

Furthermore, the main reason for building a multidimensional indoor index is to obtain an index that can efficiently support queries regarding cells but at the same time can support the multifloor queries such as the wing queries and the multifloor RNN queries and pool queries. Wing queries have been explained in detail previously. The multifloor RNN queries, usually in indoor spaces, take the interests of a certain item then locate the objects that are nearest to it. For example, we may want the location of a moving object that is the nearest to Lift A. Here, the floor is not important, since a lift is basically located on all floors. Therefore, grouping the moving objects on both the same floor and on the floor above can obtain an efficient result for this type of query (the multifloor RNN queries). Another important query that can take advantage of our approach is a pool query. This type of query usually occurs in a multifloor indoor space; hence, it is a range query that intersects with many cells on different floors in order to retrieve the moving objects within that range. For example, in Figure 5, the dash lines show the retrieval of objects that are located within that range, which is shaped like a pool. Vertical and horizontal grouping is appropriate for all these queries and others that have moving objects in a multifloor environment, regardless of the floor(s) on which they are located.

4.1. Multidimensional Indoor Spaces. Our task, in this context, can be stated as follows: in addition to the primary queries that are based on cells as locations, how can we support multifloor queries such as wing queries, or multifloor RNN (for simplicity, we will use the term "wing" to include "section" and similar entities).

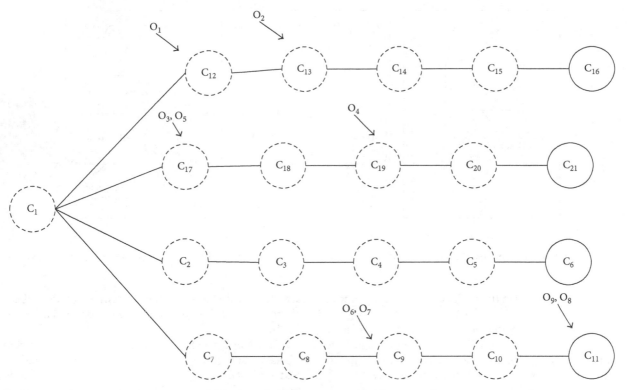

FIGURE 9: Occupancy of objects in the indoor space cells (shown on the connectivity tree).

Considering wing queries as an example, several issues arise. How are we to represent, or capture, the concept of "wing" in our model?

We will address this issue first. In doing this, we will consider, as an example, an indoor space which is clearly applicable to the queries.

Consider the indoor space in Figure 5. Observe that it has two wings connected by a single node and each of the wings has rooms on more than one floor.

For a multifloor building with wings, our proposed solution is introduced as an additional edge. Thus, the cells can be connected by primary edges and secondary edges. The primary edges are the same as those in the previous section: two cells (rooms) are connected by a primary edge if there is a door or staircase between them. The secondary edges, in this case, represent the "is_above" relationship. If two cells are on two adjacent floors and one is partly above another, we say that they are connected by a secondary edge. In our example (see Figure 5), cell C_{20} is directly above cell C_5; hence, there is a secondary edge between them. Recall that we will use the term *"multidimensional"* to refer to the existence of more than one type of edge.

4.2. Indoor Multidimensional Connectivity Graph.

Given a multidimensional indoor space, that is, one for which we can conceive of two or more types of edges, our first step is to convert it into a multidimensional (MD) connectivity graph. Figure 11 shows the MD connectivity graph that represents the indoor space in Figure 5. The graph has primary edges, shown by solid lines between the cells, and secondary edges, shown by dotted lines. The primary

edges are derived from the indoor space (Figure 5) as described in the previous section (see Table 1). The secondary edges between two cells are obtained by virtue of one cell being directly above the other. Note that the secondary "is_above" connection refers to the cells that are located above each other. This includes the case where a cell is connected vertically with more than one cell (vertically overlapped); the "is_above" connectivity will be made to all the overlapped cells regardless of the extent of the overlap.

4.3. MD Connectivity Tree.

The MD connectivity tree is constructed from the MD connectivity graph by *ignoring* the secondary edges and applying the same procedure as described in Section 3 for constructing the basic (or 1D) connectivity tree. Figure 7 shows a connectivity tree for the MD connectivity graph shown in Figure 11. This connectivity tree on the surface looks exactly like a one-dimensional connectivity tree. Furthermore, it will play a similar role in the construction of the MD index tree. However, when using that connectivity tree in the index tree construction, we will take into account the secondary edges, which will have an effect on what we regard as the overall distance between pairs of cells (as given in Definition 2 below).

4.4. Constructing the Multidimensional Index Tree.

The construction of an MD-tree is essentially the process of inserting an object into an existing MD-tree. This task has two major subtasks: (i) in which the new object is to be inserted and (ii) in the case where we need to split a node,

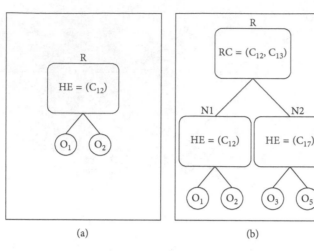
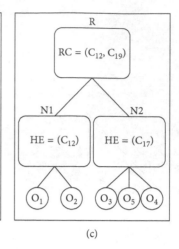

FIGURE 10: Index tree steps for inserting (O_1, O_2), (O_3, O_5), and O_4. (a) Inserting O_1 and O_2. (b) Inserting O_3 and O_5. (c) Inserting O_4.

choosing which objects (in the node) are to be grouped with the new object.

For navigation down the tree, we use exactly the same strategy as we did in Section 3. That is, suppose we need to insert an object occupying the cell C_{new}, we examine the RC and HE of the nodes, and at any particular stage,

(i) if possible, we choose the nonleaf node whose RC covers C_{new} according to the MD connectivity tree and which has an RC cell (either a lower bound or the upper bound) that is closest to C_{new};

(ii) otherwise, we examine the RC and HE of all the candidate nodes and choose the node that has an RC or HE cell which is closest to the cell C_{new}.

However, the distance between any pair of cells is now *modified* according to the definition below.

4.4.1. Definition 2. Let $d_P(x, y)$ and $d_S(x, y)$ denote the primary and secondary distances between cells x and y based on the number of primary edges and secondary edges between them. The distance between x and y is defined to be

$$d(x, y) = \begin{cases} d_P(x, y), & if \quad d_P(x, y) \le d_S(x, y) \\ d_S(x, y) & \text{otherwise.} \end{cases} \quad (4)$$

Figure 12 shows the adjacency order of C_1 horizontally and vertically.

Apart from the above modification for calculating the distance between cells, the rest of the algorithm is the same as for the basic 1-dimensional case.

The algorithm for constructing the GMI-tree is given in Algorithm 1 and Algorithm 2.

4.5. MD Indexing-Applicable Indoor Spaces. In principle, we can apply the MD index construction procedure to any indoor space that is represented by an MD connectivity; that is, it has two types of edges. However, in practice, as will be seen in Section 5, the types of indoor spaces to which the MD procedure can be applied with desirable benefits

are those with certain characteristics. To describe those characteristics, the notion of *cut node* defined below will be useful.

Consider a graph G of nodes (cells) and edges. Suppose we have a subset S of node G such that when we remove the nodes in S from the graph, what we get is a number of unconnected subgraphs. Then, we say that S is a set of cut nodes and each element of S is called a cut node. Formally, we have the following definition.

4.5.1. Definition 3. (Graph with Cut Nodes): Let G(Cells, Edges) be a connected undirected graph. Let S be a subset of nodes in cells. Then, we say that S is a set of cut nodes if the graph $G' = (\text{Cells}', \text{Edges}')$ is an unconnected graph, where

(i) Cells$'$ = Cells\S;

(ii) Edges$'$ = $\{e \in \text{Edges} : \forall x \in S, x \notin e\}$.

(Note that an edge e is an unordered pair (i.e., a set) of two nodes.)

In addition, in practice, we also choose the set S of cut nodes that is minimal in the sense that if we remove any node from S, we would get a smaller number of islands.

Intuitively, and as will be seen in Section 5, the types of indoor spaces to which the MD procedure can be applied with desirable benefits are those with the following properties:

(1) It is a graph with cut nodes.

(2) The graph after the removal of cut nodes forms a number of islands (isolated subgraphs) of reasonable sizes.

(3) There are no secondary edges among the cut nodes (this is reasonable because cut nodes should not be part of a wing: they separate wings from one another).

(4) There are no secondary edges between nodes that belong to different islands (secondary edges are confined to separate islands).

Under those conditions, we can formalize the concept of a wing as follows.

Insert_Object /* To Insert an object into the current index tree. The tree is of order $M =$ maximum number of child nodes */
Data: The connectivity tree CONNECT_TREE; the Current index tree
INDEX_TREE: the object to be inserted OBJECT; the cell that is occupied by the object,
OBJECT_CELL **Result:** The updated index tree.
1: /* Find the leaf node to insert the new object */
2: Let $p =$ root of INDEX_TREE;
3: **while** p is not a leaf node **do**
4: | Construct the set EXPANDING_CELLS from all the RC and LE of the children of p;
5: | Choose from EXPANDING_CELLS, a cell NEAREST_CELL that is nearest to the OBJECT_CELL, according to
$d(x, y) =$ IF $d_P(x, y) \leq d_S(x, y)$ THEN $d_P(x, y)$ ELSE $d_S(x, y)$;
6: | Choose a node Node that contains NEAREST_CELL as a bound of RC or LE;
7: | Let $p =$ Node;
8: **endwhile**
9: /*Insert the object into the leaf node p */
10: **if** Node p is not full, i.e., number of objects is less than m **then**
11: | /* NOTE: Add this condition to definition of Index Tree */
12: | Insert OBJECT into node p;
13: **else**
14: | Choose a set of $\lceil \frac{M}{2} \rceil$ existing objects in the node p, that are nearest to OBJECT_CELL.
15: | Call this set GROUPED_CELLS;
16: | Insert OBJECT and GROUPED_CELLS into a sibling node of p;
17: | Split the node, using the standard node-splitting procedure for B+Tree, and insert OBJECT and GROUPED_CELLS into a sibling node of p;
18: **endif**
19: For nodes that contain new objects, update RC and LE

ALGORITHM 1

CONSTRUCT_INDEX_TREE /* To construct an index tree for a set of objects */
Data: The connectivity tree CONNECT_TREE; set of objects OBJECTS; function
OCCUPIES : OBJECTS®CELLS **Result:** The index tree.
1: Let Index_Tree = ∅;
2: each object O_i of OBJECTS
3: | Call algorithm INSERT_OBJECT to insert O_i into INDEX_TREE;
4: **endfor**
5: **return** *Index_Tree*;

ALGORITHM 2

4.5.2. Definition 4. Assuming the context of the conditions above, two cells X and Y are in the same wing if and only if they belong to the same island.

Examples: Figure 11, which is the connectivity graph of an indoor space (Figure 5), shows that C_1 is the cut node: by removing C_1, we will have two unconnected subgraphs. Other examples of the cut nodes are shown in Figure 13.

As another example, Figure 14 shows a set of moving objects $O_1, O_2, \ldots, O_{10}$ in a multifloor indoor space. The GMI-tree will group the objects based on their section/wing as follows: The GMI-tree begins by grouping the moving objects that are located in the same cell and then starts to evaluate the adjacency levels in case of overflow or underflow. Therefore, O_4 is grouped with the above cell entity which is O_3. Figure 14 shows the GMI-tree of objects $O_1, O_2, \ldots, O_{10}$. Note that the objects in the west wing are grouped together ($O_1, O_2, O_3,$ and O_4) and east wing has the objects ($O_5, O_6, O_7, O_8, O_9,$ and O_{10}). In this grouping technique, the distance will be based on the number of the

hops between the cells (on both horizontal and vertical adjacent levels). Consequently, with this resulting index, queries that concern the objects' wing locations are processed easily with a lower access cost.

Regarding the search operation efficiency, the GMI-tree is very similar to the R-tree [1, 6] in three crucial aspects: (a) *the tree structure*, which is B-tree like; (b) *the tree construction process* in which the nodes are split in a similar manner to those of the B-tree; and (c) *the search procedure* (from the root, the search examines the children of a node N if the searched object is "contained" in the RC of N (for GMI-tree) or the MBB (for R-tree)). Consequently, similar to the R-tree, the worst case complexity of a GMI-tree search is $O(n)$ due to overlapping RCs, and the average case complexity can be expected to be $O(\log(n))$. In addition, for a given connectivity graph, different choices of the default cell can result in connectivity trees of different shapes. This presents the possibility of performing a pre-tree-construction exploration to find a connectivity tree that is wide and shallow

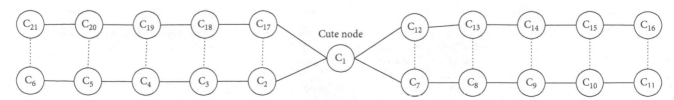

FIGURE 11: MD connectivity graph for the indoor space in Figure 5.

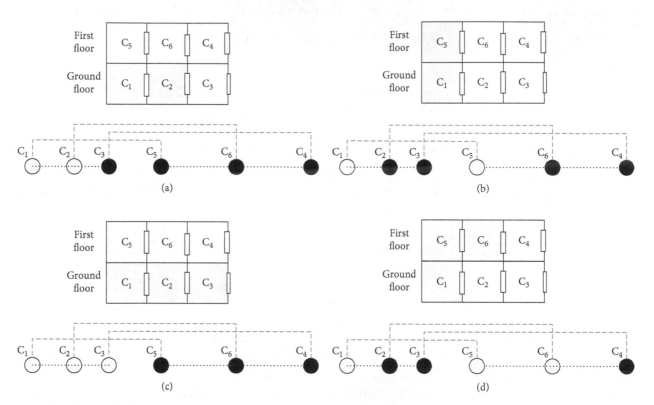

FIGURE 12: The adjacency levels of C_1. (a) First level adjacent of C_1. (b) Vertical level adjacent of C_1. (c) Second level adjacent of C_1. (d) Second vertical level adjacent of C_1.

because such a connectivity tree will tend to produce a GMI-tree with fewer overlapping RCs. We can also note that the cell connections, which are fixed for an indoor space, can be stored in an adjacency matrix and can be looked up very quickly for tree construction and querying.

5. Experimental Results and Performance Analysis

In this section, under a simulation environment, we present the results of experiments that have been conducted in order to evaluate the proposed index structure, the Graph-based Multidimensional Indoor-tree (GMI-tree). We compared this new structure with the Basic Index (C-tree) (which only groups the moving objects horizontally based on a single type of edge) [24]. The experiment was carried out on an Intel Core i5-2400S processor 2.50 GHz PC, with 4 GB of RAM running on 64-bit Windows 7 Professional. The maximum number of entries per node is $M = 80$ and the minimum is $m = 40$. The data structure was implemented in Java. The data set size ranged from 20 to 5000 moving objects in multifloor indoor

spaces. We used synthetic datasets of moving objects due to the lack of real data for indoor environments. In the experiment, we used a real case of a 20-cell indoor space.

We will focus on the following features. First, we aim to compare the capacities of the GMI-tree and the basic C-tree in grouping the moving objects according to their primary distance and secondary distance. The grouping on primary distance is referred to as "horizontal grouping," and the grouping on secondary distance, "vertical grouping." Second, we compare the number of the crossover nodes between the two index trees. A crossover node is the one that groups together objects from different wings of the indoor space. Crossovers are regarded as undesirable "false hits." Third, we compare the costs of construction of the GMI-tree and the C-tree. And finally, we compare their insert and search performances. For all operations, the execution time was measured. Each operation was performed five times, and the average was calculated.

Figure 15(a) shows the number of nodes of the GMI-tree and the C-tree that group together the objects that are in close proximity according to their primary distance

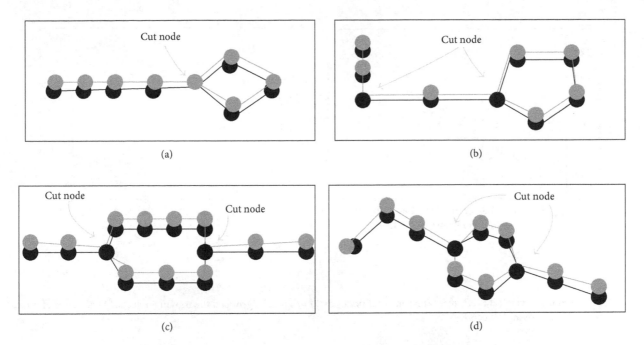

FIGURE 13: Cut nodes or articulation nodes.

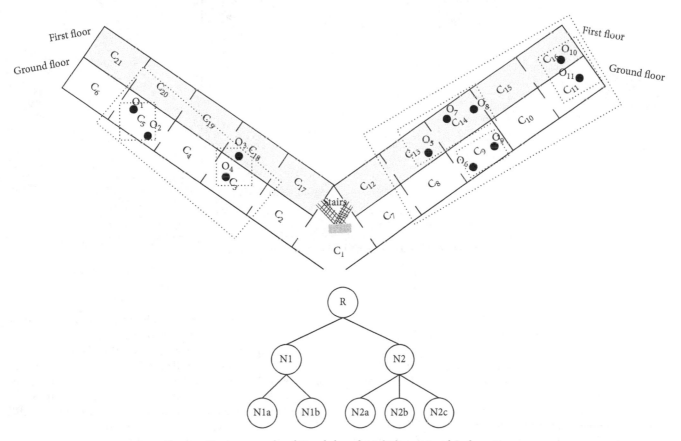

FIGURE 14: An example of Graph-based Multidimensional Indoor-tree.

("horizontal grouping"). The result shows that the GMI-tree (which is based on both the primary and secondary distances) performs virtually as well as the basic C-tree (which is based on the primary distance only). This result is very encouraging because we would want to maintain good efficiency for the primary horizontal grouping. Figure 15(b) shows the number of nodes that the GMI-tree and the C-tree group the moving objects vertically; that is, the number of

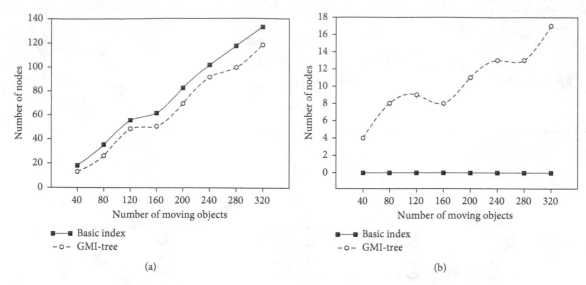

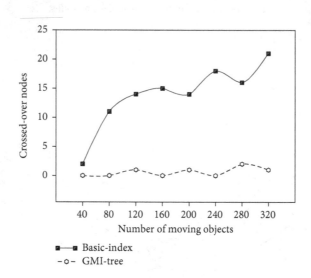

FIGURE 15: Horizontal and vertical grouping. (a) Number of nodes that horizontally grouped the moving objects. (b) Number of nodes that vertically grouped the moving objects.

FIGURE 16: Crossed-over nodes between the building wings.

nodes which group together the objects that are close to one another according to their secondary (vertical) distances. The result shows that the GMI-tree performs clearly better than the basic C-tree in this respect. Though expected, this result proves the decidedly positive effect of the vertical grouping of the GMI-tree.

Taking both results together, they clearly illustrate that the GMI-tree has been successful in grouping the moving objects both horizontally and vertically. Consequently, it successfully groups objects that are close to each other in each of the wings of this indoor space with a cut node. Moreover, Figure 16 compares the crossover nodes of the GMI-tree with those of the basic C-tree. The crossover nodes are those that group together objects from the two different wings of the indoor space. The result shows that the GMI-tree

groups the moving objects in each wing with a significantly very low crossover between the wings of the building.

Furthermore, here we investigate the measurement of the tree construction in both the R-tree and the proposed GMI-tree. The TP2R or RTR trees basically used R-tree through RFID readers. As explained in Section 2, the TP2R or RTR trees have a recordID on which the area of the MBR will be based. Here, the criteria are different from our prospective. They are entirely based on RFID in order to control the area of the MBRs. Therefore, we will not compare our work with TP2R or RTR trees, although we compare it with their baseline which is R-tree which similarly uses the Euclidean distance to group the moving objects. Here, we calculate the false hits of the mobile objects in an indoor environment for both the GMI-tree and the R-tree in order

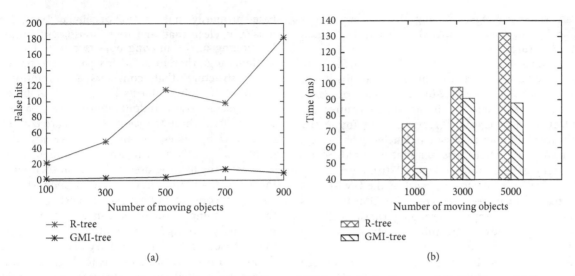

(a)

(b)

FIGURE 17: Metric performance (R-tree) compared with the GMI-tree. (a) False hits in the R tree and the GMI-tree. (b) Insert costs for the R-tree and the GMI-tree.

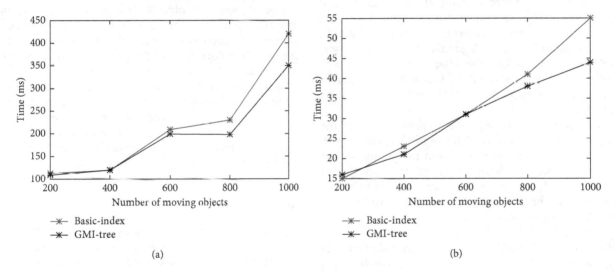

(a)

(b)

FIGURE 18: Construction and insert costs. (a) Construction cost. (b) Insert cost.

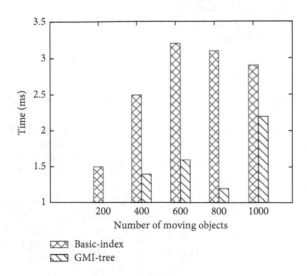

FIGURE 19: Search costs.

to illustrate the advantage of using the cell-based data structure in indoor space compared with any Euclidean-based data structures.

Figure 17(a) shows that many objects have been forced to be grouped based on the Euclidean distance when the R-tree data structure is used. However, in indoor environments, there are many walls and partitions which control the movement of moving objects. Therefore, using any metric index structures in indoor may lead to deficiency of the data structure through the many false hits that occurred. Moreover, the insert costs are shown in Figure 17(b). We notice in Figure 17(b) that in most cases the cost of the GMI-tree is lower than that of the R-tree insert costs. The GMI-tree takes into account the two ways of grouping (horizontally or vertically) which give the data structure more options, thereby reducing the cost significantly.

As the next objective in our experiment, we compared the construction costs and the insert costs of the GMI-tree and the C-tree. The result is shown in Figures 18(a) and 18(b). As we can note from the graph, the construction cost for the GMI-tree is no different from that of the Basic Index. The basic point here is that with the new method of indexing the mobile objects on the basis of two links of the indoor graph, we find that construction is still good. In fact, in most cases, the construction costs and the insert costs of the GMI-tree are less than those of the Basic Index. For example, in Figure 18(a), for 800 objects, the GMI-tree is decreased by around 28%.

As the last result to be reported here, we compared the search performance of the GMI-tree and the basic C-tree. The result is shown in Figure 19. From the graph, we can observe a significant improvement in the new index structure for all density cases. The improvement in search performance can be explained thus: In the GMI-tree, the moving objects are separately grouped based on their section through two links of the connectivity tree which makes the index tree more flexible and less costly. For example, Figure 19 shows that in the case of 600 densities, the search cost is reduced by over 44.

The experimental results clearly show that the newly proposed index structure, the Graph-based Multidimensional Indoor-tree, can successfully produce a reliable, robust, cost-effective, and query-efficient index for multifloor indoor spaces.

6. Conclusion and Future Work

This paper addresses the challenge of indexing moving objects as a multidimensional grouping in multifloor indoor environments. It is clear that the exact positions of objects moving about indoors are often not needed and cannot be regarded as a primary characteristic. The indoor environments are related to the symbolic notion of cellular space (or cell-based space), which contains restriction entities (e.g., walls) that play important roles in restricting an object's movements. Hence, the indoors locationing is

based primarily on the notion of cellular space. In addition, it is also clear that in some interiors of buildings, the locationing of the moving objects can be based on their section/wing. Therefore, in this paper, we present a new index structure that considers the multidimensional grouping of mobile objects in a multifloor indoor space. More specifically, the indoor environment is a connectivity environment where the rooms/venues are connected with each other by doors; therefore, we take advantage of the graph that results from this primary indoor connectivity. We group the moving objects based on their adjacency on the same floor and in the same section (based on the adjacency/connectivity between the cells) and extend that to the grouping of the objects in each section as multidimensional grouping for the multilevel via a distance metric that is based on both the primary distance and secondary distance. The other basic idea is to determine the types of indoor spaces that can be advantageously considered for multidimensional grouping.

This work can be extended in several directions. First, the temporal aspects of objects moving in indoors are an important factor. The moving objects are expected to be more dynamic in corridors or on stairs, but more stabilized in a room. Therefore, the indexing of moving objects based on their temporal stabilization is an interesting area of study (considering vertical transits such as stairs). Another avenue of future work is the consideration of the data structure of moving objects with certain pattern movements in the indoor environment buildings. Thus, we aim to extend our index structure to involve certain movement patterns of moving objects in indoor environments.

References

[1] S. Alamri, D. Taniar, M. Safar, and H. Al-Khalidi, "A connectivity index for moving objects in an indoor cellular space," *Personal and Ubiquitous Computing*, vol. 15, no. 2, pp. 287–301, 2013.

[2] W. Yuan and M. Schneider, "Supporting continuous range queries in indoor space," in *Proceedings of the 2010 Eleventh International Conference on Mobile Data Management, MDM'10*, pp. 209–214, IEEE Computer Society, Washington, DC, USA, 2010.

[3] S. Alamri, "Indexing and querying moving objects in indoor spaces," in *Proceedings of the 2013 IEEE 29th International Conference on Data Engineering Workshops (ICDEW)*, pp. 318–321, IEEE Computer Society, Los Alamitos, CA, USA, 2013.

[4] T. Abeywickrama, M. Aamir Cheema, and D. Taniar, "k-nearest neighbors on road networks: a journey in experimentation and in-memory implementation," *Proceedings of the VLDB Endowment (PVLDB)*, vol. 9, no. 6, pp. 492–503, 2016.

[5] D. Lin, *Indexing and querying moving objects databases [Ph.D. Thesis]*, National University of Singapore, Singapore, 2006.

[6] S. Alamri, D. Taniar, M. Safar, and H. Al-Khalidi, "Spatiotemporal indexing for moving objects in an indoor cellular space," *Neurocomputing*, vol. 122, pp. 70–78, 2013.

[7] C. Jensen, H. Lu, and B. Yang, "Indexing the trajectories of moving objects in symbolic indoor space," in *Advances in Spatial and Temporal Databases Lecture Notes in Computer Science*, N. Mamoulis, T. Seidl, T. Pedersen, K. Torp, and I. Assent, Eds., vol. 5644, pp. 208–227, Springer, Berlin, Germany, 2009.

[8] M. Muñoz-Organero, P. J. Muñoz Merino, and C. Delgado Kloos, "Using bluetooth to implement a pervasive indoor positioning system with minimal requirements at the application level," *Mobile Information Systems*, vol. 8, no. 1, pp. 73–82, 2012.

[9] D. Sidlauskas, S. Saltenis, and C. S. Jensen, "Processing of extreme moving-object update and query workloads in main memory," *The VLDB Journal: The International Journal on Very Large Data Bases*, vol. 23, no. 5, pp. 817–841, 2014.

[10] Y. Li, H. Chen, R. Xie, and J. Z. Wang, "Bgn: a novel scatternet formation algorithm for bluetooth-based sensor networks," *Mobile Information Systems*, vol. 7, no. 2, pp. 93–106, 2011.

[11] H. Zhou, S. Xu, D. Ren, C. Huang, and H. Zhang, "Analysis of event-driven warning message propagation in vehicular ad hoc networks," *Ad Hoc Networks*, vol. 55, pp. 87–96, 2017.

[12] T. A. Dionti, K. M. Adhinugraha, and S. M. Alamri, "Interbuilding routing approach for indoor environment," in *Proceedings of the International Conference on Computational Science and Its Applications*, pp. 247–260, Springer, Cham, Switzerland, 2017.

[13] S. Alamri, D. Taniar, and M. Safar, "A taxonomy for moving object queries in spatial databases," *Future Generation Computer Systems*, vol. 37, pp. 232–242, 2014.

[14] K. Raptopoulou, A. N. Papadopoulos, and Y. Manolopoulos, "Fast nearest-neighbor query processing in moving-object databases," *Geoinformatica*, vol. 7, no. 2, pp. 113–137, 2003.

[15] S. Alamri, D. Taniar, M. Safarb, and H. Al-Khalidi, "Tracking moving objects using topographical indexing," *Concurrency and Computation: Practice and Experience*, vol. 27, no. 8, pp. 1951–1965, 2015.

[16] Q. Zhang, L. T. Yang, X. Liu, Z. Chen, and P. Li, "A tucker deep computation model for mobile multimedia feature learning," *ACM Transactions on Multimedia Computing, Communications, and Applications*, vol. 13, no. 3s, pp. 1–18, 2017.

[17] J.-W Chang, J.-H. Um, and W.-C. LeeP, "A new trajectory indexing scheme for moving objects on road networks," *Flexible and Efficient Information Handling*, vol. 4042 of Lecture Notes in Computer Science, pp. 291–294, Springer, Berlin, Germany, 2006.

[18] D. Wu, B. Choi, J. Xu, and C. S. Jensen, "Authentication of moving top-k spatial keyword queries," *IEEE Transactions on Knowledge and Data Engineering*, vol. 27, no. 4, pp. 922–935, 2015.

[19] S. Saltenis, C. S. Jensen, S. T. Leutenegger, and M. A. Lopez, "Indexing the positions of continuously moving objects," *ACM SIGMOD–SIGMOD Record*, vol. 29, no. 2, pp. 331–342, 2000.

[20] Y. Tao, D. Papadias, and J. Sun, "The TPR*-tree: an optimized spatio-temporal access method for predictive queries," in *Proceedings 2003 VLDB Conference*, pp. 790–801, Berlin, Germany, September 2003.

[21] E. Frentzos, "Indexing objects moving on fixed networks," in *Proceedings of the 8th International Symposium on Spatial and Temporal Databases (SSTD)*, pp. 289–305, Springer, Santorini Island, Greece, July 2003.

[22] S. Alamri, D. Taniar, and M. Safar, "Indexing moving objects for directions and velocities queries," *Information Systems Frontiers*, vol. 15, no. 2, pp. 235–248, 2012.

[23] C. S. Jensen, D. Lin, B. Chin Ooi, and R. Zhang, "Effective density queries on continuously moving objects," in *Proceedings of the 22nd International Conference on Data Engineering (ICDE'06)*, p. 71, IEEE Computer Society, Atlanta, GA, USA, April 2006.

[24] S. Alamri, D. Taniar, and K. Nguyen, "Efficient cell-based indexing of indoor mobile objects," *Information Systems Frontiers*, 2017.

[25] H. Lu, X. Cao, and C. S. Jensen, "A foundation for efficient indoor distance-aware query processing," in *Proceedings of the 2012 IEEE 28th International Conference on Data Engineering (ICDE)*, pp. 438–449, IEEE Computer Society, Washington, DC, USA, 2012.

10

Mobile Hardware-Information System for Neuro-Electrostimulation

Vladimir S. Kublanov ⓘ**, Mikhail V. Babich** ⓘ**, and Anton Yu. Dolganov** ⓘ

Research Medical and Biological Engineering Centre of High Technologies, Ural Federal University, Mira 19, 620002 Yekaterinburg, Russia

Correspondence should be addressed to Vladimir S. Kublanov; kublanov@mail.ru

Guest Editor: Giuseppe De Pietro

The article describes organizational principles of the mobile hardware-informational system based on the multifactorial neuro-electrostimulation device. The system is implemented with two blocks: the first block forms the spatially distributed field of low-frequency monopolar current pulses between two multielement electrodes in the neck region. Functions of the second block, specialized control interface, are performed by a smartphone. Information is exchanged between two blocks through a telemetric channel. The mobile hardware-informational system allows to remotely change the structure of the current pulses field, to control its biotropic characteristics and to change the targets of the stimulation. Moreover, it provides patient data collection and processing, as well as access to the specialized databases. The basic circuit solutions for the neuro-electrostimulation device, implemented by means of microcontroller and elements of high-level hardware integration, are described. The prospects of artificial intelligence and machine learning application for treatment process management are discussed.

1. Introduction

What has the twenty-first century brought to the humanity? Scientific and technological progress in modern society has led to an increase in the duration and improvement of the quality of human life, as well as maintenance of high efficiency and intellectual activity. These processes are taking place at a time of growing mental stress caused by unstable economic development and unpredictable crisis situations, local wars, interethnic conflicts, and natural disasters. The health of the population, which is the basis of the well-being and harmony of human civilization, is deteriorating. The most disturbing is the growth of chronic stress and mental disorders, personality disorders. As a result, a person is losing the ability of efficient information processing, cognitive control, and decision-making, the basic mechanisms of the social version are violated. In the field of neurology and psychiatry, there has been a catastrophic increase in the number of lost years due to movement, coordination, sensitivity, speech, intelligence, and memory disorders [1].

As noted by World Health Organization, among 56.9 million deaths worldwide in 2016, ischemic heart disease and stroke are the world's biggest killers, accounting for a combined 15.2 million deaths. These diseases have remained the leading causes of death globally in the last 15 years. Deaths due to dementias more than doubled between 2000 and 2016, making it the 5th leading cause of global deaths in 2016 compared to 14th in 2000 [2].

Every year, more than 795,000 people in the United States have a stroke. About 87% of all strokes are ischemic strokes, in which blood flow to the brain is blocked. Stroke is a leading cause of serious long-term disability. Stroke reduces mobility in more than half of stroke survivors age 65 and over. Stroke costs the United States an estimated $34 billion each year. This total includes the cost of health care services, medicines to treat stroke, and missed days of work [3].

The most common approach for treating such diseases is a neuroprotective therapy, which helps normalize and strengthen the physiological activity of brain tissue. During neuroprotective therapy, medicines are predominantly used. But physiotherapeutic methods of restorative medicine can be also applied [4].

Of all the variety of physical fields and methods, the most promising are spatially distributed fields of monopolar low-frequency current pulses whose structure and characteristics are adequate to endogenous processes in the human body [5–8].

2. Materials and Methods: Multifactorial Neuro-Electrostimulation of Neck Nervous Structures and Organization of Control Process

Personalized multidisciplinary approach to the organization of the patient's treatment process is promising for increase of the neuro-electrostimulation effectiveness. It implies to actively use neuro-electrostimulation in addition to various procedures of neurorehabilitation for triggering mechanisms of neuroplasticity in management of the brain functional processes [9].

The choice of the neck as a target for neuro-electrostimulation is determined by the location in it: centers of segmental control for vital functions (*cervical sympathetic ganglia*) and the conducting pathways of the suprasegmental centers of the homeostasis regulation (*glossopharyngeal* and *vagus nerves* and their branches, as well as the *cervical plexus* of the spinal nerves) [10]. In the deep muscles of the neck there are nodes of the *sympathetic trunk*, formed by the nervous processes of the *autonomic nuclei* of the spinal cord. The *upper*, *middle*, and *lower* (*stellate*) *sympathetic nodes* have numerous branches that enable sympathetic innervation of glands, meninges, vessels of the head, neck, and spine. The afferent fibers of the *spinal plexus* located on the posterior surface of the neck pass through the *posterior horns* of the spinal cord and end in the sensitive nuclei of the brainstem and the reticular formation. Near the main arteries of the neck lies the *vagus nerve*. The nuclei of the *vagus nerve* are located in the brainstem and are common to the *glossopharyngeal nerve*. They have extensive connections with the *hypothalamus*, olfactory system, and reticular formation. Together, the *glossopharyngeal* and *vagus nerves* activate parasympathetic innervation of most organs. Nerve formations in the neck are closely related to the *brainstem*, through which they have two-way links to the *pons*, *middle brain*, *cerebellum*, *thalamus*, *hypothalamus*, and *cerebral cortex*. The presence of these relations ensures the involvement of the neck nervous structures in the analysis of sensory stimuli, the regulation of the muscle tone, and autonomic and higher integrative functions [11].

With electrostimulation of the *cervical spinal plexus*, branches of the *vagus nerve*, *nervus accessorius*, and *glossopharyngeal nerve*, the gray matter of the brainstem can be stimulated along the afferent pathways. Through the reticular formation, the effect in this case extends to the *thalamic structures* and the *cerebral cortex*. The stimulation of the nodes of the *sympathetic trunk* makes it possible to influence both the vascular tone of the cerebral arteries and the autonomic nuclei of the spinal cord. As a result of these actions, it is possible to influence various functional processes in the brain tissues, modulate autonomic processes, and influence motor control and cognitive functions.

The next step in creating a promising neuro-electrostimulator suitable for providing comprehensive rehabilitation is the selection of the best solutions for organizing the architecture of the neuro-electrostimulator, taking into account the characteristics of the conducting pathways of the neck nervous formations.

3. Results: Selection of Basic Circuit, Engineering, Hardware, and Software Solutions

The analysis of tasks that are implemented in modern physiotherapy devices for recovery medicine shows that, as a rule, two tasks are performed in them:

(1) Formation of a physical field in the problem area of the body

(2) Regulation of characteristics of the physical field, which form a biological effect

Generally, such devices are constructed as the single block units and tend to have relatively high mass-dimensional characteristics [12–15].

Let us note that operationally, the first task is functionally "tied" to the patient and the second to the physician. In our case, we divide the neuroelectrostimulation device into two blocks, one of which will solve only the first task; the second block will only solve the second task. The information exchange between them will be provided by a telemetric communication channel, like Bluetooth. Then, according to this principle, a new architecture of the promising neuro-electrostimulator can be organized, which will make it compact and mobile [16]. This applies equally to the first block and to the second.

The implementation of the first block as compact and mobile one is quite realistic, as only the following components are mandatory:

(i) Two multielement electrodes, between which a spatially distributed field of current pulses is formed

(ii) Multichannel impulse current source, whose functions are performed by two multiplexers and a controlled current source

(iii) Accumulator

(iv) Bluetooth transmitter

(v) Flash memory

(vi) Microcontroller unit

Core features of the first block:

(a) Number of partial cathodes: 13

(b) Number of anodes: 13

(c) Mass, 200 g

(d) Dimensions, 90 × 50 × 18.5 mm

(e) Current pulse amplitude, 0–15 mA

(f) Partial pulse duration, 15–60 μs

(g) Modulation frequency, 5–150 Hz

(h) Minimal time of autonomic work, 24 h

(i) Accumulator charging socket, USB Mini B

Diagram of the neuro-electrostimulator is presented on Figure 1, photo of the first block on Figure 2, and photo of the first block's printed circuit board on Figure 3.

The flowchart of the first block functioning algorithm is shown on Figure 4.

The program of the algorithm application is implemented as a set of tasks. Tasks that are not critical to the launch period are performed in the main program loop. Such tasks include first block unit testing, synchronizing cathodes pattern, and stimulation targets between first and second blocks, calculating amplitude for each cathode.

The tasks that are critical to the launch period include starting a new pulse packet and starting a new partial pulse inside pulse packet. This tasks forms current pulses field structure, sets up biotropic parameters, and determines stimulation targets. The critical to the launch period tasks has a higher priority and their starts are initiated by interrupt signals from the built-in microcontroller peripherals.

The current pulses field structure changing is possible only in a determined time points.

$$t = \frac{a}{v} + n * \tau, \qquad (1)$$

where $a \in N$, $n \in N, 0 \le n \le K$, K is the number of partial cathodes participating in field structure, τ is the partial pulse duration, and $T = 1/v$ is the current pulses field structure modulating period.

When the current pulses field structure changing time point t occurs, microcontroller in the first block performs the following steps:

(1) Switching off the current partial cathode and switching on the new one according to neuro-electrostimulation program. If the current partial cathode is the last one in accordance with neuro-electrostimulation program, then a new partial cathode will not be connected.

(2) If the anode needs to be changed according to the neuro-electrostimulation program or by the physician's command from the second block, the current connected anode will be disconnected and a new anode will be connected.

(3) If current amplitude and time characteristics of current pulses field structure (such as modulating period T, partial impulse duration τ, and partial impulse amplitude A) differ from the target ones, then the characteristics is changing according to following equations:

$$A_{i+1} = \begin{cases} A_{\text{target}}, & |A_i - A_{\text{target}}| < \Delta_A, \\ A_i + \Delta_A, & A_i + \Delta_A < A_{\text{target}}, \\ A_i - \Delta_A, & A_i - \Delta_A > A_{\text{target}}, \end{cases}$$

$$T_{i+1} = \begin{cases} T_{\text{target}}, & |T_i - T_{\text{target}}| < \Delta_T, \\ T_i + \Delta_T, & T_i + \Delta_T < T_{\text{target}}, \\ T_i - \Delta_T, & T_i - \Delta_T > T_{\text{target}}, \end{cases} \qquad (2)$$

$$\tau_{i+1} = \begin{cases} \tau_{\text{target}}, & |\tau_i - \tau_{\text{target}}| < \Delta_\tau, \\ \tau_i + \Delta_\tau, & \tau_i + \Delta_\tau < \tau_{\text{target}}, \\ \tau_i - \Delta_\tau, & \tau_i - \Delta_\tau > \tau_{\text{target}}. \end{cases}$$

The use of restrictions on the growth rate of the current pulses field structure parameters of neuro-electrostimulation avoids the appearance of patient's painful sensations during treatment procedure. The application for control of the field structure of current pulses and its characteristics of a microcontroller makes it possible to implement a large number of programs for neuro-electrostimulation.

Aforementioned computational procedures are required to implement the functions of the second block: when specifying the structure of the spatially distributed field of current pulses and the characteristics of this field, as well as the formation of various commands. These tasks can be handled on the basis of a computer or any specialized computation units that, in essence, will perform the functions of a specialized interface of the neuro-electrostimulator. To ensure the compactness and mobility of this specialized interface, we have chosen a smartphone.

The second unit of the neuro-electrostimulator is implemented in the form of an original cross-platform application for mobile devices based on Android, iOs, and Windows Phone. The application is structurally implemented in the form of two activities: the search for the first block and the control of the stimulation process. To organize the operation of the telemetric communication channel, the Bluetooth low energy API is used. In this case, a virtual control panel for the medical process is formed, which allows the physician to monitor the battery charge level in real time, the telemetry communication channel serviceability, the current pulse field structure, their biotropic parameters, and the position of the stimulation targets. Figure 5 shows a picture of specialized neuro-electrostimulator interface display in the virtual control panel mode of the treatment process.

Thus, the implementation of a neuro-electrostimulator in the form of two blocks will allow for the performance of the functions of restorative medicine:

(1) For a patient to form a spatially distributed field of current pulses for the organization of a multifactorial neuro-electrostimulation of the neck nervous

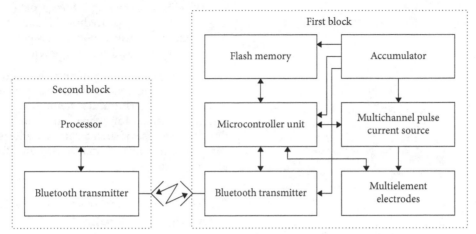

FIGURE 1: Diagram of the neuro-electrostimulator.

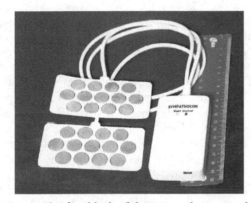

FIGURE 2: The first block of the neuro-electrostimulator

FIGURE 3: Printed circuit board of the first block.

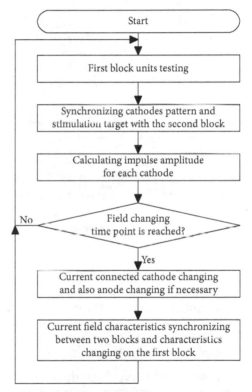

FIGURE 4: The first block functioning algorithm.

(2) For the physician to obtain wide opportunities for virtual management and control of the medical process, including the following:

(a) In real time to monitor the operation of the first block of the neuro-electrostimulator, including monitoring the level of charge of its battery

(b) Change the structure of the spatially distributed field of current pulses in the neck region, their parameters (amplitude, frequency, and duration)

(c) Choose targets for the impact in the projection of the *sympathetic trunk*, *carotid plexus*, *cervical spinal plexus*, *vagus nerve*, *nervus accessories* and branches of the *glossopharyngeal nerve* by selecting respectable functioning anodes

(d) Change the number of partial cathodes participating in the formation of the field

(e) Control the formation of a spatially distributed field of current pulses in the neck region in several patients (up to 10) via a telemetry channel using a single smartphone

(f) Use the potential of telemedicine technology through the organization of remote monitoring of the rehabilitation process by highly qualified medical personnel

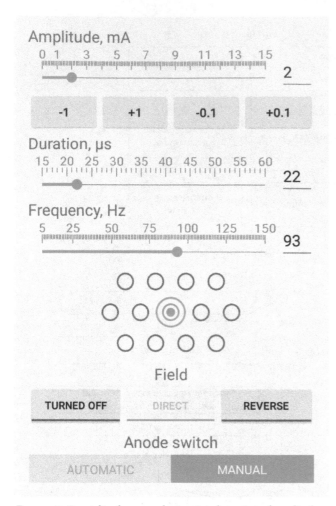

FIGURE 5: Specialized neuro-electrostimulator interface display.

(g) Ensure the collection and processing of data on changes in the functional status of patients with an option to monitor the treatment process

(h) Access to specialized databases of neuro-rehabilitation, storing personalized information about the course of the treatment process

The structure of such specialized database, named the neuro-electrostimulation service, implemented as a database model in the notation "Entity-Relationship" is shown in Figure 6.

Core elements of the database are entities (tables):

(i) «Physician», having lines physician_id; Name, Surname

(ii) «Patient», having lines patient_id; Name, Surname; Age; Sex; physician_id

(iii) «Procedure», having lines procedure_id, physician_id, patient_id, Date, procedure type (examination, neuro-electrostimulation procedure, functional load), device_id

(iv) «Device», having lines device_id, physician_id, patient_id, Stimulation features

(v) «Data», having lines data_id, physician_id, patient_id, procedure_id, Data type (arterial pressure, electrocardiography signal, biochemical tests, psychological tests), Content

The proposed structure provides quick access to information on the treatment process available for a particular patient, allows storing and systematizing registered data, and making decisions for management of treatment based on this data. The use of such a database allows the formation of complex search queries that can be used for further analysis and processing.

4. Discussion: Prospects of Artificial Intelligence Application for Neurorehabilitation Management

At present, high hopes are placed on the use of artificial intelligence and machine learning for use in the diagnosis and control of the therapeutic process [17–19]. Thus, in our early work on the clinical example of arterial hypertension, it was shown that the application of quadratic discriminant analysis and methods for selecting diagnostic features of heart rate variability signals allows not only to perform express diagnostics of arterial hypertension, but also to evaluate the effectiveness of the therapeutic process with the use of neuro-electrostimulation [20]. Thus, it is possible to create an information decision support system for a physician.

The use of artificial intelligence in determining the paradigm of rehabilitation personally for each patient is made possible by taking into account the opportunities of telemedicine. As noted earlier, the specialized interface of the neuro-electroimulator control is implemented as an application for a smartphone. A smartphone can interact with a global computer network. This allows not only to transmit the information generated in the neuro-electrostimulator, but also to obtain information from the specialized databases, to support the decision-making of the physician in treatment. Thus, the aforementioned information decision support system can be integrated with the neuro-electrostimulation service for the purpose of information exchange. The interaction of the neuro-electrostimulation service with the information decision support system provides express diagnostics of the cardiovascular system regulation disorders.

Creation of the neuro-electrostimulation service allows to close the contour of the physician and patient interaction and implements the functions of the biotechnical system for neurorehabilitation. The structural diagram of the biotechnical system is shown in Figure 7.

Such biotechnical system implements a number of principles of the patient-oriented approach in health care, such as personalized medicine and active involvement of the patient in the medical process. The presence of the neuro-electrostimulation service solves the problem of storing registered diagnostic data centrally on the server of the medical institution, simultaneous work with several patients

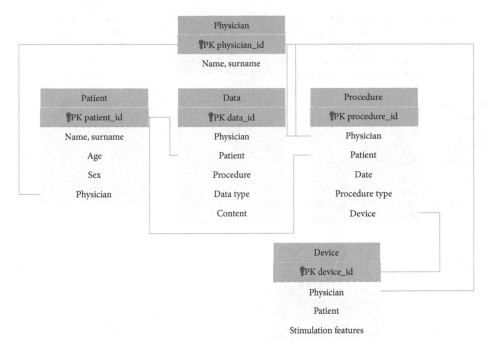

FIGURE 6: The neuro-electrostimulation service.

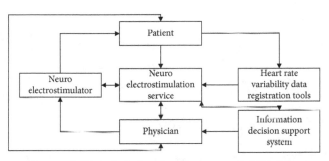

FIGURE 7: Biotechnical system for neurorehabilitation.

and effective use of the resources of the medical institution, and protection of patients' personal data from unauthorized access. The result of the interaction between the neuro-electrostimulation service and the information decision support system is the processing and automated analysis of the patient's data by means of machine learning to obtain express assessments for the diagnosis of arterial hypertension and the effectiveness of the therapeutic process, tracking the dynamics of changes in patient data, and information support by means of artificial intelligence for a physician.

5. Conclusion

As suggested in the article, principles of organization, circuit, and engineering solutions allowed to create mobile and compact hardware-information system for neurorehabilitation. Application of artificial intelligence and machine learning opens possibilities for treatment process management in accordance with the personalized medicine principles.

At present, the neuro-electrostimulation device has undergone clinical approbation in the treatment of depressive anxiety disorders, children with attention deficit disorder, and rehabilitation of patients after traumatic brain injuries. Clinical studies have shown that in comparison with known methods, a higher effectiveness of treatment is achieved through involvement in the regulatory process in addition to the autonomic nervous system and brain structures responsible for cognitive, motor, visual, auditory, vestibular, and other brain functions. These results are presented in more detail in the specialized publications of our physician co-authors [21, 22].

Acknowledgments

This study was supported by the Act 211 of the Government of the Russian Federation (contract no. 02.A03.21.0006) and was funded by RFBR (project no, 18-29-02052).

References

[1] P. A. Lapchak and J. H. Zhang, *Neuroprotective Therapy for Stroke and Ischemic Disease*, Springer, Berlin, Germany, 2017.

[2] Global Health Estimates 2016, *Disease burden by Cause, Age, Sex, by Country and by Region, 2000-2016*, World Health Organization, Geneva, 2018.

[3] E. J. Benjamin, M. J. Blaha, S. E. Chiuve et al., "American heart association statistics committee and stroke statistics subcommittee," *Heart Disease and Stroke Statistics—2017 Update: A Report From the American Heart Association*, vol. 135, no. 10, pp. e146–e603, 2017.

[4] Q. Ashton Acton, *Advances in Central Nervous System Research and Treatment: 2013 Edition*, ScholarlyEditions, Atlante, Georgia, 2013.

[5] V. S. Kublanov, "A hardware-software system for diagnosis and correction of autonomic dysfunctions," *Biomedical Engineering*, vol. 42, no. 4, pp. 206–212, 2008.

[6] J. C. Wildenberg, M. E. Tyler, Y. P. Danilov, K. A. Kaczmarek, and M. E. Meyerand, "Electrical tongue stimulation normalizes activity within the motion-sensitive brain network in balance-impaired subjects as revealed by group independent component analysis," *Brain Connectivity*, vol. 1, no. 3, pp. 255–265, 2011.

[7] D. Adair, M. Bikson, D. Q. Truong, L. Ho, and H. Borges, "Cognition and electrical stimulation of cranial nerves," *Brain Stimulation*, vol. 10, no. 2, p. 477, 2017.

[8] A. K. Srivastava and C. S. Cox Jr, *Pre-Clinical and Clinical Methods in Brain Trauma Research*, Springer Science+Business Media, LLC, part of Springer Nature, Houston, TX, USA, 2018.

[9] E. Krames, P. H. Peckham, and A. R. Rezai, *Neuromodulation: Comprehensive Textbook of Principles, Technologies, and Therapies*, Academic Press, Cambridge, MA, USA, 2018.

[10] R. S. Orlov and A. D. Nozdrachev, *Normal Physiology*, A. Textbook (in Russian). M., Geotar-Media, Moscow, Russia, 2010.

[11] S. S. Michailov, A. V. Chukbar, and A. G. Tsybul'kin, *Human Anatomy*, (in Russian). M., Geotar-Media, Moscow, Russia, 2013.

[12] V. S. Kublanov, V. I. Shmirev, A. S. Shershever, and J. E. Kazakov, "About innovative possibilities of device "SIMPATOCOR-01" in management of functional disorders of vegetative and central nervous system in neurology, kremljovskaya medicine," *Clinichesky Vestnik*, vol. 4, pp. 60–64, 2010.

[13] R. Nonis, K. D'Ostilio, S. Sava, J. Schoenen, and D. Magis, "Non-invasive vagus nerve stimulation with gammaCore (R) in healthy subjects: is there electrophysiological evidence for activation of vagal afferents?," *Headache*, vol. 56, p. 56, 2016.

[14] A. Straube, J. Ellrich, O. Eren, B. Blum, and R. Ruscheweyh, "Treatment of chronic migraine with transcutaneous stimulation of the auricular branch of the vagal nerve (auricular t-VNS): a randomized, monocentric clinical trial," *Journal of Headache and Pain*, vol. 16, no. 1, p. 63, 2015.

[15] M. I. Johnson, *Transcutaneous electrical nerve stimulation (TENS). eLS*, John Wiley, Hoboken, NJ, USA, 2012.

[16] V. S. Kublanov, M. V. Babich, and T. S. Petrenko, "New principles for the organization of neurorehabilitation," *Biomedical Engineering*, vol. 52, no. 1, pp. 9–13, 2018.

[17] E. E. Tripoliti, T. G. Papadopoulos, G. S. Karanasiou, K. K. Naka, and D. I. Fotiadis, "Heart failure: diagnosis, severity estimation and prediction of adverse events through machine learning techniques," *Computational and Structural Biotechnology Journal*, vol. 15, pp. 26–47, 2017.

[18] M. Chen, Y. Hao, K. Hwang, L. Wang, and L. Wang, "Disease prediction by machine learning over big data from healthcare communities," *IEEE Access*, vol. 5, pp. 8869–8879, 2017.

[19] M. Espinilla, J. Medina, A.-L. García-Fernández, S. Campaña, and J. Londoño, "Fuzzy intelligent system for patients with preeclampsia in wearable devices," *Mobile Information Systems*, vol. 2017, Article ID 7838464, 10 pages, 2017.

[20] A. Y. Dolganov, V. S. Kublanov, D. Belo, and H. Gamboa, "Comparison of machine learning methods for the arterial hypertension diagnostics," *Applied Bionics and Biomechanics*, vol. 2017, Article ID 5985479, 13 pages, 2017.

[21] V. S. Kublanov, K. Y. Retyunskii, and T. S. Petrenko, "A new method for the treatment of korsakoffs (amnestic) psychosis:

neurostimulation correction of the sympathetic nervous system," *Neuroscience and Behavioral Physiology*, vol. 46, no. 7, pp. 748–753, 2016.

[22] T. Petrenko, V. Kublanov, and K. Retyunskiy, "The role of neuroplasticity in the treatment of cognitive impairments by means multifactor neuro-electrostimulation of the segmental level of the autonomic nervous system," *European Psychiatry*, vol. 41, p. S770, 2017.

11

Designing an Android-Based Application for Geohazard Reduction using Citizen-Based Crowdsourcing Data

Chaoyang He [ID],[1] Nengpan Ju [ID],[1] Qiang Xu,[1] Yanrong Li,[2] and Jianjun Zhao[1]

[1]*State Key Laboratory of Geohazard Prevention and Geoenvironment Protection, Chengdu University of Technology, No. 1 Dongsanlu, Erxianqiao, Chengdu, Sichuan 610059, China*
[2]*College of Mining Engineering, Taiyuan University of Technology, Taiyuan, Shanxi 030024, China*

Correspondence should be addressed to Nengpan Ju; jnp@cdut.edu.cn

Academic Editor: Salvatore Carta

Application development based on mobile platform is regarded as one of the major trends in information communication technology. However, only a few cases of mobile application are available for geohazard reduction using citizen-based crowdsourcing data. With the development of geohazard informatization and the rapid progress of mobile technology, the design and implementation of phone-based applications that could be used to monitor and prevent geohazards have been received increasing attention. Aiming at minimizing the threat of geohazards to people's lives and assets, this paper presents an android-based application named Geohazards Group Measurement and Guards against System (GGMGAS). Local villagers use the GGMGAS to collect field data, including photos and videos, and transmit them to a database server. Therefore, the efficiency and stability of the data exchange between the mobile phone and the database server is very important. A design method and system solution of a data-exchange scheme was designed based on the WebService technology. Through trial operation, it has been found out that this data-exchange scheme could greatly improve the communication efficiency and the stability of collected field data. Practice has proved that this method based on citizens' crowdsourcing data can effectively reduce the losses caused by geohazards.

1. Introduction

Geohazard, including landslide, collapse, debris flow, ground subsidence, and so forth, has been seriously threaten people's life and properties. Data from multiple studies suggest that geological background is complex in China, especially in the south of Anhui Province [1–3]. Studies also confirm that the geological environment of Anhui Province is fragile, creating favorable conditions for the formation and development of sudden geological disasters [4, 5]. In addition to geological environment, there has also been a debate among scholars concerning whether the frequent occurrence of disasters is associated with human activities [6–12]. Bozzano et al. [10] have found out that human activities, especially the construction of numerous engineering sites, may cause serious geological disasters. Therefore, the development of geohazard guards against systems has gradually started to become the focus of the government and researchers [13, 14]. Disaster monitoring computerized software system has been attached great attention, since the data transmission of mobile equipment has already been achieved today [15, 16].

Most researchers recently have shown an increased interest in developing mobile disaster monitoring and alerting systems [17–19]. It has been proven by field-testing results that crowdsourcing-based system could increase the speed and efficiency of data collection [20]. In geological disaster field, Frommberger and Schmid [21, 22] presents a disaster alert system that are developed based on the concept of crowdsourcing. By gathering information from the disaster-affected citizens, the Mobile4D is proven to be helpful to build a bilateral contact between the local government and residents. It has also been pointed out by other studies that crowdsourcing-based applications are able to deliver "real-time" warnings to local residents, since the bilateral contact has already been established [21–23]. In addition, Coz et al. [24]

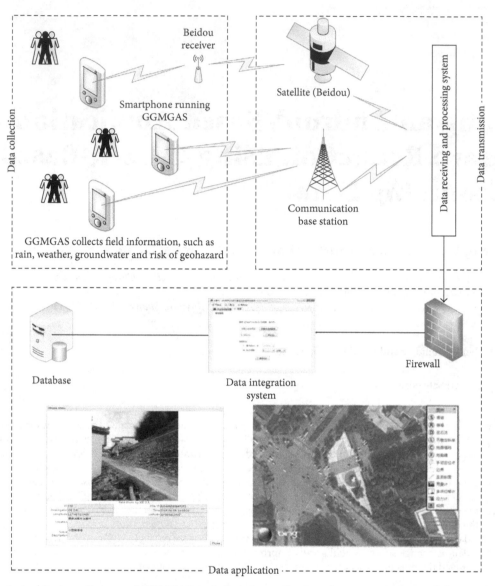

FIGURE 1: Architecture diagram of GGMGAS, including data collection, data transmission, and data application.

have also noted that the crowdsourced data collection process could help to improve local people's understanding of geological disasters. People's increasing understanding of geohazards could in turn improve the efficiency and stability of crowdsourced information that has been collected by local citizens [23].

Although the crowdsourcing-based system could improve the efficiency of data collection and information transmission, Tsai et al. [23] have also discovered that it is difficult to ensure the data quality, since the crowdsourcing-based data are collected by local people, who do not receive any professional training or learn any knowledge related to geological disasters. Coz et al. [24] also emphasized that the successful application of crowdsourcing-based system requires a simple and easy operation process, suitable data processing system, as well as people's good understanding of geological disasters.

Based on the researches which had been done by other scholars, this study aimed at exploring a geohazards against system that could be operated by citizens, especially those

who have little or no professional knowledge. To reduce the time of information transferring, this study proposes an android-based application, which could be used to collect field data, support field investigation, and report potential geohazards. To improve the quality of collected data and data exchange, a data-exchange scheme was designed based on the WebService technology. The application was designed to be a versatile operating system, the main interface of which is intuitive and user-friendly. This paper introduces the architecture design, the function design, and the development process of the application and discusses how to improve the data communication efficiency and stability. Analyze and evaluate the performance of the GGMGAS through the field testing in Huangshan City.

2. Android-Based Application Design

2.1. Architecture Design. As shown in Figure 1, the overall architecture of the GGMGAS could be divided into three

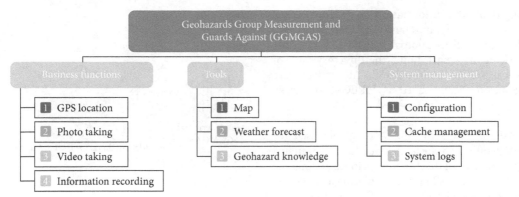

FIGURE 2: Functions of the GGMGAS could be divided into business functions, tools, and system management.

parts, which are data collection, data transmission, and data application. Data collection part is primarily designed for local citizens to collect the field data, while data transmission is set up for them to send the collected data to data server via wireless communications or Beidou satellite. As long as the mobile terminal supports Beidou communication, the collected data could be successfully transmitted to the data server. After receiving the data from the data server, duty officers are required to use the collected data to analyze the geohazard risk, and to decide whether it is necessary to issue an early warning to residents.

2.1.1. Data Collection. The field data, such as rainfall, groundwater level, and weather photos or videos, could be collected by local people. Given the fact that field investigations are often conducted in areas outside the range of cellular networks [25], it is vital to ensure that the necessary data could be gathered and stored in offline mode.

To address this issue, a database has been designed based on SQLite, which is a small but powerful relational database management system that is popularly used and could be compatible with multiple mobile operating systems [26, 27]. The establishment of this database has ensured all field data could be captured and saved with or without the Internet.

2.1.2. Data Transmission. The collected data could be automatically synchronized to the data server if the networks are available. However, if network connectivity is lost, the data will be temporarily stored in the database, which is designed based on SQLite. After reconnecting to the Internet, the data could be synchronized to the data server by data collectors manually, and the data that were stored in the smartphone would be deleted automatically once the data transmission is completed. The design of the database has guaranteed the safety and integrity of the collected data during data transmission and has also assured the feasibility and efficiency of data collection.

2.1.3. Data Application. The data will be integrated into the data center by the Geohazard Multi-Source Monitoring Data Integration System [28] immediately once received. The collected data, including the data of weather, photos, and

videos, will be analyzed by the duty officer, who is responsible for making qualitative risk assessments of geological hazards and determining whether to issue an early warning of geological disasters.

2.2. Function Design. The function design of GGMGAS is as essential as the architecture design. Most local villagers, who are the primary users of GGMGAS, generally have low education background. It is therefore vital for GGMGAS to provide simple, intuitive, and user-friendly functions.

As shown in Figure 2, multiple functions have been added to the GGMGAS, and they could also be divided into three parts, including business functions, tools, and system management.

2.2.1. Business Functions. Business functions have been developed as the core function of the GGMGAS, which is mainly designed to achieve the comprehensive collection of field information. As illustrated in Figure 2, the business functions of the GGMGAS includes GPS location, photo taking, video taking, and information recording. The implementation of these functions not only ensures that the collected data could be more diversified, but also raises the convenience of data collection.

(1) GPS Location Function. It mainly provides location information such as longitude, latitude, and altitude. Since the smartphone that is used to collect field data already has the Global Positioning System (GPS) module installed, the location information could be automatically tagged to each photo, video, and other data that has been taken in that location. The coordinate system is set as WGS84, and the coordinate accuracy depends on the GPS module in the smartphone.

(2) Photo-Taking Function. It is designed for data collectors to take photos by using the camera of the smartphone and to save the images to the disk in the jpeg format. Before saving the images to the disk, data collectors could review the photos by zooming in and rotating the images so as to decide whether it is necessary to do a retake or not.

(3) Video-Taking Function. It is considered as a critical function of the GGMGAS, because video information is

more convincing than other information. In order to ensure all recordings could be replayed and analyzed after data collection, videos (as well as photos) will be automatically saved in the disk of the smartphone, the directory path of which is "/sdcard/GGMGAS/media/." All videos are designed to be automatically saved as MPEG-4 format so that the video quality could be ensured.

(4) Information-Recording Function. It is mainly used for reminding the duty officer to check the data that has been just received. The primary role of this function is to ensure that the duty officer, who has responsibility for analyzing all collected data, would check and analyze the field data in time.

2.2.2. Tools. The tools of GGMGAS consist of map, weather forecast, and geohazard knowledge modules.

To obtain positional information during the field investigation, the Baidu Map has been embedded into the *map* module of GGMGAS. This tool guarantees that users of GGMGAS could have access to online maps, as well as local high-definition (HD) remote-sensing image maps. With the help of this tool, data collectors could get a preliminary understanding of the investigation area, obtain basic geographic information, and measure the length and area of the investigation area.

The *weather forecast* module provides weather data such as temperature, rainfall probability, PM 2.5, and so forth. All weather data come from the China Meteorological Administration. The GGMGAS is also designed to automatically read the weather data. If the investigation area faces heavy rain in the coming days, the GGMGAS will automatically notify data collectors to pay significant attention to geohazards and hidden dangers.

The *geohazard knowledge* module is developed for data collectors, who are also local villagers. Considering that most local villagers do not have any professional knowledge of geohazards, this module collects a few frequently asked questions, such as what is a landslide, and provides correspondence answers. By transferring geohazard knowledge in this way, this module is intended to increase data collectors' theoretical knowledge of geohazards.

2.2.3. System Management. In this section, data collectors can manage the system configuration, caches, and logs and reset their passwords. They can also browse the collected data and transfer them through cellular networks, Wi-Fi, or even Beidou satellite.

3. Data Communication

3.1. Data Exchange. A successful data exchange between the smartphone and the database server generally involves network data communication technology. To ensure a stable and reliable data exchange, WebService, a kind of protocol standard of remote procedure call, has been applied in the GGMGAS [29]. WebService is based on the Simple Object Access Protocol (SOAP), and it is well known as a platform-independent, loosely coupled, and web-based application

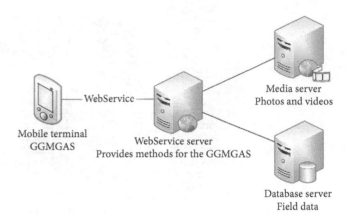

FIGURE 3: Deployment of the GGMGAS.

described by Extensible Markup Language (XML), which is also mainly used to develop distributed heterogeneous applications.

The reason for choosing WebService to provide data services is that WebService could improve the security and reliability of the GGMGAS. WebService provides an encapsulated environment in which users could only access the interface provided by the WebService, but the specific internal functional logic is not visible to users. Practice has proven that the system's security has been guaranteed by these features. Therefore, WebService has been selected to provide data services for the mobile terminal. The system deployment chart is demonstrated in Figure 3.

3.1.1. Mobile Terminal. It is the android-based smartphone in which the GGMGAS has already been installed.

3.1.2. WebService Server. It is the main bridge between the database and the mobile terminal. The WebService provides GGMGAS methods. Mobile termination could carry out operations by the WebService, such as access authentication, data uploading, and data downloading.

3.1.3. Media Server. It stores the photos and videos that are taken by the mobile terminal.

3.1.4. Database Server. It stores the data of the entire system, including basic geohazard information, monitoring data, GGMGAS-collected data, and system configuration. Oracle database (version: Oracle 11g R2) has been applied in this study.

3.2. WebService Methods. The data exchange of WebService uses XML by default. However, given that mobile termination is normally working on a cellular data network, it cannot store and parse massive amounts data, such as XML data. To accelerate the loading speed of the data and save data traffic, data compression should be the first consideration.

Compared with XML, the JavaScript Object Notation (JSON) data have a simpler structure. Most JavaScript programmers find it simpler and more intuitive to reference

TABLE 1: The data size in XML format and JSON format.

#	Data (rows)	XML (Kbytes)	JSON (Kbytes)	JSON/XML (%)
1	1	1.74	0.27	15.28
2	10	5.17	1.74	33.72
3	20	9.00	3.39	37.67
4	30	12.84	5.04	39.26
5	40	16.68	6.69	40.12
6	50	20.51	8.34	40.65
7	60	24.35	9.99	41.02
8	70	28.19	11.64	41.29
9	80	32.03	13.29	41.49
10	90	35.86	14.94	41.65
11	100	39.70	16.59	41.78

JSON data structures than to access an equivalent XML Document Object Model structure. Thus, the JSON format is applied in this study to compress data, and the overload method is used to convert data into JSON format, combined with data characteristics.

To test the performance of JSON data, 10 rows of geohazards data, which are obtained from the WebService named GetGeohazardList, have been collected and further analyzed. It could be clearly seen from Table 1 that the size of XML data is 5.17 Kbytes, while the size of JSON data is 1.74 Kbytes, taking only 33.72% of the XML data. With the increase of the data, the proportion that the amount of JSON data accounted for XML data size has maintained around 41%, as shown in Table 1. It could be detected from the above example that the amount of data could be greatly reduced when using JSON data for data exchange, even though the data size depends on the size of the field data.

Considering the function design and architecture requirements of the GGMGAS, a WebService is compiled based on the Microsoft Visual Studio 2010 and C#, as shown in Figure 4. The interactive data between mobile termination and media/database server are formatted by JSON. Eleven methods, including permission validation, are involved in the WebService, and the details of all eleven methods are listed in Table 2.

4. Android Application Development

Android platform is an open architecture that includes the operating system, middleware, and several key platform applications [16, 30]. To develop the GGMGAS, the android software developer kit has been applied in this project. The android software developer kit that has been selected to develop the GGMGAS is provided by Google [15]. Since developers are more familiar with Java programming language, the Eclipse, an integrated development environment, is selected to develop the GGMGAS.

The main interface of the GGMGAS has a clean layout with functions ordered logically on the main screen, as shown in Figure 5. Textual labels such as weather forecast, group measurement and guards against, and danger report are displayed in the center of the main screen. Image-based labels at the bottom of the screen perform actions, such as

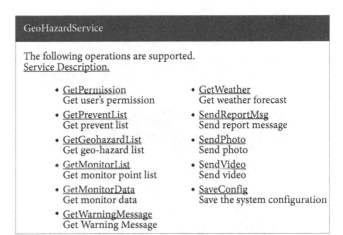

FIGURE 4: WebService provided for the GGMGAS.

the globe icon that opens a high-resolution map screen of the current position, as shown in Figure 6.

The user operation interface of the group measurement and guards against (GM&GA) module and the danger report modules is shown in Figures 7 and 8, respectively. As illustrated in Figure 7, a list of various data fields has already been provided on the operational interface of the GM&GA. With the help of the list, data collectors could collect sufficient field data simply by filling in the blanks. It has also guaranteed the availability and quality of the collected data. Field information such as location information, rainfall amount, groundwater level, and risk level could be clearly documented, by using the GM&GA.

The danger report modules also allow data collectors to upload photos and videos, as shown in Figure 8. This module could be tremendously helpful. Given that primary users of GGMGAS, who are usually local villagers, are not professionals, the duty officer may obtain more useful information from pictures or videos.

5. Field Testing

5.1. *Study Area.* To verify the capability of the GGMGAS, a field testing was conducted in Huangshan City, which is in the southern mountainous area of Anhui Province, China.

TABLE 2: WebService methods provided for the GGMGAS.

ID	Method name	Parameters	Main function
1	GetPermission	uid: PDA Id	Get user permission
2	GetPreventList	uid: PDA Id	Get a prevention list
3	GetGeohazardList	uid: PDA Id	Get a geohazard list
4	GetMonitorList	uid: PDA Id pid: Geohazard Id	Get a monitoring point list
5	GetMonitorData	uid: PDA Id pid: monitor Id stime: start time etime: end time	Get monitoring data
6	GetWarningMessage	uid: PDA Id	Get a warning message
7	GetWeather	uid: PDA Id	Get weather forecast
8	SendReportMsg	uid: PDA Id msg: encoding string of report message	Send a report message
9	SendPhoto	uid: PDA Id p: encoding string of photo	Send a photo
10	SendVideo	uid: PDA Id v: encoding string of video	Send a video
11	SaveConfig	uid: PDA Id cfg: encoding string of configuration of the system	Save the system configuration

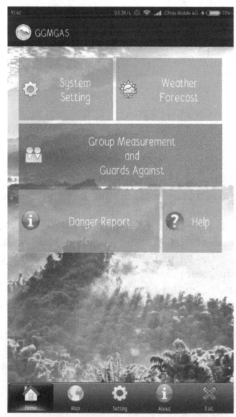

FIGURE 5: Main interface.

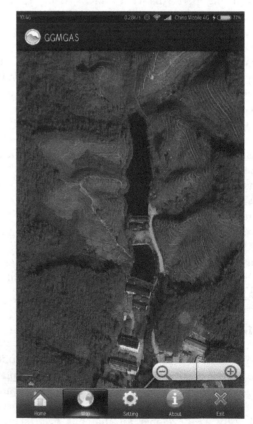

FIGURE 6: Electronic map module (based on Baidu Map).

As illustrated in Figure 9, the geographic coordinates of Huangshan City are 29°24′N to 30°31′N and 117°12′E to 118°53′E, and it covers an area of 9,807 km² and consists of three districts (Huangshan, Tunxi, and Huizhou) and four counties (Xiuning, Yixian, Qimen, and Shexian). The Huangshan City is a geohazard-prone area in Anhui Province. The geohazards in the Huangshan City are characterized by their high frequency, wide distribution, and threat to the population. Therefore, the government attaches great importance to the control and prevention of geo-hazards. Considerable work has been conducted on geo-hazard prevention, monitoring, and early warning. Emergency response and engineering management have also been strongly promoted by local government. In addition,

Figure 7: Group measurement and guards against module.

Figure 8: Danger report module.

the establishment of disaster warning systems in various districts and counties has also been taken into great consideration.

5.2. Data Collection. During the data collection process, it has been found out that local people could quickly pick up the basics of how to use the GGMGAS. According to an interview with a member of local community, GGMGAS is a user-friendly system. Most local people hold the opinion that the android-based smartphone with GGMGAS is simple and easy to use, even though they are not acquainted with electronic equipment.

The testing results also suggest that the implementation of GGMGAS could significantly reduce government spending. As shown in Figure 10, intuitive photos and videos of the geohazard scene could be collected by residents themselves. The government only needs to pay monthly mobile data traffic charges, which in Huangshan City is usually 10 to 15 yuan per user.

5.3. Data Application. In the process of data analysis, the Geohazard Monitoring and Early Warning Platform that is independently developed [28] was used. With the help of this platform, the field data that are collected by local people could be easily viewed and managed.

Figure 11 shows the data lists of collected data. Detailed information such as PDA ID, longitude, latitude, time, and location is provided in the list. During the data analysis, each data could be marked as "Untreated" or "Treated." To make unread information more obvious, "Untreated" data are set

up to be displayed on the top of the platform, and the text color of "Untreated" information is red.

All final three icons are clickable and direct duty officers to more details on disaster areas. For example, a new page named "Photo View" will open after right-clicking the first globe icon, as shown in Figure 12. The new webpage contains detailed information, including investigator, time, location, and scene description.

After nearly a year of trial operation, more than 170 rows (Figure 11) of valid data were collected by local residents. In the process of data analysis, it has been discovered the GGMGAS was significantly useful in helping the duty officer to grasp the situation at the scene, with the aid of Geohazard Monitoring and Early Warning Platform. It has also been found out that the GGMGAS could greatly improve the prevention of the geohazards.

6. Discussion and Conclusion

The purpose of this paper is to present a simple and low-cost method to reduce the losses caused by geohazards. An android-based application named GGMGAS was developed for residents to collect field data. The architecture of GGMGAS includes data collection, data transmission, and data application. In addition to the architecture design, business functions such as GPS location function, photo-taking function, and video-taking function are also developed to increase the usability of the GGMGAS. Tools, including map and weather forecast, are designed to make the process of data collection more simple and accessible.

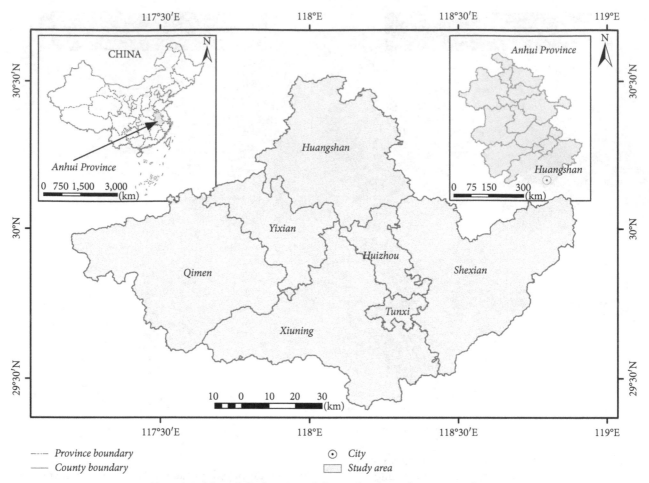

FIGURE 9: Map of the location of the study area and its surroundings.

(a)   (b)

FIGURE 10: Photos taken with GGMGAS by safety-responsible individual. (a) Location: 29°46′37.4520″N, 118°34′51.8160″E. Description: the cracks in Xiaochuan landslide are covered with plastic film by the villager. (b) Location: 29°52′41.1240″N, 118°41′18.4200″E. Description: damage of the house caused by Gaoshan landslide deformation.

One of the main objectives of the GGMGAS is to provide sufficient field data for decision-making of local government. To achieve this goal, the GGMGAS is designed based on the concept of crowdsourcing. Enough field data could be collected by local people, and a stable and reliable data exchange is guaranteed since the WebService technology has been applied in the GGMGAS. Another objective of the GGMGAS is to ensure the quality and integrity of field data. For this objective, several business functions such as map and geological knowledge modules have been developed to advance local villagers' understanding of geological disasters. In addition, the design of A group measurement and

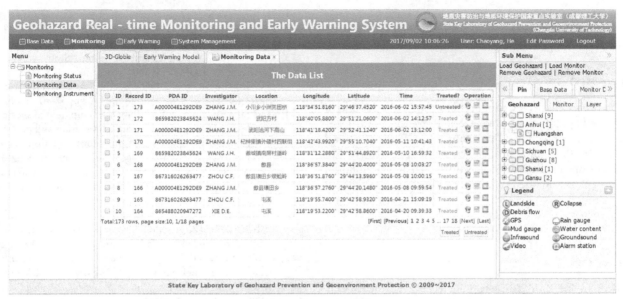

Figure 11: The data collected by the GGMGAS.

Figure 12: Photo view page in the geohazard real-time monitoring and early warning system.

guards against (GM&GA) module not only could improve the convince of data collection, but also could assure the quality of collected data.

To detect the performance of the application, the GGMGAS has been tested in Huangshan City, which is typically characterized by geological hazards. Based on test results, it could be found out that the realization of the GGMGAS could greatly improve the reliability and authenticity of the data and satisfy the function requirement of practical work. Test results also prove that the GGMGAS could gather sufficient valid information from local citizens, and it could also help to reduce the government spending on the prevention of geological hazards. However, further studies and testes are needed. Future works will mainly focus on developing the iOS version of the GGMGAS. A more effective utilization of the crowdsourced data will also be discussed in a future article.

Acknowledgments

This study was financially supported by the Research Fund of State Key Laboratory of Geohazard Prevention and Geo-environment Protection (Grant nos. SKLGP2017Z017 and SKLGP2015Z006) and the Science Fund for Creative Research Groups of the National Natural Science Foundation of China (Grant no. 41521002). The authors are also grateful to the anonymous referees for their useful comments and careful review of the manuscript.

References

[1] N. P. Ju, J. J. Zhao, H. Deng, R. Q. Huang, and H. P. Duan, "Analysis of deformation mechanism of sliding to bending slope and study of deformation emergency control at Huangshan Expressway," *Advances in Earth Science*, vol. 23, no. 5, pp. 474–481, 2008.

[2] J. Sun, H. Tao, S. W. Yang, X. L. Geng, and Y. X. Wei, "Development characteristics and prevention measures of geological hazards in mountain area of southern Anhui Province," *Hydrogeology and Engineering Geology*, vol. 38, no. 5, pp. 98–101, 2011.

[3] R. N. Parker, A. L. Densmore, N. J. Rosser et al., "Mass wasting triggered by the 2008 Wenchuan earthquake is greater than orogenic growth," *Nature Geoscience*, vol. 4, no. 7, pp. 449–452, 2011.

[4] X. D. Wang and H. Liu, "Typical cases study on meteorological forecasting and alarming of geological disasters in Wannan mountainous area," *Journal of Changchun Institute of Technology*, vol. 12, no. 4, pp. 84–88, 2011.

[5] B. R. Wu, K. J. You, G. L. Pan et al., "Failure mechanism of Yangtai landslide in mountain area of South Anhui Province," *Journal of Engineering Geology*, vol. 21, no. 2, pp. 136–142, 2013.

[6] H. F. Yin and C. G. Li, "Human impact on floods and flood disasters on the Yangtze River," *Geomorphology*, vol. 41, no. 2, pp. 105–109, 2011.

[7] J. Remondo, J. Soto, A. González-Díez et al., "Human impact on geomorphic processes and hazards in mountain areas in northern Spain," *Geomorphology*, vol. 66, no. 1, pp. 69–84, 2005.

[8] U. Kamp, B. J. Growley, G. A. Khattak et al., "GIS-based landslide susceptibility mapping for the 2005 Kashmir earthquake region," *Geomorphology*, vol. 101, no. 4, pp. 631–642, 2008.

[9] X. U. Gang, D. X. Zheng, L. I. Shu-Jing et al., "Remote sensing images and distribution characteristics of avalanche and landslide geohazards in the western part of the Weibei Plateau, Shaanxi Province, China," *Geological Bulletin of China*, vol. 27, no. 11, pp. 1837–1845, 2008.

[10] F. Bozzano, I. Cipriani, P. Mazzanti et al., "Displacement patterns of a landslide affected by human activities: insights from ground-based InSAR monitoring," *Natural Hazards*, vol. 59, no. 3, pp. 1377–1396, 2011.

[11] J. J. Zhang, D. X. Yue, Y. Q. Wang et al., "Spatial pattern analysis of geohazards and human activities in Bailong River Basin," *Advanced Materials Research*, vol. 518–523, pp. 5822–5829, 2012.

[12] F. Gutiérrez, M. Parise, J. D. Waele et al., "A review on natural and human-induced geohazards and impacts in karst," *Earth-Science Reviews*, vol. 138, pp. 61–88, 2014.

[13] C. Z. Liu, M. X. Zhang, and H. Meng, "Study on the geohazards mitigation system by residents' self-understanding and self-monitoring," *Journal of Disaster Prevention and Mitigation Engineering*, vol. 26, no. 2, pp. 57–61, 2006.

[14] H. Huang, B. Luo, and X. Y. Rao, "Development of specialized remote monitoring system of mass prediction and prevention for geological disasters based on internet of things," *Technology of Highway and Transport*, vol. 6, pp. 20–24, 2012.

[15] Y. H. Weng, F. S. Sun, and J. D. Grigsby, "GeoTools: an android phone application in geology," *Computers and Geosciences*, vol. 44, no. 13, pp. 24–30, 2012.

[16] W. Liu, S. Wang, Y. Zhou et al., "An android intelligent mobile terminal application: field data survey system for forest fires," *Natural Hazards*, vol. 73, no. 3, pp. 1483–1497, 2014.

[17] C. Bianchizza and S. Frigerio, "Il coinvolgimento dei cittadini nella gestione del territorio. Il laboratorio del progetto MAppERS," *Rendiconti Online Societa Geologica Italiana*, vol. 34, pp. 110–113, 2015.

[18] S. Frigerio, L. Schenato, and G. Bossi, "Crowdsourcing with mobile techniques for crisis support," *PeerJ Preprints*, vol. 4, article e2274v2, 2016.

[19] S. Frigerio, C. Bianchizza, L. Schenato et al., "A mobile application to engage citizens and volunteers. Crowdsourcing within natural hazard," *Rendiconti Online Societa Geologica Italiana,*vol. 42, pp. 70–72, 2017.

[20] J. R. Jambeck and K. Johnsen, "Citizen-based litter and marine debris data collection and mapping," *Computing in Science and Engineering*, vol. 17, no. 4, pp. 20–26, 2015.

[21] L. Frommberger and F Schmid, "Crowdsourced bi-directional disaster reporting and alerting on smartphones in Lao PDR," 2013, http://arxiv.org/abs/1312.6036.

[22] L. Frommberger and F. Schmid, "Mobile4D: crowdsourced disaster alerting and reporting," in *Proceedings of International Conference on Information and Communications Technologies and Development: Notes*, vol. 2, pp. 29–32, Cape Town, South Africa, December 2013.

[23] Y. F. Tsai, C. H. Chan, C. Y. Huang et al., "Crowdsourcing oriented ontology applies in instant debris-flow disaster information platform in web and smart phone application," *EGU Geophysical Research Abstracts*, vol. 17, p. 2371, 2015.

[24] J. L. Coz, A. Patalano, D. Collins et al., "Crowdsourced data for flood hydrology: feedback from recent citizen science projects in Argentina, France and New Zealand," *Journal of Hydrology*, vol. 541, pp. 766–777, 2016.

[25] S. Lee, J. Suh, and H. D. Park, "Smart compass-clinometer: a smartphone application for easy and rapid geological site investigation," *Computers and Geosciences*, vol. 61, no. 6, pp. 32–42, 2013.

[26] X. Q. Dong and Q. G. Liu, "Design of police affairs terminals based on embedded database SQLite," *Journal of Sichuan University of Science and Engineering*, vol. 23, no. 4, pp. 428–429, 2010.

[27] R. X. Li, S. P. Cheng, and Y. M. Zhou, "Design and development of vehicle-embedded POS machine based on SQLite," *Journal of University of Shanghai for Science and Technology*, vol. 32, no. 2, pp. 187–190, 2010.

[28] C. Y. He, N. P. Ju, and J. Huang, "Automatic integration and analysis of multi-source monitoring data for geo-hazard warning," *Journal of Engineering Geology*, vol. 22, no. 3, pp. 405–411, 2014.

12

A Fuzzy Logic-Based Personalized Method to Classify Perceived Exertion in Workplaces using a Wearable Heart Rate Sensor

Pablo Pancardo ⓘ**, J. A. Hernández-Nolasco** ⓘ**, and Francisco Acosta-Escalante** ⓘ

Informatics and Information System Academic Division, Juarez Autonomous University of Tabasco, Cunduacán, TAB, Mexico

Correspondence should be addressed to J. A. Hernández-Nolasco; adan.hernandez@ujat.mx

Academic Editor: Ljiljana Brankovic

Knowing the perceived exertion of workers during their physical activities facilitates the decision-making of supervisors regarding the worker allocation in the appropriate job, actions to prevent accidents, and reassignment of tasks, among others. However, although wearable heart rate sensors represent an effective way to capture perceived exertion, ergonomic methods are generic and they do not consider the diffuse nature of the ranges that classify the efforts. Personalized monitoring is needed to enable a real and efficient classification of perceived individual efforts. In this paper, we propose a heart rate-based personalized method to assess perceived exertion; our method uses fuzzy logic as an option to manage imprecision and uncertainty in involved variables. We applied some experiments to cleaning staff and obtained results that highlight the importance of a custom method to classify perceived exertion of people doing physical work.

1. Introduction

Advances in miniaturization, mobile communication, and sensor technologies make Mobile Health (mHealth) system development possible. mHealth is the intersection between Electronic Health (eHealth) and smartphone technologies. This means that the practice of eHealth is assisted by smartphones, which are used to capture, analyze, process, and transmit health-based information from sensors and other biomedical systems [1]. mHealth systems provide healthcare services with cost-effective, flexible, and efficient ways [2]. A mHealth system implemented on a mobile device enables a portable and nonobstructive solution; in addition, the computing and wireless capabilities allow real-time monitoring. This technology allows application deployment on mobile devices for continuous monitoring of people in order to determine, for example, the effort in their physical daily activities.

Humans possess a well-developed system for sensing the strain involved in physical effort. This is called perceived exertion (PE), which is the act of detecting and interpreting the sensations arising from the body during physical exertion [3].

Continuous measurement of physiological parameters in individuals while performing daily or labor activities allows health and well-being preservation or improvement.

Personal exertion estimation during labor activities has a particular interest, given that the effort to perform an activity is different for each person. Misallocation of an activity can affect a person's welfare and health. Workers may have risks associated with the disparity between high physical work demands and capacity/labor skills. These risks include musculoskeletal disorders, cardiovascular disease, prolonged absences, stress, burnout, and early retirements from the labor market [4]. Furthermore, physical strength assessment in ergonomics has additional benefits such as worker selection and placement and job design [5].

The estimation of workers' physical efforts in workplaces can be useful for allocation of employees in the appropriate position, adequacy of physical activities inherent to a job, prevention of accidents due to job demands, disease prevention related to physical demands, etc.

Generic methods known to estimate the physical effort do not take into account important physiological characteristics of individuals [6–8]. For many years, cardiac cost and metabolic expenditure from physical labor are calculated using formulas and generic tables [6]. Physical exertion is then set, based on standards, such as the maximum heart rate (220-age). While in many cases this may be agile and convenient, it is not always true, as in the case of overweight or habituated people to perform an activity. It is necessary to develop methods that can provide higher accuracy for predicting energy consumption for a wide range of physical activities. This would allow a greater chance of being accurate on when to compare them to scientifically validated methods as doubly labeled water method [9].

Most available solutions for health monitoring offer a generalized physiological measurement, that is, by reference to generic formulas or tables that are not customized to individuals [7, 10]. Many other solutions are focused on predefined activities such as walking and running without considering physiological parameters of each person, giving results that are not clearly differentiated [9, 11].

In [12], a method based on personalized maximum heart rate was proposed as an extension of Chamoux method. This method allows continuous monitoring effort, taking into account the particular physical condition of each person by measuring the heart rate. The goodness of this proposal was evaluated in [13] through a comparative study with the other two methods (original Chamoux and Borg) [10, 14]. It can be stated from these results that the heart rate reflects health conditions (sick, tired, and acclimatized), but to our knowledge, this has not been proven objectively and formally, it can also be stated that the personalized maximum heart rate method allows a better result distribution than that obtained in previous works. However, these results do not consider the habituation to specific work that a person may have, nor the perception of experts about the nature of effort levels.

In this work, we propose a method considering both of these important factors in personalized effort evaluation: the habituation to perform a specific job and expert perception about the nature of effort levels assessment.

Expert knowledge refers to the estimates or judgments made by experts of the analysis and interrelations of problem's quantitative parameters. Usually, the expert knowledge must face situations of vagueness and imprecision. It is because it is complex or not possible to have a complete list of all variables involved in the problem domain. That is, there is no exhaustive list of all factors to take into account for the problem domain. Even knowing all the variables, it can be difficult to obtain concrete data. In addition, this information may be incomplete or even erroneous [15].

Expert perception of effort level is needed because of the nature of effort values reported in previous works based on relative cardiac cost (RCC), which is defined into a rank of values, RCC = [0, 69], and grouped in sets of 10 values—these sets are named as intense = [60, 69], heavy = [50, 59], slightly heavy = [40, 49], and so on [14]. The problem is when we have a value, let us say, RCC = 49, which is considered as slightly heavy, but which could be considered as heavy instead. In order to better define the effort magnitude, we propose to consider RCC sets as diffuse ones, given that there is a gradual progression of values from one set to the next, which allows us to define the membership degree of values to each set.

The habituation of a person to perform a specific activity is needed, because we must consider if this person has the skills needed to execute the activity with a good performance, that is, good performance in the execution of an activity depends more on habituation than on other factors as good physical condition. The habituation of a person to the execution of job activities affects the job after assignment in an important way.

2. State of the Art

For many years, cardiac cost and metabolic expenditure from physical labor are calculated using formulas and generic tables [6]. The use of a custom method becomes more important when monitoring physical activities that require a lot of effort, such as heavy lifting, since such activities are those that can compromise the welfare and health of workers [16].

As established in the ISO 8996 standard [17] for estimating metabolic cost, the use of the heart rate is an option that provides an estimation of effort with a margin of error as plus or minus 10 percent. This method of analysis is surpassed only by custom measurements that require the use of specialized equipment commonly available in laboratories. The latter very precise methods are equipment of indirect calorimetry (oxygen consumption test using a mask) and doubly labeled water (water consumption and urine analysis).

Measuring the heart rate is a valid option to estimate the effort which represents a work activity for an individual, although some limitations must be considered [18]. It is also important to consider that there are other factors influencing significantly, such as environmental conditions (temperature and humidity), weight, age, acclimation, mental stress, and personality [19].

2.1. Fuzzy Logic. A fuzzy logic provides an inference mechanism that allows us to simulate human reasoning into knowledge-based systems. The theory of fuzzy logic provides a mathematical framework that allows modeling the uncertainty of human cognitive processes in a way that can be treatable by a computer [15].

In accordance with [20], two important reasons to employ fuzzy logic are (1) data obtained from sensors measurements could be imprecise and imperfect and (2) fuzzy logic can deal with imprecision and uncertainty due to its properties of performance and intelligibility necessary for the classification process.

2.1.1. Fuzzy Logic Steps. Many solutions of real-world problems require dealing with inaccurate and imprecise data. Humans are able to solve these problems because they make use of cognition but also make use of fuzzy judgments and reasoning. Diffuse classification techniques have the advantage that require a soft decision, that is, a value that describes the degree to which an element belongs to a class. Instead of a hard decision, where one must say precisely whether an element belongs to a class or not, fuzzy logic is a very attractive field within artificial intelligence because it

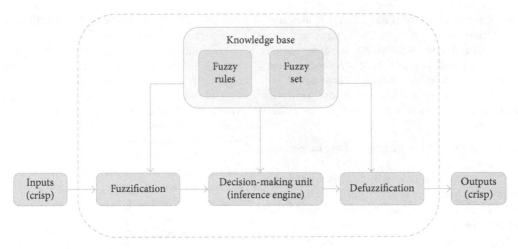

FIGURE 1: Fuzzy inference system steps.

is based on natural language. That is, it allows us to use linguistic terms to describe problems in a natural way. It does not use terms of relations between precise numerical values.

A fuzzy set can be defined as a set without clear and defined boundaries, in which elements that it contains can have a certain degree of membership ranging from total membership (value 1) to nonmembership (value 0). From this perspective, conventional sets (or crisp sets) can be seen as a particular case of fuzzy sets, a diffuse set that only admits two degrees of membership (one and zero).

Therefore, a diffuse set extends a standard set allowing degrees of membership of an element to the set, measured by the real numbers in the interval [0; 1]. If X is the universe of discourse and its elements are denoted by x, then a fuzzy set A on X is defined as a set of ordered pairs $(x, \mu_A(x))$ such that

$$A = \left\{ x, \frac{\mu_A(x)}{x}, \quad 0 \leq \mu_A(x) \leq 1 \right\}, \tag{1}$$

where $\mu_A(x)$ in (1) is the membership function of each x in A. In contrast to classical logic where the membership function $\mu_A(x)$ of an element x belonging to a set A could take only two values: $\mu_A(x) = 1$ if $x \in A$ or $\mu_A(x) = 0$ if $x \notin A$, fuzzy logic introduces the concept of membership degree of an element x to a set A and $\mu_A(x) \in [0; 1]$; here we speak about the truth value.

A typical fuzzy logic inference system has four components: the fuzzification, the knowledge base (rules and fuzzy sets), the inference engine, and the defuzzification [15]. Figure 1 shows those main fuzzy inference system steps.

2.1.2. Fuzzification.
The first step in fuzzy logic is to take the measured data (crisp data) and determine membership degree of these inputs to associated fuzzy sets. It is done by giving a value to each variable to a membership function set. Naturally, crisp value will be limited to the universe of discourse. Membership functions take different shapes. The two most common functions are triangular and trapezoidal. A triangular membership function with straight lines can formally be defined as follows:

$$\Lambda(x, a, b, c) = \begin{cases} 0, & x \leq a \\ \dfrac{x-a}{b-a}, & a \leq x \leq b \\ \dfrac{c-x}{c-b}, & b \leq x \leq c \\ 0, & x \geq c. \end{cases} \tag{2}$$

Trapezoidal function is shown in the following equation:

$$f(x, a, b, c, d) = \begin{cases} 0, & x \leq a \\ \dfrac{x-a}{b-a}, & a \leq x \leq b \\ 1, & b \leq x \leq c \\ \dfrac{d-x}{d-c}, & c \leq x \leq d \\ 0, & x \geq d. \end{cases} \tag{3}$$

A Gaussian membership function with the parameters m and σ to control the center and width of the function is defined by

$$G(x, m, \sigma) = e^{-(x-m)^2/2\sigma^2}. \tag{4}$$

The generalized Bell function that depends on three parameters a, b, and c is given by

$$f(x, a, b, c) = \frac{1}{1 + ||(x-c)/a||^{2b}}. \tag{5}$$

Other membership functions are sigmoid-shaped functions and delta functions (single functions). Selecting the membership function will depend on the nature of the problem, the type of data, and the experimental results. A knowledge expert is important to decide which shape will be used.

2.1.3. Knowledge Base (Rules and Fuzzy Sets). Rules are constructed from linguistic variables. Rules are structured in a IF-THEN format. The IF part of the rule is the antecedent and the THEN part of the rule is the consequent. These variables take on the fuzzy values that are represented as words and modeled as fuzzy subsets of an appropriate domain. There are several types of fuzzy rules, we mention only the two main rules:

(i) *Mamdani rules* [21]: These rules are of the following form: if x_1 is A_1, x_2 is A_2, ..., x_p is A_p, then y_1 is C_1, y_2 is C_2, ..., y_p is C_p, where A_i and C_i are fuzzy sets that define the partition space. The conclusion of a Mamdani rule is a fuzzy set. It uses the algebraic product and the maximum as T-norm and S-norm, respectively, but there are many variations by using other operators.

(ii) *Takagi/Sugeno rules* [21]: These rules are of the following form: if x_1 is A_1, x_2 is A_2, ..., x_p is A_p, then $y = b_0 + b_1 x_1 + b_2 x_2 + \cdots + b_p x_p$. In the Sugeno model, the conclusion is numerical. The rules' aggregation is in fact the weighted sum of rules' outputs.

2.1.4. Inference Engine. The fuzzy inference system uses fuzzy equivalents of logical AND, OR, and NOT operations to build up fuzzy logic rules. An inference engine operates on rules to evaluate them. Inference engine takes inputs and applies them to the antecedent part of the rule. If a rule has multiple antecedents, then logical AND, OR, and NOT operations are used to obtain a unique value representing evaluation result. This result (truth value) is applied to the consequent part. The outputs are then added. It is the process of unification of the outputs of all rules, that is, the membership functions of all consequent previously trimmed or scaled outputs are combined, to obtain a single fuzzy set for each output variable.

2.1.5. Defuzzification. The final step of a fuzzy logic system consists of transforming the fuzzy variables obtained by the fuzzy logic rules into crisp values again that can then be used to take a decision or perform some action. There exists different defuzzification methods: centroid of area (COA), bisector of area (BOA), mean of maximum (MOM), smallest of maximum (SOM), and largest of maximum (LOM). In our system, we used COA, and the following equation illustrates it:

$$Z_{\text{COA}} = \frac{\sum_{i=1}^{n} \mu_A(x_i) x_i}{\sum_{i=1}^{n} \mu_A(x_i)}. \tag{6}$$

2.2. Habituation. Habituation is a form of learning in which an organism decreases or ceases its responses to a stimulus after repeated presentations [22]. In perceived exertion, context is about how much a person has repeated a physical activity. Habituation as a state of training affects the heart rate [23]. In labor context, it refers to how frequently workers perform a specific physical activity related to their job.

Habituation to the performance of physical work activities is important because a person not being accustomed to perform a specific physical activity has a perceived effort of about twenty percent higher than a person accustomed to performing such an activity [24, 25].

Several methods have been used to quantify workload, including questionnaires, diaries, physiological monitoring, and direct observation [23]; in this sense, direct observation method can be considered to determine habituation, based on intensity and frequency (workload) of individual daily activities' performance.

3. Related Work

There are several works related to the proposal that we present, but none with the approach (personal perceived exertion), combination of factors (habituation, relative cardiac cost, and degree of membership to a fuzzy group), and application domain (prevention of labor accident risks due to workload fatigue) that is proposed.

The first group contains studies in workplaces oriented to estimate energy expenditure or activity recognition using technological devices. For example, Hwang et al. [26] proposed a measurement approach in energy estimation field. It is expected to provide in-depth understanding and continuous monitoring of worker's physical demands from construction tasks. Their solution was to use the heart rate (HR) to estimate EE according to a linear relationship between HR and EE. Their proposal was to achieve reliable field EE measurement through automatic action recognition using an embedded accelerometer and applying HR-EE relationships for corresponding actions with acceptable HR monitoring accuracy.

Hwang's proposal is based on identifying physical activities, which to date is limited to certain activities such as walking, running, and climbing stairs. That is, we could not identify any physical activity derived from a job; this makes Hwang's proposal not suitable for any type of work where physical activities are performed. On the contrary, our proposal focuses on identifying the personal physical effort involved in the work activity, without needing to identify which is the activity that the worker performs. Another example is shown in [27]; in this case, authors estimate and try to predict energy expenditure predictions based on the heart rate. On the contrary, we are compelled to estimate perceived exertion.

The second group contains works aimed at preserving health at work. For example, Migliaccio et al. [28] used sensors to monitor physical bends performed by construction workers, so it is identified that those physical activities can be risky to health. In this experiment, a heart monitor was used to detect high heart rates which were directly associated with a subject carrying a load. Fusing heart rate data and posture data provided the capability of differentiating safe from unsafe material-handling activities. The main objective of this research was to assist future decision makers in designing ergonomically safe and healthy work environments. Migliaccio's work focuses on detecting high levels of heart rate and unsafe postures, but the proposal is not personalized.

Aryal et al. [29] present a method for real-time monitoring of physical fatigue in construction workers using heart rate monitoring and infrared temperature sensors. Boosted tree classifiers were trained using the features extracted from the heart rate and temperature sensor signals and used to predict the level of physical fatigue from 12 participants. The study lacks a personalized classification of effort since it uses the Borg scale, which is extremely generic and does not contribute to the personalized detection of the efforts. There is a non-personalized classification because during physical activity, relative effort regarding resting heart rate and personalized maximum heart rate is not considered.

The third group contains those researches based on the fuzzy logic. The fuzzy logic-based tool for modeling human sensitivity to thermal sensation developed by Shimizu and Jindo [30] demonstrated that membership functions capture the ambiguity of classes to categorize thermal sensations. In the same sense, in [31] the theory of fuzzy sets and systems was applied to assess perceived workload involved in manual lifting tasks. In [32] a fuzzy logic-based risk assessment framework to evaluate physiological parameters is proposed; this model is used to avoid emergency situations during sport activity; however, personalized heart rate thresholds used in this proposal are based on generic values [10] from runners and triathletes.

These results support that our hypothesis about the fuzzy logic is convenient for classifying humans' effort perceptions. Additionally, no proposal considers the impact of habituation to work on physical effort, nor the degree of membership that has a cardiac cost value to a defined effort class.

3.1. Heart Rate-Based Methods to Estimate Physical Effort.
In this paper, we use methods based on the heart rate because this type of parameter has a 90% accuracy in estimating physical efforts, as it is stated in safety and health standards at work [17].

There are several methods that rely on measuring the heart rate to establish which is the physical effort that a work activity can represent for people [33]. We selected two of them: the Borg rating scale of exertion [10] and the Chamoux method [14].

The Borg scale is widely known and applied in sport and medical domains; it is generic and based on a table where, if a person has a certain value of heart rate, then it has a certain level of effort, and it is called rating of perceived exertion. In Table 1, the Borg scale shows 14 (6 to 20) values grouped in six categories.

In order to interpret the Borg scale, the numbers in the left column correspond to the number of beats of one person during physical activity divided by 10, and the corresponding value in the right column is the perceived exertion (level of effort); for example, if a worker has 110 beats per minute, the level on the scale is 11 and it belongs to slight effort. In this method, it is assumed that the maximum heart

TABLE 1: Borg's scale.

Scale	Description
6	No exertion
7	—
8	—
9	—
10	—
11	Light
12	—
13	Somewhat hard
14	—
15	Hard (heavy)
16	—
17	Very hard
18	—
19	—
20	Maximal exertion

TABLE 2: Different levels of effort for RCC under Chamoux.

RCC	RCC level	Effort
0–9	RCC1	Very light
10–19	RCC2	Light
20–29	RCC3	Slightly moderate
30–39	RCC4	Moderate
40–49	RCC5	Slightly heavy
50–59	RCC6	Heavy
60–69	RCC7	Intense

rate of a person is 220 minus his/her age in years. A real effort test is not required; therefore, it is a generic value.

Otherwise, Chamoux [14] proposes a lesser-known method, and as far as we know, it is not frequently used. This method requires to measure resting and the maximum heart rate for each person, taking into account several physiological parameters.

The method consists of two steps to estimate the physical effort. This first step is to obtain labor activity's absolute cardiac cost (ACC), which is obtained using the average cardiac frequency (ACF) and the resting cardiac frequency (RCF) for a person at every moment. ACF is obtained from the average value of the frequency of the worker during a day of conventional job. RCF is obtained after a person has slept (8 hours) and is resting.

ACC is obtained by subtracting the resting cardiac frequency (RCF) from the average cardiac frequency (ACF), as shown in the following formula [14]:

$$ACC = ACF - RCF. \qquad (7)$$

The second step is to compute the relative cardiac cost (RCC). Therefore, we should get theoretical maximum cardiac frequency (TMCF). Conventionally, the TMCF value is obtained by subtracting the person's age in years from 220. The formula for RCC is as follows [14]:

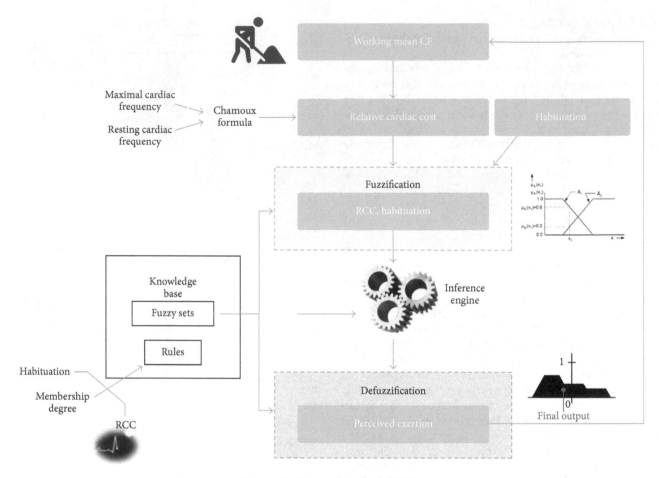

FIGURE 2: Proposed method (FPC).

$$RCC = \left(\frac{[ACC * 100]}{[TMCF - RCF]} \right). \tag{8}$$

Effort levels for a worker according to the method of Chamoux are shown in Table 2.

4. Materials and Method

We used a Basis B1 Fitness Wristband as a heart rate monitor, an Omron Sphygmomanometer Model HEM-742INT, and a common stethoscope. We used a treadmill mark BH Fitness Model Prisma M60 to measure personalized maximal cardiac frequency. It was operated without inclination. The prototype to estimate perceived exertion was developed with the Java 6.0 language using the ADT tool v22.3.0-887826. The prototype was implemented over a Samsung Galaxy S4, an Android 4.2.2 (Jelly Bean) Operation System, an octa-core chipset, and a 1.6 GHz Quad + 1.2 GHz Quad CPU.

We propose a method based on the method of Chamoux as it was explicitly created for the work environment, while the Borg method is used in sports. The fuzzy personalized Chamoux-based method (FPC) we propose is illustrated in Figure 2. Our fuzzy inference method is Mamdani type.

The first step of the proposed FPC method is taking cardiac frequency at rest, personalized maximal cardiac frequency, and habituation level. As we decided to customize the Chamoux method, that is, obtaining the value of TMCF parameter for each person, we required each user to perform a maximal exercise stress test using an electric treadmill and we took the value of the heart rate as their TMCF. We refer to this as a personalized Chamoux method [12]. Habituation value was assigned considering how frequent and experienced the user is about a specific labor physical activity.

Users will carry a wearable heart rate monitor to have a continuous monitoring of cardiac frequency during labor activity. From this monitoring, we obtain media cardiac frequency per minute. Having these data, we apply the Chamoux formula, using as maximum cardiac frequency, the personalized value that was obtained during the test with the treadmill. Chamoux formula gives us relative cardiac costs (RCCs) for each worker.

Later, RCC variables were assigned to fuzzy sets, as shown in Figure 3.

In accordance with knowledge obtained in [25], it was used as a condition that establishes that nonhabituated workers increase their perceived exertion by 20% for evaluated activity (sweeping, cleaning windows, and stacking chairs). Another condition was implemented for moderately habituated workers; in this case, their PE was increased 10%. For habituated workers, there is no need to increase

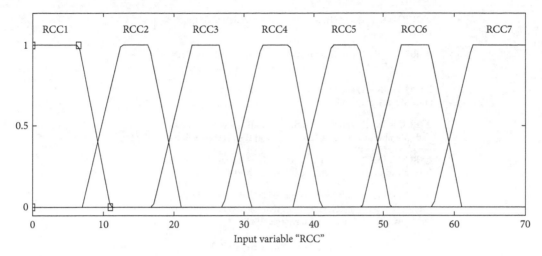

FIGURE 3: RCC membership function.

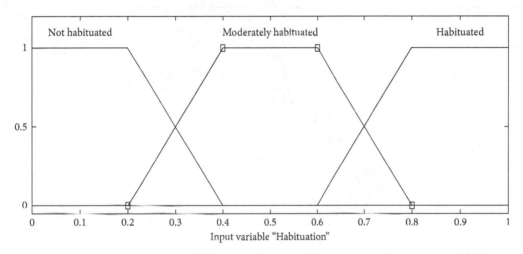

FIGURE 4: Habituation function.

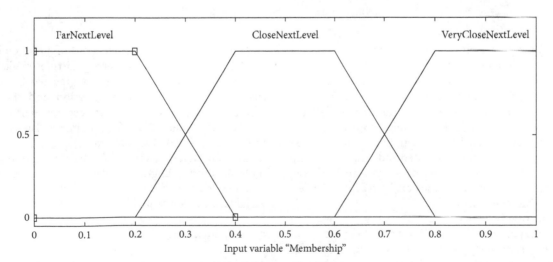

FIGURE 5: Level of membership function.

If (RCC is RCC1) and (Habituation is habituated) then (perceived
Exertion is PE1)

If (RCC is RCC1) and (Habituation is ModeratelyHabituated)
and (Membership is FarNextLevel) then (Perceived Exertion is PE1)

If (RCC is RCC1) and (Habituation is ModeratelyHabituated)
and (Membership is CloseNextLevel) then (Perceived Exertion is PE1)

If (RCC is RCC1) and (Habituation is ModeratelyHabituated)
and (Membership is VeryCloseNextLevel) then (Perceived Exertion is PE2)

If (RCC is RCC1) and (Habituation is NotHabituated) and (Membership
is FarNextLevel) then (Perceived Exertion is PE1)

If (RCC is RCC1) and (Habituation is NotHabituated) and
(Membership is CloseNextLevel or Membership is VeryClose
NextLevel) then (Perceived Exertion is PE2)

FIGURE 6: Rules for RCC1.

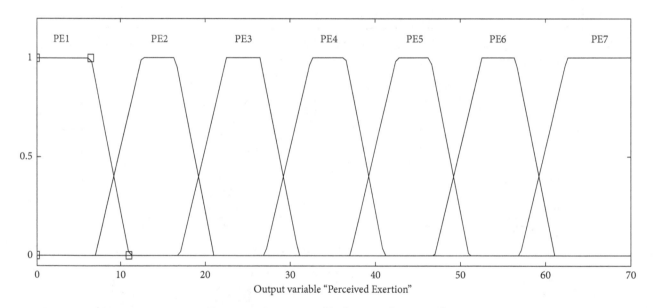

FIGURE 7: Output variable "perceived exertion."

(compensate) the perceived exertion. Membership function for habituation variable is shown in Figure 4.

Another criterion used to conform the rules is a variable called membership. This variable is used to define when a PE result must be located in the next level. That is, if a worker is moderately habituated and his membership variable is VeryCloseNextLevel, then his PE is upgraded to the next level of PE. If a worker is nonhabituated and his Membership variable equals to CloseNextLevel or VeryCloseNextLevel, then his PE result is upgraded to the next level of PE. Figure 5 illustrates the Membership function.

After that, rule base is constructed, rules are based on knowledge or experience in the domain and these are useful for the inference engine to carry out the process of defuzification. In our proposal, rules make use of the fuzzification of efforts scalar sets defined by Chamoux and habituation impact on the worker.

An extract of the rules used in the proposal is illustrated in Figure 6, specifically for the first level of relative cardiac

costs (labeled as RCC1). For each one of the seven RCC levels [RCC1, RCC7] were built a group of rules similar to these.

Later, we use the inference engine fed by the defined rules, where the level of habituation and the degree of membership to relative cardiac costs are part of the rules. The last step is the defuzzification phase. The COA method was applied for defuzzification. The COA defuzzification method effectively calculates the best compromise between multiple output linguistic terms [15]. In this phase, we obtained PE, which is one of all possible outputs (linguistic variables), as shown in Figure 7.

5. Experiments

The tests were conducted on a university campus, and users were potential janitors and janitors. In the experiments, a group of 20 research participants conducted a series of work activities, and heart rate measurements were taken during those activities. These data sets were collected using a population of 20

TABLE 3: Participants' characteristics.

Subject	Genre	Age	BMI	Habituation level
Worker 1	Male	23	29.62	Habituated
Worker 2	Female	23	21.98	Habituated
Worker 3	Female	23	20.95	Moderately habituated
Worker 4	Male	22	24.72	Habituated
Worker 5	Male	23	28.27	Habituated
Worker 6	Male	23	20.03	Not habituated
Worker 7	Female	24	19.27	Not habituated
Worker 8	Female	33	31.24	Moderately habituated
Worker 9	Female	34	21.68	Habituated
Worker 10	Male	25	28.44	Habituated
Worker 11	Male	28	28.33	Habituated
Worker 12	Male	27	24.38	Habituated
Worker 13	Male	24	33.64	Not habituated
Worker 14	Female	28	29.36	Moderately habituated
Worker 15	Male	34	23.63	Not habituated
Worker 16	Female	36	24.35	Not habituated
Worker 17	Male	33	24.68	Habituated
Worker 18	Female	22	26.29	Not habituated
Worker 19	Female	36	30.44	Not habituated
Worker 20	Male	51	23.12	Habituated

TABLE 4: Activities in the experiments.

Activity	Description
Sweep the floor	One broom (1 kg) was used in this activity. A hallway (42 m long × 0.5 m width) was the area to sweep. The volunteers started in one corner of the hallway and swept in overlapping strokes in towards the end of the hallway.
Washing windows	The total dimensions of the window were 110 cm × 90 cm. The research participants started at the top and worked down the window. This activity was executed in indoor environments.
Stacking chairs	Placing the entire stack of chairs had a short walk away (3 m). This activity was done using iron chairs (7 kg). During these activities were created several stacks, each stack with 8 chairs; all experiments were done in an indoor hallway. Never were stacked more than ten chairs at a time.

participants; 11 male (28.4 ± 8.5 years, BMI 26.26 ± 3.77) and 9 female (28.7 ± 5.97 years, BMI 25.06 ± 4.45). Participants' characteristics are shown in Table 3.

Three physical activities were defined for every research participant. These activities are described in Table 4.

Personal characteristics and physical conditions (such as age, sex, acclimation, and physical condition) are the attributes that are indirectly reflected when we measure the maximal theoretical heart rate being their maximal personal effort for each user. Together with the heart rate at rest and individualized monitoring in real time during the execution

of physical activities, they allow customized estimations. During analysis, these characteristics' results allow us to see that two people with similar characteristics do not necessarily perform the same effort to perform the same activity.

Heart rate was measured using an unobtrusive Basis B1 fitness tracker band. Basis' precision is enough to know how many beats per minute a user heart has. Basis B1 measures our blood pressure, steps, intensity and exertion of our workout, and sleep metrics. This device was placed on the wrist of each worker. The first activity was to sweep a floor using a broom, the second activity was to clean glass windows with a rag, and the last activity was stacking metal structure chairs.

Heart rate values used in all methods (Borg–Chamoux–personalized Chamoux–fuzzy personalized Chamoux) were the average heart rates during the activities.

Experiments related to the three labor activities are shown in Figure 8.

6. Results

In order to compare the resulting values of all methods tested, we made a mapping of the Borg's perceived exertion values (Table 1) with labels used in Chamoux method (Table 2). Scales 6-7 are no exertion (NE), 8-9 are very light (VL), 10-11 are light (L), 12 is slightly moderate (SM), 13 is moderate (M), 14 is slightly heavy (SH), 15-16 are heavy (H), and over 16 is intense (I).

A frequency analysis of results of perceived exertion of the participants obtained for each physical activity was included. In order to do this, we obtained some values describing the features of a collection of data from physical activities performed. For stacking chairs activity, Table 5 shows the number of users for each perceived exertion level grouped by the method.

In Table 5 we can see that the estimated perceived exertion of people using the Borg method is only two levels, the common Chamoux method classifies them into three levels, and the personalized Chamoux and our proposal (FPC) classify them into five levels. The Borg method classifies all people into very light (VL) and light (L); conventional Chamoux classifies 20% into SM, as it only takes into account the age of the people; personalized Chamoux distributes 60% of workers between SM and SH, this is because it takes into account personal maximum effort, in addition to the age of the individual; while the proposed method makes a small rearrangement of the number of people at every level, which results from applying the fuzzy logic for handling uncertainty membership groups and the effect of habituation variable. This indicates that our proposal has a better effort discrimination because of measuring their personal maximum effort, fuzzy sets without clear and defined boundaries, rules base, and habituation-level variable.

In Figure 9(a), the results of perceived exertion are scalar (diffuse for FPC), whereas in Figure 9(b) the results of perceived exertion are linguistic (crisp for FPC). The objective is that the decision-maker can appreciate not only the level of final perceived exertion obtained (after the whole process) but also the level of belonging to that level (scalar values). The same criterion applies for Figures 9(c) and 9(d).

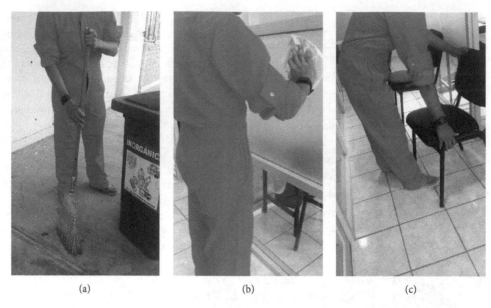

(a)   (b)   (c)

FIGURE 8: Activities developed by participants: (a) sweeping floors, (b) cleaning windows, and (c) stacking chairs.

TABLE 5: Number of users for each effort level during stacking chair activity, grouped by method.

Perceived exertion	Borg	Chamoux	Personalized Chamoux	Fuzzy personalized Chamoux
VL	11	4	0	0
L	9	12	8	6
SM	0	4	6	6
M	0	0	4	5
SH	0	0	2	3

These results can be used in decision-making to preserve or improve the health and quality of life of the worker. This can be done by adjusting their work environment or by measuring physical performance based on their effort for a better allocation of their workload.

As we can see in Figures 9(a) and 9(b), a female worker who is moderately habituated to physical job maintained her perceived exertion level obtained using FPC with respect to the personalized Chamoux with sweeping and cleaning windows activities; however, while she was stacking chairs (which demands more physical effort), her perceived exertion level increased. With regard to not habituated male Worker 6 (Figures 9(c) and 9(d)), his perceived exertion level obtained using FPC increased with respect to the personalized Chamoux with all activities (sweeping, cleaning windows, and stacking chairs). All his FPC perceived exertion levels were higher than the personalized Chamoux perceived exertion levels. We attribute this behavior to the level of habituation. One objective of this proposal is to illustrate how the habituation factor impacts the perceived effort, and the proposal is not focused on an accurate calculation of physical effort or energy expenditure.

Figures 10 and 11 show personalized Chamoux and FPC methods to classify perceived exertions during sweeping.

As we can see, results clearly reflect different perceived exertion levels for individuals even though they perform the same activity. In Figure 10, the results of the FPC method are fuzzy, and in Figure 11, the results of the FPC method are defuzzified.

The statistical results allow us to know that when the activity is physically demanding (activity of stacking chairs), variance and standard deviation values are much higher. This shows that the many factors involved in the process of classifying perceived exertion are clearly reflected in the increase in cardiac frequency.

Figures 12 and 13 illustrate an activity that can be physically demanding if we are not habituated, and they show how the fuzzy personalized Chamoux method is more efficient for classifying individual perceived exertion, which is appreciated particularly for the activity of stacking chairs (Figures 12 and 13). Figure 12 can be very useful for a decision-maker to appreciate how a worker is being impacted for a specific physical activity.

All participants were directly observed during experiments to estimate their physical effort level. Additionally, they were asked about their perceived exertion just at the end of each activity. We obtained that perceived exertion classification using our proposed method is coincident (75% or higher) with respect to our direct observation and answers from participants.

Workers' personal perceived exertion (PPE) was a linguistic label (belonging to Table 2) that participants assigned

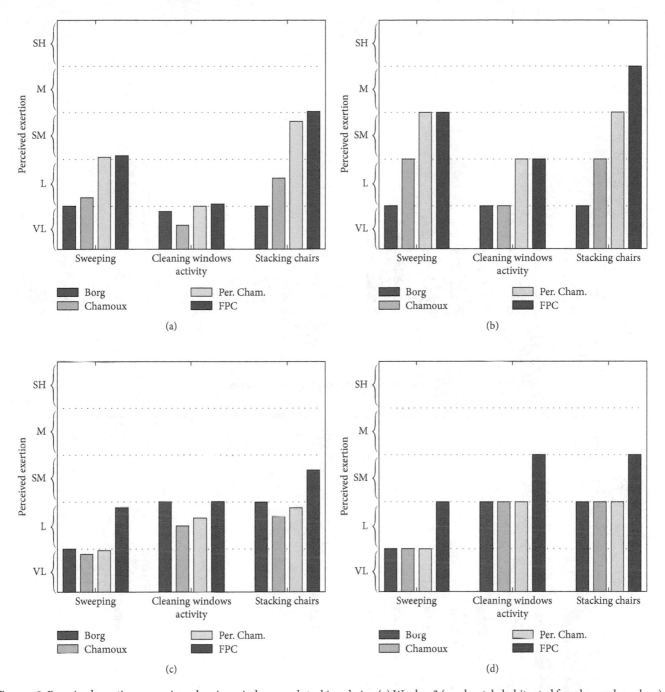

FIGURE 9: Perceived exertion: sweeping, cleaning windows, and stacking chairs. (a) Worker 3 (moderately habituated female—scalar values), (b) Worker 3 (moderately habituated female—linguistic values), (c) Worker 6 (not habituated male—scalar values), and (d) Worker 6 (not habituated male—linguistic values).

to each developed activity, representing their effort perception. We compare PPEs with FPC results to evaluate our proposal. Matching percentages were 75%, 75%, and 80% for sweeping, cleaning windows, and stacking chairs, respectively. As an example, in Figure 14, it is appreciated a comparison of workers' PPE versus linguistic outputs provided by our proposal for the sweeping activity.

We have designed a prototype for logging and informing users about their perceived exertion levels and historical records during activities. Figure 15 shows the prototype for Android devices.

The disk located at the bottom of the interface simulates a semaphore. The colors used represent the different levels of perceived exertion (from very light to intense). The green color represents the lowest levels of effort, and the red color represents the intense effort. The yellow color is used for moderate efforts. The purpose of the disk in the interface is that a given user can visualize in each moment and, in real time, the percentage of monitoring time that he/she has been in each level of perceived exertion, in accordance with our proposed method. Recording of perceived efforts is useful for rapid decision-making by the supervising manager, for

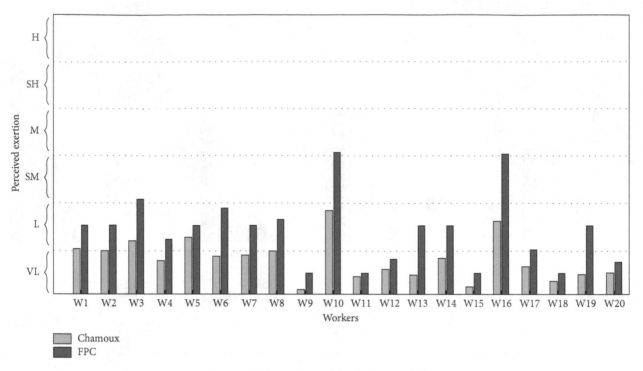

FIGURE 10: Sweeping activity (scalar results).

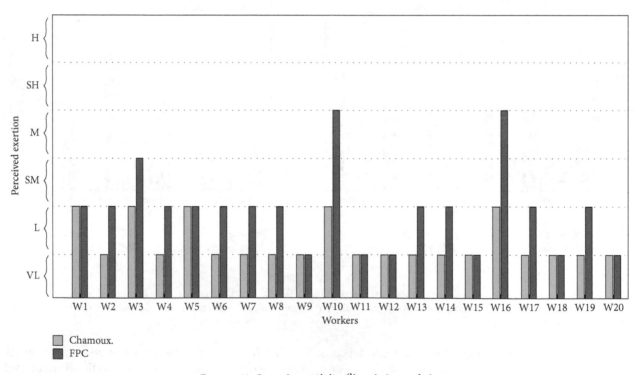

FIGURE 11: Sweeping activity (linguistic results).

example, for reassignment of tasks or scheduling of rest periods.

7. Discussion

The smartwatch presented several failures when data started to be captured, that is why a period of at least three minutes was monitored before the value of cardiac frequency was taken. However, as cardiac frequency values entered to formulas were averaged, some noise effects do not impact the results. We think that technological advances will let that future devices be more precise in sensing.

Considering habituation as a factor in the method of estimating perceived effort allows in turn improving

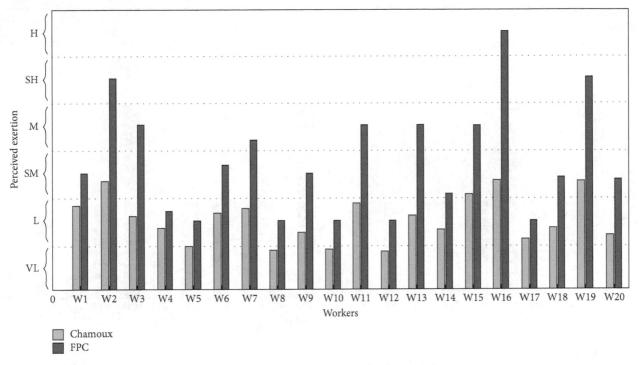

FIGURE 12: Stacking chair activity (scalar results).

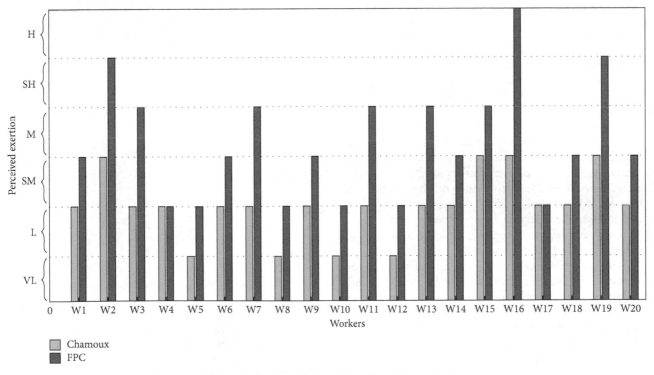

FIGURE 13: Stacking chair activity (linguistic results).

decision-making, for example, when a worker should be selected for a job with physical activities. Habituation is important because an unhabituated worker will have a greater perceived effort with respect to another worker who is accustomed, as studies reveal [24, 25].

Although recent proposals have determined rates in perceived exertion, these results do not consider individual factors related to worker experience or the physical activity performance. This is, for activities that cannot be controlled in terms of the intensity with which users perform them

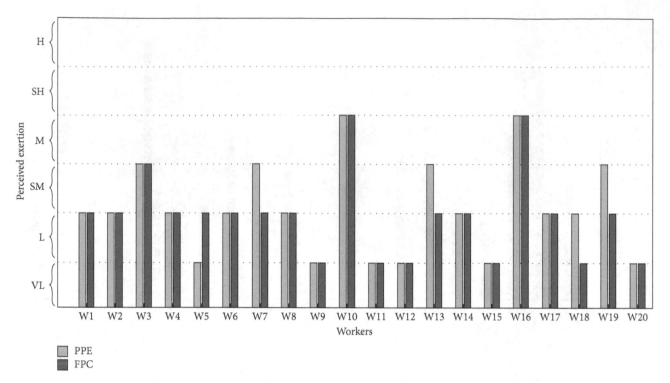

FIGURE 14: Sweeping activity (personal perceived exertion versus FPC method results).

(e.g., sweeping), each user executes them according to their personality, unlike activities performed on an electric treadmill where the speed at which they walk or run is controlled, so many studies only offer average energy expenditure values for daily activities. For this reason, in some cases for the same activity, a moderately habituated person may have a perceived exertion slightly greater than an unhabituated person.

Perceived exertion assessment in labor physical activities must consider factors such as physical condition, obesity, and hypertension; environmental factors like temperature, humidity, and altitude; or even factors affecting individual physical response in the performance of physical activities such as habituation and acclimatization. Recent proposals do not include these factors in perceived exertion assessment, which can lead to inaccurate decision-making in the allocation of a job post, for example.

The proposed method can handle any of these factors; habituation is an example of how this can be done. To handle other factors (like nutrition), variables and their domains have to be known (such as the quantity (kg and liters) and quality (calories) of food ingested and the time (hours and min) spent between the consumption of food and the performance of the activity), as well as their impact on perceived exertion, that is, the weight to be given to each variable in estimating the effort.

Habituation is considered as the training experiences based on tasks repetition, which conduces to a better physical activities' performance and changes in perceived exertion.

It has been stated in recent works that considering individual characteristics like maximum effort in activities'

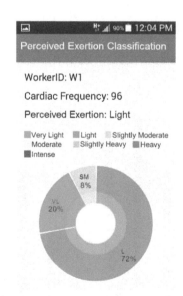

FIGURE 15: Perceived exertion prototype.

performance conduces to a better perceived exertion assessment. Published results of perceived exertion are based on one of the following methods: Borg method which considers a HR = [60, 220] to define a 14-value scale [22, 28] going from no exertion to maximal exertion, Chamoux method considering person age (220 − age) as the baseline to define a 70-value scale RCC = [0, 69], grouped in sets of 10 values each going from very light to intense, and extended Chamoux which considers individual maximum exertion as the baseline. However, effort level transition in those scales based on HR values may not correspond to perceived exertion (as perceived by the worker), due to lack of habituation, that is, when considering habituation, a compensation value has to be added to personal exertion for less habituated ones.

Since the assessment of perceived effort and habituation are based on human experience, the fuzzy logic can be used in such evaluations, given that discrete and continuous membership functions of a fuzzy set are intended to capture a person's thinking. Fuzzy membership functions can be determined subjectively in practical problems based on an expert's opinion. Membership functions can be considered as a technique to formalize empirical problem solving that is based on experience rather than the knowledge of theory.

Fuzzy membership function of habituation takes one of three values: no habituated, moderate habituation, and habituated. Fuzzy set values are defined in [0, 1] interval: border values are for a nonhabituated person and a habituated one, respectively. The membership degree was determined by worker experience and direct observation of workers performing physical activities. Values from fuzzy membership function of habituation, CCR, 20% compensation for nonhabituated and 10% compensation for moderate habituated, are inputs for fuzzy membership function of perceived exertion. Fuzzy membership function of perceived exertion takes one of 7 values: very light, light, slightly moderate, moderate, slightly heavy, heavy, and intense, each one taking ten values in [0, 69] interval.

Habituation contribution to perceived exertion assessment is a more realistic result in terms of human experience. As it can be seen in the results (Figure 9), perceived exertion can change to the next level when considering habituation. We think by experience that when a person is not accustomed to perform labor physical activities, the higher the hardness of activities is, the higher the level of perceived effort is. This is true when considering that the membership of one value to a set is binary, that is, a person is habituated or not to perform an activity; however, when considering fuzzy sets, the membership is defined by a function that takes its values in the interval [0, 1]. The closer the degree of membership is to 1, the more the element will be in the set, and the closer the degree of membership is to 0, the less the element will be in the set.

Results obtained in this study clearly establish the importance of considering factors such as habituation to physical activities performance in the evaluation of perceived exertion of workers. Adjustment of perceived exertion levels achieved with fuzzy logic allows us to improve decision-making for the allocation of jobs, the planning of workloads, or even the reduction of risks of fatigue accidents.

8. Conclusions

The contributions of this proposal are the ability to classify perceived exertion of people in daily activities, to improve their safety and health. This is because it is formally established that the effort of a person can be estimated based on his/her cardiac frequency. A standard effort can be estimated for each activity as a reference to analyze the gap with the personalized perceived exertion estimated by our proposed method to perform those activities; the usefulness of measuring the personalized effort of workers in their work environment to preserve their health; and the possibility to determine that a person is conducting his/her activities in a comfortable way, that is, in accordance with his/her personal capacities, abilities, and habituation to improve performance, safety, and welfare state.

This is not a proposal to accurately measure the physical effort but emphasizes the importance of customizing the measurement process and mentions that it is hardly possible to have a generic method, given a large number of variables that must be considered. The intention is to show how the effort estimation varies when considering a custom value as the maximum personal cardiac frequency, as well as imprecision and uncertainty of variables affecting methods to classify perceived exertion.

Using the fuzzy logic, it was possible to verify the importance of the degree of membership of a variable to a fuzzy set, because depending on the degree of membership it is possible that the perceived exertion can be increased (next label) as a result of the rules used by the inference engine. This situation is more suited to real life where although a variable belongs to a certain group, there is a level of belonging to that group, which should be considered because it may be more correct to classify the variable as belonging to a nearby set.

The proposed method for the classification of perceived exertion considers how to add possible variables, as exemplified by the inclusion of habituation and the way it affects, as obtained in related studies. Analysis of our results reveals that an objective method of estimating individual effort should consider custom values in the parameters to capture the widest possible set of variables involved in the estimation of perceived exertion. Therefore, the decision to perform a stress test for obtaining the maximum heart rate is important, because with this action, indirectly, we are including many factors such as age, sex, body mass index, and acclimation.

We conclude that the use of a wearable device with capacities of measurement of physiological parameters together with fuzzy logic computational methods provokes expert knowledge that represent a viable automatic solution for perceived exertion classification.

Future work includes other factors involved such as environment, gender, body mass index, and mental stress. Another type of sensors must be considered, as well as the combination of heterogeneous sensors. The perceived exertion should be objective; direct observation gives an idea of the results, but it is based on experience and questionnaires. Habituation to physical effort requires further study; to our knowledge, there are no studies analyzing the impact of habituation to perform physical activities in the perceived exertion of workers. Additionally, it is important to extend FPC method definition to integrate the implementation into a smartphone.

Acknowledgments

This paper was supported by Universidad Juárez Autónoma de Tabasco through Grant no. UJAT-2014-IA-01.

References

[1] S. Adibi, *Mobile Health. A Technology Road Map*, Springer International Publishing, Cham, Switzerland, 2015.

[2] R. S. H. Istepanian, C. S. Pattichis, and S. Laxminarayan, *Ubiquitous M-Health Systems and the Convergence Towards 4G Mobile Technologies*, pp. 3–14, Springer, Boston, MA, USA, 2006.

[3] B. J. Noble and R. J. Robertson, *Perceived Exertion*, Human Kinetics Publishers, Champaign, IL, USA, 1996.

[4] A. Holtermann, M. B. Jørgensen, B. Gram et al., "Worksite interventions for preventing physical deterioration among employees in job-groups with high physical work demands: background, design and conceptual model of finale," *BMC Public Health*, vol. 10, no. 1, p. 120, 2010.

[5] S. Gallagher, J. S. Moore, and T. J. Stobbe, *Physical Strength Assessment in Ergonomics*, pp. 1–61, American Industrial Hygiene Association, Falls Church, VA, USA, January 1998.

[6] AIHA Technical Committee, "Ergonomics guide to assessment of metabolic and cardiac costs of physical work," *American Industrial Hygiene Association Journal*, vol. 32, no. 8, pp. 560–564, 1971.

[7] S. Nogareda-Cuixart and P. Luna-Mendaza, *Ntp 323: Determination of Metabolic Rate*, Instituto Nacional de Seguridad e Higiene en el Trabajo. Ministerio de Trabajo y Asuntos Sociales, Espaa, Madrid, Spain, 2005.

[8] K. Parsons, "Occupational health impacts of climate change: current and future iso standards for the assessment of heat stress," *Industrial Health*, vol. 51, no. 1, pp. 86–100, 2013.

[9] S. E. Crouter, J. R. Churilla, and D. R. Bassett, "Estimating energy expenditure using accelerometers," *European Journal of Applied Physiology*, vol. 98, no. 6, pp. 601–612, 2006.

[10] G. A. Borg, "Psychophysical bases of perceived exertion," *Medicine and Science in Sports and Exercise*, vol. 14, no. 5, pp. 377–381, 1982.

[11] D. W. Esliger, A. V. Rowlands, T. L. Hurst, M. Catt, P. Murray, and R. G. Eston, "Validation of the genea accelerometer," *Medicine and Science in Sports and Exercise*, vol. 43, no. 6, pp. 1085–1093, 2011.

[12] P. Pancardo, F. D. Acosta, J. A. Hernández-Nolasco, M. A. Wister, and D. López-de Ipiña, "Real-time personalized monitoring to estimate occupational heat stress in ambient assisted working," *Sensors*, vol. 15, no. 7, pp. 16956–16980, 2015.

[13] P. Pancardo, J. A. Hernández-Nolasco, F. D. Acosta, and M. A. Wister, "Personalizing physical effort estimation in workplaces using a wearable heart rate sensor," in *Proceedings of the 10th International Conference on Ubiquitous Computing and Ambient Intelligence (UCAmI 2016)*, Part II 10, pp. 111–122, Springer, San Bartolomé de Tirajana, Gran Canaria, Spain, December 2016.

[14] P. Frimat, M. Amphoux, and A. Chamoux, "Interprétation et mesure de la fréquence cardiaque," *Revue de Medicine du Travail XV*, vol. 147, no. 4, p. 165, 1988.

[15] L. A. Zadeh, "Outline of a new approach to the analysis of complex systems and decision processes," *IEEE Transactions on Systems, Man and Cybernetics*, vol. 3, no. 1, pp. 28–45, 1973.

[16] International Labour Organization, "Safety and health at work," 2016, http://www.ilo.org.

[17] ISO Standard, 9886, *Ergonomics-Evaluation of Thermal Strain by Physiological Measurements*, International Standard Organization, Geneva, Switzerland, 2nd edition, 2004.

[18] L. G. Sylvia, E. E. Bernstein, J. L. Hubbard, L. Keating, and E. J. Anderson, "A practical guide to measuring physical activity," *Journal of the Academy of Nutrition and Dietetics*, vol. 114, no. 2, pp. 199–208, 2014.

[19] S. J. Strath, A. M. Swartz, D. R. Bassett Jr., W. L. O'Brien, G. A. King, and B. E. Ainsworth, "Evaluation of heart rate as a method for assessing moderate intensity physical activity," *Medicine and Science in Sports and Exercise*, vol. 32, no. 9, pp. S465–S470, 2000.

[20] H. Medjahed, D. Istrate, J. Boudy et al., "A fuzzy logic approach for remote healthcare monitoring by learning and recognizing human activities of daily living," *Fuzzy Logic-Emerging Technologies and Applications*, InTech, London, UK, 2012.

[21] J.-S. R. Jang, C.-T. Sun, and E. Mizutani, "Neuro-fuzzy and soft computing-a computational approach to learning and machine intelligence," *IEEE Transactions on Automatic Control*, vol. 42, no. 10, pp. 1482–1484, 1997.

[22] M. E. Bouton, *Learning and Behavior: A Contemporary Synthesis*, Sinauer Associates, Sunderland, MA, USA, 2007.

[23] J. Borresen and M. I. Lambert, "The quantification of training load, the training response and the effect on performance," *Sports Medicine*, vol. 39, no. 9, pp. 779–795, 2009.

[24] E. M. Heath, J. R. Blackwell, U. C. Baker, D. R. Smith, and K. W. Kornatz, "Backward walking practice decreases oxygen uptake, heart rate and ratings of perceived exertion," *Physical Therapy in Sport*, vol. 2, no. 4, pp. 171–177, 2001.

[25] J. F. Patton, W. P. Morgan, and J. A. Vogel, "Perceived exertion of absolute work during a military physical training program," *European Journal of Applied Physiology and Occupational Physiology*, vol. 36, no. 2, pp. 107–114, 1977.

[26] S. Hwang, J. Seo, J. Ryu, and S. Lee, "Challenges and opportunities of understanding construction worker's physical demands through field energy expenditure measurements using a wearable activity tracker," in *Proceedings of Construction Research Congress 2016*, pp. 2730–2739, San Juan, Puerto Rico, May–June 2016.

[27] A. Kolus, D. Imbeau, P.-A. Dubé, and D. Dubeau, "Adaptive neuro-fuzzy inference systems with k-fold cross-validation for energy expenditure predictions based on heart rate," *Applied Ergonomics*, vol. 50, pp. 68–78, 2015.

[28] G. C. Migliaccio, J. Teizer, T. Cheng, and U. C. Gatti, "Automatic identification of unsafe bending behavior of construction workers using real-time location sensing and physiological status monitoring," in *Proceedings of the Construction Research Congress*, vol. 2123, p. 633642, West Lafayette, IN, USA, May 2012.

[29] A. Aryal, A. Ghahramani, and B. Becerik-Gerber, "Monitoring fatigue in construction workers using physiological measurements," *Automation in Construction*, vol. 82, pp. 154–165, 2017.

[30] Y. Shimizu and T. Jindo, "A fuzzy logic analysis method for evaluating human sensitivities," *International Journal of Industrial Ergonomics*, vol. 15, no. 1, pp. 39–47, 1995.

[31] W. Karwowski and M. M. Ayoub, "Fuzzy modelling of stresses in manual lifting tasks," *Ergonomics*, vol. 27, no. 6, pp. 641–649, 1984.

13

IoT Services and Virtual Objects Management in Hyperconnected Things Network

Israr Ullah ⓘ,[1] Muhammad Sohail Khan,[2] and DoHyeun Kim ⓘ[1]

[1]Computer Engineering Department, Jeju National University, Jeju City, Republic of Korea
[2]Department of Computer Software Engineering, University of Engineering and Technology, Mardan, Pakistan

Correspondence should be addressed to DoHyeun Kim; kimdh@jejunu.ac.kr

Academic Editor: Maristella Matera

In recent past, Internet of Things- (IoT-) based applications have experienced tremendous growth in various domains, and billions of devices are expected to be connected to the Internet in near future. The first step for development of IoT-based applications is to virtualize the physical devices by abstracting device properties in virtual objects. Later, these virtual objects can be combined to compose different services for diverse applications. Many existing systems provide virtualization service for physical devices and service composition. But, with the growth of the network, when too many devices and services are added in the IoT network, its management will become a cumbersome task. This paper presents an architecture of IoT services and virtual objects management in hyperconnected things network to facilitate the management tasks. We also have implemented a Service and Virtual Objects Management (SVOM) system prototype to effectively organize and monitor the physical devices through corresponding virtual objects and services composed in the IoT environment. The proposed system also provides interface for user interaction to perform supported control operations on selected device and check device operational and fault status. For scalability analysis of the proposed system, we have performed simulation in the OMNeT++ simulator to study impact of the IoT network size on key performance measures like response time, throughput, and packet delivery ratio. Simulation results reveal that with the growing network size, the gateway nodes become the performance bottleneck. We have also performed resources requirement analysis for virtual objects and control overhead analysis of the proposed management system. Simulation results reveal that control overhead is insignificant in normal scenarios; however, in extreme network conditions, we may have to sacrifice fewer bits which is, in fact, worth nothing when compared to the flexibility and control offered by the proposed management system.

1. Introduction

Recent developments in communication technologies have enabled the small computing devices to communicate and share information anytime, anywhere. Majority of the conducted and ongoing research is centered around the same objective, that is, to enable seamless usage of computing devices in daily life. This is made possible by integration of many underlying enabling technologies including Internet, tiny devices, sensors, and operating system, protocols, and interoperability standards. Still, there are many open challenges and opportunities, inviting research attention for investigation and exploitation; for example, the recently coined term Internet of Things (IoT) has opened a new avenue for research and development in many different fields [1]. IoT is mainly focused on connectivity of

things (daily life objects with attached sensors or actuators) to the Internet so that users can remotely monitor and control a particular activity or device.

Internet of Things (IoT) is designed to attach a small communicating device with everything that we want to monitor or control using the Internet. The IoT device may be a sensing device that collects some desired information, or it can be an actuating device that can accept commands to perform some desired tasks. IoT devices have limited communication, computation, and battery power, so specialized lightweight protocols are designed for efficient resource utilization and communication over the Internet, for example, CoAP protocol [2]. IoT Systems have tremendous capabilities and applications [3]. In the recent past, many giant manufacturing and development organizations have

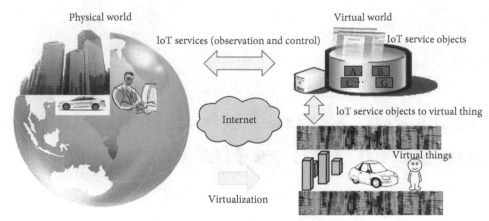

FIGURE 1: Physical world observation and control through virtual world in the IoT environment.

made investment in this technology to realize its potential. Many projects are initiated to address different aspects of IoT-based systems.

The development of IoT composition tools is one of the key areas of research to enable mass participation in realization of the IoT vision [4]. The objective is to enable a common user to utilize IoT-based system in order to achieve his/her desired task without any programming skills. These systems will also enable managers and designers to use the system on their own without bothering IoT experts to achieve some tasks. Many Do-It-Yourself (DIY) IoT projects are initiated in this connection to develop IoT composition toolboxes using standard business process modeling (BPM) notations. The user of this system is expected to be aware of the BPM notation and will only require slight training to utilize the system in his/her domain.

Many existing systems provide virtualization service for physical devices by creating its virtual object (VO). Later, VOs are combined to compose services which can be used to build various applications [5]. Figure 1 is a typical illustration of physical world observation and control through the virtual world in the IoT environment. Virtual world is also known as cyberworld, and the complete system is then referred as cyberphysical system (CPS). This strategy works fine when the system has limited number of registered devices and services, but when the system grows and too many virtual objects are added, devices management becomes a cumbersome task. Similarly, when too many services are composed, services management will be a challenging task. To resolve this issue, we propose "*Services and Virtual Objects Management (SVOM)*" system as a solution. The main objective of our proposed system is to effectively organize the service and virtual objects to facilitate the management task. Furthermore, we have performed simulation of the proposed system in OMNeT++ for scalability analysis to study the impact of the IoT network size on key performance measures like response time, throughput, and packet delivery ratio. We have also conducted experiments for the analysis of resources requirement and control overhead generated by the proposed system.

Rest of the paper is organized as follows. Section 2 presents an overview of some related works in the literature. Detailed description of the proposed system design and

functionality is covered in Section 3. System implementation prototype is presented in Section 4. Scalability analysis of the proposed system is performed via simulation in OMNeT++, and simulation results are presented in Section 5. Towards the end, we conclude this paper in Section 6 with an outlook to our future work.

2. Related Work

Since inception, IoT has attracted too much research attention, and it is considered among the future disruptive technologies having the potential to transform every aspect of human life. Various IoT-based applications are developed for building smart environment in home, cities, health, education, security, entertainment, and industry. To enable rapid application development, several standard platforms are introduced. Philips company, known for its home appliances manufacturing, has introduced an IoT management platform for their products called Philips Hue which allows the users to easily connect home appliances to the Internet [6] for remote monitoring and control, thus realizing the concept of smart homes. The IoT.est project is an effort towards building intelligent IoT-based solution using semantic technologies to support interoperability among distributed and diverse sources [7]. They have developed a test bed for the IoT service creation and validation through several use cases. Both Philips Hue and IoT.est are focused on realization of IoT and do not consider management and scalability issues. Management functionality is given due consideration in the IoT architecture reference model (IoT-ARM) [8]. The functional model for IoT as proposed in the IoT-A project includes management functionality group having five components, that is, configuration, fault, reporting, member, and state. In this paper, we are focused on fault and configuration management in hyperconnected IoT systems with too many virtual objects and services.

Finding a suitable service required for a particular application development over Internet is a challenging task. Normally, a dynamic service discovery option does not satisfy the complex user requirements for exceeding number of requests. Reference [9] presents an idea of on-demand service creation by combining existing services to meet

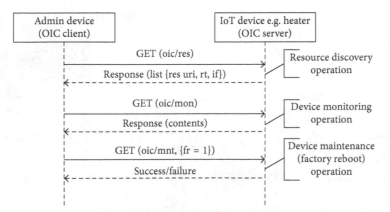

FIGURE 2: Typical interaction between OIC client and server for device management operation.

complex user needs using visual and interactive interface. User-desired objective is decomposed into subgoals, and the attempt is made to satisfy each subgoal in an iterative fashion. In [10], the authors present a semiautomatic mechanism for service filtering using semantic ontology. Their proposed system consists of two key components, composer and inference engine. The inference engine helps in the selection of best matching service by performing service filtering which is then connected by the composer component to produce desired service. A similar system is reported in [11] for automatic service composition. Intelligent solutions based on AI algorithms are also explored for automatic service composition in [12]. A framework for IoT objects naming and management is proposed in [13], based on the IoT-IMS platform. However, their main focus is on addressing the issue due to lack of proper rules or specification for naming things.

Device management, diagnostics, and fault recovery capabilities are considered among the core requirements in standards developed for IoT technologies. For instance, the most popular standard developed by Open Connectivity Foundation (OCF) defines guidelines for device management, diagnostic, and maintenance through two OIC core resources /oic/mon and /oic/mnt that shall be supported by all devices [14]. The monitoring resource (/oic/mon) is used for collection of device statistics, for example, packets sent, packets received, last operation time, and so on. This maintenance resource (/oic/mnt) has two important properties: (a) factory reset "fr" is used to update the device configuration to its original (default) state (factory state and equivalent to hard reboot), and (b) reboot "rb" triggers a soft reboot of a device while maintaining most of the configurations intact. Figure 2 shows typical interaction between OIC client and server for device management operation. The OCF is also sponsoring an open source project IoTivity to provide reference implementation for OCF technical specifications [15]. Likewise, oneM2M is a global organization that aims at the development of functional architecture, API specifications, security solution with interoperability for M2M communication, and IoT technologies. The oneM2M standard architecture defines three main entities, that is, common service entity, network service entity, and application entity [16]. The common service entity has two main components, that is, common service functions (CSFs) and

enabler functions (EFs). CSF includes *Device Management* among core components to utilize the information for administrative purposes, that is, diagnostic and troubleshooting. The oneM2M specifies four key functions for device management, that is, device diagnostic and monitoring function (DDMF), device configuration function (DCF), device firmware management function (DFMF), and device topology management functions (DTMFs). Similarly, ITU-T also considers device management, diagnostic, and fault recovery capabilities among the common service and application support functions [17].

Recently, Do-It-Yourself- (DIY-) based projects are initiated in many fields to enable mass involvement and promote rapid development without requiring any special training. Arduino [18], Intel Edison [19], and Raspberry Pi [20] boards are very popular for customized hardware-based application development but users need to learn their respective programming languages in order to build and execute applications using these boards. Thus, only programmers can benefit from it. The SAM project by the Kickstarter [21] company is a useful initiative towards DIY-based development for normal users to build applications for fun and help students in learning basics of electronics through demonstration. Reference [22] presents an improved DIY-based service composition toolbox using the CoAP protocol. They have developed a visual interface for composition of services by combining registered virtual objects using drag and drop operations.

Many IoT projects and research contributions are geared towards prototypes development, protocols, standards, and process automation. This work is an extension of [22], and our proposed system is an effort to address scalability and management issues in the future IoT world with anticipated growth and hyperconnectivity.

3. Proposed Management System for IoT Service and Virtual Objects

The conceptual layering structure of the proposed management system for IoT service and virtual objects is given in Figure 3. There are four main layers: physical layer, virtual object layer, service composition layer, and management layer. Brief description of each layer is given below.

Physical Layer is mainly composed of two types of devices: (a) sensors are electronic and/or electromechanical

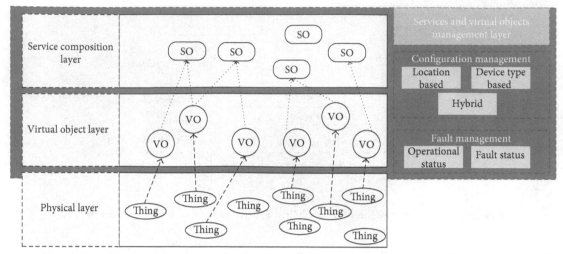

FIGURE 3: Conceptual layering structure of the proposed management system for IoT service and virtual objects.

devices which acquire data from their surroundings; (b) actuators are used to control the contextual parameters through their actuation. In the figure, things represent both set of sensing and actuating things.

The *Virtual Object Layer* represents the physical layer things in the form of virtual objects (VOs). VOs are the in-system representation of a thing at the physical layer which encapsulates the information associated with a physical thing. Through VO manipulation, users can interact with the system environment. We have developed a virtual device manager (VDM) application to create corresponding virtual objects for each physical device in our system. The virtual objects at the virtual object layer are utilized by the *Service Composition Layer* in order to compose service objects (SOs) by combining the functionality offered by two or more virtual objects. A simple SO may thus contain an input VO joined with an output stream to display the collected data. A more complex example of a service object would be to join a temperature sensor VO with a fan VO with the settings that when the temperature value exceeds x degrees Celsius, the fan shall be turned ON. The acquisition of the temperature value and the actuation of the fan depend on the functionality encapsulated in their corresponding VOs. The Specialized Service Composition Manger (SCM) application is used to perform tasks of this layer.

An IoT system having these three basic layers (i.e., physical, virtualization, and service composition) will work fine when the system has a limited number of registered devices and services. But, when the system grows and too many virtual objects are added, then devices management will become a cumbersome task. Similarly, when too many services are composed, then services management will also be a challenging task. To resolve this issue, we propose *Services and Virtual Objects Management* (SVOM) system as a solution. The main objective of our proposed SVOM system is to effectively organize the service and virtual objects to facilitate the management task, and it will work across the two layers (i.e., second and third layers) as shown in Figure 3.

The proposed system architecture is shown in Figure 4. Through device virtualization process, we capture properties

and behavior of physical IoT devices (sensors and actuators) in form of virtual objects and stored them in a database. Information of virtual objects is then utilized by the service composition process in order to build service objects. The proposed SVOM reads stored VOs and SOs information to facilitate fault and configuration management. The SVOM system also provides interactive services for device access and control through virtual objects. Management functionality can be exposed through API to external customized applications and service composition module.

The SVOM system internal functionality regarding services and virtual objects management can be grouped into two broad perspectives as shown in Figure 5. Brief detail of each component is given in the following subsections.

3.1. Configuration Management.
Under configuration management, the system provides an interface to explore specifications of registered virtual objects and services in three different ways as shown in Figure 6.

Location-based management will enable the users to display the virtual objects and services inside a selected region. Users can choose diameter of the circle and then click over the map to select the center of the region of interest.

All devices and services located within the circular region will be displayed. Users can interact with any device to see its current status and use the device in service composition. *Service/device type-based* management is useful when too many devices are registered in the system, and it becomes very difficult to find/choose a particular device needed by the user. This option simply provides a facility to the user to specify his/her desired type of device/service to visualize a particular type of devices or services. *Hybrid* is just a combination of aforementioned two approaches. Users can search a particular type of device or service within a selected region by choosing the radius of circular area and clicking over the map to define its center.

Configuration-Management algorithm pseudocode is given in Figure 7. It takes a list of registered virtual objects as an input along with optional parameters, that is, device type,

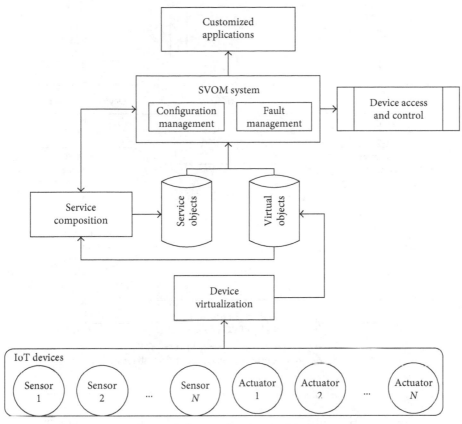

FIGURE 4: Proposed system architecture.

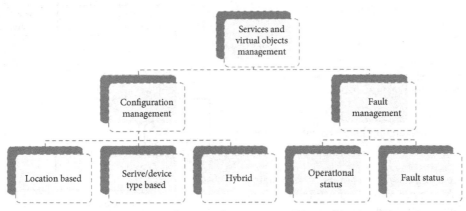

FIGURE 5: Structure of proposed system management functionalities.

location, and range. Every registered device type and location is checked if it meets user-desired parameter values, and then it is added into the *outputList* which is finally returned by this algorithm.

3.2. Fault Management. This component is focused on locating the working/not working and idle/busy devices and services. Through CoAP communication, we can easily get the current status of the registered devices and services. The flow diagram of the fault management is shown in Figure 8.

Operational status management can be used if the user is interested in finding the current idle/busy state of registered devices or services. If a device or service is currently being used by some application, then the status of that device or service is set to busy; otherwise, it becomes idle if not used by any application for a certain amount of time.

Fault status management will provide a list of nonfunctional devices to easily locate such devices for repair or replacement. A simple keep alive query (CoAP GET command) is sent to every device, and if no response is received within certain amount of time, then retry attempts are made for specified number of times. If all retry attempts are failed, then the corresponding device is labeled as nonfunctional. Any service using a nonfunctional device is also marked as notworking.

Fault Management algorithm as given in Figure 9 takes a list of registered virtual objects as an input and tries to

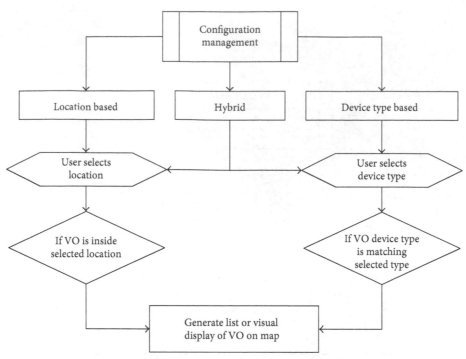

FIGURE 6: Configuration management flow diagram.

```
Algorithm Config-Management ()

    Input:

        InputList List of Registered Virtual Objects

        desiredType = arg[0] default (any)

        desiredLoc  = arg[1] default (center)

        searchRange = arg[2] default (max)

        OutputList  = new VOList[]

    Foreach vo in InputList

    {

        If (vo.devType = desiredType)

            If(isDevinRange(vo.devLoc, circle(desiredLoc, searchRange))=TRUE)

                OutputList.Add(vo)    %Make output List

    }

        return OutputList
```

FIGURE 7: Pseudocode for configuration management algorithm.

connect to each device using its URI to get its current status information. Threshold defines a maximum number of attempts for connection establishment. If no response is received, then the respective device is considered to be "*Not Working.*" The output list holds fault status information with each virtual object and can be used by the application to identify defective devices for repair or replacement.

4. Development of Proposed Management System Prototype

We have developed a prototype for management of IoT services and virtual objects in Visual Studio 2015 using C#. CoAP.NET library [23] is used for accessing IoT resources attached with Intel Edison Board. CoAP.NET implementation is based on the Californium (Cf) framework implemented in Java. Microsoft SQL Server is used to store profile information of registered IoT services and virtual objects. Table 1

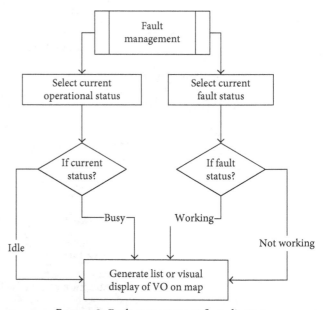

FIGURE 8: Fault management flow diagram.

summarizes the key functions list of our proposed system with brief explanation.

In the following subsections, we present the working of three main modules of our proposed SVOM system, that is, virtual objects management, service objects management, and VO-based interactive access to physical devices.

4.1. Virtual Objects Management. Screenshot of the virtual objects management system interface is given in Figures 10 and 11. The interface has two main tabs. The first tab is used to display virtual objects information for registered IoT

```
Algorithm Fault-Management (InputList List of Registered Virtual Objects)
    //Create empty List for holding output
    OutputList= new VOStatusList[]
    Foreach vo in InputList
    {
            FaultStatus="Not Working"        %assume device is not working
            OpStatus="Null"                  %assume device is not working
            attemptNo=0
            While attemptNo < Threshold      % attempt to get device status
            {
                If (getStatus(vo.DeviceUri) = TRUE)
                    FaultStatus="Working"        %TRUE when device is working
                    If(getLastAccessTime(vo.DeviceUri) < MaxActiveTime)
                            OpStatus="Busy"
                    Else
                            OpStatus="Idle"
                    Exit While Loop
                Else
                        attemptNo++
            }
            OutputList.Add(vo, FaultStatus, OpStatus)   %Make output List working
    }
    return OutputList
```

FIGURE 9: Pseudocode for fault management algorithm.

TABLE 1: List of SVOM system APIs.

Category	API function	Explanations
Common	GetSensorsNum	Get total number of registered sensing devices in a system
	GetActuatorsNum	Get total number of registered actuating devices in a system
	GetMapServiceURI	Get map service information for visual display of virtual objects
	ConfigUI	Build user interface for a selected virtual object to provide interactive access and control
	ExecCommand	Execute supported operation on selected device using its virtual object profile
Virtual objects management	GetVOStatus	Get current status of virtual objects, for example, idle, busy, functional, and nonfunctional
	AddVObject	Add virtual object profile information to the database
	UpdateVObject	Modify existing virtual object profile information in the database
	DelVObject	Delete the selected virtual object from the database
	VOConfigManagement	Perform configuration management on the virtual object to return the selected type of virtual objects in the given area
	VOFaultManagement	Perform fault management on registered virtual objects to identify faulty and operational devices
Service objects management	GetSOStatus	Get current status of the service object by checking the status of its associated virtual objects
	AddSObject	Add service object profile information to the database
	UpdateSObject	Modify existing service object profile information in the database
	DelSObject	Delete the selected service object from the database
	SOConfigManagement	Perform configuration management on service objects to return the selected type of service objects in the given area
	SOFaultManagement	Perform fault management on registered service objects to identify faulty and operational services

devices in a tabular format as shown in Figure 10. The second tab is used to visually display IoT devices in the form of icons over the map at their respective location as shown in Figure 11. Icons are chosen as per the device type for making it easy to visually identify the desired type of device in a given region/area over map. Before displaying the VOs information, first we need to connect to the database to read virtual objects information. Virtual objects' view can be changed from list to map by clicking the respective tab. Once VOs information is loaded, then various types of management tasks can be

performed by the user. Brief description of management tasks related with VOs is given below.

In the application windows given in Figure 10, the first group box (top left) holds controls to perform configuration management-related tasks. Users can display all VOs registered in the system. When devices are geographically spread over a large area (multiple cities), users can choose to display the device only in a particular region. This is done by selecting the radius of the desired area and clicking over map to specify center of the selected region, then only devices

FIGURE 10: VOMS showing devices within a circular region of radius 10 km (tabular view).

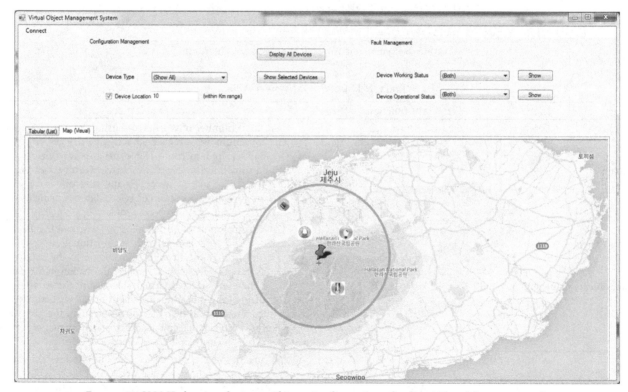

FIGURE 11: VOMS showing devices within a circular region of radius 10 km (view over map).

located within selected area will be displayed. During registration of devices in the VDM, we need to provide exact location coordinates (latitude and longitude) in order to facilitate management tasks. Furthermore, if there are too many devices in a particular area, then users can view only selected type of devices. Thus, users can view all or just selected type of VOs using this interface.

In Figure 11, through the fault management panel (top-right group box), users can choose to view VOs based on their working status (working, not working, or both). The virtual object status is set not working if no response is received from the corresponding physical device after specified number of attempts. A list of not working devices can easily be generated and handed over to the system maintenance department to quickly locate and resolve the issue. Common reasons for not

working status of the device include network connectivity issues and device power depletion. Furthermore, users can also choose to view VOs having selected operational status (busy, idle, or both). The device status is set to busy if it is currently being used by a running application. If no query is received from any application within a specified amount of time, then the device status is set to idle. A list of idle state devices can easily be generated to facilitate users while creating a new service in order to use idle devices to have better response time. This also helps in load balancing while restricting the shared access to a particular device.

4.2. Service Objects Management. Figures 12 and 13 present screenshots of the Service Objects Management System

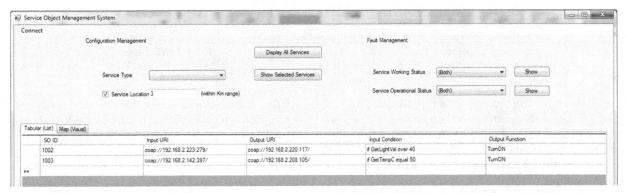

FIGURE 12: SOMS showing services within a circular region of radius 3 km (tabular view).

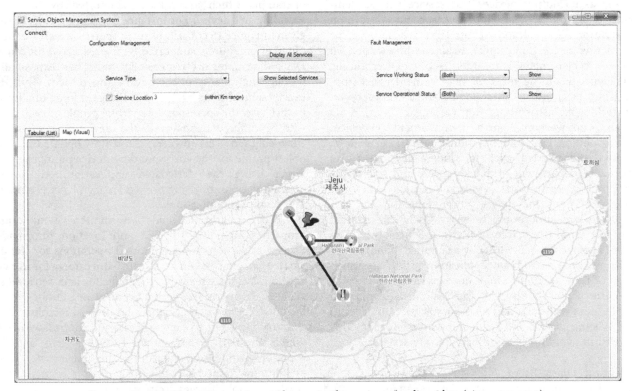

FIGURE 13: SOMS showing services within a circular region of radius 3 km (view over map).

interface. Like VOMS, it also has two main tabs. The first tab is used to display service objects information of composed service in a tabular format as shown in Figure 12. The second tab is used to visually display registered services in the form of connected icons by joining the constituent VOs over map at their respective location as shown in Figure 13. A service is composed of one or more VOs and icons of those VOs are connected to express a service over map. Before displaying the SOs information, first we need to connect to the database to read service objects information. Service objects view can be changed from list to map by clicking on the respective tab. Once SOs information is loaded, then various kinds of management tasks can be performed by the user. Brief description of management tasks related with SOs is given below.

The first group box (top left) in the application interface given in Figure 12 holds control to perform configuration management related tasks. Users can display all SOs

registered in the system. When system devices are geographically spread over a large area (across multiple cities), users can choose to display the device only in a particular region. This is done by selecting the radius of the desired area and clicking over the map to specify the center of the selected region; then only services located within the selected area will be displayed. During composition of service in SCM, we need to connect appropriate VOs in order to facilitate management tasks. Furthermore, if there are too many services in a particular area, then users can choose to view service having the selected type of VOs as its input or output. Thus, users can view all or selected type of SOs using this interface. We can see in Figure 13 that only 2 services are available within the selected region of radius 3 km. A service is listed if at least one of its constituent devices is located within the selected region. Brief description of the two services is given in Table 2.

TABLE 2: Details of the selected service.

Service ID	Input device	Output device	Execution condition
1002	Light sensor	Buzzer	If GetLightVal over 40, then TurnON buzzer
1003	Temperature sensor	Serve motor	If GetTempC over 50, then TurnON serve motor

Service ID 1002 is an example of a typical alarm system for lighting control in a certain environment. It has a light sensor as its input and a buzzer as its output device. This service simply gets illumination data from the light sensor and will turn on the buzzer if its value is over 40. Service ID 1003 is an example of a typical temperature control system for monitoring overheating of a certain environment. It has a temperature sensor as its input and a serve motor (an actuator) as its output device. This service will get temperature data from the temperature sensor and will turn on the serve motor if its value is over 50. The serve motor can be any actuating device, for example, an air conditioner or a fan that needs to be turned ON in order to control overheating.

In Figure 12, using the fault management panel (top-right group box), users can choose to view SOs based on their working status (working, not working, or both). A SO status is set not working if one of its constituent VO devices is not responding. List of not functional services can easily be generated and handed over to system developers and maintenance department to quickly locate and resolve the issue. Common reasons for service failure include network connectivity issues and device power depletion. Furthermore, users can also choose to view SOs having selected operational status (busy, idle, or both). A SO status is set to busy if it is currently being used by a running application. If no query is received from any application within a specified amount of time, then corresponding service status is set to idle. A list of idle state service can easily be generated to facilitate users while creating a new application in order to utilize existing service and reduce development time. This also helps in avoiding creation of duplicate services.

4.3. Virtual Object-Based Interactive Access to Physical Devices. In this section, we show how users can interact with IoT devices using virtual objects in the proposed management system. Users can select any device to perform supported interactive operations through the configuration management. As shown in Figure 14, users will select the desired device. Afterwards, the current operation status of the device is checked, and if the device is not working, then appropriate error message is displayed. If the device is working properly, then the application uses the device profile information and builds a user interface to allow users to perform supported interactive operations. User commands are sent to the respective device using device URI.

We have tested temperature, humidity, and wind sensors along with the fan control using Intel Edison board and CoAP protocol. For the sake of brevity, we only show interaction with an IP camera used for experimental purposes as demonstration. In order to create a virtual object for the IP camera, we build its profile in *Virtual Device Manager* application. A typical virtual object profile for the camera has information as shown in the XML format in Figure 15.

The virtual object profile for IoT devices is a generic description which is shared by the individual devices. We have developed a specialized tool *Virtual Device Manager* application for creating the virtual object profile for any IoT device. End users can use this application to create and publish virtual object profile information of their respective devices. Moreover, it is worth mentioning here that the virtual object profile shall contain all those properties and operations which are actually supported by the corresponding IoT device. For instance, the virtual object profile given in Figure 15 consists of six properties which are the six different operations supported by the respective IP camera. Depending upon the requirement, users can expose all or partial functionality of their respective devices. Thus, two exactly same devices can provide different functionality, but in that case, the corresponding virtual profile of each device will be different. Finally, if the device functionality is changed, then users (owners) can simply update the virtual object profile for the corresponding device on management server using the designated application. All services depending upon or using the old virtual object profile may also require modifications.

A camera profile holds information about camera properties including its URI and location information. Properties sections hold supported operations for the designated camera. We can get stream from camera for live view and can save the stream in a video file for later retrieval and analysis. Furthermore, various control operations are also included to move the camera in four directions to get a desired view. For IP camera access and control, we need to double click on its icon in the SVOM system, and then a pop-up window is opened for the camera view. After establishing connection with the camera, a frame queue is created to hold frames from streaming object. Streaming object runs in a separate loop to get continuous frames from camera as per frame rate which are then stored in the frame queue. If we want to save the stream, then camera thread is initiated to get the frames from the queue and store it. This sequence of operations is illustrated in Figure 16. Once streaming is initiated, then users can execute various supported commands to move the camera through its virtual object.

In the SVOM system, when a list of registered devices is displayed, then by hovering mouse over the device icon, a tool tip is appeared showing the name of virtual object. Double click on IP camera icon to open a new pop-up window for interaction as shown in Figure 17. Windows form controls in the pop-up window is dynamically linked with corresponding properties of selected VO. We use Afroge.NET library for getting live camera stream. Cisco WVC200 Wireless-G PTZ Internet Video IP camera is used in this experiment, and this camera model is Onvif complaint and supported by Ozeki Camera SDK to perform

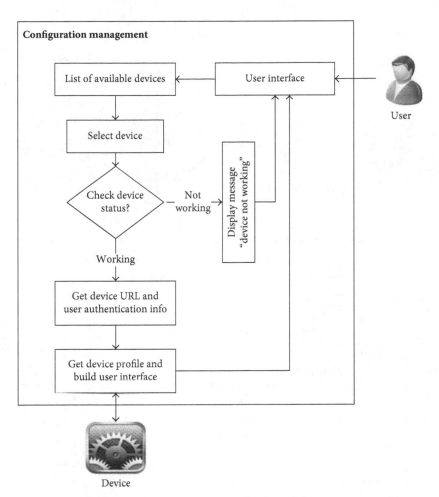

FIGURE 14: Mechanism for virtual object-based interaction with physical devices using configuration management.

```xml
<?xml version="1.0" encoding="UTF-8"?>
- <Devices>
  - <Device>
      <VO_ID>16</VO_ID>
      <Uri>coap://10.102.42.125</Uri>
      <Type>IPCamera</Type>
      <Location>Room123</Location>
      <LocLat>33.455</LocLat>
      <LocLong>126.74</LocLong>
    - <Properties>
        <P>GetStream</P>
        <P>SaveStream</P>
        <P>MoveUp</P>
        <P>MoveDown</P>
        <P>MoveLeft</P>
        <P>MoveRight</P>
      </Properties>
    </Device>
  </Devices>
```

FIGURE 15: Typical IP camera profile (xml view).

interactive operation on the camera. For sake of demonstration, only camera movement operations are implemented, and zooming buttons are disabled as this camera

VO profile (given in Figure 15) does not have zooming operations. Users can record the stream on some online storage for later retrieval and analysis. Furthermore, we have developed customized interfaces for known types of registered IoT devices that share same profile information. For new and unknown type of IoT devices, the system support dynamic creation of interactive interface where elements on the interface is created during run time. For every property in the registered device virtual profile, we create a button on the interface with a clickable event. When a button is clicked, the event will be triggered to execute corresponding operation on the IoT device. This will just provide end users to test properties included in the virtual profile of registered IoT devices.

5. Scalability Analysis of Proposed System via Simulation

We have performed simulation of proposed system in OMNeT++ for scalability analysis to study the impact of IoT network size on key performance measures like response time, throughput, and packet delivery ratio. In addition, we also tried to analyze resource requirement for proposed management system along with analysis of control overhead introduced due to centralized management. OMNeT++

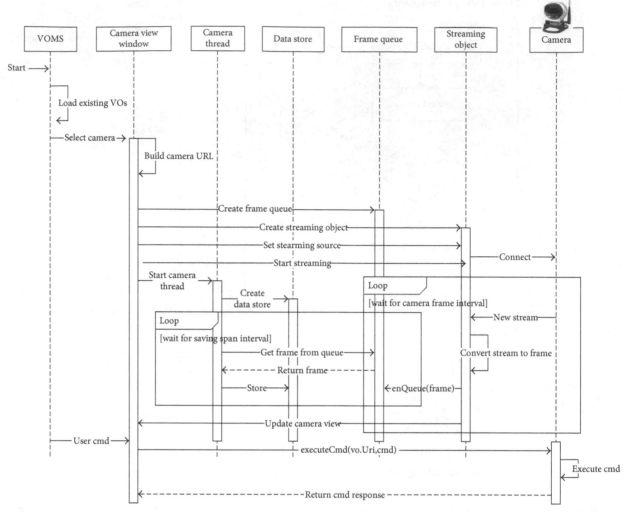

FIGURE 16: Sequence diagram for IP camera access and control.

(Objective Modular Network Testbed in C++) is a well-designed discrete event simulation environment [24]. To perform network simulation in OMNeT++, an open-source framework INET is developed which includes various protocols for wired, wireless, and mobile networks [25]. These simulations are performed in OMNeT++ 5.2 with INET framework version 3.6.

5.1. Protocol Implementation in OMNeT++. To achieve proposed management system functionality for scalability analysis, we have implemented two application layer protocols in OMNeT++; one for management server and another for IoT devices. Figure 18 shows typical simulation setup for evaluation of the proposed management system. IoT devices are connected to the local gateway node through wireless link with data rate of 54 Mbps and gateway nodes are connected to management server over a 100 Mbps wired link through intermediate routers. For sake of illustration, graphical view of nodes' internal layered architecture is highlighted (red color rectangle) in Figure 18 for management server and an IoT node. At management server, an instance of management protocol *mgtServerApp[0]* is used at the

application layer (highlighted in yellow rectangle). Likewise, an instance of IoT device protocol *ioTDeviceApp[0]* is used at application layer of IoT nodes. At simulation start-up, all IoT nodes send registration request to management server containing its profile information. Upon registration, management server creates a virtual object (VO) for each IoT device to hold its profile information which is also used for onwards communication and control with corresponding IoT devices. Screenshot given in Figure 18 is taken when registration process of all IoT devices was completed as indicated by the tag on application layer of management server *Registered VOs* = 10 (means 10 IoT devices are registered). Similarly, the tag on application layer of IoT device is changed to *Registered* = *yes* indicating its registration with server is successfully completed. After registration, management servers can send various commands to registered IoT devices using its VO, for example, to get its operational status, to initiate data transmission, and so on.

5.2. Performance Measures and Simulation Parameters. We have selected three key performance measures, that is,. response time, throughput, and packet delivery ratio to study the impact of IoT network size on these metrics.

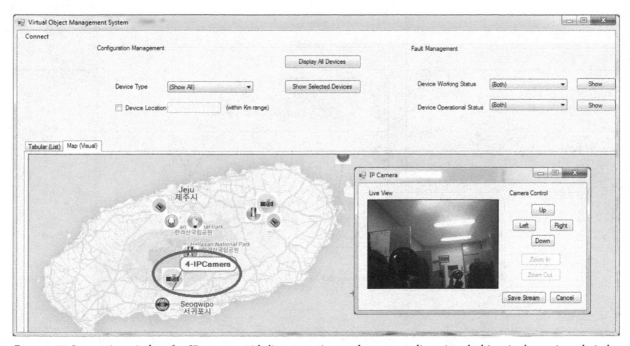

FIGURE 17: Interactive window for IP camera with live streaming, and corresponding virtual object is shown in red circle.

Response time is computed by measuring the time taken to receive a response from an IoT node to a query generated by management server. Throughput is the total data received at server in per unit time from all sources, that is, active IoT devices. Packet delivery ratio is computed by considering the ratio between total number of data packets received at server versus the total number of data packets generated in the network. Table 3 presents the configuration for various parameters used in simulation.

5.3. Performance Analysis. We have conducted simulations in two phases: (a) with single gateway node and (b) with multiple gateway nodes. Following subsection presents results for each phase with brief discussion.

5.3.1. Results with Single Gateway Node. First, we performed a set of experiments by varying the number of IoT devices in the network with varying packet sending rates. In this phase, all IoT devices are connected with management server through a single gateway node. The gateway node is connected with management server via a 100 Mbps wired link through a router as shown in Figure 18. To compute IoT device response time, management server sends an operational status query to all IoT devices through a broadcast message. In response to the status query message, every IoT device sends its status information (idle or busy) to management server. First, experiments are performed with 30 IoT devices in the network. The average response time was about 5 msec with network size of 30 nodes. Similar experiments were performed with network size of 60, 90, 120, and 150. Linear growth in average response time was observed with growing network size as shown in Figure 19(a). There were two choices to evaluate the impact of network size on throughput: (a) increase the number of sources, that

is, active IoT device to generate more data in the network and (b) increase the data rate, that is, packets/sec while keeping number of sources fixed. The latter approach was used here to evaluate network performance in terms of throughput. For throughput calculation, we have used fixed network size of 60 nodes with 6 sources, that is, active IoT devices. For these simulations, the data rate for each active IoT device was varied from 200 to 1000 packets/sec (with step of 200). With six sources, a date rate of 200 packets/sec, and a packet size of 1000 bytes, data generated in the network become $6 \times 200 \times 1000 \times 8/10^6 = 9.6$Mbps. Data throughput computed at management server node was also around 9.6 Mbps as shown in Figure 19(b). It means that with a data rate of 200 packets/sec, packet delivery ratio in the network was 100% which is confirmed from packet delivery ratio graph given in Figure 19(c). Throughput results are given in the box-plot graph format, which also captures the variation in throughput during simulation time. When packet sending rate was doubled, that is, 400 packets/sec, we get data throughput around 15 Mbps, not doubled as expected. Packets delivery ratio graph in Figure 19(c) shows that only 76.40% packets are delivered with a data rate of 400 packets/sec; therefore, throughput was not doubled. Further increase in data rate to 600 packets/sec results slight improvement in throughput results, that is, 16.5 Mbps but no improvement in throughput was observed for date rate of 800 and 1000 packets/sec as shown in Figure 19(b). On the other hand, the results given in Figure 19(c) show significant degradation in packet delivery ratio with an increase in data sending rate. Upon investigation, it was revealed from simulation trace files that with increase in data sending rate, most of the packets gets dropped at MAC layer of IoT device nodes. Packets are dropped because nodes are unable to get access to the shared wireless channel due to contention. This is due to the fact that all IoT devices are using single gateway

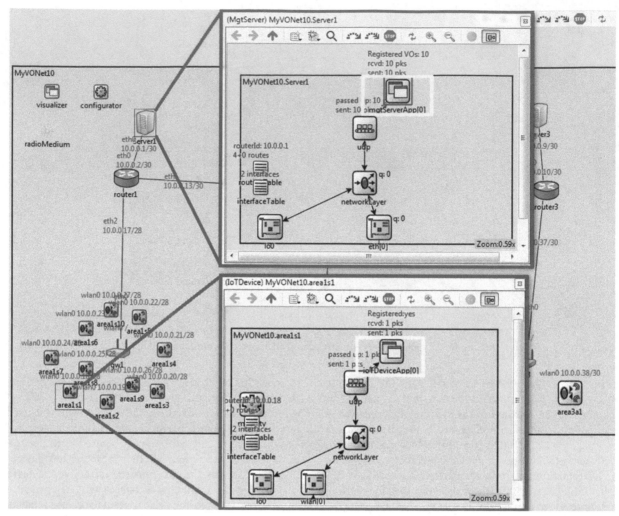

FIGURE 18: Simulation setup in OMNeT++.

TABLE 3: Simulation parameters.

| Parameter | Value/range | | |
	IoT device(s)		Management server
Nodes count	30, 60, 90, 120, 150		1
Gateway nodes		1, 2, 3	
Application layer	IoTDeviceApp		MgtServerApp
Packet size	1000 bytes		NA
Packet sending rate (per node)	200, 400, 600, 800, 1000 packets/sec		NA
Transport layer		UDP protocol	
Routing layer		Fixed routing IP protocol	
MAC layer	IEEE802.11		Ethernet
Bit rate	54 Mbps		NA
Communication range	100 m		NA
Area size		1000 m × 1000 m	
Mobility type		No mobility	
Simulation time		20 sec	

node which is overloaded. Simulations results reveal that with growing network size and data load, the gateway node becomes the performance bottleneck. Hence, we performed another set of experiments with multiple gateway nodes to verify this assertion.

5.3.2. Results with Multiple Gateway Nodes. In the second phase, the same set of experiments is repeated with multiple gateway nodes, that is, 2 and 3. Gateway nodes are placed in the network at suitable locations to have uniform distribution of IoT nodes.

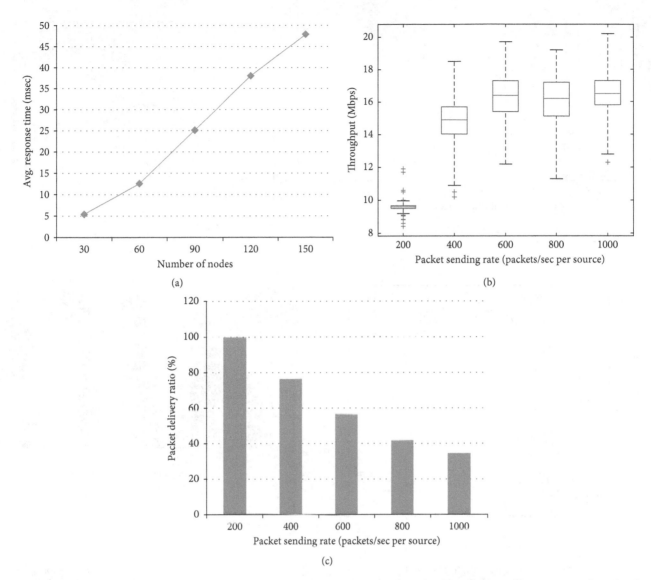

FIGURE 19: Simulation results with single gateway node. (a) Average response time of IoT device with respect to varying number of nodes in the network. (b) Network throughput with respect to varying packet sending rate. (c) Packet delivery ratio in the network with respect to varying packet sending rate.

With 30 IoT devices in the network, the average response time was almost the same (around 5 msec) with 1, 2, and 3 gateway nodes. However, with increase in network size from 60 to 150 nodes, significant difference between response time was observed as shown in Figure 20(a). With 2 gateway nodes and 150 nodes in the network, the average response time recorded was around 20 msec which is almost 60% reduction in average response time as compared to the case of single gateway node. Average response time was further reduced to 10 msec when we used 3 gateway nodes with network size of 150 nodes (almost 77% reduction in average response time as compared to the case of single gateway node). For throughput calculation, we have used fixed network size of 60 nodes with 6 sources, that is, active IoT devices. With 2 gateway nodes and 6 active IoT nodes, the recorded throughput was (9.6, 19.2, 28.8, 37.6, and 38.1 Mbps) with packet sending rate (200, 400, 600, 800 and 1000 packets/sec), respectively, as shown in Figure 20(b). This shows linear increase in throughput

until packet sending rate of 800 packets/sec. However, there is no significant difference between throughput for 800 and 1000 packets/sec. Packet delivery ratio results for two gateway nodes in Figure 20(d) indicate that 100% packets were delivered for packet sending rate 200–600 packets/sec. However, for 800 and 1000 packets/sec, packets delivery ratio was 97.88% and 79.30%, respectively. In other words, increase in packet sending rate from 800 to 1000 packets/sec only results in packet loss in the network, as there was no improvement in the throughput. Finally, with 3 gateway nodes, linear increase in throughput results was observed with increase in packet sending rates as shown in Figure 20(c). Packet delivery ratio results with three gateway nodes are given in Figure 20(d) indicating that 100% packets were delivered for packet sending rate 200–1000 packets/sec. Thus, with given network conditions and data load, three gateway nodes seem to be good choice. Significant improvement in results is observed by using multiple gateway nodes.

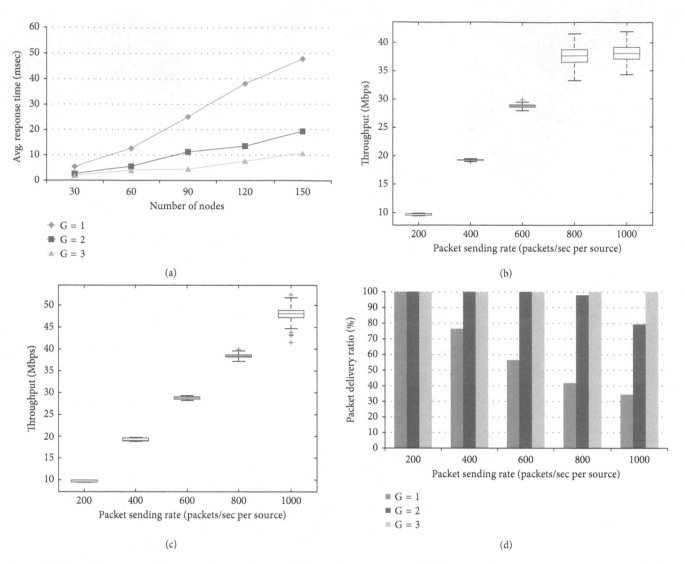

FIGURE 20: Simulation results with multiple gateway nodes. (a) Average response time of IoT device with respect to varying number of nodes in the network. (b) Network throughput with two gateway nodes. (c) Network throughput with three gateway nodes. (d) Packet delivery ratio in the network with respect to varying packet sending rate.

5.3.3. Analysis of Virtual Objects Resources Requirement.

We have conducted another set of experiments through simulations to analyze resources requirement (memory) at management server with growing network size. As stated earlier, virtual object for any IoT device is created using a specialized tool *Virtual Device Manager* application. Figure 15 shows typical representation of virtual object profile (IP camera in this example) in XML format. It is worth mentioning here that structure of virtual object profile will remain the same; however, memory requirement may vary depending upon the recorded properties of registered IoT devices. In the simulation setup, we consider seven different types of IoT devices, that is, camera, serve motor, temperature sensor, green led, axis sensor, light sensor, and buzzer where memory requirement for virtual object profile of each type device is 170, 154, 122, 122, 122, 106, and 122 bytes, respectively. Multiple simulation runs were tested with growing number of IoT devices from 200 to 1000 (step size of 200). In each simulation run, IoT devices of aforementioned types were created using uniform distribution.

Memory requirement for holding virtual objects profile information was recorded at management server after completion of registration of all IoT devices. Figure 21 shows the total memory required for holding virtual objects profile information at management server with growing number of IoT devices.

Memory requirement at management server exhibits linear growth with growing number of IoT devices in the network as depicted in Figure 21. Computation requirement may vary depending upon the type of operation that we want to perform. Computation complexity of the current supported operations in existing system is between $O(n)$ and $O(n^2)$. However, complex operations will require more computation and will certainly demand intelligent and distributed solutions as conventional approaches will not be scalable when performed at large scale with millions of registered IoT devices.

5.3.4. Analysis of Control Overhead.

To analyze overhead traffic due to centralized management server, we have conducted several set of experiments. Experiments are performed with

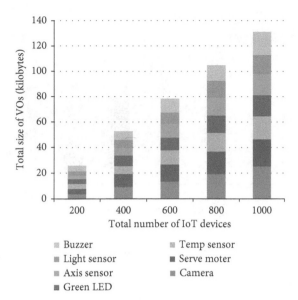

FIGURE 21: Analysis of memory requirements with growing number of IoT devices.

varying network size and data sending rates. Proposed management system generate various control packets in the network which includes initial registration packets, periodic status enquiry messages for registered IoT devices, and command message to initiate and terminate various active flows in the network. To quantify network overhead of proposed system, normalized control overhead (NCO) metric is used which is computed as below:

$$\text{normalized control overhead}(\%) = \frac{\text{control packets}}{\text{data packets}} \times 100. \tag{1}$$

Normalized control overhead (NCO) is the ratio between total control packets and total number of data packets generated in the network. As given in (1), this metric measures the control overhead in terms of control packets required for generating 100 data packets. Control packets generated in network mainly depends upon the network size and number of active flows, while NCO depends on two factors, that is, control packets and data packets. In other words, if the network size is growing without increase in active flows and data sending rate, then NCO will increase. The same behavior is exhibited in the experimental results presented in Figure 22(a). As the number of active source nodes and data sending rate were kept fixed, data generated in the all network sizes were the same. However, increase in network size causes increase in network control packets. Therefore, we can observe that NCO increases linearly with growing network size. In these experiments, the highest value of NCO was recorded as 16 (approximately) as shown in Figure 22(a) which means that with a network of size 180 IoT devices, the proposed management system generates around 16 control packets for every 100 data packets. In real world scenarios, increase in data rate is also expected with growing network size which will then compensate for increasing control overhead. To further validate this assertion,

we have conducted another set of experiments with growing data sending rate, but this time network size was kept fixed, that is, 60 IoT devices. With the increase in data sending rate, more data packets are injected into the network with same number of control packets which is results in decrease in NCO as shown in Figure 22(b).

Furthermore, we have also performed experiments to analyze the impact of overhead injected by proposed management system on network performance measures, that is, end-to-end delay and throughput. For this purpose, we conducted simulations with and without management system while keeping all other parameters the same. We consider a network of 60 nodes divided into two areas, namely, area-1 and area-2. Nodes in each area are wirelessly connected to a local gateway node, and the gateway nodes are connected via routers using wired network. Management server is also connected to an intermediate router. Five nodes in area-1 are selected to send data to five other nodes in area-2. Nodes are randomly selected and activated for specific period of time (e.g., 5 sec). Another set of nodes are selected when activation time is over. In the first round of experiments, communication is initiated by management server, and all data are routed through the proposed management system. While in the second round, same experiments are repeated by establishing a direct (fixed) communication route between randomly selected source and destination nodes, thus by-passing the management system. With increasing data rate, gradual increase in end-to-end delay can be observed for both cases as shown in Figure 23(a) which is due increase in contention between active source nodes while access shared wireless channel. Comparatively more increase in end-to-end delay statistics can be observed for management system as shown in Figure 23(a). This is due to the fact that the data packets have to traverse a longer route including protocol stack at management server which induces slight increase in end-to-end delay. However, throughput results for both cases remain almost the same as shown in Figure 23(b). The difference between throughput results only become slightly visible when data sending rate was set to 120 packets/sec per source, that is, $120 \times 5 = 600$ packets/sec are generated in the network, and the size of each packets is 1000 bytes. In highly congested network conditions, the probabilities of packets collision get increased for experiment with management system as the scenarios has relatively more packets competing for channel access thus resulting in slight degrading in overall network throughput.

Finally, these simulation results reveal that the impact of communication overhead due to centralized management system is insignificant on network performance measures. However, in extreme network conditions, we may have to sacrifice fewer bits which is in fact worth nothing when compared to the flexibility and control offered by proposed management system over registered IoT devices.

6. Conclusions

This paper presents a management architecture for effective organization of services and virtual objects in

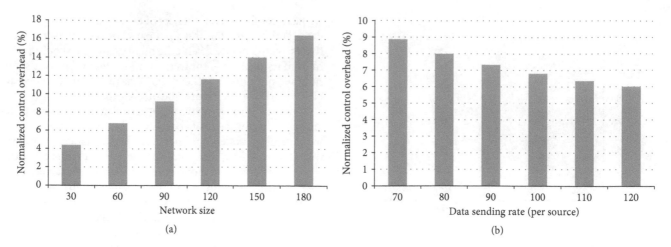

(a)   (b)

FIGURE 22: Simulation results with five active sources sending data @100 packets/sec. (a) Normalized control overhead with growing network size. (b) Normalized control overhead with increasing data rate.

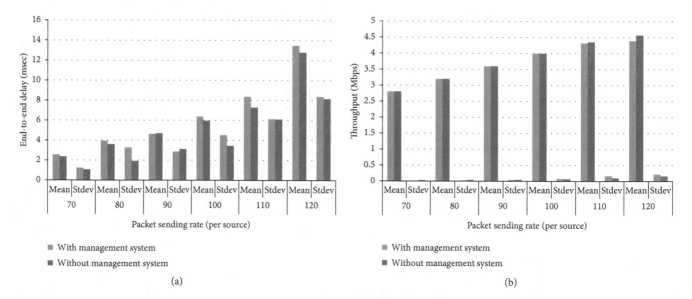

(a)   (b)

FIGURE 23: Simulation results with fixed network size of 60 nodes and five active sources. (a) End-to-end delay with increasing data rate. (b) Network throughput with increasing data rate.

hyperconnected IoT environment to facilitate management tasks, for example, locating devices in particular region, identifying faulty devices and services. For better visualization, services and devices are displayed over the map at their corresponding locations. The system also allows live interaction with device through their corresponding virtual objects to perform supported operations. We have performed the analysis of the proposed system performance with growing network size by implementing two application layer protocols in OMNeT++ simulator. Simulation results indicate that gateway nodes will become the performance bottleneck when the network size grows beyond certain extent. One way to improve the performance of hyper connected networks is by utilizing multiple gateway nodes as demonstrated through simulations results in this paper. Other solution includes improvement in wireless connectivity protocols for IoT devices. We have also performed resources requirement analysis

for virtual objects along with control overhead of the proposed management system. Simulation results reveal that control overhead is insignificant in normal scenarios; however, in extreme network conditions, we may have to sacrifice fewer bits, which is in fact worth nothing when compared to the flexibility and control offered by the proposed management system over registered IoT devices. Furthermore, the current setup only supports those IoT devices with CoAP protocol. We are also working on the development of an interworking proxy to enable communication with IoT devices that do not support CoAP protocol. In future, we are also looking forward to integrate this system with an IoT-based application development tool and incorporate security module. This will enable common users to rapidly build their customized IoT-based applications by quick selection of desired devices and services. Furthermore, we will try to integrate IoTivity framework in our current system for sake of interoperability.

Acknowledgments

This research was supported by the MSIT (Ministry of Science and ICT), Korea, under the ITRC (Information Technology Research Center) support program (2014-1-00743) supervised by the IITP (Institute for Information & Communications Technology Promotion), and this work was supported by Institute for Information & communications Technology Promotion (IITP) grant funded by the Korea government (MSIT) (no. 2017-0-00756, Development of interoperability and management technology of IoT system with heterogeneous ID mechanism).

References

[1] L. Coetzee and J. Eksteen, "The internet of things—promise for the future? An introduction," in *IST-Africa Conference Proceedings, 2011*, pp. 1–9, Gaborone, Botswana, May 2011.

[2] Z. Shelby, K. Hartke, and C. Bormann, "The constrained application protocol (coAP)," Internet Engineering Task Force, Fremont, CA, USA, 2014.

[3] D. Miorandi, S. Sicari, F. De Pellegrini, and I. Chlamtac, "Internet of things: vision, applications and research challenges," *Ad Hoc Networks*, vol. 10, no. 7, pp. 1497–1516, 2012.

[4] P. P. Jayaraman, D. Palmer, A. Zaslavsky, and D. Georgakopoulos, "Do-it-yourself digital agriculture applications with semantically enhanced iot platform," in *Proceedings of the 2015 IEEE Tenth International Conference on Intelligent Sensors, Sensor Networks and Information Processing (ISSNIP)*, pp. 1–6, Singapore, April 2015.

[5] D. Mazzei, G. Fantoni, G. Montelisciani, and G. Baldi, "Internet of things for designing smart objects," in *Proceedings of the 2014 IEEE World Forum on Internet of Things (WF-IoT)*, pp. 293–297, Seoul, Korea, March 2014.

[6] Philipse Hue, 2016.

[7] S. De, F. Carrez, E. Reetz, R. Tonjes, and W. Wang, "Test-enabled architecture for IoT service creation and provisioning," in *The Future Internet Assembly*, pp. 233–245, Springer, Berlin, Germany, 2013.

[8] A. Bassi, M. Bauer, M. Fiedler et al., Enabling Things to Talk, Springer, Berlin, Germany, 2016.

[9] M. Naeem, R. Heckel, and F. Orejas, "Semi-automated service composition using visual contracts," in *Proceedings of the 7th International Conference on Frontiers of Information Technology*, ACM, Abbottabad, Pakistan, December 2009.

[10] S. Evren, H. James, and P. Bijan, "Semi-automatic composition of web services using semantic descriptions," in *Proceedings of the Web Services: Modelling, Architecture and Infrastructure Workshop in ICEIS 2003*, pp. 17–24, Angers, France, April 2002.

[11] G. Li, S. Deng, H. Xia, and C. Lin, "Automatic service composition based on process ontology," in *Proceedings of the Third International Conference on Next Generation Web Services Practices (NWeSP 2007)*, pp. 3–6, Seoul, Republic of Korea, October 2007.

[12] D. Wu, B. Parsia, E. Sirin, J. Hendler, and D. Nau, "Automating DAML-S web services composition using SHOP2," in *Proceedings of the Second International Conference on Semantic Web Conference*, pp. 195–210, Springer-Verlag, Sanibel, FL, USA, October 2003.

[13] K.-D. Chang, C.-Y. Chang, H.-M. Liao, J.-L. Chen, and H.-C. Chao, "A framework for IoT objects management based on future internet IoT-IMS communication platform," in *Proceedings of the 2013 Seventh International Conference on Innovative Mobile and Internet Services in Ubiquitous Computing (IMIS)*, pp. 558–562, Taichung, Taiwan, July 2013.

[14] Open Connectivity Foundation (OCF), *OIC Core Specifications*, 2017, https://openconnectivity.org/specs/OCF_Core_Specification_v1.3.0.pdf.

[15] Linux Foundation, *IoTivity–Open Source Project*, Linux Foundation, San Francisco, CA, USA, 2016, https://www.iotivity.org/.

[16] oneM2M, *Technical Specifications—Functional Architecture*, Version 2.10.0 Release 2, October 2016, http://www.etsi.org/deliver/etsi_ts/118100_118199/118101/02.10.00_60/ts_118101v021000p.pdf.

[17] ITU-T, *Requirements and Reference Architecture of the Machine-to-Machine Service Layer*, ITU-T, Geneva, Switzerland, 2015.

[18] Arduino, October 2016, https://www.arduino.cc/.

[19] Intel Edison Board, October 2016, https://software.intel.com/en-us/iot/hardware/edison.

[20] Raspberry Pi, October 2016, https://www.raspberrypi.org/.

[21] SAM: The Ultimate Internet Connected Electronics Kit, October 2016, https://www.kickstarter.com.

[22] M. S. Khan and D. Kim, "DIY interface for enhanced service customization of remote IoT devices: a CoAP based prototype," *International Journal of Distributed Sensor Networks*, vol. 2015, p. 8, 2015.

[23] A C Implementation of the CoAP Protocol, September 2016, https://github.com/smeshlink/CoAP.NET.

[24] A. Varga, "OMNeT++," in *Modeling and Tools for Network Simulation*, pp. 35–59, Springer, Berlin, Germany, 2010.

[25] A. Varga, *INET Framework for the OMNeT++ Discrete Event Simulator*, December 2012, https://inet.omnetpp.org/.

14

The Intention to use Mobile Student Portal: A Mobile Human Computer Interaction Study in a University Context in Egypt

Ghada Refaat El Said ⓘ

Department of Management Information Systems, Future University in Egypt (FUE), 90th Street, Fifth Settlement, New Cairo, Egypt

Correspondence should be addressed to Ghada Refaat El Said; ghada.refaat@fue.edu.eg

Academic Editor: Michael Vassilakopoulos

Mobile devices are increasingly being used as platforms for interactive services. However, factors affecting adoption of mobile services in some specific contexts, such as student portals, are still underresearched. This paper reports thematic analyses of semistructured interviews conducted with 52 undergraduate users of mobile student portal in a developing country. The results uncover design features affecting the use of mobile student portals, such as (1) *Content Sharing*, comprising an Integrative Design to share posts from the mobile portal to social media, (2) *Personalized Content and Notification*, for personalized notification based on student's academic status, (3) *Location-Aware notification*, providing location-based updates, (4) *User Control*, allowing to choose content formats and details level, and (5) *Context Switching and Interrupted Behavior*, leading to the need for displaying content in small, meaningful chunks to help pick up after interruptions of messages and calls. The findings suggest design recommendations for mobile student portal, in specific.

1. Introduction

The demand for a single integrated, easy-to-use, access to information applications and people within a network of users is increasing more and more. In the higher education context, mobile student portals are designed to increase accessibility to almost everything that a student associated with the campus needs. Once logged in, students have access to a variety of tools and information about their classes, teachers, office hours, test scores, extra credit, and extracurricular activities [1].

One obvious reason for universities to adopt mobile portals is to improve students' productivity and satisfaction, which is not always the case for reasons related mainly to portals design [2, 3]. A considerable body of Information Systems research is currently taking place to explore acceptance factors in mobile web services adoption. There is also a growing concern that certain novel technologies, such as mobile web, may bring additional adoption issues that will not necessarily be uncovered by simply testing existing theories in a new context [3].

Another concern is the suitability of some design factors in particular application areas, such as university context, compared with other application areas [4].

Most of previous research in student portal context focused on web usability, mainly from desktop and laptop computers [5]. On the other hand, many of universities already built a separate mobile-optimised design for their student portal. As costly as it could be, these mobile sites, when implemented without assessing user preference, could hold usability challenges.

The study took place in Egypt, while classified as a developing country, has a high penetration of mobile devices [6]. A main aim of this research is to reveal mobile educational portal experiences for students from underresearched users. This paper begins by discussing past literature on adoption of mobile student portals, as well as previous research on student portals in developing countries. This is followed by a description of the methodology and data collection and a presentation of the results. Finally, the findings and their implications are discussed.

2. Background

2.1. Previous Research on Mobile Student Portal. The last decade has seen substantial investments in technology infrastructure for higher education enterprises; mobile applications in specific are currently widely used in educational environments [7]. Resource constrains and accreditation requirements oblige higher education institutions to set their technology priority and select the most appropriate systems [8]. The immense availability of mobile devices among students offers opportunities to integrate them into educational context [7], taking an important role in the day-to-day life of students inside and outside the university campus. According to Zbick et al. [9], competitive advantages of mobile educational context portals, compared to desktop ones, are related to, namely, the mobility, portability, and the fact that it offers immediate help to students. Nevertheless, most of researches reveal dissatisfaction and negative student evaluation, for reasons mainly related to mobile portal design issues [9].

According to Zhang and Adipat [10], usability of mobile applications is an emerging research area that faces a variety of challenges due to unique features of mobile devices, such as changing connectivity conditions and mobility. Traditional guidelines and methods used in usability testing of desktop applications may not be directly applicable to a mobile environment [10]. Additionally, there is a severe shortage in the usability of mobile student portals. One of the few studies on mobile educational portal suggests that students' motivation can be stimulated if authenticity is introduced in the portal's content and design [7].

Previous research on student web portal interface in developing countries asserts weaknesses of these applications concerning usability and user acceptance. Student portals studied in these research works were lacking sufficient information, were anything but user-friendly, and were rarely updated [2].

A university's website satisfaction model was suggested by Rezaeean et al. [11]. They conducted a survey among 270 university students in Iran, and results suggest that greater innovation and perceived usability have significant impact on student's perceived usefulness, trust, and satisfaction in university portal [11].

In their usability evaluation study on student portal, Zazelenchuk and Bolind [12] raise the question of how well efficiency relates to user satisfaction for recent technologies, such as web-based portal applications. The usability study, conducted with 45 undergraduate university students, involves completing a series of tasks that required location information and personalizing the portal system [12]. The study reveals significant relationship between students' satisfaction and a number of design features of portals, such as portal responsiveness, interface organization and consistency, and timely informative and corrective feedback [12]. Booi and Dista [2] studied user acceptance of South African Universities Web Portal Interfaces. Their results suggest that interaction and invisibility are the most important factors affecting user acceptance and usability, respectively.

3. Main Focus of the Article

The current research aims to explore the factors that affect the use of mobile student portals. The focus was on user perception of portal features, as the main intent is to provide design recommendations to ensure better use of students' mobile portal. The study took place in the context of a developing country—Egypt.

In Egypt, the demographic of Internet users is young and active; with 45 million users, one half of them are under age 25. Egypt has an Internet penetration rate of 52%, representing a 1.68% share of world Internet users, and the largest population of Internet users in the Middle East and North Africa region [6]. Smart phone users in Egypt reached 25.8 million in 2018 and expected to reach 27.9 million in 2019 with a penetration rate of 31% [13]. Although the potential benefits of mobile web application for educational purposes are particularly high for economically and academically disadvantaged societies [14], many aspects of such platforms are developed without considering preferences of users from these societies. This article is aiming to reveal mobile student portals experiences for users from Egypt.

4. Research Methodology

4.1. Semistructured Interviews. This research represents a descriptive, qualitative study employing semistructured interviews with university undergraduates. Web service research has been undergoing a major movement toward quantitative approaches [4], where the semistructured interview techniques are most preferred for disclosure of self-reflected data from individual sources [15]. The mobile student portal of the university, where the interviewees are registered was used during discussions within the interviewees. In the selected university, all students are required to use the portal for academic registration each semester. The portal used in the current research is bilingual, students can select/switch between Arabic and English at any page of the portal. Thematic analysis of data collected during the interviews was used to draw out the main adoption themes.

4.2. Sample. The target sample for this study covers undergraduate university students. Convenience sampling was used due to the need to identify a study context in which there was a clear academic rationale to invite students to discuss the mobile portal provided by their university. In this research, undergraduates were full-time students from different specializations (finance, business, information technology, management, and marketing) enrolled in a private university in Cairo, Egypt. The sample includes 52 students who were willing to participate in an individual interviewing session. Gender was almost equally distributed throughout the overall sample (24 males and 28 females), and age range varied between 16 and 24. Students were informed that this interview is part of a study aiming to better design their mobile portal. They were also informed of their right to withdraw from completing the interview at any time. No compensation was provided to students.

4.3. Procedures. The interviews were conducted face-to-face by the author of this paper in the months of January and February 2018. An announcement was posted on the portal of the university, where the author works as teaching professor, asking for students who are frequent users of the student mobile portal to volunteer in a research concerning better design of mobile student portal. Volunteered students applied by e-mail and schedules were arranged for interviews at the university students' study room.

The interviewing sessions started by informing participants that the length of each session would be 30 to 40 minutes long and that they can stop the session at any time. With the participant's permission, interviews were recorded using a portable recorder. Data collection was completed by saturation, which occurs when a feeling of closure is obtained from noticing repeated information.

The interviews started with a guiding question: "What is your experience with the mobile student portal?" This question was followed by a series of reflective questions to elicit in-depth responses and derive implications for the practical experience with the portal. The questions aimed to investigate the participants' general experience, how much of the portal content they usually check, why and when they use the mobile version of the portal versus the desktop one, and what issues, if any, they experienced when working with the mobile portal, trying to link these issues with their use. Throughout the interview sessions, participants were asked to indicate what they like or dislike about their mobile student portal and to suggest ways to enhance it. Some of the questions used in the interviews included:

> How frequent do you login to the mobile student portal?
>
> When and where do you usually use the mobile portal and the desktop portal?
>
> What data do you usually retrieve from the portal?
>
> How do you evaluate the system in general?
>
> What do you dislike the most about the system?
>
> What do you like the most about the system?
>
> What do you propose to be added to the system?

In general, interviewees did not have any problem comprehending the questions.

Interviews were conducted in Arabic language, the mother tongue of the interviewer (the author of this paper) and all of the interviewees. In the closing comments, interviewees were encouraged to add anything that was left unsaid in the session and they were thanked and informed that the interview was successfully completed.

4.4. Data Recording and Analysis. The sessions were recorded, transcribed, and coded through thematic analysis. The thematic analysis technique is widespread in analyzing qualitative data [16]. Unlike textual analysis, thematic analysis goes beyond counting phrases or words and moves on to identifying patterns, themes, across datasets, describing the phenomenon under investigation [17]. Through a process of six phases, thematic analysis creates meaningful patterns to identify

unfolded themes emergent from the data [18]. In the first phase, the researcher becomes familiar with the dataset through several readings of the transcript of the collected data to identify repeating issues and patterns. In the second phase, codes were generated by labeling relevant words, phrases, sentences, or sections. Following the guidelines of Braun and Clarke [19], data can be found relevant to code because it is repeated in several places (e.g., the mobility issue of the mobile portal); it surprises the researcher (e.g., the idea to integrate the mobile portal with student own social media); the interviewee explicitly states that it is important (e.g., reliability); and it is referenced in the literature (as for the case of perceived value). These relevant codes are combined in phase three into overarching themes. Identifying a theme does not necessarily yield the frequency at which a theme occurs. Ideally, the theme will occur numerous times across the dataset, but a higher frequency does not necessarily mean that the theme is more important to understanding the data (e.g., student control features). The identified themes are reviewed in phase four, in which some existing themes can be grouped together (e.g., perceived value and reliability); others might be split into subthemes (such as course personalized notification was split into personalized content and location aware). This process is repeated until the researcher is satisfied with the thematic map. In phase five, themes are defined and given names, providing a full sense of the theme beyond surface meanings of the data. In phase six, results are reported by integrating themes to convey the story of the data in a logical manner. Interviews' quotes are included to provide sufficient evidence that themes within the data are relevant to the dataset. Conclusion is interpreted in light of results from similar previous studies and newly uncovered themes.

5. Results and Discussion

Based on thematic analysis of the interview sessions, a number of themes and associated categories were revealed concerning intention to use mobile student portal. Some of these themes support findings of previous literature; others were novel finding in the context of mobile human computer interaction, as discussed in the following sections.

5.1. Theme 1: Perceived Value. Values define the key features of the system that are appreciated by the target users; they represent the main reasons why the users are interested and intending to use a system. Defining the users' perceived values helps in focusing the design on the most essential features. The current research highlights the importance of perceived value as a broad mobile student portal use driver. During interviews, participants envisaged the student portal would provide value to them throughout: *Reliability*, *Content Sharing*, and *Mobility*, as discussed in the following sections.

5.1.1. Reliability. As alternatives to other students' information dissemination channels within their universities, participants of the current research expressed that mobile portals have the benefit that they are always available and accessed. Since students cited that they check their phones several times a day, for them, mobile student portals is the best way to keep up to date with what is going on in campus. All of the interviewees expressed the importance that the students' portal includes updated and comprehensive information, sufficient enough to rely on as the main source of information, as cited below in the following quotes:

"I am checking my mobile phone several times during the day and I rely on the mobile portal to get updated and comprehensive information about social and academic events in campus."

"I totally depend on the mobile portal to get updates about courses registration, drop and add, as well as students activities . . . I don't need any more to collect bits and pieces of data from students affair office, or the school bulletin board. . . ."

5.1.2. Content Sharing.

Content Sharing is explained by the interviewees as the preference to share posts from mobile student portal to other student's own account on social media. Some of the interviewees (13 out of the 52) expressed the need to be able to share the news and information from the portal to other students on the faculty Facebook, in case of student's activity announcement and academic deadlines. Few students expressed that sometimes they like to share videos, images, and text included in the portal to their own account on facebook.

"It would be great if I can share important news from the portal, such as academic calendar, and dates of social activities and events... and post it on the faculty facebook," as stated by an interviewee. A second interviewee expressed the preference to *"When a celebrity visits the university, photos are posted on student's portal... I would be great if I am able to share photos, video, links from the portal to my facebook....."*

Those interviewees expressed that their accounts on social media, most of the time, are open on their mobile, when accessing the student's portal, they like to easily share some posts from the portal to these accounts. The ability to share posts from the portal to social media, gives competitive advantage to the mobile portal, as explained by those interviewees.

5.1.3. Mobility.

Mobility was expressed by interviewed students as the degree of connectivity that allows them to access the portal via mobile phones anywhere, anytime, and under various connectivity conditions. The highest majority (45 out of 52) praised the mobile portal as a movable source of information they can access anywhere and anytime. Many of the interviewed students mentioned that mobile portal already reduced their attendance in the faculty information office and student affair department. This suggests that mobility is a key factor affecting the use of mobile students' portal.

On the other hand, the frustration from loading photos and videos included in the mobile portal in public areas within and outside campus, with unreliable and low-speed Internet connectivity, was cited as the main reason for not using the mobile portal.

"I am checking the student portal from my phone on the run, in the university shuttle bus and between class breaks. This is great, but in areas with weak connectivity it freezes." expressed an interviewee. *"In area with low Wi-Fi, on my smart phone, videos and large pictures won't load or won't even appear, this is very frustrating"* as stated by an interviewee. This suggests that while the mobility feature is suggested to be an important antecedent of use for mobile student portal, it also can limit its use in cases of low-connectivity conditions. Offline features can deal with this issue by giving users the option to download videos and large pictures beforehand with a reliable Internet coverage, to watch them later when they move to a nonreliable coverage. On the other hand, portal can be designed to save state and remember what users were doing when signals drop to accommodate users who might lose signals during browsing.

It could be concluded that mobility and Internet coverage would affect usage of the portal, though this could be somewhat handled by appropriate portal's design.

5.2. Theme 2: Personally Relevant Content.

Personalization was perceived by the participants of the current research as the capability of portal to reflect the students' own personality, also the ability to display personalized content, based on individual student's location and academic status. During interviews, participants envisaged the student portal would provide personally relevant content throughout: *Genuine Photos, Personalized Notification,* and *Location aware,* as discussed in the following sections.

5.2.1. Genuine Photos.

All of the interviewees explained that they would use the mobile portal more if it includes videos and photos from the students activities and events, not only the academic posts. Students' activities photos are kept on the university website and not the mobile portal. On the other hand, the majority of interviewed students (30 out of 52) complained that the current look of the portal does not reflect them, as most of the photos used in the portal interface are not genuine and are not for students from their university.

"What is the idea of using photos of American/European students, who do not look like us. We are all Egyptians here!... It is true we are having few international students, but they are also from Africa. I expect to find photos of real students," as cited by a student.

The students expressed the need to feel that the portal reflects their identity, and they appreciated authentic photos, reflecting what they actually see in their campus.

5.2.2. Personalized Notification.

Some interviewees showed preference that the mobile student portal provides personalized notification based on student's academic status and relevant deadlines. Examples of these personal notifications were given by the interviewees, as following: changes in the timetable of the student's specific bus, warning for the student's own absenteeism rate, deadline for registration and add and drop courses, and notification for events of the student's faculty or class.

5.2.3. Location Aware.

Few users (8 out of 52) suggested that the mobile portal can provide location-award notification. The dynamically generated information based on the student's mobility within campus or on the way to campus is a feature that could be appealing to students. Some of the examples of location awareness were given by an interviewee, as following:

> "Using Wi-Fi at different places on campus, I'd like to be notified about news related to the place... for example, in the library, to notify me of new book arrivals. In food court to notify me of meals new offers. Near the university theater, to notify me of events currently taking place...."

Another student suggested that this location-aware notification feature can be useful to inform students of working hours and rules of public places in campus, once they step in these places, such as library and computer labs.

5.3. Theme 3: User Control.

User control is expressed by the current research participants as the extent to which mobile portal users can control content amount, whether detailed or brief, as well as enable or disable features such as location track and notifications. User control was primarily mentioned by interviewees who have extensive experience with web and mobile applications. The interviewees provided interesting ideas for adding more user control over the mobile portal, such as those discussed in the following sections.

5.3.1. User Control over Content.

Students expressed that they use mobile for various purposes at the same time, with an interrupted and multitasking behavior; they expressed a preference for easy-to-scan small chunk content.

> "With the mobile portal, I am not expecting overwhelming content, I expect small and meaningful chunks," as cited by an interviewee. "While checking the mobile portal, I frequently get interruptions with text messages and calls, I also tend to switch to check my e-mails and Facebook, I need to be able to catch-up when I return back to the portal," as stated by another interviewee.

On the other hand, same students expressed that in some specific cases, they "rely on the mobile portal to get detailed and comprehensive information," and this is related to the Reliability theme cited above. Hence, many of the interviewees suggested a control over content, enabling the user to select between detailed versus brief text and text versus videos, for each content included in the mobile students' portal.

5.3.2. User Control over Features.

While some of the interviewees who expressed the importance of getting location-related and academic-related notifications, as cited in the *Personally Relevant Content* theme discussed above. Many of those also suggested that these features be optional. It was recommended by those students that the user should have the option to enable/disable the location identification and academic status identification.

6. Conclusion and Implications

This exploratory study investigates factors affecting the intention to use mobile student portal for university students. The study was conducted in a university context in Egypt. The study aims to provide practical mobile student portal design guidelines for educational entities, designers, and implementers, to enhance students' willingness to use. Series of semistructured interviews were conducted with undergraduate of a private university in Egypt. Thematic analysis of the interviews revealed three themes (*Perceived Value*, *Personally Relevant Content*, and *User Control*); within these, a number of contributing items are suggested to affect students' intention to use mobile portals, as listed in Table 1. Some of these factors were identified in previous studies, such as *Perceived Value* [20, 21], *Reliability* [3], *Mobility* [8], and *Location Aware* [5]. Other factors were newly introduced in the mobile students' portal adoption context, such as *Content Sharing*, *Personalization*, and *User Control*. Additionally, some students' behaviors in mobile portals were newly discovered, such as the *Context Switching and Interrupted Behavior*. The current study provides a number of theoretical and practical contributions to the existing understanding of mobile student portal adoption, as in the following sections.

6.1. Theoretical Implications.

This research provides a number of theoretical implications which contribute to the existing understanding of mobile portal adoption, as shown in the following sections.

6.1.1. Perceived Value.

Perceived value was identified as an important determinant of intention to use mobile student portal. The construct was extensively discussed by all interviewees, supporting the applicability of previous findings on mobile application use to the mobile student portal context [3, 20, 21]. In the current study, authentic insights collected from the interviews suggested that reliability is considered as a value that mobile portal would provide to the users. As alternatives to other services, mobile services, in general, have the benefit that they are available most of the time, allowing to provide users with updated information [5]. In the student portal case, updated content would include opening and closure of courses registration, updated academic calendar, and last-minute changes to students' event schedules. Students use the portal usually at registration and exam time, and this is when there is need of updated, comprehensive, and sufficient information. If the students cannot rely on the mobile portal information to complete the task, they will look at it elsewhere.

TABLE 1: Suggested factors affecting the intention to use mobile student portal.

Adopting factors	Contributing items
Perceived value as discussed below:	Reliability
	Content Sharing
	Mobility
Personally relevant content	Genuine Photos
	Personalized Notification
	Location aware
User control	User Control over Content
	User Control over Features

6.1.2. Personally Relevant Content and Notification. Being on the top of personal communication devices, key values for mobile systems include personally relevant content and communication. Features such as personally relevant and interesting content and communication are highly valued. Individual notifications based on student's academic status, such as relevant deadline and warning, were cited as preferable features. Additionally, providing students with location-based information to notify students at a certain time at a certain location was suggested by a number of interviewees, as additional value of the mobile portal. Such construct may enrich the service, bring in additional users, and encourage a sense of community among users.

6.1.3. User Control. User control is expressed by participants of the current research not only as the extent to which they can chose between different alternatives of content format and details, but also to be able to switch on and off some of the portal personalized features, such as the location-aware notifications.

6.2. Practical Implications. Students in general are overconfident in their mobile-based web browsing abilities; nevertheless, the current research revealed some of their weakness, such as lower reading levels and impatience. These issues reduce students' task success and require simple, relatable student portal design. This study provides suggestions for designers of mobile student portals, to ensure better adoptions within students, and they are given in the following sections.

6.2.1. Redirect Mobile Users to the Mobile Site Version. The majority of participants indicated that in most cases, when they search for their student portal using their mobiles, search engines guide them to full site version instead of the mobile ones. Therefore, it is important to offer a clear link from the university full site to the mobile site for users who end up at the full site.

6.2.2. Clearly Identify Link to Student Portal on Every Page of the University Website. The link to student portal should be clearly visible on every page of the university website. Some of the participants indicate that they did not access the student portal from the university website, rather from internal pages via search.

6.2.3. Use Genuine Photos Reflecting User's Values. In the interviews, participants praised the fact that the university site includes photos and video gallery of sporting and art events. Two issues were raised concerning the use of photos. First, most of participants commented that photos about student life and activities are kept on the main home page of the university's website, and none are included in the student portal part of the site. Second, participants commented that they can easily tell the difference between genuine photos of real students in their university and advertising photos. Users appreciate photos that look authentic and representative of what they actually see in their university.

6.2.4. Design for Interruptive Behavior. Almost all participants expressed that their access to the student portal via their mobiles is been interrupted by text messages, calls, and message and e-mail alerts. Describing their interaction with the student portal as interrupted and multitasking, they expressed a preference for rapid scanning of content, with less effort. Display content in small, meaningful chunks with plenty of white space helps students retain information and pick up where they left off after the interruptions of text messages and phone calls.

A main challenge in mobile site design is to eliminate features and word count without limiting the selection of main tasks. A mobile site should have less information about each task, but the range of tasks should remain the same as that on the full site. On the other hand, most of the participants dislike tiny font sizes. Even though they're sufficiently sharp-eyed, most participants move too quickly and are too easily distracted to attend to small text.

6.2.5. Design for Mobility. Participants complained that the student portal includes lengthy videos, and with variable connectivity, uploading videos is very frustrating. Therefore, captions and a transcript of the video could be helpful in the mobile portal. The main issue with such mobility access is the frustration from loading materials, namely, videos, via smart phone in public areas with slow connectivity. Within the university, efforts should be made to ensure that Wi-Fi coverage and mobile Internet connectivity is adequate for students in campus. Killing time is often mentioned as one of the main contexts of use for the mobile Internet [5]. This motivation for use was also cited in the current study. Interviewees accessed the mobile portal when taking a break between lectures, waiting for the university bus, waiting for their friends, or sitting on the bus. Loading the portal needs to be fast on different connectivity conditions.

6.2.6. Follow the Student Changing Priorities along the Semester. Participants reported that with their mobile, they scan pages, rarely read text, and expect to find the need data in small comprehensive chunk. Therefore, it is recommended to identify the top tasks that students need to accomplish in different times along the semester, clearly show the task deadlines, and offer a step-by-step description of how to accomplish the task. Participants of the current research indicated that their priorities, when using the student portal, vary from one time to another along the semester. At the start of the semester, registration deadline, process, and fees should be the main icon on the screen, while on exam times, exam schedule should be the main icon. Depending on the seasonal priority of students along the semester, these priority tasks need to be clearly labelled and easy to spot.

6.2.7. Integrative Design and Content Sharing. Students are heavy users of social media with their mobiles. Integrative design with social media, Web 2.0 tools, and other web resources would be a good employment of web technology on mobile student portals, as suggested by an interviewee. Mobiles are personal communication devices and hence, services that enrich communication add good potential [5]. A suggestion was raised by an interviewee to integrate student portals with professional network, such as LinkedIn, and knowledge management of the university's industrial and academic partners. The integrative features are best to be designed in the mobile site as high majority of interviewees explained that they access their social media, read materials, and access their student portal via the same mobile device.

7. Limitations and Future Work

As with any empirical study, there are some limitations to the current research. One limitation is that the interviews sample was limited to the same geographical and cultural context. All participants were undergraduate students from a single university in Cairo, Egypt, which affects the generalization of the results. Egypt, though it is a developing country, owns a relatively high penetration of mobile technology, which might not be the case in other developing countries. Additionally, the private university, of which the student portal is used in this study, is still relying on manual systems in few of its process. For example, courses registration is done manually, as well as borrowing books from library. On the other hand, checking course schedule, downloading course materials, and getting course grades can be solely retrieved from the student portal. Hence, dependence of students on the portal is partial.

The interviewing method, used in this study, brought out users' authentic reactions and ideas about the system. However, the method does present limitations [4], as there are often differences between what users say about the system and what they actually do on the system. Hence, direct observation via usability testing or web analytic data on the usage of mobile portal might be sometimes needed to supplement interviews. It therefore remains a question for future research to explore the extent to which factors identified in this study will also hold for mobile university systems adoption for other samples and with other research tools. The implications of the current research suggest number of research questions which would be suitable for future quantitative examination. It would also be interesting to investigate some of the newly identified themes in a wider range of mobile technology applications.

References

[1] R. Katz, *Web Portals and Higher Education: Technologies to Make It Personal*, Educause and Nacubo, Jossy-Bass A Wiley Company, San Francisco, CA, USA, 2006, ISBN-13: 978-0787961718.

[2] V. Booi and G. Dista, "Usability and user acceptance of university web portal interfaces: a case of South African Universities," in *Communications in Computer and Information Science (373)*, C. Stephanidis, Ed., pp. 91–95, Springer Publication, Las Vegas, NV, USA, 2013.

[3] S. Alfaresi and K. Hone, "The intention to use mobile digital library technology: a focus group study in the United Arab Emirates," *International Journal of Mobile Human Computer Interaction*, vol. 7, no. 2, pp. 23–42, 2015.

[4] N. Mallat, "Exploring consumer adoption of mobile payments: a qualitative study," *Journal of Strategic Information Systems*, vol. 16, no. 4, pp. 413–432, 2007.

[5] E. Kaasinen, "User acceptance of mobile services," *International Journal of Mobile Human Computer Interaction*, vol. 1, no. 1, pp. 79–97, 2008.

[6] Internet Live Stats, *World Wide Web Consortium (W3C)*, 2018, http://www.internetlivestats.com.

[7] S. Ruth, "Is E-learning really working? The trillion-dollar question," *IEEE Internet Computing*, vol. 14, no. 2, pp. 78–82, 2010.

[8] G. R. El Said, "Understanding how learners use massive open online courses and why they drop out: thematic analysis of an interview study in a developing country," *Journal of Educational Computing Research*, vol. 55, no. 5, pp. 724–752, 2017.

[9] J. Zbick, I. Nake, M. Milrad, and M. Jansen, "A web-based framework to design and deploy mobile learning activities: evaluating its usability, learnability and acceptance," in *Proceedings of the IEEE 15th International Conference on Advanced Learning Technologies (ICALT)*, pp. 88–92, Hualien, Taiwan, July 2015.

[10] D. Zhang and B. Adipat, "Challenges, methodologies, and issue in usability testing of mobile applications," *International Journal of Human Computer Interaction*, vol. 18, no. 3, pp. 293–308, 2015.

[11] A. Rezaeean, S. Bairamzadeh, and A. Bolhari, "The importance of website innovation on Students' Satisfaction of University," *World Applied Sciences Journal*, vol. 18, no. 8, pp. 1023–1029, 2012.

[12] T. W. Zazelenchuk and E. Bolind, "Considering user satisfaction in designing web based portals," *Educause Quarterly*, vol. 26, no. 1, pp. 35–43, 2003.

[13] Statista, *The Portal of Statistics*, 2018, http://www.statista.com.

[14] C. Zhenghao, B. Alcorn, G. Christensen, N. Eriksson, D. Koller, and E. J. Emanuel, *Who's Benefiting from MOOCs, and Why*, 2015, https://hbr.org/2015/09/whos-benefitingfrom-moocs-and-why.

[15] H. Mariampolski, *Qualitative Market Research*, Sage Publications, Thousand Oaks, CA, USA, 2001.

[16] P. Yu and T. Hai, "A focus conversation model in consumer research: the incorporation of group facilitation paradigm in in-depth interviews," *Asia Pacific Advances in Consumer Research*, vol. 6, pp. 337–344, 2005.

[17] G. Guest, *Applied Thematic Analysis*, Sage Publications, Thousand Oaks, CA, USA, 2012.

[18] H. R. Bernard and G. W. Ryan, *Analyzing Qualitative Data: Systematic Approaches*, Sage Publications, Thousand Oaks, CA, USA, 2009.

[19] V. Braun and V. Clarke, "Using thematic analysis in psychology," *Qualitative Research in Psychology*, vol. 3, no. 2, pp. 77–83, 2006.

[20] D. Mugo, K. Njagi, B. Chemwei, and O. Montanya, "The technology acceptance model (TAM) and its application to the utilization of mobile learning technologies," *British Journal of Mathematics and Computer Science*, vol. 20, no. 4, pp. 1–8, 2017.

[21] J. Dong, H. Yin, L. Yongqiang, H. Li, and W. Wang, "TAM: a transparent agent architecture for measuring mobile applications," *Computing in Science and Engineering*, vol. 19, no. 1, pp. 54–61, 2017.

15

Dynamic Spectrum Pricing with Secondary User's Normal Demand Preference

Li Wang ⓘ[1] and Feng Li ⓘ[2]

[1]*College of Information Engineering, Zhejiang University of Technology, Hangzhou, Zhejiang 310023, China*
[2]*School of Electronic Science and Engineering, Nanjing University, Nanjing, Jiangsu 210023, China*

Correspondence should be addressed to Feng Li; fenglzj@zjut.edu.cn

Academic Editor: Mariusz Glabowski

During secondary user's dynamic access to authorized spectrum, a key issue is how to ascertain an appropriate spectrum price so as to maximize primary system's benefit and satisfy secondary user's diverse spectrum demands. In this paper, a scheme of pricing-based dynamic spectrum access is proposed. According to the diverse qualities of idle spectrum, the proposed scheme applies a Hotelling game model to form the spectrum pricing problem. Firstly, establish a model of spectrum leasing, among which the idle spectrum with different qualities constitutes a spectrum pool. Then, divide the idle spectrum into equivalent width of leased channels, which will be uniformly sold in order. Secondary users can choose proper channels to purchase in the spectrum pool according to their spectrum usage preferences which are subject to normal distribution and affected by the spectrum quality along with market estimation. This paper analyzes the effect of spectrum pricing according to the primary system's various tendencies to spectrum usage and economic income. Numerical results evaluate the effectiveness of the proposed pricing method in improving the primary system's profits.

1. Introduction

With the rapid development of wireless communication technology and the establishment of next-generation 5G communication standard, high-quality idle spectrum is more scarce which has become one of the bottlenecks restricting the development of wireless communication technology [1–4]. Cognitive radio which is based on dynamic spectrum access has attracted more and more attention of academy and engineering in recent years [5, 6]. Various kinds of emerging network technologies have begun to adopt dynamic spectrum detection and dynamic spectrum access to improve the efficiency of spectrum utilization. In the process of dynamic spectrum access, primary users owning licensed spectrum can lease the idle channels to secondary users to gain incomes. For primary users, how to identify an optimal channel pricing to maximize its own profit has become a significant issue. In this paper, we directly price the idle spectrum of authorized users according to the secondary user's diverse preferences. The spectrum pricing scheme has a prior estimate to the spectrum market. Compared with the spectrum auction, it does not need many overheads and improves the convenience of the spectrum access.

Spectrum trading provides an efficient way for secondary users to dynamically access licensed bands while the financial gains can encourage primary users to lease unused spectrum temporarily. Generally, the participants can perform the deal by auction-based method or pricing-based method. The spectrum auction mechanism can be divided into many kinds according to different application circumstances, such as trust-based auction which relaxes the credit limit appropriately in return for a higher economic efficiency to balance the honesty and the efficiency [7–10]. To be specific, Gao et al. [7] raised a proposal by being against the integrated contract and auction design for secondary spectrum trading, in the premise of the dependence of spectrum in time and space while spectrum spatial reuse is not allowed. A two-level dynamic game framework is developed in [8], which can achieve optimal benefit when both secondary providers and secondary users are made dynamically by competition. Sung and Richard [9] analyzed both the cooperative and noncooperative games and listed the maximum thresholds of the benefits received.

On the other hand, to lower the overhead and time cost for spectrum pricing, pricing-based spectrum trading has also been widespread concerned either [11–14]. In [11], the authors considered that secondary users access idle spectrum in LTE architecture with a base-station-centric framework and introduced a pricing model based on benefit motivation. Zhong and Wang [12] analyzed the scheme of power and spectrum allocation to improve the energy efficiency through spectrum sharing. Moreover, Tan et al. [13] introduced the concept of user preference which obeys the uniform distribution to proceed spectrum pricing. Actually, a random and actual user's preference parameter should be a normal distribution. Thus, more deep research on this case should be extended to address the optimal spectrum pricing.

During dynamic spectrum access, most of current research studies extend their technical roadmaps with an underlying assumption that all the leased channels are homogeneous and undergo uniform interference. However, as the available spectrum to be leased is not predictable and always appearing in nonconsecutive bands, it may have various fading characteristics. Furthermore, due to secondary users' diverse positions in heterogeneous cells, even the same spectrum band does not mean the same utility for different users sometimes. Thus, heterogeneous spectrum and differential user selection on the spectrum deserve full investigation which is the main concern of this paper.

In this paper, we investigate how to price the spectrum especially when heterogeneous spectrum and stochastic secondary user's preference are under consideration. A concept of spectrum pool constituted by the idle bands to be leased is introduced to facilitate the following spectrum deal. Suffering from different levels of interference, these channels have various qualities. In this case, secondary users are supposed to select channels for usage based on their preference. It can be envisioned that a secondary buyer with sufficient capital or urgent demand for ideal QoS can pick a high-quality channel. A secondary spectrum customer will pick a high-quality channel for usage when its capital is ample or broadband is required to support essential service. We adopt Hotelling model which is proper to describe the product pricing issue in heterogeneous market. By analyzing the secondary user's preference parameter, an iterative algorithm for spectrum pricing is obtained after fixing the Nash equilibrium. Numerical results are further provided to evaluate how the pricing parameters affect the primary system's profits.

The remainder of this paper is organized as follows. We introduce the system model for dynamic spectrum pricing in Section 2. Section 3 gives the utility function and finds the Nash equilibrium. Furthermore, numerical results are supplied to analyze the performance of the pricing algorithm in Section 3. Finally, we conclude this paper in Section 4.

2. System Model

Suppose the idle spectrum leased by the primary system forms a spectrum sharing pool, where the spectrum can be divided into many uniform channels for selling. Besides, the qualities of these channels are not homogeneous. For high-quality channels, the secondary users suffer lower channel fading or adjacent channel interference. Thus, secondary users choose these channels according to their diverse preferences. The preference parameter is determined by the channel quality and channel price.

In this case, we cast the pricing problem into the model of duopoly competition where two suppliers, similar to high-quality spectrum and low-quality spectrum, competing in prices and products, tend to attract more potential buyers which will finally lead to a dynamic balance. This idea became known among economists as the principle of minimum differentiation which was first proposed by Hotelling [15]. In fact, a mature market is always controlled by only few huge corporations which likely come into being a monopoly economy. Hotelling generalized Bertrand's model by considering different firms' locations in geographic space, and later this model was more often interpreted as a model of product differentiation which is an important feature of actual business.

To be specific, when applying Hotelling model to formulate an optimization problem, product price and product diversity should be considered during the process of building objective function. Besides, after solving the convex function and identifying the Nash equilibrium, the existence and rationality of the Nash equilibrium should be discussed.

Due to the spectrum quality diversity, secondary users should make rational choices on the channels since an ideal channel corresponds to a higher cost. On the other side, the primary system needs to set a proper pricing mechanism to optimize its profits according to the secondary customers' purchasing behaviors.

2.1. Utility Functions. In this paper, we consider that the spectrum trading is performed without auction activities. During the course, primary systems have no prior knowledge of the secondary customer's spectrum preference. In spectrum trading, the utility function of a secondary user can be expressed as

$$U = \theta s - p, \tag{1}$$

where θ denotes the secondary user's preference, s denotes the channel quality, and p is the channel price. In the spectrum sharing pool, there are two kinds of channels with diverse qualities to be chosen by secondary users as shown in Figure 1. We use s_1 to denote the high-quality channel and s_2 to denote the low-quality channel. Apparently, we have $s_1 > s_2 > 0$. In this case, different channel qualities mean various transmission capacities. Furthermore, we suppose that the secondary user's preference parameter θ is subject to the normal distribution expressed as $g(\theta)$. θ locates in the region of $[\theta_L, \theta_H]$, and ρ is the corresponding

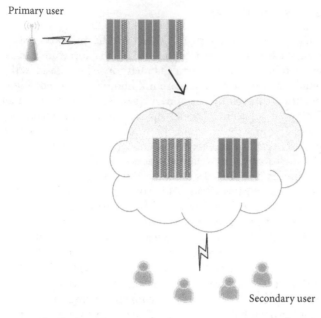

Primary user

Idle channel

Low-quality channel

High-quality channel

Secondary user

FIGURE 1: Spectrum pool.

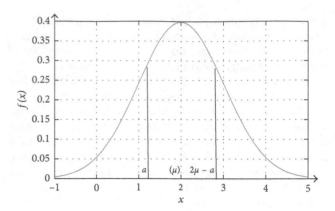

FIGURE 3: General normal distribution.

secondary user's preference shows the relation of demand and supply in current market. It is natural that a user's preference θ_i will increase when the spectrum pricing decreases or budget fund becomes abundant. In this situation, we consider when a user's preference locates at the region $[\theta_1, \theta_2]$, then the user will select a channel between high-quality spectrum and low-quality spectrum with qualities s_1 and s_2, respectively.

Besides, in this case, we assume that the user's preference complies with normal distribution since a discrete random variable can be supposed to approximately obey normal distribution when the sample number is sufficient enough.

2.2. Spectrum Pricing. Secondary user's preference parameter is considered to be subject to the normal distribution for practical application. Figure 2 shows the density curve of the standard normal distribution. The probability density can be given as

$$\varphi(x) = \frac{1}{\sqrt{2\pi}e^{-x^2/2}}. \tag{2}$$

Then, the distribution function is

$$f(x) = \int \varphi(x) = \frac{1}{2\pi} \int_{-a}^{a} e^{-t^2/2} \, dt. \tag{3}$$

According to [16], $f(a)$ can be simplified as

$$f(a) = \sqrt{1 - e^{-a^2/1.6058}}. \tag{4}$$

Thus, the probability can be approximately calculated in the given region $[-a, a]$. Besides, according to [16], the conclusion obtained from (4) can also be applied to the case of general normal distribution as shown in Figure 3.

Furthermore, when the distribution mean is μ, the probability calculated approximately in $[a, 2\mu - a]$ is obtained as

$$f(a) = \sqrt{1 - e^{-(\mu-a)^2/1.6058}}. \tag{5}$$

As shown in Figure 4, the secondary customer whose preference parameter θ locates in $[\theta_L, \theta_0]$ will purchase low-quality channels. The user with the preference parameter $\theta \in [\theta_0, \theta_H]$ chooses a high-quality channel.

Then, we figure out the distribution probabilities for the two cases. Divide the part in red in Figure 4 into two parts,

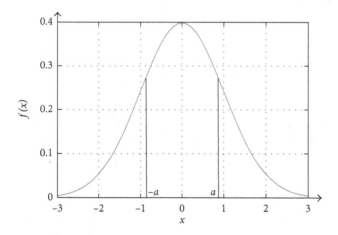

FIGURE 2: Standard normal distribution.

probability distribution function denoted as $\rho = G(\theta)$. We adopt θ_0 to express the nonpreference parameters of cognitive users when there is no demand difference for the secondary customers between the high-quality channel and low-quality channel. Then, it can be calculated as $\theta_0 = (p_1 - p_2)/(s_1 - s_2)$, where p_1 and p_2 represent the two kinds of channel prices. From the above analysis, when a secondary user's spectrum preference θ_i is higher than θ_0, the user prefers to choose the high-quality channel. Otherwise, the user would rather prefer to choose the low-quality channel for purchasing.

Furthermore, a secondary user's selection preference is impacted by many factors, such as available budget, spectrum quality, and spectrum pricing denoted as (1). In fact,

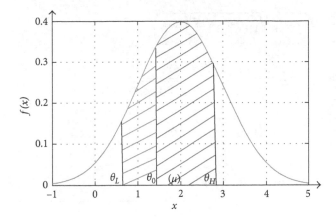

FIGURE 4: Divide the channels into two kinds of qualities.

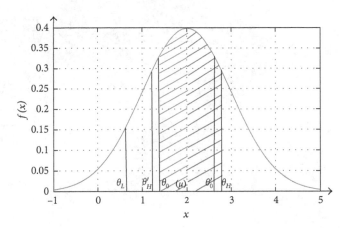

FIGURE 5: Divide the high-quality channels into two parts.

wherein there are $\theta_0' = \theta_0 + \mu$ and $\theta_H - \theta_H' = \mu$, as shown in Figure 5.

According to the corresponding regions of high-quality and low-quality channels, we have the probability densities as follows:

$$\varphi(H) = \frac{1}{2} \times \left(\sqrt{1 - e^{-(\mu - \theta_0)^2/1.6058}} + \sqrt{1 - e^{-(\theta_H - \mu)^2/1.6058}} \right),$$

$$\varphi(L) = \frac{1}{2} \times \left(\sqrt{1 - e^{-(\mu - \theta_L)^2/1.6058}} + \sqrt{1 - e^{-(\mu - \theta_0)^2/1.6058}} \right). \tag{6}$$

Besides, it is essential to take the opportunity cost of the primary system into account which means the primary system abandons the potential benefits in future to promote current spectrum trading. Thus, assume that the marginal cost of the

primary user is related to the quality of the channel which can be expressed as $c_i = \alpha s_i$ $(i = 1, 2)$, where α is the marginal factor. Formulating the problem by a Berland game model, the profit functions of systems H and L can be given as

$$\pi_H(p_1, p_2) = N(p_1 - \alpha s_1) \times \frac{1}{2} \times \left(\sqrt{1 - e^{-(\mu - \theta_0)^2/1.6058}} + \sqrt{1 - e^{-(\theta_H - \mu)^2/1.6058}} \right), \tag{7}$$

$$\pi_L(p_1, p_2) = N(p_2 - \alpha s_2) \times \frac{1}{2} \times \left(\sqrt{1 - e^{-(\mu - \theta_L)^2/1.6058}} + \sqrt{1 - e^{-(\mu - \theta_0)^2/1.6058}} \right), \tag{8}$$

where N is the number of secondary users. The nonpreference parameter θ_0 is not fixed and changing in $[\theta_L, \theta_H]$. Besides, whether $\theta_0 > \mu$ matters which will affect the deductions. The

profits obtained above are subject to the situation when θ_0 locates at the left side of μ. Similarly, when θ_0 locates at the right side of μ, the corresponding profit functions can be deduced as

$$\pi_H(p_1, p_2) = N(p_1 - \alpha s_1) \times \frac{1}{2} \times \left(\sqrt{1 - e^{-(\theta_H - \mu)^2/1.6058}} + \sqrt{1 - e^{-(\theta_0 - \mu)^2/1.6058}} \right), \tag{9}$$

$$\pi_L(p_1, p_2) = N(p_2 - \alpha s_2) \times \frac{1}{2} \times \left(\sqrt{1 - e^{-(\mu - \theta_L)^2/1.6058}} + \sqrt{1 - e^{-(\theta_0 - \mu)^2/1.6058}} \right). \tag{10}$$

Based on the marginal utility functions, by taking derivatives of (7) and (8), we can achieve the iterative optimal channel pricing to be

$$p_1^{(t+1)} = p_1 + \beta \times N \times \frac{1}{2} \times \left(\sqrt{1 - e^{-(\mu-\theta_0)^2/1.6058}} + \sqrt{1 - e^{-(\theta_H-\mu)^2/1.6058}} \right)$$

$$+ \beta \times N \times e^{-(\mu-\theta_0)^2/1.6058} \times \left(2\alpha - p_1^{(t)}\right) \times \frac{2\mu - 2p_1^{(t)} - 2p_2^{(t)}}{6.4232 \sqrt{1 - e^{-(\mu-\theta_0)^2/1.6058}}},$$

$$p_2^{(t+1)} = p_2 + \beta \times N \times \frac{1}{2} \times \left(\sqrt{1 - e^{-(\mu-\theta_L)^2/1.6058}} + \sqrt{1 - e^{-(\mu-\theta_0)^2/1.6058}} \right)$$

$$+ \beta \times N \times e^{-(\mu-\theta_0)^2/1.6058} \times \frac{1}{6.4232} \times \left(2p_2^{(t)} - 2p_1^{(t)} + 2\mu\right). \tag{11}$$

To be similar, we can achieve the optimal channel pricing when $\theta_0 > \mu$.

As shown from the primary systems' utility functions expressed from (7) to (10), a key point to fix the final pricing solution is to ascertain that the utility function is consistent integrable. Then, we provide Theorem 1 to prove the essential condition.

Theorem 1. *For the primary system's utility function π_i, if there is $\tau \geq 0$ satisfying $\sup_{i \in N} E(\pi_i)^\tau < \infty$, then we conclude π_i, $i \in N$, is consistent integrable.*

Proof. When $\sup_{i \in N} E(\pi_i)^\tau < \infty$ can be met, we have the following inequality in the condition of $\chi > \chi_\varepsilon$:

$$P\left(|\pi_i| \geq \chi\right) \leq \frac{E|\pi_i|}{\chi} \leq \frac{\sup_{i \in N} E|\pi_i|^\tau}{\chi} < \delta_\varepsilon, \tag{12}$$

where π_i denotes the spectrum preference of the secondary user i. Therefore, $E(\pi_i)I_{\{(\pi_i) \geq \chi\}} \leq \varepsilon$ holds for any $t \in N$, then we have

$$\sup_{i \in t} E(\pi_i)^\tau I_{\{(\pi_i) \geq \chi\}} \leq \varepsilon, \quad \tau \geq 0, \tag{13}$$

wherein for $\omega \in \Omega$,

$$I_A(\omega) = \begin{cases} 1, & \omega \in H, \\ \\ 0, & \omega \in H^C := \dfrac{\omega}{H}. \end{cases} \tag{14}$$

Besides, for any $H \in \mathfrak{R}$ and $\chi > 0$, we have

$$\sup_{i \in N} E(\pi_i)^\tau I_H$$
$$= \sup_{i \in N} \left(E(\pi_i)^\tau I_{H \cap \{(\pi_i) < \chi\}} + E(\pi_i)^\tau I_{H \cap \{(\pi_i) \geq \chi\}} \right) \tag{15}$$
$$= \chi P(H) + \sup_{i \in N} E(\pi_i)^\tau I_{H \cap \{(\pi_i) \geq \chi\}}.$$

If $\{\pi_i, i \in N\}$ is consistent integrable, $H = \Omega$ can be set which makes χ_0 larger to obtain $\sup_{i \in N} E(\pi_i)^\tau I_{H \cap \{(\pi_i) \geq \chi_0\}} < 1$,

then we further have $\sup_{i \in N} E(\pi_i)^\tau \leq \chi_0 + 1 < \infty$. Furthermore, for any $\varepsilon > 0$, letting χ_ε large enough can guarantee

$\sup_{i \in N} E(\pi_i)^\tau I_{H \cap \{(\pi_i) \geq \chi_\varepsilon\}} < \varepsilon/2$. Let $\delta_\varepsilon = \varepsilon/(2\chi_\varepsilon)$, for any $A \in \mathfrak{R}$, only if $P(H) < \delta_\varepsilon$, we can achieve

$$\sup_{i \in t} E(\pi_i)^\tau I_H \leq \chi_\varepsilon P(H) + \frac{\varepsilon}{2} < \varepsilon. \tag{16}$$

Thus, the sufficient conditions can be satisfied to ensure the consistent integrability of the proposed utility function.

Besides, as the utility function may lead to multiple solutions, it is essential to remove the surplus solutions and find the optimal one for the rationality of the deduced Nash equilibrium. The proof for the existence of a pure Nash equilibrium is provided as follows.

Theorem 2. *For a given utility function $f_i = \pi_i$ and strategy function $s_i = p_i$, a pure Nash equilibrium for the proposed pricing game algorithm exists.*

Proof. Based on the theorem of Debreu's equilibrium existence [17], for the functions s_i and f_i given above, a pure strategy Nash equilibrium exists once the following sufficient conditions can be satisfied: (1) in limited Euclidean space, the strategy function s_i is a nonempty and compact subset and (2) for a strategy combination S, f_i is continuous and concave. First of all, we define $S : \Sigma \to \Sigma$ to be a Cartesian direct product for s_i, and Σ_i is a simplex in dimension (s_i). s_i can be a compact subset in limited Euclidean space only when the condition that s_i is symmetrically bounded and continuous functions is met. In order to prove that s_i is symmetrically bounded, thus $\forall \varepsilon_1$, it requires certifying that $\exists \delta = \delta(\varepsilon_1)$ can make $\forall \psi \in F$ workable which can be

$$|\psi(x_1) - \psi(x_2)| < \varepsilon_1 \quad (\text{when } \rho(x_1, x_2) < \delta), \tag{17}$$

where $\rho(x, y) \triangleq \max_{a \leq t \leq b} (x(t) - y(t))$ and $\psi(x_i) \Rightarrow s_i$. As the subset $\varepsilon_1/3$ is finite $N(\varepsilon_1/3) = \{\psi_1, \psi_2, \ldots, \psi_n\}$, then based on the characteristic of continuity, we have $\exists \delta = \delta(\varepsilon/3)$. Therefore, in the condition of $\rho(x_1, x_2)$, we achieve the following inequality:

$$|\psi_i(x_1) - \psi_i(x_2)| < \frac{\varepsilon_1}{3} \quad (i = 1, 2, \ldots, n). \tag{18}$$

As $\forall \psi \in F$, $\psi_i \in N(\varepsilon/3)$ enables $d(\psi, \psi_i) < \varepsilon/3$, we can obtain

$$\left|\psi(x)-\psi(x')\right|$$

$$\leq \left|\psi(x)-\psi_i(x)\right|+\left|\psi_i(x)-\psi_i(x')\right|+\left|\psi_i(x)-\psi(x')\right|$$

$$\leq 2d(\psi,\psi_i)+(\psi_i(x)-\psi_i(x'))<\varepsilon_1 \quad (\text{when } \rho(x,x')<\delta),$$

$$(19)$$

where $d(u,v)=\max(u(x)-v(x))$. Besides, it is apparent that s_i should be continuous and differentiable; thus, we can conclude that s_i is a nonempty and compact subset in limited Euclidean space.

Furthermore, since the requirement for the concave function is that $f(tx+(1+t)y)\geq tf(x)+(1-t)f(y)$ and concave f_i holds, we need the following equation for the high-quality channels:

$$\pi_i^{''}<0. \quad (20)$$

Obviously, proper parameter settings can satisfy this condition. Hence, we can conclude that the existence of a unique Nash equilibrium for our proposed algorithm is satisfied [18].

3. Numerical Results

In this section, numerical results are provided to testify the effects of the proposed pricing method. In dynamic access networks, we suppose that the idle spectrum is controlled by the licensed users. The secondary users who aim to access the spectrum must participate in the spectrum trading and pay for the cost to the primary systems. As the proposed pricing solution is an iterative algorithm, we thus give the initial spectrum pricing for two kinds of channels to be $s_1=2$, $s_2=1$, $N=100$, $\alpha=1$, $\mu=2.2$, and $\beta\in(0,0.028)$. The cognitive user's preference locates in $[1,3]$ which means $\theta_L=1$ and $\theta_H=3$. Furthermore, since the proposed pricing method is an iterative algorithm, we set the initial spectrum pricing for two kinds of qualities of channels as $p_i^{(0)}=0.01$. Then, we give the performances of the channel prices and system profits in the following tests.

In Figure 6, we give the performances of the channel prices obtained in this paper with different marginal factors α. We can achieve from the figure that the optimal price of the high-quality channel is much higher than that of the low-quality channel. Furthermore, the channel pricing rises with increasing marginal factor α, since higher marginal cost needs to be compensated for the primary system. We further obtain that the iterative algorithm converges very fast which will attain a stable value within 15 iterations. In the counterpart, Figure 7 gives the performances of the system profits under the optimal pricing with different marginal factors α. It is apparent in Figure 7 that the system profits decrease with increasing marginal factor α, which means the close relation between spectrum cost and system profit. Besides, it should be noted that the profit received on the high-quality channel overcomes that on the low-quality channel which is understandable since the primary system in nature expects to reap more profits through more excellent products.

Then, we give the presentations of channel prices and system profits under different preference distribution means

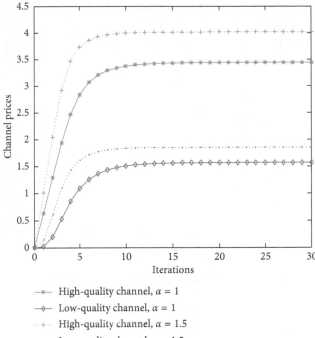

FIGURE 6: Channel prices with different marginal factors.

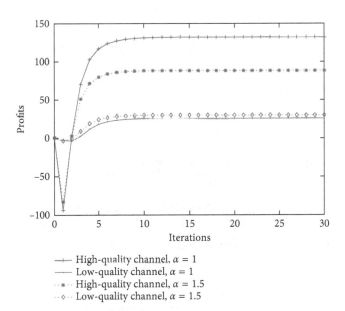

FIGURE 7: System profits with different marginal factors.

in Figures 8 and 9. Due to the cognitive user's preference factor θ locating in $[1,3]$, it would prefer a high-quality channel when θ approaches to 3. Otherwise, it will choose a low-quality channel. As shown in Figure 8, there are two curves in response to one kind of color. We can obtain from the figure that the optimal channel price rises with the increasing distribution mean. It can be understood that the primary system considering the secondary customers with a higher preference factor would endure more expensive spectrum. As a result, the system profits upgrade with an

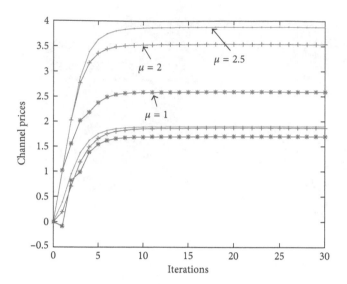

FIGURE 8: Channel prices with different distribution means.

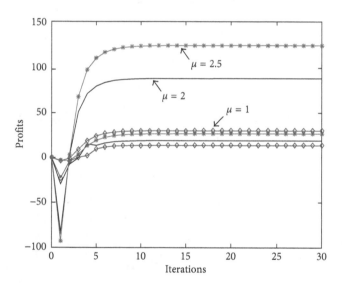

FIGURE 9: System profits with different distribution means.

increasing distribution mean. Meanwhile, the primary system can reap more profits when its high-quality spectrum attracts plenty of attention.

We can conclude from Figures 6–9 that the pricing curves for channel I to channel IV converge no more than 20 iterations. In fact, by choosing proper parameters, the proposed pricing algorithm can be guaranteed to converge at a fixed point.

Based on the pricing algorithm given in (11), the equations can be rewritten in the following matrix form:

$$P^{k+1} = U^{-1}WP^k + U^{-1}b, \quad k = 0, 1, 2, \ldots . \quad (21)$$

According to [19], if $\rho(U^{-1}W) < 1$ holds, the iterative algorithm p^k will be convergent. Based on the proposed pricing algorithm, we can easily achieve the Jacobi matrix and the corresponding maximal eigenvalue. Hence, by properly setting the algorithm's parameter, we can ensure

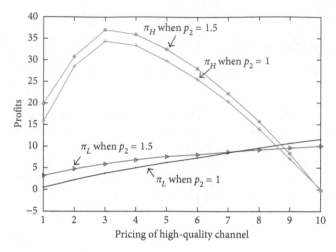

FIGURE 10: System profits with changing channel pricing.

$\rho(U^{-1}W) < 1$. In addition, the oscillating point appears when $\rho(U^{-1}W) = 1$.

At last, we testify the performances of system profits with different channel prices as shown in Figure 10. We can obtain from the figure that the system profits of the high-quality channels do not grow continually with the increasing price of high-quality channel. Similar to the conclusions we deduced before, the utility functions of the system profits are convex with respect to corresponding channel pricing. Thus, the system profits of the high-quality channels can attain a maximum. Besides, the performances of low-quality channel's profits differ from that of the high-quality channel as the argument in x-axis is the pricing of high-quality channel. On the other hand, the increase of the high-quality channel's pricing will lead to the loss of potential customers to the high-quality channel which in turn improves the low-quality channel's profits.

4. Conclusion

In this paper, we investigate how to price the heterogeneous spectrum in condition of secondary users' stochastic selection preferences. The main contribution of this paper lies in that we introduce a Hotelling game model to formulate and address the differential spectrum pricing. In the proposed model, we assume that the idle spectrum is collected and leased to potential secondary users centrally so that a centralized spectrum pricing can be carried out by the primary system. Various qualities of idle spectrum constitute a spectrum pool in which the bands are divided into numbers of uniform channels for leasing. It is foreseen that the high-quality channels can incur more profits for the primary system by offering a high price. On the other hand, a preference factor is introduced to describe the secondary user's selection tendency on the channels. We analyze the impact of secondary users' preference on spectrum trading and propose an iterative algorithm for pricing. Proofs of the integrability of the utility function and existence of Nash equilibrium used in the proposal are also given. Numerical results are provided to testify the performances of the proposed optimal spectrum pricing and the corresponding system profits as a result.

Acknowledgments

This work was supported by the National Natural Science Foundation of China under Grant no. 51404211.

References

[1] N. Zhao, F. R. Yu, H. Sun, and M. Li, "Adaptive power allocation schemes for spectrum sharing in interference-alignment-based cognitive radio networks," *IEEE Transactions on Vehicular Technology*, vol. 65, no. 5, pp. 3700–3714, 2016.

[2] F. Li, X. Tan, and L. Wang, "An uplink power control algorithm using traditional iterative model for cognitive radio networks," *Journal of Central South University*, vol. 19, no. 10, pp. 2816–2822, 2012.

[3] C. Yang, J. Li, and A. Anpalagan, "Hierarchical decision-making with information asymmetry for spectrum sharing systems," *IEEE Transactions on Vehicular Technology*, vol. 64, no. 9, pp. 4359–4364, 2015.

[4] X. Liu, F. Li, and Z. Na, "Optimal resource allocation in simultaneous cooperative spectrum sensing and energy harvesting for multichannel cognitive radio," *IEEE Access*, vol. 5, pp. 3801–3812, 2017.

[5] F. Li, X. Tan, and L. Wang, "A new game algorithm for power control in cognitive radio networks," *IEEE Transactions on Vehicular Technology*, vol. 60, no. 9, pp. 4384–4392, 2011.

[6] X. Liu, M. Jia, and X. Tan, "Threshold optimization of cooperative spectrum sensing in cognitive radio network," *Radio Science*, vol. 48, no. 1, pp. 23–32, 2013.

[7] L. Gao, J. Huang, Y. Chen, and B. Shou, "An integrated contract and auction design for secondary spectrum trading," *IEEE Journal on Selected Areas in Communications*, vol. 31, no. 3, pp. 581–592, 2013.

[8] K. Zhu, N. Dusit, P. Wang, and Z. Han, "Dynamic spectrum leasing and service selection in spectrum secondary market of cognitive radio networks," *IEEE Transactions on Wireless Communications*, vol. 11, no. 3, pp. 1136–1145, 2012.

[9] C. H. Sung and J. L. Richard, "Secondary spectrum trading-auction-based framework for spectrum allocation and profit sharing," *IEEE/ACM Transactions on Networking*, vol. 21, no. 1, pp. 176–189, 2012.

[10] W. Wang and X. Liu, "List-coloring based channel allocation for open-spectrum wireless networks," in *Proceedings of 2005 IEEE 62nd Vehicular Technology Conference 2005*, pp. 690–694, Dallas, TX, USA, 2005.

[11] D. Soumitra, P. Shalini, and Y. Halim, "Secondary user access in LTE architecture based on a base-station-centric framework with dynamic pricing," *IEEE Transactions on Vehicular Technology*, vol. 62, no. 1, pp. 284–296, 2012.

[12] W. Zhong and J. Wang, "Energy efficient spectrum sharing strategy selection for cognitive MIMO interference channels," *IEEE Transactions on Signal Processing*, vol. 61, no. 14, pp. 3705–3717, 2013.

[13] X. Tan, Y. Liu, and S. Wei, "Game-based spectrum allocation in cognitive radio networks," *Journal of South China University of Technology*, vol. 38, no. 5, pp. 22–38, 2010.

[14] Y. Liu, M. Jiang, X. Tan, and F. Lu, "Maximal independent set based channel allocation algorithm in cognitive radios," in *Proceedings of IEEE Youth Conference on Information, Computing and Telecommunication 2009*, pp. 78–81, Beijing, China, 2009.

[15] H. Hotelling, "Stability in competition," *Economic Journal*, vol. 39, no. 153, pp. 41–57, 1929.

[16] M. Li, *Research of Cognitive Radio Spectrum Allocation Algorithm Based on Graph Theory*, Southwest Jiaotong University, Chengdu, China, 2012.

[17] G. Debreu, "A social equilibrium existence theorem," *Proceedings of the National Academy of Sciences*, vol. 38, no. 10, pp. 886–893, 1952.

[18] A. M. Colell, M. D. Whinston, and J. R. Green, *Microeconomic Theory*, Oxford University Press, Oxford, UK, 1995.

[19] Y. Saad, *Iterative Methods for Sparse Linear System*, Society for Industrial and Applied Mathematics, Philadelphia, PA, USA, 2nd edition, 2003.

16

Cluster-Based Device Mobility Management in Named Data Networking for Vehicular Networks

Moneeb Gohar (iD),[1] **Naveed Khan,**[1] **Awais Ahmad** (iD),[1] **Muhammad Najam-Ul-Islam,**[1]
Shahzad Sarwar,[2] **and Seok-Joo Koh** (iD)[3]

[1]*Department of Computer Science, Bahria University, Islamabad, Pakistan*
[2]*College of Information Technology, Punjab University, Lahore, Pakistan*
[3]*School of Computer Science and Engineering, Kyungpook National University, Republic of Korea*

Correspondence should be addressed to Seok-Joo Koh; sjkoh@knu.ac.kr

Academic Editor: Mohamed Elhoseny

Named data networking (NDN) is an emerging technology. It was designed to eliminate the dependency of IP addresses in the hourglass model. Mobility is a key concern of the modern Internet architecture, even though the NDN architecture has solved the consumer mobility. That is, the consumer can rerequest the desired data contents, while the producer mobility remains as an issue in the NDN architecture. This paper focuses on the issue of producer mobility and proposes the cluster-based device mobility management scheme, which uses the cluster heads to solve the producer mobility issue in NDN. In the proposed scheme, a cluster head has all information of its attached devices. A cluster head updates the routes, when a device moves to the new access router by sending all the attachment information. The proposed scheme is evaluated and compared with the existing scheme by using the *ndnSIM* simulation. From the results, we see that the proposed scheme can decrease the numbers of interest packets in the network, compared with the existing scheme.

1. Introduction

NDN is a common networking model for all applications and network environment, and it is still under the developing phase. It has been designed as an alternative to the IP address-based network. IP was designed for conversation between endpoints, and it is used enormously for content distribution [1–3]. NDN uses data names instead of IP addresses. The NDN network removes the restriction of IP datagram which can only use both IP destination addresses and source addresses. NDN application removes middleware which causes inefficiency because middleware uses mapping application for interaction. In NDN, data looping is prevented via memory because every chunk of data has a unique name, while IP is used for single-path forwarding.

The NDN architecture uses the two types of packets [4], *interest packet* and *data packet*. A consumer uses the interest packet to request the desired contents, while a producer or NDN router uses the data packet to send the desired content to the consumer by using the reverse path. Each NDN router maintains the three tables for processing of interest packets and data packets [5]. These tables are content store (CS), pending interest table (PIT), and forwarding information base (FIB).

Initially, when an interest packet reaches the NDN router, the NDN router first checks the desired content in CS. If the content is found in the CS table, the NDN router will send the content back to the consumer. Otherwise, it is forwarded to PIT. When PIT waits for the same content from FIB, it only marks an entry in the PIT table. PIT forwards the desired content to the consumer upon reception. If PIT did not send the desired interest packet to FIB, it will forward it to FIB, and FIB will look for the desired content in the other NDN router. When the content is found, it will be delivered to the consumer by using the reverse path.

The producer mobility is a major issue in NDN. The consumer mobility is automatically solved by the NDN architecture since a consumer can rerequest the desired contents. If the consumer nodes are interested in a desired data content, the producer nodes will offer the content to the consumers. Problems may occur when a consumer requests the desired content and the producer moves to the new access router by handover. One of the problems may occur when the interest packets reach the previous access router, and thus the interest packets cannot be delivered to the producer. Based on this, in this paper, we introduce a cluster-based device mobility management (CB-DMM) so as to locate the devices in NDN that may possibly move from the previous access router to a new access router.

The remaining parts of this paper are organized as follows. Section 2 will briefly review the related work. In Section 3, we will explain the existing scheme. The proposed CB-DMM model will be described in Section 4. We will evaluate the performance of the CB-DMM models in Section 5. Finally, Section 6 will give conclusions and future works.

2. Related Work

NDN is a new emerging networking model that can be applied in various networking areas. Specially, NDN provides a lot of advantages such as network caching, security, and efficient response time in the vehicular ad hoc networks (VANETs) [2, 3, 6–8]. There are two types of mobility considered in NDN: consumer mobility and producer mobility. A lot of studies have been done on consumer mobility. However, there are not many studies on producer mobility.

The producer mobility issue is often addressed by using the mobile IP [9]. However, it suffers from the problems, such as a single-point failure, nonoptimal routing and so on. In [1], a distributed scalable mobility management (SMM) mechanism is introduced to solve the issues of MIP-based solution for NDN mobility without changing the original NDN paradigm. SMM protocol separates the content locator and the identifier. The hierarchical MIP [10] is used to support the intradomain and interdomain handover. However, the use of mapping systems on a global scale brings latency and complexity in the network.

An anchor-based mobility support method was proposed in [5]. Mobility tracking node, called anchor, was used to redirect the consumer request to the producer from the old location to the new location. When the producer handover happens and the interest packet ends up with being undeliverable, the traveling interest packet is immediately redirected toward the anchor node instead of being dropped at the old point of attachment.

The content provider mobility is solved in [11] by providing the locator and the mapping system. The locator is used because we do not know where the information is located, and the mapping system is used to map an identifier to the locator. An identifier is used for matching in CS and PIT, and a locator is used for forwarding in FIB. The provider gets a locator when it joins the network. A locator represents the address of the provider in the access point. A mapping system, such as DNS, will resolve the query so as to map the name to the locator. These extra labels may cause more complexity and burden on the network.

In [12], the authors tested the named data network for mobility support in the wireless access network and provided the simulation-based results by using *ndnSIM*. This work focuses on delay-sensitive and delay-tolerant traffics by using different network topologies. These topologies are based on autonomous systems (ASs). The authors give the four scenarios. The first scenario is for a single mobile host and a single static host, which are assigned to the same AS. The second scenario is based on the first scenario with modification that allows both hosts to be mobile. The third scenario has a single mobile host and a single static host, and each host is assigned to different ASs. In the last scenario, the third scenario is modified, which allows both hosts to be mobile. In these scenarios, the application with delay-tolerant and delay-sensitive traffics may experience worse performance in the viewpoint of message overhead and throughput. NDN is not suitable for small size networks. The authors want to introduce the location-routing policies in NDN to satisfy the requirements of the different applications and to reduce the burden on network infrastructure.

In [13], the authors have divided the existing solutions for producer mobility in NDN into the three categories: routing, mapping, and tracking. A mobile node (MN) can keep its IP address while moving to another network, but MN must update the other routers in the routing-based approach. In mapping-based solution, whenever MN changes the network, it must update the current IP address at previous routers. The tracing-based approach is mainly used to reach the producer in the hop-by-hop manner by using the reverse path. The authors mainly concentrate on the producer mobility and give a detailed mechanism of the already available proposed solution. For producer mobility, the authors present the two chase mechanisms of the moving producer and also the two data-centric ways to find interest data.

In [14], a trace-based scheme is proposed for NDN mobility, called Kite. In Kite, a new forwarding mechanism is introduced for the producer mobility. A trade name field is used. Tracing flags are used to forward the tracking interest. The Kite is locator-free and based on application. The developer can make changes in its application to achieve better performance. But, the authors have not provided any simulation to validate the proposed approach. Trace-based solution also causes huge traffic in the network, and it is time-consuming.

In [15], the producer mobility problem is solved by data replication. The authors provided the two main strategies to handle the producer mobility. In the first strategy, they handle the producer mobility through data replication. Secondly, they evaluate when data replication improves the producer mobility in NDN. The producer mobility issue is divided into the two categories: unavailability period and reattachment to the network. In the unavailability period, they suggested replicating the content when the producer is unavailable. Through different parameters, they evaluate the performance for unavailability period and for reattachment to the network. But, the replication techniques can cause more storage and overhead in the network.

In [16], the authors minimize data loss in the real-time application which is caused by mobility in the NDN network. They used the three approaches to minimize the loss which is caused by mobility. In the first approach, the point of access (PoA) is used, where a mobile node (MN) registers itself with a nearby PoA. This PoA sends interest packets and data packets to the MN. In the second approach, the rendezvous points are used. Rendezvous points represent the strategically located routers. The authors used the rendezvous point for seamless mobility. In the last approach, multipath interest and multipoint content are used to solve the mobility issue in NDN.

In [17], the producer mobility is solved by using the cache techniques. Before the producer handover occurs, data can be cached to offer seamless operation in NDN.

In [18], the authors built a prototype of NDN in the ns-3 simulation. A forwarding hint is used for the producer mobility. The forwarding hint was used in the previous IP mobility solution. The authors argue that this new element can be used for content-centric data transmission.

3. Existing SMM Scheme

Scalable mobility management (SMM) for content source in NDN is proposed in [1]. It solved the producer mobility issue in NDN. The authors used the mapping system on a global scale which may cause huge latency and bring more complexity to the network. The authors proposed the two handover models. In the first model shown in Figure 1, a producer is attached to a new access router, and it sends a special message to the mapping system by using a binding update (BU). The mapping system sends a binding acknowledgment (BA) to the producer. The mapping system also sends BU to the previous access router. The previous access router (PAR) sends data packets with BA, and the communication continues. In the second handover model, the producer sends the BU packet to both mapping system and PAR at the same time. The BA is sent from PAR to the producer. The second handover model introduced the mobility option (MO) packet which is a modification of NDN interest packets. The MO interest is sent from PAR to the new access router (NAR). We solve the mobility issue through the cluster-based device mobility in NDN. The device may be a producer or a consumer, which will further be discussed in Section 4.

4. Proposed CB-DMM Model

In this section, we will discuss the proposed CB-DMM model, including topology, handover procedure, selection of cluster heads, responsibilities of cluster heads, and NDN routers.

4.1. CB-DMM Topology Model. We have designed the cluster-based device mobility management (CB-DMM) to support the device mobility in NDN. In Figure 2, it is assumed that a consumer requests contents "contentsource/realtime/video1." The problem occurs when the interest packet reaches the previous access router and the producer moves to the new access router, and the interest packet cannot be delivered to the producer. To solve this problem, the cluster-based device mobility management scheme is

used. Our model has the strength to solve other mobility issues such as consumer mobility. In CB-DMM, when the device moves from one access router to another, it will send its current location information to the cluster head, and the cluster head diverts the pending interest packets toward the intended device.

In Figure 2, a group of NDN routers selects cluster heads. There are different techniques available for selection of cluster heads based on the nature of network type. In a wireless network, we need more storage capacity, energy, and the location of the cluster head, while the situation is different for the wired network. Our topology is based on the mixed network. We use both wireless and wired networks in our model for simulation. The selection of cluster will be further discussed in Section 4.3.

4.2. CB-DMM Handover Procedure. A producer moves from PAR (previous access router) to NAR (new access router) in Figure 3. The moving device (producer) sends the attachment information to NAR. The NAR sends the attachment information to the cluster head and informs it about the producer. The cluster head updates its cached table and saves the current location of the producer. The cluster head sends the binding acknowledgment to NAR, and NAR sends BA to the content producer. The cluster heads exchange periodic updates with each other. When a request reaches the cluster head for producer, it simply checks its cache and sends a request to the current location of the producer. The producer sends the contents through the reverse path to the consumer.

4.3. Selection of Cluster Heads. Different approaches can be taken to select the cluster heads. The wired network is different from the wireless network. Selection of cluster heads in the wired network is easy, while selection in wireless is difficult. Our scenario is based on both wired and wireless networks. In our scenario, the consumer is connected to the wired network, and the producer is connected to the wireless network. The AP is connected to a cluster head via a wired link. Based on our approach, we select the cluster head on the following approaches. First, we use the existing algorithm [19] for the selection of cluster head, based on memory. Secondly, the cluster heads must provide easy connectivity to other cluster heads. Third, each cluster head knows the addresses of the other cluster head. Fourth, the cluster heads are connected with each other directly. In [19], the authors proposed an algorithm for selection of cluster heads. We will also use that algorithm for selection of cluster heads in a wireless network.

4.4. Operations of Cluster Head. In our scenario, different operations are possible for each cluster head. The different routers can be connected to the same cluster head. Now, User A is connected to router R1, and User B is connected to R2, and both (i.e., R1 and R2) are connected to the same cluster head R. User A requests the contents "contentsource/realtime/video1" and sends the interest packet for content toward R1. Then, R1 will forward the interest packet to the cluster head R.

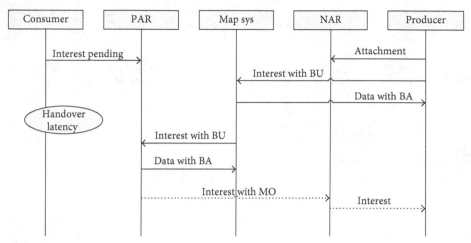

FIGURE 1: SMM handover model.

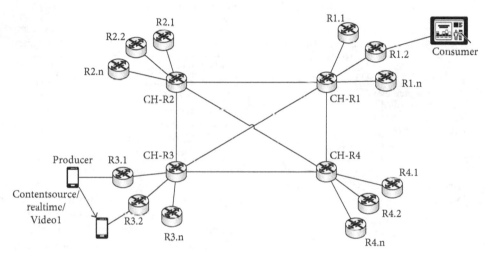

FIGURE 2: CB-DMM network topology model.

The "contentsource/realtime/video1" is sent through the data packet using the reverse path to User A. Now, User B sends interest packets for the same data through different router R2, when the interest reaches the cluster head. The cluster head simply sends data packets to User B from it CS table. Through this process, a lot of network resources can be saved, and overhead can be decreased from the network. Our model can also solve the consumer mobility because whenever a device moves to a new access router, it will send its current location information to cluster heads. Now, for both cases, the data packets will be sent to a new location. In case of a producer, the interest packets will be sent to the new location. The cluster heads in our scenario also send a periodic update about connected devices to each other. Through this process, the contents can be easily found in the network. The mobility problem can also be solved through periodic updates, which the cluster heads share with each other.

5. Performance Analysis

We simulate the CB-DMM model in *ndnSIM* [20] and compare our results with the SMM model. The SMM model is an existing scheme that is presented in Section 3. We used the two scenarios to simulate CB-DMM and SMM models in *ndnSIM*.

Figure 4 shows the basic network topology for CB-DMM and SMM models. For scenarios 1 and 2 in CB-DMM, the producer is initially connected to AP1. Both APs are connected to cluster heads, and the cluster heads are connected with each other through a direct link. The consumer is connected to an NDN router, and the NDN router is connected to a cluster head. For the SMM model, the mapping system is placed three hops away from the producer node for scenario 1. While for scenario 2, the mapping system is six hops away from the producer. In the SMM model, the mapping system is used to locate the desired contents in the NDN network. We placed the mapping system in a different position because according to [1], the mapping system can be placed globally in the NDN Network.

Table 1 shows the basic network parameters for both CB-DMM and SMM models. The SMM model uses the mapping system to locate the producer. The location of the mapping system in the network is a big challenge for the SMM model.

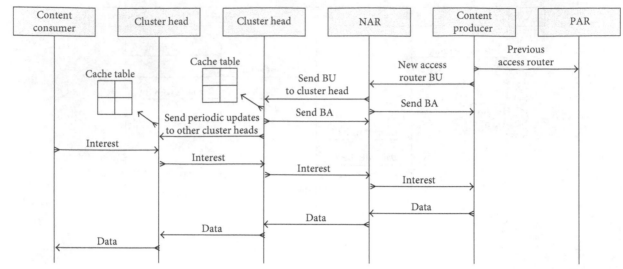

FIGURE 3: CB-SMM handover procedure.

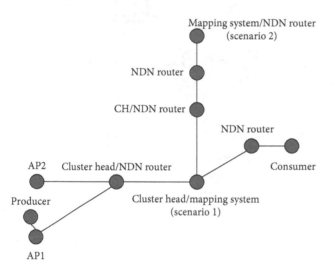

FIGURE 4: Models for CB-DMM and SMM network simulation: scenarios 1 and 2.

TABLE 1: Network parameters.

Parameters	Values
Number of nodes	11
Link capacity	100, 50, 10 Mbps
Link delay	1,10, 20 ms
Mobility model	*RandomWalk2Mobility*
Wi-Fi AP bandwidth	24 Mbps
Simulation time	15 seconds

We use the two scenarios for the SMM model, where the mapping system is located 3 and 6 hops away from the producer. According to the SMM model, the mapping system is placed on a global scale in the network. The topology of Figure 4 is used for simulation of CB-DMM and SMM models. The difference occurs in the node functionality. That is, when we simulate the SMM model, the node has the functionality of the mapping system; whereas for the CB-DMM model, some nodes have the functionality of cluster heads. The number of nodes in the networks is 11. The capacity of the link is set to 100, 50, and 10 Mbps, and the link delay is set to 1, 10, and 20 ms, respectively. The *RandomWalk2Mobility* model is used as a mobility model. The Wi-Fi bandwidth is set to 24 Mbps, and the simulation time is 15 seconds.

Figure 5 shows the performance of CB-DMM and SMM models. We used two scenarios for the SMM model and compared the results with the CB-DMM model. The performance measurement is based on the interest satisfied ratio. At the start of simulation for the CB-DMM model, the interest satisfied ratio was 30 percent at 0.2 seconds, and the interest satisfied ratio reached 100 percent at 1 second. For the SMM model (scenario 1), the communication started at 1 second, and the interest satisfied ratio was 20 percent; whereas for scenario 2, the communication started at 2 seconds, and the interest satisfied ratio was 20 percent. The SMM scenario 1 reached 100 percent approximately in 2.2 seconds, and the SMM scenario 2 reached 100 percent in 4 seconds.

At 7 seconds, in the CB-DMM and SMM model, the producer moves to another network. Both models use their handover procedures to locate the producer node. The CB-DMM model locates the producer in 0.2 seconds, whereas the SMM model scenario 1 takes 1 second, and the SMM scenario 2 takes 2 seconds.

In Figure 6, we reduce the link speed to 50 Mbps and increase the link delay to 10 ms, and then compare the CB-DMM model with the SMM scenarios. The CB-DMM model starts communication at 0.2 seconds, and the interest satisfied ratio is 20 percent. Compared to Figure 5, the interest satisfied ratio was less at 0.2 seconds. For SMM scenario 1, the communication started at 1 second, and the interest satisfied ratio was around 8 percent; whereas for scenario 2, the interest satisfied ratio was the same but the communication started at 2 seconds. The CB-DMM model reached 100 percent of the interest satisfied ratio at 0.8 seconds, while the SMM model reached 100 percent at 2 seconds and 3.6 seconds, respectively. When a handover happened again at 7 seconds,

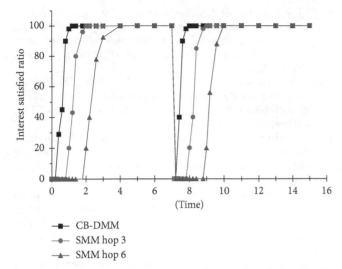

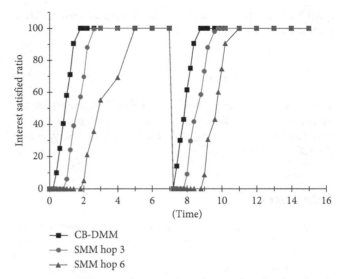

Figure 5: Comparison of CB-DMM and SMM (3 and 6 hops) with 100 Mbps and 1 ms.

Figure 7: Comparison of CB-DMM and SMM (3 and 6 hops) with 10 Mbps and 20 ms.

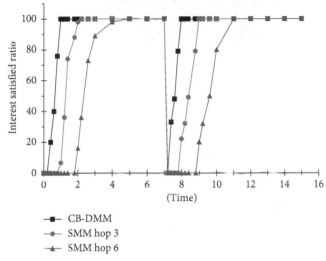

Figure 6: Comparison of CB-DMM and SMM (3 and 6 hops) with 50 Mbps and 10 ms.

both models went down to 0 percent. The CB-DMM model started communication again at around 7.2 seconds, while the SMM model started the communication at 8 seconds and 9 seconds, respectively.

In Figure 7, we reduce the link speed to 10 Mbps and increase the link delay to 20 ms, and then compare the CB-DMM model with both the SMM scenarios. Initially, the interest satisfied ratio for the CB-DMM model was around 10 percent; whereas for the SMM model scenario 1, the interest satisfied ratio was approximately 7 percent, and for scenario 2, the ratio was around 5 percent. In the CB-DMM model, the interest satisfied ratio was good, and after around 1 second, the ratio reached 100 percent; whereas for the SMM model, the interest satisfied ratio for scenario 1 reached 100 percent in 1.8 seconds, and for scenario 2, the ratio reached 100 percent in 4 seconds. When the producer changed the network, both models started searching for the producer node to get data contents. After around 7 seconds,

the producer moved to another network. The CB-DMM model started communication again after 7.2 seconds, and the interest satisfied ratio was 12 percent. In the SMM model, for scenario 1, the communication started again in around 8 seconds, and for scenario 2 the producer started communication approximately in 9 seconds. After around 8 seconds, the CB-DMM model reached 100 percent, and in the SMM model, the first scenario reached 100 percent in approximately 8.4 seconds, while scenario 2 reached 100 percent after around 10.2 seconds. We can see that the CB-DMM model is better than the SMM Model in terms of the interest satisfied ratio and time.

6. Conclusions and Future Work

This paper proposes the solutions to locate the producer in the NDN network. In the proposed CB-DMM model, devices send their information to a cluster head after handover. The cluster head keeps that information for future use. We have compared our results with the existing SMM model. In the SMM model, the producer sends the new location information to the mapping system. Then, the mapping system sends the information to the previous access router to divert the interest packets toward the new access router. In our solution, we send the device information to the cluster head, and the cluster head is responsible for diverting the interest packets toward the new access router. There is no need to tell the previous access router to divert the interest packets.

The proposed scheme provides better performance than the existing SMM model in terms of diversion of interest packets toward producer and the interest satisfied ratio. The diversion of interest packets toward producer is quicker in our proposed model, compared with the existing scheme. The interest packet satisfied ratio is also good in our proposed scheme.

The future work will be made to reduce the overhead of the cluster head in the network and to use the cluster head for other purposes, which can solve the network query very quickly. We also plan to move the producer into different cluster heads in the network.

Acknowledgments

This research was supported by the BK21 Plus project funded by the Ministry of Education, School of Computer Science and Engineering, Kyungpook National University, Korea (21A20131600005).

References

[1] S. Gao and H. Zhang, "Scalable mobility management for content sources in Named Data Networking," in *Proceedings of IEEE Annual Consumer Communications and Networking Conference (CCNC)*, Las Vegas, NV, USA, January 2016.

[2] M. F. Majeed, S. Ahmed, S. Muhammad, H. Song, and D. B. Rawat, "Multimedia streaming in information-centric networking: a survey and future perspectives," *Computer Networks*, vol. 125, pp. 103–121, 2017.

[3] S. Isa and P. Kadam, "Named data networking in VANET: a survey," *International Journal of Scientific Engineering and Science*, vol. 1, no. 11, pp. 45–49, 2017.

[4] X. Jiang, J. Bi, and Y. Wang, "What benefits does NDN have in supporting mobility," in *Proceedings of IEEE Symposium on Computers and Communication (ISCC)*, Messina, Italy, June 2014.

[5] X. Jiang, J. Bi, Y. Wang, P. Lin, and Z. Li, "A content provider mobility solution of named data networking," in *Proceedings of IEEE International Conference on Network Protocols (ICNP)*, Austin, TX, USA, October 2012.

[6] S. Ahmed, D. Mu, and D. Kim, "Improving bivious relay selection in vehicular delay tolerant networks," *IEEE Transactions on Intelligent Transportation Systems*, vol. 19, no. 3, pp. 987–995, 2018.

[7] S. H. Bouk, S. Ahmed, D. Kim, K. J. Park, Y. Eun, and J. Lloret, "LAPEL: hop limit based adaptive PIT entry lifetime for vehicular named data networks," *IEEE Transactions on Vehicular Technology*, vol. 67, no. 7, pp. 5546–5557, 2018.

[8] S. Ahmed, S. Hussain Bouk, M. A. Yaqub, D. Kim, and H. Song, "DIFS: distributed interest forwarder selection in vehicular named data networks," *IEEE Transactions on Intelligent Transportation Systems*, 2018.

[9] IETF RFC 6275, *Mobile IPv6*, IETF, Fremont, CA, USA, 2011.

[10] IETF RFC 5380, *Hierarchal Mobile IPv6*, IETF, Fremont, CA, USA, 2008.

[11] J. Su, X. Tan, Z. Zhao, and P. Yan, "MDP-based forwarding in named data networking," in *Proceedings of Chinese Control Conference (CCC)*, Chengdu, China, July 2016.

[12] Y. Zhang, H. Zhang, and L. Zhang, "Kite: a mobility support scheme for ndn," in *Proceedings of International Conference on Information-Centric Networking*, Paris, France, September 2014.

[13] D. Kim and Y. Ko, "On-demand anchor-based mobility support method for named data networking," in *Proceedings of International Conference on Advanced Communication Technology (ICACT)*, Pyeongchang, Republic of Korea, 2017.

[14] A. Aytac, R. Ravindran, and G. Wang, "Mobility study for named data networking in wireless access networks," in *Proceedings of IEEE International Conference on Communications (ICC)*, Sydney, Australia, June 2014.

[15] M. Lehmann, M. Barcellos, and A. U. Mauthe, "Providing producer mobility support in NDN through proactive data replication," in *Proceedings of Conference on Network Operations and Management Symposium (NOMS)*, Istanbul, Turkey, April 2016.

[16] R. Ravishankar, S. Lo, X. Zhang, and G. Wang, "Supporting seamless mobility in named data networking," in *Proceedings of IEEE International Conference on Communications (ICC)*, Ottawa, ON, Canada, June 2012.

[17] F. Hesham and H. Hassanein, "Optimal caching for producer mobility support in named data networks," in *Proceedings of IEEE International Conference on Communications (ICC)*, Kuala Lumpur, Malaysia, May 2016.

[18] Z. Liu, Y. Wu, E. Yuepeng, J. Ge, and T. Li, "Experimental evaluation of consumer mobility on named data networking," in *Proceedings of International Conference on Ubiquitous and Future Networks (ICUFN)*, Shanghai, China, July 2014.

[19] S. Muhammad, "Cluster-based mobility support in content-centric networking," *Research Notes in Information Science (RNIS)*, vol. 14, pp. 441–444, 2013.

[20] A. Alexander, I. Moiseenko, and L. Zhang, "ndnSIM: NDN simulator for NS-3," Technical Report, University of California, San Francisco, CA, USA, 2012.

17

Perception-Based Tactile Soft Keyboard for the Touchscreen of Tablets

Kwangtaek Kim [ID]

Department of Information and Telecommunication Engineering, Incheon National University, Incheon, Republic of Korea

Correspondence should be addressed to Kwangtaek Kim; ktkim@inu.ac.kr

Academic Editor: Maristella Matera

Most mobile devices equipped with touchscreens provide on-screen soft keyboard as an input method. However, many users are experiencing discomfort due to lack of physical feedback that causes slow typing speed and error-prone typing, as compared to the physical keyboard. To solve the problem, a platform-independent haptic soft keyboard suitable for tablet-sized touchscreens was proposed and developed. The platform-independent haptic soft keyboard was verified on both Android and Windows. In addition, a psychophysical experiment has been conducted to find an optimal strength of key click feedback on touchscreens, and the perception result was applied for making uniform tactile forces on touchscreens. The developed haptic soft keyboard can be easily integrated with existing tablets by putting the least amount of effort. The evaluation results confirm platform independency, fast tactile key click feedback, and uniform tactile force distribution on touchscreen with using only two piezoelectric actuators. The proposed system was developed on a commercial tablet (Mu Pad) that has dual platforms (Android and Windows).

1. Introduction

With advancement in touchscreen technologies, users get used to various functions of mobile devices through touch interactions. One of the most used functions is the soft keyboard input method which is very important for productive interaction on the touchscreen of a mobile device. For this reason, studies to design a better soft keyboard have been actively conducted for the past years. One of the good examples is to analyze and optimize keystroke patterns on touchscreens in order to improve key typing productivity [1–3]. Nevertheless, most of the users are not satisfied even with a better-designed soft keyboard since lack of physical key pressing feedback is the most frustrating thing when typing on a touchscreen. To this end, a low-cost linear motor has been widely used for mobile phones to create synchronized vibrations when phone users type on the touchscreen. However, the vibration generated from a linear motor is far away from a real-like key click effect. Therefore, there is the need of developing a high-definition (HD) tactile feedback technology of key click on the touchscreen of mobile devices including tablets that become popular these days.

To provide real-like key click feedback, designing a new actuator that can mimic a real-like key click movement on a touchscreen is imperative. It is learned that the piezoelectric actuator is prominent for implementing a virtual key click effect on touchscreens since its response is not only very fast, but also precisely controlled by applying input voltage. Despite the strength of piezoelectric actuators, there is very little known about how to utilize them to key click tactile feedback on tablet-sized touchscreens because piezoelectric actuators in general require high voltage (e.g., 100 to 200 V_{pp} for a single-layer ceramic bender) to be operated. Besides, driving multiple piezoelectric actuators at the same time on the touchscreen of a tablet is a challenging issue. To tackle the problem, Han and Kim developed the first prototype of the haptic soft keyboard for a tablet (Microsoft Surface Pro) with four piezoelectric actuators for high-definition key click effects [4].

For the work, a soft keyboard module was implemented under the Windows platform, and a haptic driver system that drives the four piezoelectric actuators at the same time was also developed as a portable prototype. The key pressing event was synchronized with four actuators attached under the touchscreen. The study showed how to use and drive multiple piezoelectric actuators on a commercial tablet for the first time. It also demonstrated the effectiveness of precise key click tactile feedback and the improved typing performance by conducting a user study with the developed prototype. However, the prototype had a significant time delay (over 10 ms) when driving the four piezoelectric actuators at the same time, which resulted in unsynchronized tactile feedback to fast typing. Another problem was nonuniform distribution of tactile feedback on the touchscreen, so a typist often felt unpleasantly strong tactile feedback near the actuators while felt weak at the center of the touchscreen. The other was no verification on other platforms since demanding additional work was needed to test with another platform.

In this study, a new haptic soft keyboard technology is introduced as an extended version of the previous work by Han and Kim in that three issues of the previous work—platform dependency, delayed tactile feedback, and nonuniform tactile feedback distribution on the touchscreen—have been resolved by developing a standalone microprocessor-based tactile feedback module that can be easily integrated with existing tablets. In addition, a perception study to find an optimum threshold of key click feedback strength on a touchscreen has been conducted by using a well-known psychophysical method (two interval one-up one-down adaptive method), and the result was adapted to the developed key click tactile feedback system. This study shows the first work employing perception data to the haptic soft keyboard on tablets and confirming a fast tactile feedback response on both Android and Windows. Additionally, this study showed the possibility of making uniform tactile force distribution on tablet-sized touchscreens with only two piezoelectric actuators. This paper is organized as follows. Section 2 introduces related studies that deal with improving usability of the soft keyboard by analyzing user's typing behaviors or adding haptic feedback. Section 3 presents a new platform-independent haptic soft keyboard developed on both Android and Windows. A perception study conducted by using a psychophysical experiment is described in Section 4. Experimental results for the quantitative evaluation of the developed haptic soft keyboard are reported in Section 5. Finally, discussions and conclusions are presented in Sections 5 and 6, respectively.

2. Related Work

Most of the studies for the soft keyboard focused on analyzing the position of typing fingers and key input patterns on touchscreens to design an improved key input interface. For example, Findlater et al. designed a new QWERTY layout of soft keyboard by utilizing user's typing patterns and behaviors. As a result, typing speed with ten fingers was greatly improved by achieving eyes-free touchscreen keyboard typing [1, 2]. Similarly, Sax et al. also showed that adaptively arranging the keys on the touchscreen to natural positions and movements of user's fingers can significantly improve typing performance [3]. Another research by Goel et al. introduced a new text entry model that adapts user's hand posture information such as two thumbs, the left thumb, the right thumb, or the index thumb to improve typing

performance on a mobile touchscreen [5]. From a design perspective, these efforts were all good to provide better usability for typing on touchscreens but physical key typing feedback.

An early effort adding tactile feedback to the touchscreen of a mobile device was made by Poupyrev and Maruyama [6]. They designed and implemented a tactile interface on a PDA touchscreen and tested the usability with 10 participants under two conditions: audio feedback and tactile feedback. The result of their study confirmed that tactile feedback is more effective than audio feedback on a small touchscreen. In a medical perspective, Rabin and Gordon conducted an experiment to investigate the role of tactile cues in typing. Their study showed that tactile cues provide information of the start position of the typing fingers, which is necessary to perform typing movements accurately [7]. These studies initiated the need of tactile feedback technologies on touchscreens of mobile devices.

Brewster et al. further studied the effect of tactile feedback on a mobile device by attaching a commercial actuator to the backside of the mobile device [8]. Their study showed that tactile feedback improves typing speed and accuracy even though the feedback vibrates the backside of the device. Hoggan et al. did a similar study but examined with a specific task: text typing on a touchscreen [9]. The results also showed that tactile feedback significantly improves typing performance on touchscreens. As a commercial application, Koskinen et al. compared pleasant feeling between piezoelectric actuators and linear motors [10]. They found that piezo actuators are slightly more pleasant than the linear vibration motors on touchscreens with commercial mobile phones. Jansen et al. developed a system that can provide localized tactile feedback on touching a surface [11]. Another interesting idea was to add tactile feedback to an error prevention method of existing word processors so that each key provides tactile feedback to prevent errors during text entry [12].

McAdam et al. confirmed improved typing performance on tabletop computers in terms of speed and accuracy but with a different setup attaching tactile actuators to the user's body [13]. After that, Chen et al. investigated the frequency of a real-like key click signal on a touchscreen, which was found to be 500 Hz on the touchscreen of a smart phone [14]. Most recently, Han and Kim developed a prototype of haptic soft keyboard by embedding piezoelectric actuators under the mobile touchscreen which provides high-resolution key click effects on a Windows smart phone and a tablet [4, 15]. The experimental results demonstrated that key click tactile feedback underneath the touchscreen provides better performance in terms of typing speed, accuracy, and efficiency. They also reported that there was a tactile feedback delay (about 11 ms) due to the complexity of the prototype, which needs to be improved.

3. Development of Platform-Independent Haptic Soft Keyboard for Tablets

TA platform-independent haptic soft keyboard that can be integrable to existing tablets was designed as seen in Figure 1. The key idea is how to easily integrate the additional tactile

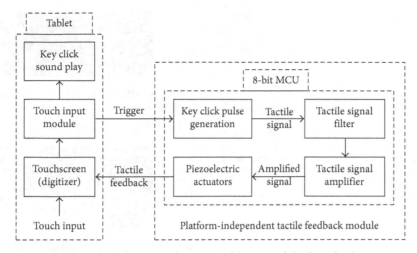

FIGURE 1: Block diagram of a proposed haptic soft keyboard scheme.

feedback module into existing tablet touchscreens in minimizing additional work. With the proposed scheme, all has to do is just to get a trigger signal (key press down) from the touchscreen (or digitizer). The trigger signal can be obtained from a key press event of the soft keyboard module or directly from the digitizer driver, regardless of the types of mobile operating systems. The trigger signal initiates generating a tactile pulse (e.g., key click, button down, and slide bar) that becomes an input to tactile feedback actuators. The generated tactile signal is then trimmed by a tactile noise filter. The role of this filter is to remove potential noise components of the generated tactile signal. In many cases, the noise components turn out to be an annoying jitter sound that is formed when piezoelectric actuators are vibrated on the touchscreen. The filtered signal is then amplified by a signal amplifier so that the amplified signal can have sufficient amount of energy to vibrate multiple piezoelectric actuators. All of these steps are synchronized by the clock of the microprocessor. The last thing is to mount actuators onto the touchscreen. In the proposed scheme, the way of mounting is flexible up to the need. For instance, the piezoelectric actuators can be integrated under the touchscreen for an embedded haptic soft keyboard [15] or attached on the touchscreen as a form of a portable cover. In the following, the detail of the development is described.

3.1. Development of Platform-Independent Tactile Feedback Module.
A platform-independent tactile feedback module (often called haptic driver) has been developed with a low-cost 8-bit microcontroller (Arduino micro) as shown in Figure 2. This module consists of four sequential blocks: tactile pulse generation, tactile signal filter, tactile signal amplifier, and tactile feedback actuators (piezoelectric actuators). The tactile pulse generation forms a key click pulse by using the pulse width modulation technique. Three parameters, frequency, duty cycle and duration, are taken as the input, and a square waveform is then generated. In the development, the three parameters were fixed to 500 Hz, 50%, and 2 ms for a tactile key click pulse by referring Han and Kim's study [4]. The second step, a tactile signal filter,

FIGURE 2: A prototype of the platform-independent haptic driver (40×40 mm) capable of driving two multilayer piezoelectric actuators at the same time.

which removes undesirable sound noise (jitters) when vibrating actuators, was implemented by using a digital smooth filter function of the Arduino library. However, there is a trade-off between reducing the high-frequency components and maximizing the signal energy that is the source of tactile feedback strength on the touchscreen. Finding an ideal trade-off value is another research topic that needs to be studied further in the future.

A tactile signal amplifier plays an important role to vibrate multiple piezoelectric actuators since high voltage is required for a piezoelectric actuator to produce real-like key click feedback on the touchscreen. Based on a pilot study, the minimum voltage that provides a perceptible tactile feeling on the touchscreen was around 80 V_{pp}. The minimum voltage amplification was achieved by using an acoustic signal amplifier (PDU 100) that amplifies up to 100 V_{pp}. For prototyping, an amplifier was used to drive two multilayer piezoelectric actuators ($L \times W \times H$: $32 \times 7.8 \times 0.7$ mm manufactured by Noliac) on the touchscreen. The multilayer actuator generates a bending mode and produces a stroke up to $\pm 475 \mu$m when a 200 V_{pp} square wave is applied.

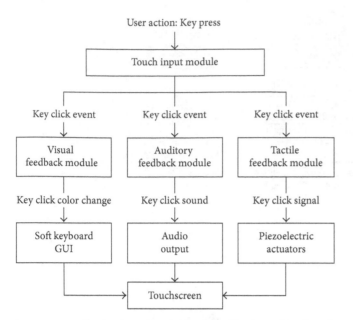

FIGURE 3: Feedback scheme for the developed haptic soft keyboard.

FIGURE 4: QWERTY soft keyboard design of the Windows platform.

FIGURE 5: Design of key typing areas (green) for key press feedback.

The proposed tactile feedback module can be integrated into either the touch input module or the soft keyboard module of any type of operation systems. For the proposed tactile feedback, a key press down event is used for sending a trigger signal to the tactile feedback module. In developing a prototype, the proposed tactile feedback module was integrated into the touch input module of a tablet (Mu Pad II, 1.8 GHz CPU, 2 GB RAM) that has dual operating systems, Android and Windows. Besides, visual and aural feedback modules were also implemented as seen in Figure 3. For the visual feedback, each key color is changed to show which key is pressed or released while the aural feedback plays a key click sound. For the haptic feedback, actuators attached to the touchscreen are simultaneously bent to make the entire touchscreen be vibrated for a real-like key click effect.

3.2. Implementation of a Soft Keyboard Module on Dual Platforms (Windows and Android). A platform-independent soft keyboard module was designed and implemented on a table device (Mu Pad) that has dual platforms, Windows and Android. For the QWERTY soft keyboard design interfacing with the tactile feedback module, the QWERTY design provided in the mobile with Windows platform (Figure 4) was used for the implementation on both platforms, Windows and Android. With implementing the same soft keyboard scheme on the different platforms, the developed tactile feedback module was able to objectively be compared in terms of performance and expendability. The implemented soft keyboard module consists of getting a key press input from the digitizer (touchscreen) and displaying feedback signals (vision, touch, and/or sound) to user's typing actions.

To reduce mistyping on the keyboard, key-pressable areas were defined as shown in Figure 5, and those areas were synchronized with feedback modules so that feedback for key press confirmation can be provided only when user's finger touches the defined areas. The feedback signals for the three modalities, vision, touch, and audio, were designed differently as seen in Figure 6. For the visual feedback, the color of a pressed key is changed to white while tactile and aural feedback signals are used for the same acoustic signal, a 500 Hz square wave (one cycle), by referring a prior study [4], but the tactile signal is generated by pulse width modulation (PWM) of an 8-bit microprocessor (Arduino micro), and the generated tactile signal is automatically sent to the developed haptic driver that drives multiple piezoelectric actuators on the touchscreen of the tablet (Mu Pad).

4. Towards Perceptible Tactile Feedback for a Key Click Effect on Touchscreens

A psychophysical experiment was designed and conducted to measure a detection threshold—barely perceptible magnitude—of key click tactile feedback on touchscreen of a commercial touchscreen. Twelve volunteers (7 males and 5 females: average age 23.75 years old) took part in the experiment. All of the participants were right handed by self-report. None of the participants had experience on haptic-assisted mobile devices or similar experiments. For the perception study, a commercial 10.1 inch touchscreen of Samsung Galaxy tab was used for the experiment. Prior to the psychophysical experiment, key click tactile feedback strength on the touchscreen driven by a multilayer piezoelectric actuator (manufactured by Noliac) was calibrated by an accelerometer to quantify haptic perception levels for a key click effect (Figure 7). The piezoelectric actuator was tightly mounted on the touchscreen, and an accelerometer (PCB 352A24, Sensitivity $10.2 \, \text{mV}/(\text{m/s}^2)$) was positioned 5 mm to the edge of the piezoelectric actuator. Acceleration was then measured with incrementing $20 \, V_{pp}$ as the input (a 500 Hz square wave), and the measured values are plotted in Figure 7. The plot shows that the acceleration on touchscreen monotonically increases to $160 \, V_{pp}$, which is the performance of the piezoelectric actuator used for this study.

Figure 8 shows the experimental setup used for conducting a psychophysical experiment that measures a detection threshold on the index finger. Participants took a five-minute

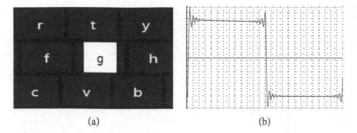

(a) (b)

FIGURE 6: Visual feedback (a) and a 500 Hz square wave for tactile and aural feedback (b).

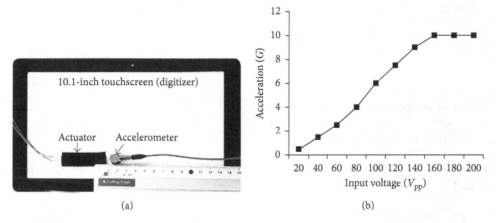

(a) (b)

FIGURE 7: A commercial touchscreen with an attached piezoelectric actuator; tactile feedback calibration on touchscreen with an accelerometer (a) and the measured acceleration values for increasing input voltage on the actuator (b).

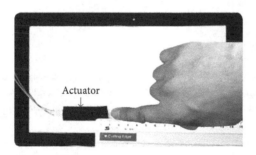

FIGURE 8: Experimental setup of a perception study on key click tactile feedback.

training session to understand the experiment procedure including the finger positioning on the touchscreen before starting the main experiment. During the experiment, the waveform (one cycle of a square wave pulse at 500 Hz) in Figure 6 was repeatedly sent to the piezoelectric actuator though the developed haptic driver and tactile feedback module. Participants wore a headphone and listened to white noise so that they can focus on the provided tactile cue during the experiment. A well-known psychophysical method called a two interval one-up one-down method (2I1U1D [16]) that adaptively measures participants' perception was employed to measure a detection threshold of tactile key click effect on touchscreen from the six participants. On each trial, the participant was asked to respond whether the presented stimulus on the touchscreen has a key click tactile feedback signal—one has a tactile feedback signal and the other has no

tactile signal. The participant had to respond yes if he/she felt the key click feedback on the touchscreen.

By the rule of the 2I1U1D method, the magnitude of input voltage (V_{pp}) was increased after each incorrect response and decreased after each correct response. For each series of trials, the initial value was set to 200 V_{pp} and then changed by 4 dB during the first 4 reversals and then changed by 1 dB for 12 reversals. Note that the initial larger step size (4 dB) allows finding the convergence level quickly while the following smaller step size (1 dB) plays a role to improve the resolution of the final perception level. Each participant repeated three trials, and the final detection threshold was estimated by taking the average of the three trials. It took each participant 20 to 30 minutes to complete all trials including the training session. From the psychophysical experiment, the estimated detection threshold of the key click tactile feedback was 1.17 ± 0.22 G (m/s^2). The detection threshold provides a guideline of perceptible key click tactile feedback on touchscreens. With the obtained perception data, a modified tactile soft keyboard was designed as shown in Figure 9. From the new design, the tactile force adjustment computes globally equalized tactile force levels on the entire touchscreen by referring the perception detection threshold. Without this function, a typist feels a stronger tactile force near the piezoelectric actuator (near the bezel of the touchscreen) but a weak force at the center of the touchscreen. The perception database provides an ideal tactile force level that can be adaptively set to personal preferences. Finally, a prototype was developed

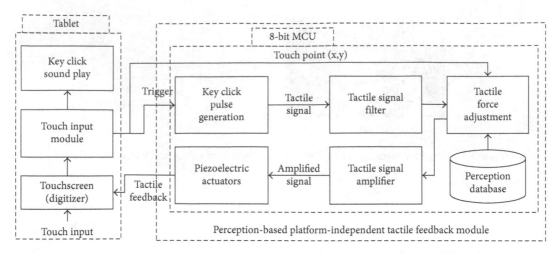

FIGURE 9: Perception-based tactile soft keyboard of tablets.

on a tablet (Mu Pad), and two piezoelectric actuators were mounted next to the home button on the bezel of the touchscreen to generate tactile key click feedback.

5. Experimental Results with the Integrated Tablet (Mu Pad)

5.1. Experimental Design. Three experimental measurements were performed to quantitatively test performance in terms of the similarity of tactile key click, force feedback distribution on a touchscreen, and delay time with the developed soft keyboard system (Windows and Android) on the Mu Pad tablet integrated with the developed tactile feedback module. For the first and second experiments, an accelerometer was used for measuring acceleration values that were recorded as waveform profiles for the similarity measured with a pre-recorded physical click waveform and as force values on the touchscreen for ensuring the force distribution on a 10.1-inch touchscreen.

5.2. Data Collection. An acceleration profile (waveform) was measured with an accurate accelerometer (PCB 352A24, Sensitivity $10.2 \, \text{mV}/(\text{m/s}^2)$) as a 500 Hz square wave (one cycle), a haptic key click signal, was sent to two actuators attached to the bezel of the touchscreen. For measuring discrete tactile feedback strength on the touchscreen, the same accelerometer was placed at six different positions that were equally spaced and premarked on the touchscreen. Acceleration values were recorded five times for each point and then averaged when one cycle of 500 Hz square wave (100 V_{pp}) was applied to the two piezoelectric actuators activated by a key press event from both Windows and Android. The last measurement was conducted to test the delay time from pressing a key on the touchscreen to driving the piezoelectric actuators through the developed haptic driver. The measurement was repeated ten times both on Android and Windows, respectively, and measured values were averaged to be compared.

5.3. Results. The first experiment was to verify whether the key click tactile feedback on the touchscreen is a real-like key

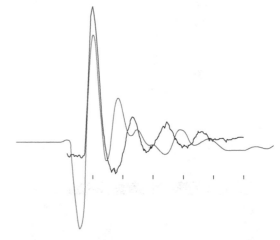

FIGURE 10: Comparison of the measured acceleration waveform (blue) on the touchscreen of Mu Pad with the acceleration waveform (black) recorded from a mechanical key pad by Chen et al. [14].

click effect. For this, the measured acceleration waveform was compared with the acceleration waveform recorded from a mechanical key pad by Chen et al. [14]. The comparison result is shown in Figure 10. The blue curve is the measured waveform in this study, and the black curve is the waveform recorded from a mechanical key pad. It is obvious that there are good matches in peaks and valleys. Note that the first peak is most important to mimic a real-like key click effect.

The second experiment was to quantify tactile force distribution on the touchscreen of the integrated tablet since vibrations generated by piezoelectric actuators on the bezel of a tablet are diminished in strength while traveling from a side to the center. So the goal of this experiment is to investigate the diminishing by visualizing tactile feedback strength on the touchscreen of the soft keyboard. As the result, all averaged values are graphically visualized in Figure 11. The stronger tactile feedback is colored in the redder. From the distribution image, it is clear that tactile feedback is not equally distributed over the soft keyboard. The reddest area on the arrow keys, right next to a piezoelectric actuator, is too strong (larger than 2 G), whereas the areas of the

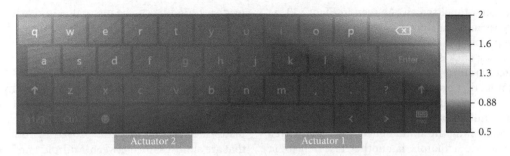

FIGURE 11: Acceleration distributed on the touchscreen of the tablet (Mu Pad): the measured values were superimposed onto the soft keyboard image to visualize the tactile strength generated from two piezoelectric actuators attached on the bezel. Note that red means stronger tactile feedback.

FIGURE 12: Equalized acceleration distributed on the touchscreen by the tactile force adjustment function that computes globally equalized tactile forces concerning the distance between actuators and key locations.

backspace key and the "q" key are relatively weak (1.3 to 1.4 G) though the strength is slightly over the estimated detection threshold (1.14 G). The issue can be resolved by the tactile force adjustment function in Figure 9. To achieve globally equalized tactile feedback over the soft keyboard, the desired tactile strength was set to 1.5 G by referring the estimated detection threshold (1.14 G) since the estimated detection threshold is barely detectable. The equalized distribution is seen in Figure 12. Overall, tactile forces are well distributed over the soft keyboard with an ignorable less force on the backspace key.

The last experiment was conducted to measure the time from pressing a key on the touchscreen to driving the piezoelectric actuators through the developed haptic driver. The results were 1.9 ms and 2.1 ms on Android and Windows, respectively, which shows that there is no big difference between Android and Windows when the proposed tactile soft keyboard system was integrated. A further experiment has been conducted to compare with the previous study by Han and Kim [4]. Han and Kim's approach was to drive piezoelectric actuators by using an audio play function with a prestored key click waveform on a Windows tablet. The time reported in their study was over 10 ms. To objectively compare the result, the same experimental condition (playing a prestored key click waveform) was implemented on the Windows platform of Mu Pad, and the result was compared with the proposed tactile key click system (i.e., generating a key click waveform directly from the developed haptic driver). The numerical result of Han and Kim approach was 3.9 ms which is slower than the new result (2.1 ms) of the proposed approach in this study. It confirms that the proposed

approach in this study outperforms in terms of a fast response of tactile feedback on touchscreens. The fast response of tactile feedback is imperative since a fast typist on a tablet may not get tactile feedback on time. This study shows a promising direction of haptic soft keyboard technologies by improving the responsiveness.

6. Discussions

To the best of my knowledge, the detection threshold measured in this study is the first result ever reported for touchscreens. The detection threshold was used as a lower bound perception value to ensure a tactile key click effect. By taking this approach, people can surely feel the tactile feedback on 10.1-inch touchscreens, and the use of energy (mobile battery) driving multiple actuators can also be optimized. This is important in that adding tactile key click feedback to existing tablets should not be a burden due to battery consumption. This study shows a practical example how to utilize human perception data though further studies are needed to apply for various form factors in terms of the size and material of touchscreens.

When designing a tactile soft keyboard for mobile devices, one of the challenging issues is how to make the tactile feeling realistic although the feeling itself could be relative. To quantify the tactile feeling, an acceleration profile (waveform) was measured and compared with the acceleration waveform reported by [14]. Based on pilot studies conducted in this study to figure out primary features that are most important to imitate a key click effect, the pattern of peaks of the acceleration waveform was a key to simulate a key click effect on a touchscreen. As seen in Figure 10, as long as the largest and the second largest peaks are well formed like the physical key click, the tactile feedback was felt as a real-like key click on a planar touchscreen surface. However, the acceleration waveform is determined by piezoelectric actuators that provide accurate force bending the mounted touchscreen. Actuators used in this study were all best-performed multilayer actuators manufactured by Noliac. Therefore, making the similar effect with even lower quality of piezoelectric actuators is another research topic that will be done in the near future.

Equalizing force feedback on a 10.1-inch touchscreen is not simple since the vibration force is diminished as the distance from an actuator increases. Figure 11 shows the stronger forces near the attached actuators, which is not desirable. There are two solutions to solve this issue. One is to directly control the input power of the piezoelectric actuator with respect to the location where a key click effect should be delivered. In general, the larger voltage is required to get the bigger movement from the actuator (Figure 7). The other is to change the amplitude of an input tactile signal (e.g., a square wave) that will determine the movement of the actuator in the end. In this study, the first solution was used since it was learned that the resolution of the tactile feedback force with a piezoelectric actuator is significantly low with the second approach. This is because the mapping between the magnitude of the input signal and the input voltage of the actuators is not linear.

In addition, the performance of key click tactile feedback on touchscreens is greatly influenced by the characteristics of actuators to be mounted. The actuators should be able to provide high-definition tactile forces that make various types of virtual touch feelings on touchscreens. Piezoelectric actuators are in general precision actuators that convert electric energy into linear motions with high speed and resolution. Due to this reason, piezoelectric actuators are suitable for implementing a virtual key click effect on touchscreens of mobile devices. However, high voltage (e.g., 200 V_{pp} for a single-layer piezoelectric plate) is typically required for a piezoelectric actuator to be sufficiently vibrated on a touchscreen to imitate a mechanical key click effect. Due to the limitation of input voltage with a tablet device, handling multiple piezoelectric actuators is a challenging problem. Han and Kim developed a most advanced tactile key click feedback with multiple piezoelectric actuators on a Microsoft Surface Pro tablet [4]. However, there was over 10 ms delay time to get tactile feedback from pressing a key and so tactile feeling was not synchronized well. The prototype of a haptic driver was also a bit bulky to be integrated with existing commercial tablets. The last problem was that the developed haptic soft keyboard module was not completely independent from the Windows platform. The present study can be considered as an improved version of the Han and Kim's work by resolving those issues of the prior study.

The present study focused on developing a platform-independent haptic soft keyboard system so that the tactile feedback module can be integrated into existing commercial tablets (or mobile devices) by putting the least amount of effort. For this reason, a dual platform tablet with a 10.1-inch touchscreen, widely used in these days, was chosen as a test device. As explained earlier, the developed tactile key click feedback module can be simply integrated by using a pulse-generating function of each platform that sends a trigger signal to the haptic driver generating a key click signal. The platform independency was proved by results of delay time that are almost same between Android and Windows. This is because a tactile signal is created from the separated haptic driver but not from the operating system like Han and Kim's work. Further, the proposed scheme outperforms the prior study in terms of response time, which also resulted from being less dependent on the operating system. One of the important contributions in the present study is to employ human perception on key click tactile feedback on a commercial touchscreen. According to a prior study, Han and Kim [4], one cycle of square waveform at 500 Hz was used for a real-like key click tactile effect, and the effect was quantitatively proved by analyzing the acceleration profile.

7. Conclusions

In the present study, a platform-independent haptic soft keyboard module that has the least dependency to mobile operating systems has been designed and developed. The proposed haptic soft keyboard module consists of three parts: soft keyboard with feedback, a mini haptic driver, and piezoelectric actuators. The soft keyboard with feedback (visual, tactile, and aural feedback) was implemented on a dual platform tablet to prove the platform independency. A mini haptic driver that can generate tactile key click pulses and remove noise was developed with an 8-bit microprocessor (Arduino) so that it can be simply integrated into existing tablets. The haptic driver was specially designed to drive multiple piezoelectric actuators that produce sufficient tactile forces on the touchscreen. In addition, a psychophysical experiment has been conducted to estimate the human perception (detection threshold) on key click tactile feedback. By applying the obtained perception data to the haptic soft keyboard module, perceivable and uniformly distributed tactile feedback was implemented on the touchscreen. Experimental results confirm that the proposed haptic soft keyboard outperforms the previous study by Han and Kim in terms of platform independency, uniform tactile feedback, and synchronized tactile feedback (delay time). The knowledge learned through this study can be an informative guideline to engineers, researchers, and designers who are actively involved in design or development of soft keyboard on mobile devices. Tactile key click on touchscreens must be a promising technology that greatly improves the usability of mobile input methods or multimedia-related interaction. However, there are still many open questions that need further research. One of them is localized tactile feedback with less number of piezoelectric actuators. As future work, a further study will be conducted to investigate a feasible solution on the topic.

Acknowledgments

This research was supported by Basic Science Research Program through the National Research Foundation of Korea (NRF) funded by the Ministry of Education (2015R1D1A1A01060715).

References

[1] L. Findlater, J. O. Wobbrock, and D. Wigdor, "Typing on flat glass: examining ten-finger expert typing patterns on touch surfaces," in *Proceedings of the SIGCHI Conference on Human Factors in Computing Systems (CHI'11)*, pp. 2453–2462, ACM, Vancouver, BC, Canada, 2011.

[2] L. Findlater and J. Wobbrock, "Personalized input: improving ten-finger touchscreen typing through automatic adaptation," in *Proceedings of the SIGCHI Conference on Human Factors in Computing Systems (CHI'12)*, pp. 815–824, ACM, Austin, TX, USA, May 2012.

[3] C. Sax, H. Lau, and E. Lawrence, "Java goes TLA+," in *Proceedings of the Fifth International Conference on Digital Society (IARIA Conference)*, Guadeloupe, France, 2011.

[4] B. Han and K. Kim, "Typing performance evaluation with multimodal soft keyboard completely integrated in commercial mobile devices," *Journal on Multimodal User Interfaces*, vol. 9, no. 3, pp. 173–181, 2015.

[5] M. Goel, A. Jansen, T. Mandel, S. N. Patel, and J. O. Wobbrock, "ContextType: using hand posture information to improve mobile touch screen text entry," in *Proceedings of the SIGCHI Conference on Human Factors in Computing Systems (CHI'13)*, pp. 2795–2798, ACM, Paris, France, 2013.

[6] I. Poupyrev and S. Maruyama, "Tactile interfaces for small touch screens," in *Proceedings of the 16th Annual ACM Symposium on User Interface Software and Technology*, pp. 217–220, ACM, Vancouver, BC, Canada, November 2003.

[7] E. Rabin and A. M. Gordon, "Tactile feedback contributes to consistency of finger movements during typing," *Experimental Brain Research*, vol. 155, no. 3, pp. 362–369, 2004.

[8] S. Brewster, F. Chohan, and L. Brown, "Tactile feedback for mobile interactions," in *Proceedings of the SIGCHI Conference on Human Factors in Computing Systems (CHI'07)*, pp. 159–162, ACM, San Jose, CA, USA, 2007.

[9] E. Hoggan, S. A. Brewster, and J. Johnston, "Investigating the effectiveness of tactile feedback for mobile touchscreens," in *Proceedings of the SIGCHI Conference on Human Factors in Computing Systems (CHI'08)*, pp. 1573–1582, ACM, Florence, Italy, 2008.

[10] E. Koskinen, T. Kaaresoja, and P. Laitinen, "Feel-good touch: finding the most pleasant tactile feedback for a mobile touch screen button," in *Proceedings of the 10th International Conference on Multimodal Interfaces (ICMI'08)*, pp. 297–304, ACM, Chania, Crete, Greece, October 2008.

[11] Y. Jansen, T. Karrer, and J. Borchers, "MudPad: localized tactile feedback on touch surfaces," in *Adjunct Proceedings of the 23nd Annual ACM Symposium on User Interface Software and Technology (UIST'10)*, pp. 385-386, ACM, New York, NY, USA, October 2010.

[12] A. Hoffmann, D. Spelmezan, and J. Borchers, "TypeRight: a keyboard with tactile error prevention," in *Proceedings of the SIGCHI Conference on Human Factors in Computing Systems (CHI'09)*, pp. 2265-2268, ACM, Boston, MA, USA, April 2009.

[13] C. McAdam and S. Brewster, "Distal tactile feedback for text entry on tabletop computers," in *Proceedings of the 23rd British HCI Group Annual Conference on People and Computers: Celebrating People and Technology*, pp. 504–511, British Computer Society, Cambridge, UK, September 2009.

[14] H. Y. Chen, J. Park, S. Dai, and H. Z. Tan, "Design and evaluation of identifiable key-click signals for mobile devices," *IEEE Transactions on Haptics*, vol. 4, no. 4, pp. 229–241, 2011.

[15] B. K. Han, K. Kim, K. Yatani, and H. Z. Tan, "Text entry performance evaluation of haptic soft QWERTY keyboard on a tablet device," in *Proceedings of the International Conference on Human Haptic Sensing and Touch Enabled Computer Applications*, pp. 325–332, Springer, Versailles, France, June 2014.

[16] H. Levitt, "Transformed up-down methods in psychoacoustics," *Journal of the Acoustical society of America*, vol. 49, no. 2, pp. 467–477, 1971.

18

Insect Identification and Counting in Stored Grain: Image Processing Approach and Application Embedded in Smartphones

Chunhua Zhu [iD],[1] Jiaojiao Wang,[1] Hao Liu,[2] and Huan Mi[3]

[1]*College of Information Science and Engineering, Henan University of Technology, Zhengzhou, China*
[2]*Institute of Industrial Technology, Zhengzhou University, Zhengzhou, China*
[3]*Department of Electronic Engineering, University of York, York, UK*

Correspondence should be addressed to Chunhua Zhu; zhuchunhua@haut.edu.cn

Academic Editor: Raul Montoliu

Insects can cause a major loss in stored grain, and early identification and monitoring of insects become necessary for applying corrective action. Considering the effectiveness and practicability, an image processing approach and the corresponding application embedded in smartphones are proposed to identify and count the insects. For the insect images acquired by mobile phones, one sliding window-based binarization is adopted to release their nonuniform brightness, and then connected domain-based histogram statistics is presented to identify and count the insects in stored grain. Finally, the experiments are performed on the corresponding application based on Android, and it has shown that the proposed approach can be applicable for different random insect images from mobile phones with the counting accuracy of 95%, which is superior to the traditional approach.

1. Introduction

Detecting the insects in stored grain quickly and accurately is the basis of preventing and controlling storage grain insects and avoiding severe grain losses and unnecessary excessive treatment. Current standards of international trade are used as insect-free detection by standard method (ISO 6639-3,2001). Recently, several detection techniques have been developed for insect detection in stored grain such as electromagnetic spectrum-based methods [1–6], acoustic-based methods [7], conductance-based methods [8], and probes [9]. However, some of these techniques are time-consuming, expensive and less efficient to detect the dead insects. The image processing-based method is nondestructive and convenient in application design, which has been one of the hot topics in recent years [10–12]. There have been some methods that use image processing to count insects, which mainly include counting the morphological features of the grain insects [13, 14], the binary sketch of the grayscale image [15, 16], and counting the insect pixels [17, 18]. However, these methods have lower accuracy in counting smaller grain pests, the hardware of image acquisition and monitoring

system are expensive, and the higher cost in computation cannot ensure the real-time detection. Therefore, considering the accuracy and practicability of insect detection, the image processing approach and application embedded in smartphones are researched. The focus is to preprocess the acquired insect image with nonuniform brightness and dark background and to separate the different insect pixels for higher accuracy, especially for tiny storage grain insects. The main work and innovation is as follows:

(i) Sliding window with changeable optimal threshold is used to binary processing the acquired original insect image with uneven brightness, which affects the insect identification accuracy based on pixels difference.

(ii) The probable occupied connected-domain pixels area of one insect is analyzed, thereby identifying and counting the insects, which is applicable for the booklice and other tiny insects.

(iii) The application based on Android is portable to install in cell phones, and less memory space is occupied.

To verify the effectiveness, the traditional insect detection based on image processing [15] is compared.

2. Algorithm Descriptions

The overall structure of the automatic identification and counting system of storage grain insects based on the smartphone image is shown in Figure 1. Modular design is adopted, including original photo collection module, image capture module, image preprocessing module, data statistics module, and so on. In the first two modules, the original photos are collected in mobile phones with the high-resolution camera which can be clipped into different size to be detected to obtain the detected area.

The test environment is shown in Table 1.

While the system is used in the barn, mobile phone photos are easily affected by external environmental factors, including insufficient illumination and noise interference; therefore, the quality of images cannot be guaranteed. In order to solve the aforementioned problem and increase the difference between the insects and the background, it is necessary to preprocess the acquired insect image.

2.1. Preprocessing Algorithm Based on Sliding Window.
For the acquired insect image, the main preprocessing units include the color space transformation, binary processing, boundary tracing, and so on, which are adopted to extract the contour of grain insects in the white wall of barn, as shown in Figure 2.

Obtaining the optimal threshold for the following binarization is the key preprocessing unit. In existed references, the fixed threshold with standard weighted average was often used [11], which is helpless for distinguishing the insect pixels area with different brightness, further maximizing the difference between the insect areas and the background. Therefore, the optimal threshold should be changeable with the brightness of different insect areas. Thereby, the key difficulty is to select a series of segmentation thresholds corresponding to different insects' areas.

Assume that the insect image is $I(m, n)$, where m and n are its row and column separately. One square window with a size of $3*3$ pixels is adopted as the basic template operation. In each area with a size of $3*3$ pixels, the optimal threshold is equal to the weighted average of the nine pixels; for the first $3*3$ pixel area, the optimal threshold is

$$T_1 = \frac{1}{9} \sum_{m=1}^{3} \sum_{n=1}^{3} w(m,n) I(m,n). \tag{1}$$

Here, $w(m, n)$ is the weighted coefficients, typically take 1. In a similar operation, the second optimal threshold is

$$T_2 = \frac{1}{9} \sum_{m=1}^{3} \sum_{n=4}^{6} w(m,n) I(m,n). \tag{2}$$

Similarly, $T_i, i = 1, 2, ..., N$ can be obtained, where N is the number of $3*3$ pixel areas in the whole insect image.

The pixels whose gray value is bigger than the optimal threshold will be assigned to "255" and the converse will be

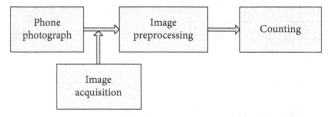

FIGURE 1: Insect identification and counting system.

TABLE 1: Test environment.

Hardware environment	Android smart machine (OPPO R7 rear 13 million HD camera, MT6752 processor, 3GB RAM memory space, 16 GB storage space)
Software environment	Android 6.0
Software language	The Java language development environment based on Eclipse
Lighting conditions	Uneven lighting intensity distribution in the crowded barn environment
The test object	Booklice covered in the walls of granaries. The phone is 10–15 cm above the white wall

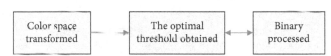

FIGURE 2: Image preprocessing procedure.

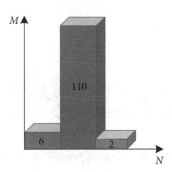

FIGURE 3: Histogram statistics by connected domains.

assigned to "0." Generally, the lower gray pixels area represents the image background.

After image binarization, the gray difference between the insect pixel and the background is maximized to an extreme, which is helpful to increase the identifying and counting accuracy.

2.2. Histogram Statistics Counting Insects by Connected Domains.
The commonly used grain pest counting algorithms mainly include template matching method [12, 13] and connected domain method [15]. The template matching method is used to identify insect body posture and body characteristics, and a matching benchmark must be established to complete the process of registration. The template matching method can obtain higher matching accuracy, but

TABLE 2: Histogram statistics of black connected domains in experimental tests.

Connected domain type	Number of pixels in one connected domain	Number of homogeneous connected domains	Proportion (%)
1	Less than 18	6	5.08
2	18–24	110	94.23
3	More than 24	2	1.69

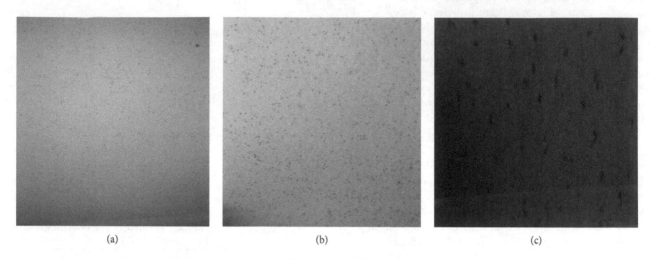

(a)   (b)   (c)

FIGURE 4: Original test images. (a) Test image 1, (b) test image 2, and (c) test image 3.

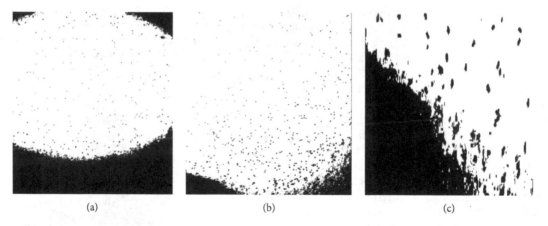

(a)   (b)   (c)

FIGURE 5: Binarization images under the fixed threshold. Test results of (a) image 1, (b) image 2, and (c) image 3.

is less efficient for more similar insect body features and the complexity will increase with the insect body samples. In the connected domain method, one center pixel and its adjacent several pixels with the same gray value of "255" will be called as one connected domain, also called as black connected domain. One black connected domain represents one insect probably. The key difficulty is to decide the number of pixels in one black connected domain occupied by one kind of grain insect. For a given grain insect image, the number of black connected domains with different pixels numbers is shown in Figure 3. Here, N is the number of pixels in one black connected domain, and M is the number of homogeneous connected domains over the whole image. M is 6 when N is less than 18, M is 110 when N is from 18 to 24, and M is 2 when N is more than 24, as shown in Table 2.

From Table 2, it has shown that one grain insect occupies 18 to 24 pixels in one connected domain with most

possibility. Therefore, the black connected domain with 18 to 24 pixels will be regarded as one insect.

3. Evaluations

3.1. Android-Based Mobile Application Development. Using the Windows system, Android Studio and SDK (software development kit) [19] are used to develop the application (APP), and the completed APK (Android package) is installed on the Android smartphone. The main functions are listed as follows:

(i) Choosing one photo. One way to obtain the photo is from the camera of the cell phone, and the other way is from the albums.

(ii) Clipping the photo. The photo is a square image with one side 10 cm to 15 cm, in which hundreds of

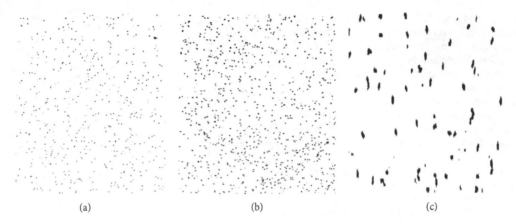

FIGURE 6: Binarization images under the sliding threshold. Test results of (a) image 1, (b) image 2, and (c) image 3.

grain insects are usually included. At this time, the sampled photo area can be chosen by clipping.

(iii) Resizing the sampled photo. In order to increase the detection resolution, the detected image should keep certain size; usually, the clipped image is enlarged.

(iv) Identifying and counting the insects. After binarization and connected domain statistics, the number of insects in stored grain is displayed.

3.2. Results. For the experiment, three original image samples with different brightness and insect density are selected as shown in Figures 4(a)–4(c). To verify the effectiveness, the traditional insect detection based on image processing [10] is compared, in which the binarization under the fixed threshold is adopted, called as the fixed threshold method. The proposed binarization in this paper is called as the sliding threshold method. The preprocessed images under the fixed threshold and under the sliding threshold are shown in Figures 5(a)–5(c) and Figures 6(a)–6(c), respectively.

From Figures 4–6, it can be seen that the gray difference between the grain insect and the background is more obvious by the sliding window preprocess and that the side identification is enhanced. According to the histogram statistical algorithm proposed in this paper, the accuracy of identifying grain insects is shown in Table 3. Obviously, the sliding threshold method can provide the higher identification accuracy.

4. Conclusion

In this paper, one insect identifying and counting approach and Android-based APP are presented, in which the sliding window is used in the preprocess unit that can maximize the difference between the detected targets and the background and remove the uneven background brightness. By adapting the sliding window size, it is possible for tiny insects to be distinguished. Compared with the existing technology, the proposed scheme can provide the higher counting accuracy and is portable with online identifying and counting the insects. Besides, in the proposed connected domain method, the insects with one same shape and size will correspond to

TABLE 3: Accuracy of identifying grain insects.

Statistical methods	Number of grain insects detected	Number of actual insects	Accuracy (%)
Fixed threshold method	72	60	80
Sliding threshold method	57	60	95

one same black connected domain, which can be applied to identify and count the other kinds of insects with different shapes and sizes. Thereby, the separation of the connected domain will be one of the key issues to improve identification accuracy in the future.

Acknowledgments

This research was financially supported by the National Science Foundation of China (61741107 and 61871176), Henan Provincial Department of Science and Technology Project (172102210230), and Key Scientific Research Projects in Henan Colleges and Universities (19A510011).

References

[1] I. Y. Zayas and P. W. Flinn, "Detection of insects in bulk wheat samples with machine vision," *Transactions of the ASAE*, vol. 41, pp. 883–888, 1998.

[2] C. Karunakaran, D. S. Jayas, and N. D. G. White, "Soft X-ray inspection of wheat kernels infested by *Sitophilus oryzae*," *Transactions of the ASAE*, vol. 46, no. 3, pp. 739–745, 2003.

[3] C. Karunakaran, D. S. Jayas, and N. D. G. White, "X-ray image analysis to detect infestations caused by insects in grain," *Cereal Chemistry Journal*, vol. 80, no. 5, pp. 553–557, 2003.

[4] N. A. Nanje Gowda and K. Alagusundaram, "Use of thermal imaging to improve the food grains quality during storage," *International Journal of Agricultural Research*, vol. 1, no. 7, pp. 34–41, 2013.

[5] K. Sheetal Banga, N. Kotwaliwale, D. Mohapatra, and S. K. Giri, "Techniques for insect detection in stored food grains: an overview," *Food Control*, vol. 94, pp. 167–176, 2018.

[6] H. Liu, S. H. Lee, and J. S. Chahl, "A review of recent sensing technologies to detect invertebrates on crops," *Precision Agriculture*, vol. 18, no. 4, pp. 635–666, 2017.

[7] P. A. Eliopoulos, I. Potamitis, D. C. Kontodimas, and E. G. Givropoulou, "Detection of adult beetles inside the stored wheat mass based on their acoustic emissions," *Journal of Economic Entomology*, vol. 108, no. 6, pp. 2808–2814, 2015.

[8] D. Brabec, F. Dowell, J. Campbell, and M. West, "Detection of internally infested popcorn using electrically conductive roller mills," *Journal of Stored Products Research*, vol. 70, pp. 37–43, 2017.

[9] D. Shuman and N. D. Epsky, "Commercialization of the electronic grain probe insect counter," in *Proceeding of an International Conference on Controlled Atmosphere and Fumigation in Stored Products*, pp. 665–667, Fresno, CA, USA, 2001.

[10] J. Wang and L. Ji, "Methods of insect image segmentation and their application," *Acta Entomologica Sinica*, vol. 54, no. 2, pp. 211–217, 2011.

[11] B. Yan, F. Chen, and J. Guo, "Automatic classification virtual system of grain pest based on image processing," *Cereal and Feed Industry*, vol. 2014, no. 6, pp. 19–26, 2014.

[12] G. Lu, Q. Man, and R. Xu, "SVM-based multi-feature fusion longicorn image recognition," *Forest Engineering*, vol. 28, no. 4, pp. 21–25, 2012.

[13] Z. Hu, Y. Zhao, Y. Bai, and F. Cao, "Fast Recognition of pests based on image processing technology," *Journal of Anhui Agricultural Science*, vol. 42, no. 30, pp. 10784–10787, 2014.

[14] D. Xian, Q. Yao, B. Yang et al., "Automatic identification of rice light-trapped pests based on images," *Chinese Journal of Rice Science*, vol. 29, no. 3, pp. 299–304, 2015.

[15] B. Yan, J. Zhao, B. Tang, and Z. Liu, "Research of stored grain pests monitoring system based on image processing and photoelectric technology," *Cereals and Oils*, vol. 29, no. 10, pp. 70–74, 2016.

[16] M. Shi and R. Michael, "Modelling mortality of a stored grain insects pest with fumigation: probit, logistic or cauchy model?," *Mathematical Biosciences*, vol. 243, no. 2, pp. 137–146, 2013.

[17] L. O. Solis-Sánchez, R. C. Miranda, J. J. García-Escalante et al., "Scale invariant feature approach for insect monitoring," *Computers and Electronics in Agriculture*, vol. 75, no. 1, pp. 92–99, 2011.

[18] Y. Yang, B. Peng, and J. Wang, "A system for detection and recognition of pests in stored-grain based on video analysis," in *Proceedings of Computer and Computing Technologies in Agriculture*, pp. 119–1246, Nanchang, China, October 2010.

[19] R. Laganière, *In-Depth Open CV Android Application Development*, Electronic Industry Press, Beijing, China, 2016.

A Study on Tracking and Augmentation in Mobile AR for e-Leisure

Seong-Wook Jang ⓘ,[1] **Junho Ko,**[1] **Hun Joo Lee,**[2] **and Yoon Sang Kim** ⓘ[1,3]

[1]*BioComputing Lab, Department of Computer Science and Engineering, Korea University of Technology and Education (KOREATECH), Cheonan, Republic of Korea*
[2]*Creative Content Research Laboratory, ETRI, Daejeon, Republic of Korea*
[3]*Institute for Bioengineering Application Technology, Korea University of Technology and Education (KOREATECH), Cheonan, Republic of Korea*

Correspondence should be addressed to Yoon Sang Kim; yoonsang@koreatech.ac.kr

Academic Editor: Maristella Matera

Recently, a mobile augmented reality (AR) system with AR technology that requires high performance has become popular due to the improved performance of smartphones. In particular, mobile AR that directly interacts with outdoor environments has been in development because of increasing interest in e-leisure due to improvements in living standards. Therefore, this paper aims to study tracking and augmentation in mobile AR for e-leisure. We analyzed the performance of human body tracking application implemented in a mobile system (smartphone) using three methods (marker-based, markerless, and sensor-based) for the feasibility examination of human body tracking in mobile AR. Furthermore, game information augmentation was examined through the implementation of mobile AR using two methods (marker- and sensor-based).

1. Introduction

PC-based augmented reality (AR) is evolving into mobile AR by the popularization of smartphones with high-resolution image sensors, GPS, and gyro sensors. In particular, mobile AR that directly interacts with outdoor environments such as Pokémon Go [1] is being noted because of increasing interest in e-leisure due to improvements in living standards. e-Leisure, the digital leisure culture that includes e-sports, e-games, and interactive media, is becoming a favorite activity by providing both sociocultural worth and enjoyment [2, 3]. Therefore, research into the mobile AR for e-leisure (i.e., e-leisure mobile AR) is required. Through this research, e-leisure mobile AR that can augment game information for outdoor sports such as baseball, basketball, and soccer in real time is being developed [4–7].

Tracking points of interest (POI) in the real world and obtaining the precise coordination of game information augmentation have become increasingly important for e-leisure mobile AR, and various studies are underway. Among the various studies on mobile AR-based object tracking, there is greater emphasis on studies in which the POI is tracking a human body [8–13].

Real-world objects (human bodies in this study) and the precise coordination of virtual data for realistic mobile AR are processed in three steps: positioning, rendering, and merging. In the positioning step, virtual data (known as virtual content) are converted in accordance with the smartphone's location. In the rendering step, 3D objects involving virtual data are projected into 2D images. Finally, virtual data projected into 2D images are combined with the real world on the smartphone screen (viewport) in the merging stage.

Coordinating these three steps requires tracking the 3D locations of POIs with precision. The POI can be tracked via widely used methods based on vision and sensors [8]. Vision-based methods are categorized into marker-based and markerless tracking methods.

Marker-based tracking methods (Figure 1) are methods of tracking color markers or markers of specific forms [8]. Wagner [9] proposed a marker pattern for mobile AR and compared the performance with mobile AR using

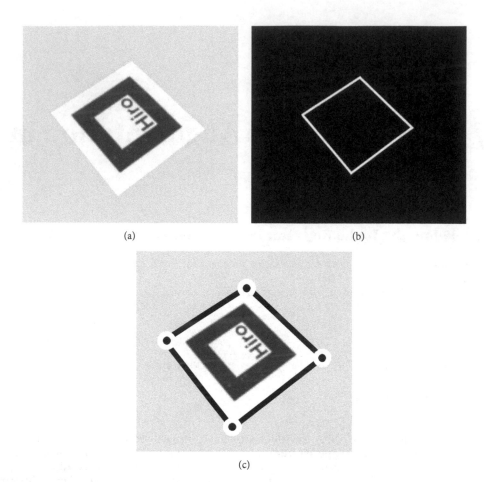

FIGURE 1: Mobile AR system procedure implemented based on marker [14]. (a) Original image. (b) Corners. (c) Extracted marker edges and corners.

conventional markers. Marker-based tracking methods have the advantages of high stability and ease of implementation compared to markerless tracking methods, but the disadvantage that it is inconvenient because the marker is restricted to the subject.

Markerless tracking (Figure 2) is a method of tracking a target's features naturally without the attaching artificial markers [10]. Ziegler [11] evaluated tracking methods based on markerless suitable for mobile AR. Markerless tracking method has an advantage of recognizing the target's rotation angle, direction, lighting changes, partial overlap, and so on based on the target's features. However, markerless tracking method has the disadvantage that it cannot guarantee its real-time performance in a smartphone environment that has lower performance than a PC because the markerless tracking method generally requires more computation than marker-based tracking methods.

The sensor-based method (Figure 3) is a method of tracking a target using various sensors including magnetic, inertial, optical, and mechanical sensors [8]. Tan [12] and Pryss [13] implemented real-time mobile AR using sensor-based tracking methods. Sensor-based tracking methods generally have the advantage of rapid processing speed and the disadvantage that calibration and matching processes are required to solve problems because physical problems such as sensor errors and communication delays affect tracking performance.

In this paper, we study human body tracking and game information augmentation in e-leisure mobile AR. We examine human body tracking by performance measurement experiments in mobile applications based on marker-based, markerless, and sensor-based methods. Game information augmentation is examined by the implementation of e-leisure mobile AR using marker- and sensor-based methods.

This paper is organized as follows. Section 2 describes the existing cases of tracking and augmentation in mobile AR for e-leisure. Section 3 presents the experiments and the results of human body tracking and game information augmentation for e-leisure mobile AR applications. Finally, Section 4 presents the paper's conclusion.

2. Tracking and Augmentation in Mobile AR for e-Leisure

This section introduces conventional studies of human body tracking and game information augmentation methods that can be applied to e-leisure mobile AR. The e-leisure mobile AR is performed through the process of detection area decisions, human body tracking, and game information augmentation, as shown in Figure 4. In the detection area decision, the POI is set at the game information augmentation location, whereas human body tracking follows the POI's movement based on the three methods (marker,

FIGURE 2: Mobile AR system procedure implemented based on the marker. (a, b) Mobile AR implemented using SIFT [13]. (c, d) Mobile AR implemented using HOG [16].

FIGURE 3: Mobile AR system example implementation using sensors [17, 18].

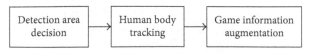

FIGURE 4: Mobile AR process.

markerless, and sensor) in real time. Finally, the game information augmentation process augments game information via the tracked POI.

Marker-based mobile AR can be implemented in various ways. Among them, the typical mobile AR implementation method uses a square marker that has easy-to-recognize three-dimensional (3D) position and rotation. Marker-based mobile AR implementation is composed of three stages as shown in Figure 1: (a) acquiring the original image

from the camera; (b) estimating the outline of the white boundary area from the connected components; and (c) augmenting the fine location of virtual data for marker patterns using extracted edges and corners.

Tracking human bodies using markers requires attaching the markers to all targets, which is impractical. Studies have been conducted on the use of environmental information of real-world data instead of markers to overcome this disadvantage [15]. There are markerless tracking methods that use the features data of natural objects in the real world to understand how to use environmental information.

Markerless mobile AR implementation methods include Scale-Invariant Feature Transform (SIFT) [13] and Histogram of Oriented Gradient (HOG) [16]. SIFT compares the original image to the feature points of objects. Even if an object is covered, as shown in Figure 2(a), it can still be identified through its feature points. HOG was proposed for tracking pedestrians using detected feature points such as color brightness or the directional distribution of area. This method is suitable if a target has been rotated or if the inner pattern is simple and the object can be identified from the target's outline. Figure 2(b) shows the results of detecting human bodies with multiple targets using HOG.

Sensor-based mobile AR provides virtual data based on location data acquired through the GPS as shown in Figure 3 [17, 18]. Since sensor-based mobile AR uses location data, it can be easily expanded to various services by replacing the augmented virtual data.

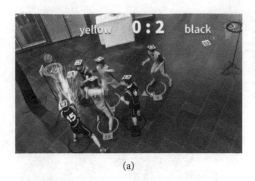
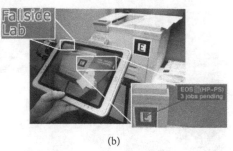

(a)   (b)

FIGURE 5: Examples of game information augmentation using highlighting and annotation. (a) Game information augmentation example using highlighting [27]. (b) Game information augmentation example using annotation [28].

TABLE 1: Summary of experiments for e-leisure mobile AR.

Process	First experiment	Second experiment
Methods	Marker-based tracking (color recognition) Markerless tracking (HOG) Sensor-based tracking (IMU sensor)	Augmentation using marker-based tracking Augmentation using sensor-based tracking

Sensor-based mobile AR provides virtual data based on location data measured by the sensor. Sensor-based mobile AR implementation is performed in two steps: (1) measuring the location of the target though the sensor and (2) matching the sensor coordinate system to the image coordinate system.

A mismatch occurs if the matching error between the sensor coordinate system and the image coordinate system is large [19–24]. A typical example of the mismatch phenomenon is mobile AR using GPS. Because GPS-based mobile AR uses a two-dimensional (2D) coordinate system that consists of latitude and longitude, it does not provide height information between the target and the ground surface. Therefore, GPS-based mobile AR has the problem that the virtual data's location in the image is inaccurate. Improving the accuracy of the sensor-based mobile AR requires calibration for mismatching. Recently, communication technologies have started being used in conventional research. An example method based on communication networks is the Wi-Fi positioning system (WPS), which tracks the location of devices by searching for their Wi-Fi access point location [25].

Game information augmentation's general aim is to provide information to users by either highlighting or annotating objects or humans [26]. Figure 5(a) shows an example [27] in which game information augmentation has been applied to a basketball game: the game information is augmented by highlighting the surroundings of the objects of interest using bright circles. Here, augmented game information includes the player number, team color, and play direction. Figure 5(b) shows an example [28] in which game information augmentation has been applied to a material management system. The marker attached to the object of interest provides material information to users via annotations, and the provided material information is used to augment the screen of the mobile system (smartpad) based on a marker that exists in the real world.

3. Experimental Results and Discussion

This section examines the human body tracking and game information augmentation methods for application to e-leisure mobile AR as shown in Table 1. Human body tracking methods are implemented in the first experiment, and the feasibility of applying such methods to mobile devices is examined based on performance measurement experiments. The second experiment examines the feasibility of applying game information visualization to mobile devices through the implementation of e-leisure mobile AR.

We examine the feasibility of human body tracking methods in mobile devices by comparing the performance of implemented applications using various human body tracking methods. Markerless and marker- and sensor-based human body tracking were implemented using color markers, HOG, and IMU sensors, respectively.

Three experiments were conducted with respect to the three conditions (capability, resolution, and the number of people). The first condition used low-capability (Galaxy S4, 1.6 GHz CPU) and high-capability (Galaxy S6, 2.1 GHz CPU) smartphones to determine the effect on performance. The second condition used low-resolution (320 × 240) and high-resolution (960 × 720) input images (30 fps) to determine the effect on resolution. The third condition checked the effect on different number of people (single user versus multiple users).

In this experiment, marker-based human body tracking applications were implemented using uniforms as color markers [29, 30], as shown in Figure 6, because those in e-leisure (game and sports) environments often wear uniforms. The color marker method extracts POI using the HSV color space and threshold value. Here, the HSV color space was selected because it is robust against shadows and unequal illumination [29, 30]. The marker-based human body tracking application was implemented using the OpenCV

FIGURE 6: An application implemented using color-marker-based human body tracking. (a) Tracking results for a single user. (b) Tracking results for multiple users (two people). (c) Tracking result for multiple users (three people). (d) Tracking result for multiple users (four people). (e) Tracking result for multiple users (five people).

Library connected to the Android software development kit (SDK) and native development kit (NDK).

Figure 6 shows the results of the color-marker-based human body tracking applications. Figure 6(a) displays the tracking result for a single user, and Figures 6(b)–6(e) display the tracking results of multiple users (two to five people). In tracking results, a white rectangle means the tracked human body, and a group means a group of users identified based on the color of the marker, red or green.

Many calculations are required for markerless human body tracking. Therefore, this section implements applications using the HOG algorithm, which has been applied to smartphones and is less complex than other markerless human body tracking methods. Markerless human body tracking is used in the OpenCV Library combined with the

Android SDK and NDK to implement applications such as marker-based tracking.

Figure 7 shows the results of markerless human body tracking applications. Figure 7(a) displays the tracking results for a single user, and Figure 7(b) displays the tracking results of multiple users (five). In the tracking results, a white rectangle indicates a tracked human body.

Experiments were conducted to measure the recognition rate of marker-based and markerless human body tracking methods in low- and high-resolution images. The sensor-based human body tracking performance was affected by the sensor's accuracy, and the measurement experiment of the recognition rate for the sensor-based human body tracking method was excluded because the sensor's accuracy is not in this paper's scope. The recognition rate was measured by

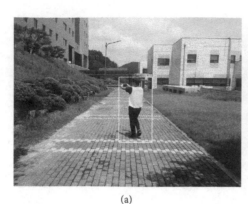 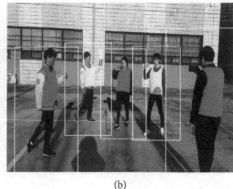

(a)   (b)

FIGURE 7: An application implemented using markerless human body tracking. (a) Tracking result for a single user. (b) Tracking result for multiple users.

TABLE 2: The recognition rate for human body tracking methods based on marker and markerless systems according to low- and high-resolution images.

	Marker-based	Markerless
Low resolution	96%	62%
High resolution	96%	82%

dividing the total number of images by the number of images that were successfully tracked.

Table 2 shows the results of the recognition rate of human body tracking methods for marker-based and markerless in low- and high-resolution images. The recognition rate of the marker-based human body tracking method was 96% for both high- and low-resolution images. These results confirm that the recognition rate can be maintained at a low resolution when using a large-size marker such as a uniform. The recognition rate of the markerless human body tracking method was 82% at high resolution and 62% at low resolution, which confirms that the recognition rate in markerless human body tracking increases when using a higher resolution.

Sensor-based human body tracking is implemented in three steps using IMU, server, and smartphone, as shown in Figure 8. In the first step, the IMU attached to the smartphone transmits the measured 3D position data to the server. In general, IMU measurement data has a large cumulative error. In this experiment, measurement data with a small error were selected through repeated experiments in the same environment. In the second step, the server converted the 3D position data received from the IMUs for calibration into 2D position data of smartphones displayed on the screen (via orthographic projection). Converting 3D position data based on a real-world coordinate system into 2D position data on the user screen requires synchronizing the coordinate system of the 3D position data. In the implemented sensor-based human body tracking, the coordinate system origin of the 3D position data (the IMU's initial position) was set the same, and the coordinate system of the 3D position data was synchronized. In the final step, the smartphone receives the converted 2D position data from the server.

Figure 9 displays the sensor-based human body tracking display. The implemented application augments the specific symbol (user identification number and white rectangle) by identifying the user as shown in Figures 9(a) and 9(b).

Table 3 shows the experimental results measuring the performance (FPS) of the human body tracking methods according to the smartphone's performance, the image resolution, and the number of objects. The measurement results show the FPS difference in human body tracking methods according to the smartphone performance and the image resolution, as indicated largely in the order of markerless, marker-based, and sensor-based. The FPS difference according to the increase in tracked targets was largely not indicated in all three human body tracking methods. Marker-based human body tracking using low-resolution (average greater than 35 fps), markerless human body tracking using low-resolution (average over 15 fps), and sensor-based human body tracking (average 60 fps or higher) considering the real-time performance (over 15 fps), that could be applied to mobile AR. However, the recognition rate in markerless human body tracking methods (Table 2) indicates a low recognition rate for low-resolution images and the disadvantage that the user cannot be identified. Therefore, we use marker- and sensor-based methods in experiments to examine game information augmentation methods for e-leisure mobile ARs.

We examined the feasibility of applying game information augmentation to mobile devices by implementing an e-leisure mobile AR using marker- and location-based human body tracking. An e-leisure mobile AR system that was developed for game information augmentation is performed through the processes of detection area decisions, human body tracking, and game information augmentation. The detection area is determined by categorizing outdoor sports into two groups (offense and defense) based on the actions involved, and the main body parts each group used were analyzed as shown in Figure 10 [31]. In the results of analysis, the hand using an object such as a sword or ball was derived as the detection area in the offensive group. The upper body with equipment such as protective gear was derived as a detection area in the defensive group.

Game information augmentation was achieved in detection areas, including the hands and upper body. Examples of game

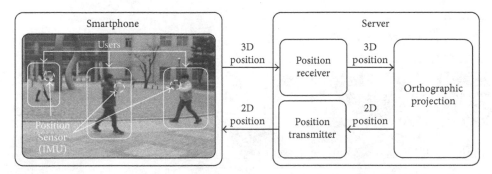

FIGURE 8: Block diagram of an application using sensor-based human body tracking.

(a)   (b)

FIGURE 9: An application implemented using sensor-based human body tracking. (a) Tracking result for a single user. (b) Tracking result for multiple users.

TABLE 3: Experimental results of human body tracking methods: performance comparisons with respect to capability, resolution, and the number of people (unit: fps).

Device capability	Number of people	Marker-based		Markerless		Sensor-based	
		Low resolution	High resolution	Low resolution	High resolution	Low resolution	High resolution
Low spec (Galaxy S4)	One	33.88	3.81	7.63	0.75	60.28	60.76
	Two	31.54	4.25	8.06	0.80	60.10	60.28
	Three	32.19	3.84	8.05	0.72	60.64	60.82
	Four	34.26	3.78	7.60	0.72	60.82	60.94
	Five	33.99	3.89	7.58	0.67	60.28	60.88
High spec (Galaxy S6)	One	37.09	7.97	16.27	1.8	60.22	60.58
	Two	33.30	5.81	14.97	1.43	60.58	60.46
	Three	38.63	6.59	16.86	1.91	60.10	60.46
	Four	37.58	7.19	14.42	1.78	60.34	60.16
	Five	37.63	6.54	14.97	1.80	60.28	60.64

information augmentation in detection areas were analyzed using conventional contents. Figure 11 shows the selected game information for augmentation from conventional content. The detected game information augmentations for the hands and upper body are as shown in Figure 11(a) (fire, sword, and flag) and Figure 11(b) (target, status, and epaulet), respectively.

Figure 12 shows the overall performance of human body tracking and game information visualization on a mobile AR system through the processes of detection-area decision, human body tracking, and game information visualization: The user's hands and upper body are set as POIs when

deciding the detection area: during human body tracking, the human body is tracked using color markers and sensors. Finally, the game information is augmented for the user of interest among the various users.

As shown in Figure 13, the mobile AR system provides functions for selecting the HOI, visualizing game information, and visualizing the first-person shooter. The function for selecting the HOI selects the activation of user visualization (users 1, 2, and 3), and the game information visualization function activates virtual game symbols (target, status (heart), and epaulet) to the HOI.

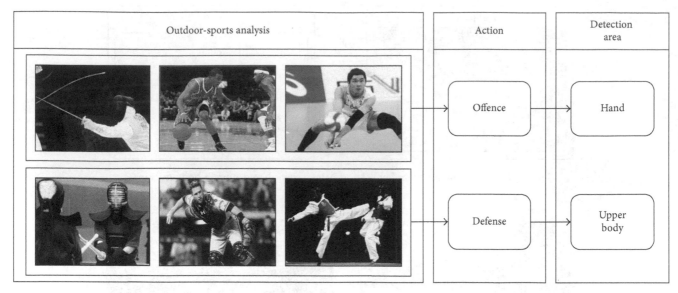

FIGURE 10: Detection area deducted from outdoor-sports analysis for game information augmentation.

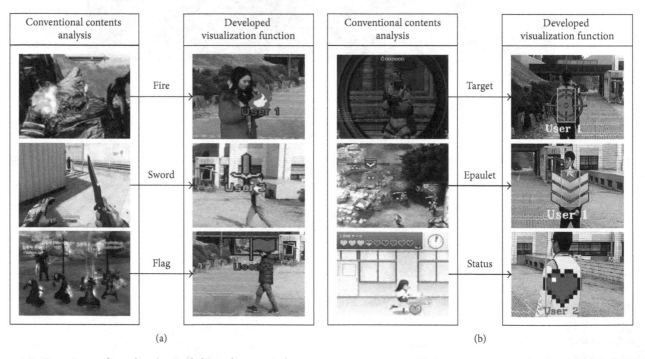

(a) (b)

FIGURE 11: Experimental results obtained through game information augmentation. (a) Augmentation on the detected hand region. (b) Augmentation on the detected upper body region.

Figure 14 shows the results of the game information augmented by the mobile AR: Figure 14(a) shows the screenshot for human body tracking in the marker-based mobile AR. Figure 14(b) shows the game information (target) obtained by identifying users in the marker-based mobile AR. Figure 14(c) shows a screenshot obtained for human body tracking in the sensor-based mobile AR. Finally, Figure 14(d) shows a screenshot for augmenting game information (sword) through user identification in the sensor-based mobile AR. The performance measurement results for the implemented mobile AR with the high-capacity smartphone

at high resolution were confirmed to have stable operation (real-time tracking and visualization were possible without breaks) at 20 fps (marker based) and 62 fps (location based).

4. Conclusions

This paper examines methods of human body tracking and game information augmentation in e-leisure mobile AR. The application of human body tracking was examined by implementing mobile AR via three methods. In the experimental results, marker-based human body tracking at

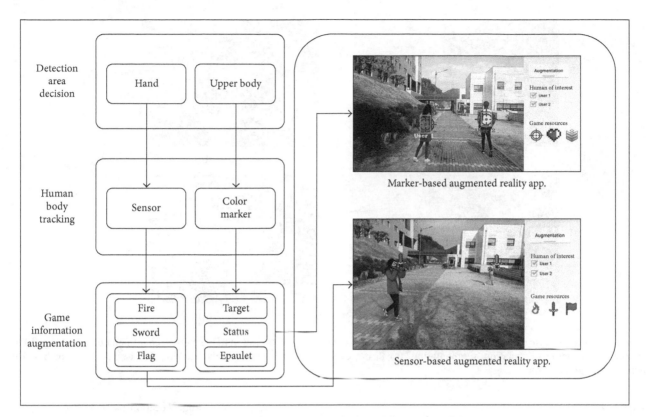

FIGURE 12: Overall block diagram of the mobile AR for e-leisure.

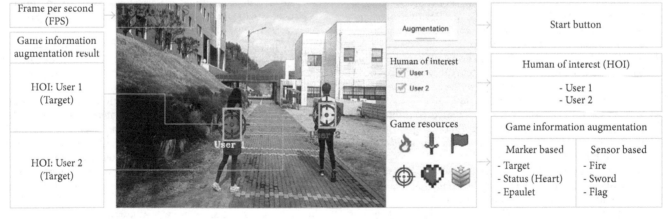

FIGURE 13: Layout of the developed mobile AR for e-leisure.

low resolution (over average 35 fps), markerless human body tracking at low resolution (over average 15 fps), and sensor-based human body tracking (over average 60 fps) considering real-time performance (over 15 fps) could be applied to mobile AR. However, it confirmed that the markerless tracking method was not suitable for the e-leisure mobile AR environment (outdoor with multiple users) considering user identification and recognition according to resolution.

Game information augmentation was examined through the implementation of marker- and location-based mobile AR systems. The performances of the marker- and location-based mobile AR systems were 20 and 62 fps, respectively,

and the results confirmed that human body tracking and game information visualization methods operated stably on the smartphone. Furthermore, we confirmed that it provides interactions among users that conventional mobile ARs could not provide and derived a methodology for selecting the game information to be augmented. These results are expected to be greatly helpful in the study of e-leisure mobile AR.

Acknowledgments

This research is supported by the Ministry of Culture, Sports, and Tourism (MCST) and Korea Creative Content Agency

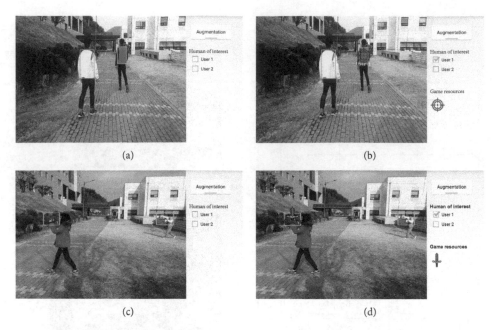

FIGURE 14: Results of game information augmentation applied to the mobile AR. (a) Result of marker-based human body tracking. (b) Result of marker-based game information augmentation. (c) Result of sensor-based human body tracking. (d) Result of sensor-based game information augmentation.

References

[1] *Pokémon Go*, https://www.pokemongo.com.

[2] G. Nimrod and H. Adoni, "Conceptualizing e-leisure," *Loisir et Société/Society and Leisure*, vol. 35, no. 1, pp. 31–56, 2012.

[3] M. E. Son, N. H. Kim, and I. D. Kong, "Positive correlation between cyber leisure time and sympathetic activity in high school students," *FASEB Journal*, vol. 26, pp. 705–707, 2012.

[4] S. O. Lee, S. C. Ahn, J. I. Hwang, and H. G. Kim, "A vision-based mobile augmented reality system for baseball games," in *Proceedings of the International Conference on Virtual and Mixed Reality*, Orlando, FL, USA, July 2011.

[5] S. Bielli and C. G. Harris, "A mobile augmented reality system to enhance live sporting events," in *Proceedings of the ACM the 6th Augmented Human International Conference*, Singapore, March 2015.

[6] A. Kraft, "Real time baseball augmented reality," Tech. Rep. WUCSE-99, Computer Science and Engineering, Washington University in St. Louis, St. Louis, MO, USA, 2011.

[7] E. Cheshire, C. Halasz, and J. Perin, *Player Tracking and Analysis of Basketball Plays*, 2015.

[8] F. Zhou, H. B. Duh, and M. Billinghurst, "Trends in augmented reality tracking, interaction and display: a review of ten years of ISMAR," in *Proceedings of the IEEE International Symposium on Mixed and Augmented Reality*, pp. 193–202, Cambridge, UK, September 2008.

[9] D. Wagner, T. Langlotz, and D. Schmalstieg, "Robust and unobtrusive marker tracking on mobile phones," in *Proceedings of the 7th IEEE/ACM International Symposium on Mixed and Augmented Reality*, Cambridge, UK, September 2008.

[10] D. Lowe, "Distinctive image features from scale-invariant keypoints," *International Journal of Computer Vision*, vol. 60, no. 2, pp. 91–110, 2004.

[11] E. Ziegler, *Real-Time Markerless Tracking of Objects on Mobile Devices*, Doctoral thesis, The Pennsylvania State University, State College, PA, USA, 2009.

[12] Q. Tan and W. Chang, "Location-based augmented reality for mobile learning: algorithm, system, and implementation," *Electronic Journal of e-Learning*, vol. 13, pp. 138–148, 2015.

[13] R. Pryss, P. Geiger, M. Schickler, J. Schobel, and M. Reichert, "Advanced algorithms for location-based smart mobile augmented reality applications," *Procedia Computer Science*, vol. 94, pp. 97–104, 2016.

[14] *ARToolkit*, https://archive.artoolkit.org/documentation.

[15] O. Jihyun, *Hybrid Augmented Reality System on the Mobile Platform*, M.S. thesis, Hanyang University, Seoul, Republic of Korea, 2008.

[16] C. J. Seo and H. I. Ji, "Pedestrian detection using HOG feature and multi-frame operation," *Transactions of the Korean Institute of Electrical Engineers*, vol. 64, no. 3, pp. 193–198, 2015.

[17] A. L. S. Ferreira, S. R. dos Santos, and L. C. de Miranda, "TrueSight a pedestrian navigation system based in automatic landmark detection and extraction on android smartphone," in *Proceedings of the 14th Symposium on Virtual and Augmented Reality (SVR)*, Washington, DC, USA, May 2012.

[18] *Wikitude Drive*, http://www.wikitude.com/en/drive.

[19] S. K. Choi, "The case analysis of augmented reality contents services and business forecast," *KSII Transactions on Internet and Information Systems*, vol. 12, pp. 51–62, 2011.

[20] G. Klein and D. Murray, "Parallel tracking and mapping for small AR workspaces," in *Proceedings of the IEEE and ACM International Symposium on Mixed and Augmented Reality (ISMAR)*, Washington, DC, USA, November 2007.

[21] A. J. Davison, I. D. Reid, N. D. Molton, and O. Stasse, "MonoSLAM: real-time single camera SLAM," *IEEE Transactions on Pattern Analysis and Machine Intelligence*, vol. 29, no. 6, pp. 1052–1067, 2007.

[22] P. Keitler, F. Pankratz, B. Schwerdtfeger et al., "Mobile augmented reality based 3D snapshots," in *Proceedings of the 8th IEEE International Symposium on Mixed and Augmented Reality (ISMAR)*, Orlando, FL, USA, October 2009.

[23] S. J. Velat, J. Lee, N. Johnson, and C. D. Crane, "Vision based vehicle localization for autonomous navigation," in *Pro-*

ceedings of the IEEE International Symposium Computational Intelligence in Robotics and Automation (CIRA), Jacksonville, FL, USA, June 2007.

[24] J. Y. Lee and J. S. Kwon, "Error correction scheme in location-based AR system using smartphone," *Journal of Digital Contents Society*, vol. 16, no. 2, pp. 179–187, 2015.

[25] H. B. Shim, "Comparative analysis for advanced technologies of the location based service," *Journal of the Korea Institute of Information and Communication Engineering*, vol. 16, no. 4, pp. 853–871, 2012.

[26] D. Schmalstieg, "Augmented reality methods in games," in *Proceedings of the 4th IEEE/ACM International Symposium on Mixed and Augmented Reality (ISMAR)*, Washington, DC, USA, October 2005.

[27] P. Baudisch, H. Pohl, S. Reinicke et al., "Imaginary reality gaming: ball games without a ball," in *Proceedings of the 26th Annual ACM Symposium on User Interface Software and Technology*, St Andrews, UK, October 2013.

[28] E. Rosten, G. Reitmayr, and T. Drummond, "Real-time video annotations for augmented reality," in *Proceedings of the International Symposium on Visual Computing (ISVC)*, Lake Tahoe, NV, USA, November 2005.

[29] H. Belghit, N. Zenati-Henda, A. Bellabi, S. Benbelkacem, and M. Belhocine, "Tracking color marker using projective transformation for augmented reality application," in *Proceedings of the IEEE International Conference on Multimedia Computing and Systems (ICMCS)*, Tangiers, Morocco, May 2012.

[30] A. Bellarbi, S. Benbelkacem, N. Zenati-Henda, and M. Belhocine, "Hand gesture interaction using color-based method for tabletop interfaces," in *Proceedings of the 7th International Symposium on IEEE Intelligent Signal Processing (WISP)*, Floriana, Malta, September 2011.

[31] S. W. Jang, J. H. Ko, H. J. Lee, and Y. S. Kim, "A study on human body tracking and game information visualization for mobile AR," *International Journal of Mobile Device Engineering*, vol. 1, no. 1, pp. 15–20, 2017.

20

The Influence of Social Networks on the Development of Recruitment Actions that Favor User Interface Design and Conversions in Mobile Applications Powered by Linked Data

Pedro R. Palos-Sanchez [iD],[1,2] Jose Ramon Saura [iD],[3] and Felipe Debasa [iD][4]

[1]Department of Business Management, University of Extremadura, Av. Universidad, s/n, 10003 Cáceres, Spain
[2]Department of Business Organization, Marketing and Market Research, International University of La Rioja, Av. de la Paz 137, 26006 Logroño, Spain
[3]Department of Business and Economics, Rey Juan Carlos University, Madrid, Spain
[4]Department of Contemporary History and Actual World, Rey Juan Carlos University, Madrid, Spain

Correspondence should be addressed to Pedro R. Palos-Sanchez; ppalos@unex.es

Academic Editor: José J. Pazos-Arias

This study analyzes the most important influence factors in the literature, which have the greatest influence on the conversions obtained in a mobile application powered by linked data. With the study of user interface design and a small user survey ($n = 101,053$), we studied the influence of social networks, advertising, and promotional and recruitment actions in conversions for mobile applications powered by linked data. The analysis of the users' behavior and their application in the design of the actions to promote and capture constitutes an important part of the current theories of digital marketing. However, this study shows that its results may be contradictory and depend on other factors and circumstances when mobile applications powered by linked data are considered. The predictive value, reached by the developed model, may be useful for professionals and researchers in the field of digital marketing and the user interface design in mobile applications powered by linked data.

1. Introduction

The growing use of digital marketing strategies has led to a great deal of research being published on this subject in the first decade of the 21st century. Research such as that of [1], "The marketing communication and the World Wide Web," gave rise to various studies of digital technologies and Internet marketing.

Also, over the last few years, there has been a great deal of academic research published in the field of digital mobile marketing that helps us understand what the influencing factors are in order to get conversions from the Internet and mobile applications.

In the work of Saura et al. [2], the concept of conversion in the field of digital marketing is explained in the following way: "Conversion depends on the marketing objective. It

could be a sent form, a click on an ad, or a purchase. It is an objective or goal." This definition helps us to understand the reasons why companies develop their strategies focusing on obtaining conversions and investigating what influences how conversions are achieved.

Research such as that in [2], comparing new forms of Internet advertising versus off-line media, presents the new digital paradigm and focuses on the relevance of the Internet for mobile phones and mobile applications powered by linked data to compare the objectives achieved both online and off-line. In the work of Järvinen and Karjaluoto [3], the use of web analytics in digital marketing techniques in web pages and mobile applications is studied, and it helps us to understand which factors to measure to obtain conversions. In the work of Jayaram et al. [4], the user's behavior in social media and the influence on mobile devices, digital campaigns like SEO, the acronym of Search Engine Optimization, and SEM, known as Search Engine Marketing, and mobile applications are analyzed and presented to give a global view of the digital ecosystem. Using the mathematical algorithm developed by Järvinen et al. [5], the effectiveness of SEO and SEM strategies in the financial sector is analyzed, and the algorithm also provides a relevant theoretical framework for the material being studied.

Also, in the study of Kannan and Li [6], a reference framework for digital marketing research that highlights each part of the online strategy process for desktop and mobile devices based on user interface design has been developed with the aim of increasing conversions. The results of the research conclude that emerging mobile technologies, such as linked data, will prospectively be the technologies that will have the greatest impact on the future of mobile digital marketing as they offer ease of use and accessibility and that, consequently, will be more effective in achieving conversions. In addition, the digital marketing strategies SEO and SEM are linked to social networks and user interface design in the framework developed for mobile and fixed devices, which is a fact that is linked to the objectives of the company with the development of these strategies.

Like the work of Saura et al. [2], studies such as [7] focus on the opportunities that digital marketing and the evolution of ICTs (Singular Scientific and Technological Infrastructures) offer to marketing in the mobile era [8] and which could be the future of the techniques that influence achieving conversions.

Likewise, Kireyev et al. [9] investigate the relevance of the brand by analyzing the queries made in search engines. This research reveals the relevance of the number of queries made on search engines that contain the brand name. They [9] also focus on the relationship between brand relevance and queries on Google by users who allowed their search behavior and search history to be monitored while specifying that SEO is a traffic capture strategy and, therefore, could influence the achievement of conversions on a web page or an application powered by linked data.

Mathews et al. [10] analyze the impact of traffic coming from queries in search engines. This research focuses on organic product searches on SERPs (Search Engine Results Pages) in Google and Bing search engines. In the research, a model for the prediction of search results in the retail sector is developed which shows that the names of retailers in organic search results are potentially useful to control the prominence and the impact on the traffic that comes from the SERPs and which is relevant to the objectives of the investigation.

Skiera et al. [11] present an analysis of the importance of "longtail" in SEM, indicating that SEM advertising is one of the most used strategies on the Internet. In the research, three SEM campaigns in three countries are analyzed, monitoring 4408 keywords in 36 weeks, covering a total of 10,014,015 searches and 492,735 clicks. The authors [11] conclude that 20% of all keywords attract 98.16% of the searches and that they also generate 97.21% of all the clicks which the campaign receives, presenting large differences compared to results from downloads by mobile devices

and apps, allowing us to understand what the influence of each type of campaign has on achieving conversions.

Like [4], the research of Roshan et al. [12] aims to analyze the use of social networks in business. It also focuses on companies in times of crisis. Communications from 17 Australian organizations made on Facebook and Twitter are analyzed, in which a total of 15,650 communications are considered. The results of the research suggest that the communications on social media of companies that are in crisis lack the potential awareness to face a crisis using communication in social networks by making use of speed when using mobile technologies powered by linked data, highlighting social networks as a source of quality traffic.

Like [4, 13], the research of Peters et al. [14] defines good practices for social network management in an organization in which a framework is proposed with three main components which define the main social media elements, based on marketing, sociology, and psychology theories, and baptize these terms as "motives," "content," "structure" and "roles and interactions," based on the theoretical framework. The literature review suggests nine steps to evaluate and design an appropriate framework in social media using mobile traffic and applications. The results of this research offer an interesting perspective for the structure of a strategy based on obtaining and increasing the number of conversions by organizing and structuring each of the analytical indicators that influence conversions.

Also, few studies [5, 7, 10] carry out a thorough review of the social networking sector in B2B companies revealing the interest this type of businesses has in social networks. In addition, the results of the investigation indicate that these companies must update their knowledge regarding digital marketing and how to measure and monitor their activity in this area to increase the recruitment actions in mobile devices based on the user interface design and how this affects achieving conversions or goals.

Chunga et al. [15] follow the line of the research of Wang et al. [16], in which an empirical model is developed so that companies can make better decisions in social networks on the management and objectives raised in the strategy of social media marketing based on the interactions of the users of mobile applications for social networks.

Lohtia et al. [17] evaluate the effectiveness of banners and display advertisements on the Internet. The authors develop a data analysis taking into account different inputs and outputs to estimate and measure the efficiency of the banners. The conclusion is that the evaluation of how banners work on the Internet is a complex task since each company has different inputs and outputs when it comes to starting an online advertising campaign. Each click on these banners was considered a conversion.

Like [17, 18], the effects of the banners on the search behavior of the users are investigated based on other investigations that suggest that banners have little or no impact on user behavior and user experience with the interface design of applications powered by linked data. García-Álvarez et al. [19] conclude that the observation and the observation frequency on the banners increase with the perception that the users have of this type of publicity in applications and mobile phones. This means that users' perception affects the number of conversions that are produced.

This research paper provides scientific evidence of interest to consultants and researchers in digital marketing and, in general, marketing managers and technicians in mobile application development who will find contributions that can help them to identify what the influencing factors are to achieve conversions in mobile applications powered by linked data and to determine a possible model of causal relations that explains why conversions occur.

This research offers the research hypothesis first and then presents and explains the methodology used, the sample, the scales and measurement of variables that form the proposed model of causal relationships, the method of data analysis, the analysis of the measurement model, and finally, the analysis of the results and conclusions.

2. Conceptual Framework and Hypothesis Development

As we have shown, the interest of researchers in the categories and subcategories present in digital marketing has been growing as a research topic during the last decade.

In this research, the study is based on the concepts of the use of social networks, Internet advertising, and promotional actions to achieve conversions in mobile applications powered by linked data.

The use of social networks is defined by [19] as an online community that makes it easy to publish, share, and disseminate information as an online collaboration to increase interactions and links to dynamic content on web pages or mobile applications powered by linked data.

Internet advertising is becoming a real fact. Aslam and Karjaluoto [20] indicate that Internet advertising has radically transformed how companies do business, especially with methodologies to increase sales of their products and services on the Internet. The paradigm of advertising now is not from the traditional to the digital but from the digital to the mobile. New advertising formats adapted to new mobile devices are highlighted.

Conversions are defined by Sumita and Zuo in their research [21] on mobile Internet access as an online indicator of particular interest, in which consumers perform a specific action on a website or an application, such as clicking on a button, making a call, or sending a form. Sumita and Zuo [21] propose a model to quantify the impact of mobile application access to the Internet and the conversions they make.

Promotional actions in the Internet are defined as different types of tactics carried out on the Internet such as discounts, coupons, or incentives. Crespo-Almendros and Barrio-García [22] analyze several investigations to determine, with respect to a sector, the level of optimization of the experience of a website or a mobile application—in this case for the sale of airline tickets—to increase sales on the Internet.

Based on the research presented, we developed the research hypotheses presented in this study:

H1: the use of social networks by users influences (+) Internet promotion actions.

Like [4, 12], the investigation of Wang et al. [16] analyzes the communications made by companies of a particular sector in social networks. The research develops a content analysis of 390 companies to examine the impact of Internet promotion actions on the Facebook social network, including metrics such as the number of likes, number of shares, and characteristics of posts and their links. The results of the research show that the tone and narrative used in the promotional actions are directly associated with the engagement of communications in social networks in mobile applications powered by linked data.

In addition, the research carried out by Bernabé-Moreno et al. [13] develops an enriched consumer recruitment system to increase retention of users in campaigns on social networks. The possibilities offered by the geolocation of mobile applications in social media open the door to new ways of listening to the consumer to improve promotional actions on the Internet. The authors develop a system that categorically extracts interactions in social networks according to location and industry and quantifies the impact over a period of time. Definitions for the capture and retention of users on social media are shown as conclusions of the research. These can improve the efficiency and profitability of the promotional actions in the Internet.

Vásquez and Escamilla [23], in their research, carry out a thorough analysis of the best practices for marketing on social networks using SMEs. The objective of the research is to propose the best practices in the use of social networks with SMEs. An exploratory study of successful case studies is carried out, providing, on one hand, the identification of best practices in the use of social networks and, on the other hand, developing a social media marketing strategy for the promotion of SMEs on the Internet. Consequently, the relationship between the use of social networks and promotional actions on mobile Internet is studied.

H2: advertising influences (+) Internet acquisition actions.

The research of Deane and Agarwal [24] in parallel to the research of Nabout and Skiera [8] shows that 23% of digital marketing strategies are based on online advertising. They [24] also propose a model to make this investment more effective by scheduling the appearance of ads at certain time slots. Therefore, we can state, according to their research, that advertising would indeed be related to the promotional actions that companies make on the Internet.

Studies [26, 2] investigate whether the Banners (Display Ads) on web pages, together with emails, have an influence on the searches that users make in search engines. This research develops a model of online advertising attribution, in which reflections are made on how advertising increases the number of clicks on search results and also on the cost of the campaigns, thus modifying the following promotional actions on the Internet.

H3: advertising influences (+) conversions on the Internet.

Other authors focus their attention on web analytics and the definition of KPIs for the optimal analysis of digital

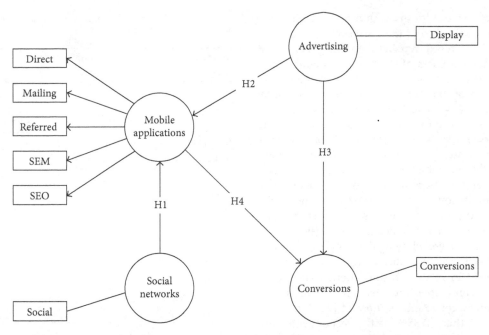

FIGURE 1: Structural model proposed for the development of hypotheses.

strategies. Condit [26] develops an investigation on the main indicators for digital analytics focusing the study on a library. Also in [27], the definition of web analytics is considered as an improvement in Internet communication with the measurement of conversions or leads achieved by the company. The work of Lee [28] focuses on the acquisition of users through the measurement of digital marketing actions by analyzing each purchase as a conversion.

The research of Nabout et al. [29] examines the optimal cost that companies as advertisers invest in SEM advertising, demonstrating that agencies achieve higher results than those demanded by advertisers by basing the analysis on the number of conversions achieved. In addition, this research provides insights on how to measure investment in SEM if earnings per conversion are not clearly defined by the client and agency.

H4: recruitment actions influence (+) Internet conversions.

Royle and Laing [30] focus their research on developing a measurement model for digital marketing techniques in search engines, taking SEO as a recruitment action on the Internet. The work of Nabout and Skiera [8] also focuses attention on improving the investment made in search engines and optimizing conversions, treating the SEO technique as an action to attract users on the Internet.

The research of Marinova [25] on permission e-mail marketing is focused on how companies use e-mail marketing to capture customers on the Internet. The research [25] also points out that it is common to create distribution lists to analyze the e-mails that reach the consumers that form the databases of the companies, indicating that it is a fact that the users are connected for more time, thanks to mobile devices, allowing the companies to acquire data on the use of traffic arriving at web pages.

In addition, the research of Ahangar and Dastuyi [31] provides solutions on the persuasive language that companies use in their communications for user recruitment. They [31] also identify and classify the types of persuasive messages that e-mails must contain and categorize them into ten types of e-mails and thirty-six steps to perform an effective e-mail marketing for recruitment of users by Internet companies.

Kim and Tse [32] conduct research in which they analyze the less popular search engines versus quality search services, aiming to improve conversions and leads on the Internet. Kim and Tse [32] conclude that the quality of the content that gets conversions depends on two variables, namely, the amount of content available on the Internet and the difference in search quality between a nonpopular search engine and a popular search engine.

With the development of these hypotheses, this research aims to identify what the influencing factors are in order to achieve conversions in mobile applications powered by linked data and find a model of causal relationships that explains why conversions occur and what influences their occurrence.

Figure 1 shows the structural model proposed for the development of hypotheses.

3. Methodology

3.1. Sample. The chosen methodology has been used to find the results of the user experience in 30 mobile applications powered by linked data and the subsequent survey answered by the users of those applications. To do this, the data were gathered with an electronically administered survey to users of 30 leading companies in mobile digital marketing which invoiced more than 3 million euros through digital marketing strategies, social media marketing, advertising, and actions of recruitment and loyalty with mobile applications in the Internet in Spain during the last year.

The individuals surveyed were between the ages of 18 and 72 and were occasional users of the selected mobile applications. A simple probabilistic sampling was carried out on users who made use of the mobile applications powered by linked data. The study was conducted between January and June 2017. The total volume of visits that made up the population universe for the study was 2,010,535 million visits that were studied as user experiences from the information provided by Google Analytics. Of all those experiences based on optimization of the user interface design, finally, the representative sample consisted of 101,053 consumers who answered a brief survey to assess the user experience in the mobile applications powered by linked data that they accessed to make their purchases, when leaving the mobile application.

Demographic characteristics such as age and gender have been very significant in relation to the Internet and in the adoption of mobile commerce. These have been examined by different investigators, for example, those of [33–35].

It was observed that 60.35% of the respondents who accessed mobile applications are men, while 39.65% are women. The people who have accessed the most mobile applications are between the ages of 29 and 39 corresponding to women, followed by men ranging from 37 to 47 years. These data can be observed in Table 1.

The 30 companies from which 1,096,770 customer IDs have been analyzed are from the sectors corresponding to education (1), distribution (2), legal (3), health (4), leisure (5), real estate (6), automobile (7), financial (8), services (9), and logistics (10) and represent the best companies in terms of results in the digital marketing sector in Spain.

Table 2 shows the number of user IDs that have been analyzed in each sector.

The sample was reduced to 101,053 IDs because of the quality required to perform the analysis based on metrics such as rebound percentage or duration of the visit.

3.2. Scales and Measurement of Variables.
The survey was performed using the Likert 5-point scale, which allowed us to measure attitudes and experiences on the degree of adequacy of the respondent to any statement we proposed (1: completely disagree; 5: completely agree) regarding the design and user experience on each website.

Data related to the user experience were extracted with web analytics measurement software on 2,010,535 customer IDs corresponding to the companies under study. When performing quality tests for each of the user IDs analyzed, the sample was reduced to 101,053 unique user IDs, mainly due to the high rebound count percentage of many of the sessions analyzed (greater than 87%). The rebound percentage is an indicator that marks the interaction percentage and the length of time the user has with the web page, and this determines the quality of the visit [8].

Any survey can have measurement errors which question the validity of the conclusions regarding the relationship that might exist between the measurements, and it is widely recognized that such errors have random as well as

TABLE 1: Samples' sex and average age.

Sex	Percentage	Average age
Women	39.65%	29–39 years
Men	60.35%	37–47 years

TABLE 2: IDs of analyzed users.

Company sector	User ID
Education (1)	134434
Distribution (2)	189201
Legal (3)	93043
Health (4)	217058
Leisure (5)	37997
Real estate (6)	17901
Automobile (7)	87867
Finance (8)	98160
Services (9)	201142
Logistics (10)	19967

systematic components. Therefore, it is important to take measurements so that there is no so-called "common method bias" associated with how to answer the various questions in the questionnaire. Thus, as a preventive measure of these errors, a number of recommendations were followed during the design of the questionnaire used in our study [36, 37]. To this end, clear and concise questions were formulated with terms that were very familiar to the users; the answers were guaranteed confidential so that users could answer as honestly as possible, and changes were also made in the way the questions were written for the different scales.

The order of some of the questions and the problem that this might entail was counteracted by changing them at random. After data collection, the Harman single-factor test was used as a measure of post hoc control of the common method bias [38].

3.3. Method of Data Analysis.
The hypotheses of the conceptual model (Figure 1) were tested using the partial least squares (PLS) technique to estimate the structural equation models based on the variance. The SmartPLS 3 software [39] was chosen to evaluate the reliability and validity of the measurement model and to test the structural model, both for its graphical resolution capability and for the set of statistical methods applied. Structural equation models based on the variance are a good methodology choice when it comes to finding the simultaneous behavior of dependency relationships and allow us to go beyond other multivariate techniques, such as multiple regression and factor analysis.

4. Result Analysis

PLS is a specially recommended method for exploratory research and allows the modeling of latent constructs with both formative and reflective indicators [40]. In addition, PLS is more appropriate when the objective is to predict and

TABLE 3: AVE and CR.

Variable	Cronbach's alpha	Composite reliability	Average variance extracted (AVE)
Recruitment actions	0.949	0.961	0.833
Conversions	1000	1000	1000
Advertising	1000	1000	1000
Social networks	1000	1000	1000

TABLE 4: Cross loads in PLS.

	Recruitment actions	Conversions	Advertising	Social networks
Conversions	0.292	1000	0.350	−0.018
Direct	0.879	0.439	0.202	0.335
Display	0.302	0.350	1000	0.060
Mailing	0.835	0.050	0.138	0.812
Referred	0.963	0.166	0.279	0.384
SEM	0.909	0.428	0.487	0.276
SEO	0.973	0.275	0.277	0.423
Social	0.511	−0.018	0.060	1000

investigate relatively new phenomena [41], such as the influence of social networks in obtaining conversions in digital marketing with mobile applications powered by linked data.

PLS was chosen for several reasons: first, PLS does not impose normality requirements on the data and is a technique that is adequate for predicting dependent variables in small samples, given a certain degree of quality in the measurement model [42, 43]. Therefore, it is a good choice for our final sample of 101,053 sample elements. In addition, PLS is more appropriate when the objective is to predict and investigate relatively new phenomena [44], as in the case of digital marketing conversions and the influence of social networks. Finally, PLS is an SEM evaluation method widely used in commercial management research in information systems [45–48], e-commerce [49], and cloud computing [49–52].

4.1. Analysis of the Measurement Model. The model was constructed with items with a reflective character, since they share concepts and, therefore, are interchangeable to be equivalent manifestations of the same construct [37, 53].

First, we measured the individual reliability of the load (λ) for the indicator, where it is usual to establish the minimum level for acceptance as part of the construct in $\lambda \geq 0.707$ [54].

However, other authors diverge from this rule, considering it to be excessively rigid in the initial stages of scale development and in little studied subjects, accepting in these cases minimum values greater than 0.5 or 0.6 [46, 55]. The commonality of a manifested variable (λ^2) is the part of the variable which can be explained by the factor or constructs [56]. All values exceeded this minimum value [53].

To test the consistency of a construct, Cronbach's alpha and its composite reliability (CR) were used. These values measure the consistency of a construct based on its indicators [57], that is, the rigor with which these items are measuring the same latent variable.

Cronbach's alpha determines a consistency index for each construct and presents values between 0 and 1 [53].

The lower limit to accept the reliability of the construct is usually set between 0.6 and 0.7 [58].

The highest validity will be in values close to 1. As can be seen in Table 3, all variables passed those minimum values for validity.

AVE is defined as the average variance extracted and reports how much variance a construct obtains from its indicators in relation to the amount of variance due to the measurement error [53, 59]. The recommendation of these authors is that AVE is ≥ 0.50, which we can interpret as more than 50% of the variance of the construct is due to its indicators.

Discriminate validity marks the extent to which a construct is different from others. A high value would indicate weak correlations between constructs. Two types of analysis are used for this test [53]. On one hand, as can be seen in Table 4 showing cross loads, no indicator shares more load with any other than that of the construct itself.

On the other hand, as can be seen in Table 5, it has been verified that the square root of the average variance extracted (AVE) is greater than the relationship between the construct and the rest of the model constructs [53, 59].

A construct should share more variance with its measurements or indicators than with other constructs in a given model [60]. To verify this, we must see if the square root of the AVE (given in bold in Table 5) is greater than the correlation between the construct and the rest of constructs of the model. In our case, this condition is true for all latent variables [53]. Therefore, we can affirm that the constructs share more variance with their indicators than with other constructs of the investigated model [60], and discriminate validity is shown based on this first analysis.

4.2. Structural Model Analysis. Standardized path coefficients (β) provide the extent to which predictor variables contribute to the explained variance of endogenous variables [53].

TABLE 5: Fornell and Larcker criteria (1981).

	Recruitment actions	Conversions	Advertising	Social networks
Recruitment actions	**0.913**			
Conversions	0.292	**1000**		
Advertising	0.302	0.350	**1000**	
Social networks	0.511	−0.018	0.060	**1000**

TABLE 6: Path coefficients and statistical significance.

	Hypothesis	Original sample	T statistic	P values	Support
H1	Social networks → recruitment actions	0.495	1932	0.027	Yes*
H2	Advertising → recruitment actions	0.272	1091	0.138	Not
H3	Advertising → conversions	0.288	0.414	0.340	Not
H4	Recruitment actions → conversions	0.205	0.326	0.372	Not

The variance explained in an endogenous construct by another latent variable can be measured from the absolute value of the multiplication of the coefficient path by the correlation coefficient of the two variables [53, 61].

The analysis of these coefficients and their statistical significance will allow us to contrast the proposed research hypotheses. Several authors, for example, those of [46], consider that a value of β is considered acceptable if it is greater than or equal to 0.2, although it is desirable that it be above 0.3 [53].

In any case, the calculation of the path coefficients must be accompanied by some measure that reports its statistical significance and, ultimately, the acceptability of the adjustment made. The acceptability of the fit has been measured based on the t-statistic resulting from applying the bootstrap resampling test to 5000 subsamples. The single-line t-distribution of Student has been used, since the direction of relationships has been specified in the model [53].

From this, the following values are used as the reference of statistical significance: $t = 1.64791345$ for 95% confidence, $t = 2.333843952$ for 99%, and $t = 3.106644601$ for 99.9%. The values reached in this test, together with the standard regression coefficients, have been collected in Table 6 and allow for the contrast of the proposed structural model hypotheses.

The influence of social networks on H1 recruitment actions is supported by their positive influence, although only having a significance of 95% ($\beta = -0.495$; $t = 1.932$).

The influence of advertising on recruitment actions reaches a minimum of 0.2, although not in terms of significance ($\beta = 0.272$; $t = 1.091$), so H2 is not fulfilled. With the influence of advertising on conversions, a very similar result ($\beta = 0.288$; $t = 0.413$) is obtained, and H3 is not confirmed; that is, advertising does not influence final conversions.

This structural analysis yields significant data that have been analyzed with the β of each construct. Thus, the influence of recruitment actions on conversions yields very low results ($\beta = 0.205$; $t = 0.326$), with H4 not being met [53].

The coefficient of determination R^2 has been calculated (Figure 2), since it is a widely used statistic with the main

purpose of predicting future results. This coefficient determines the quality of the model to replicate the results and the variation of the results that can be explained by the model [62].

According to [44], the reference values of R^2 of 0.67, 0.33, and 0.19, are considered strong, moderate, and weak, respectively. The research of Palos-Sanchez et al. [53] indicates that when the values of R^2 are below 0.1, the relationships formulated as hypotheses have a very low predictive level, in spite of being statistically significant. This is the case of the independent variable conversions and recruitment actions [61].

The obtained results indicate that the model explains 51.7% of the total variance ($R^2 = 0.517$), since this is the result obtained by the dependent variable conversions (R^2). On the other hand, the other dependent variable recruitment actions explains 48.5% ($R^2 = 0.485$). It can be seen that the values widely exceed the minimum 0.1, which is the threshold set by [53].

According to [53], the R^2 value for conversions demonstrates the existence of a moderate predictive power, while for recruitment or promotional actions (0.485) a lower predictive power is obtained, but with a similar intensity. In summary, although it is evident that there are additional factors, the model can be declared highly predictive, and a great part of the variance of the variables is explained by the model itself [53].

Figure 2 shows the final structural model.

5. Conclusions

The interest of researchers in the categories and subcategories present in digital marketing is a solid fact that has been growing as a topic for research during the last decade. This research has centered the study on the concepts of the use of social networks, Internet advertising, conversions and recruitment from promotion actions for mobile applications powered by linked data, and the optimization of the user interface design.

The results obtained show that it is a model with predictive capacity and that the model can be replicated, given

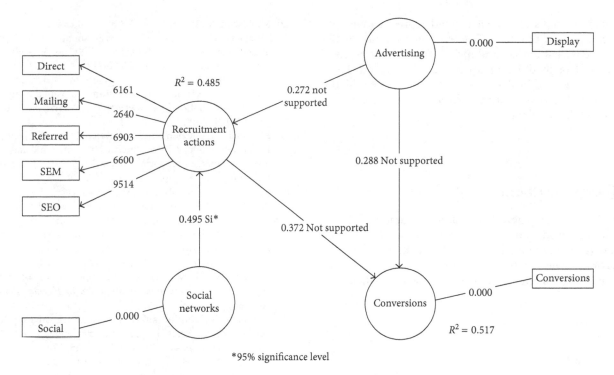

*95% significance level

FIGURE 2: Final structural model.

the results obtained by the determination coefficients of the dependent variables: conversions and recruitment actions. In this way, the results of the research serve to measure the influence factor of the variables developed to achieve conversions in mobile applications powered by linked data.

The first of the contrasted hypotheses has been validated, which is why we show that the use of social networks by users has a positive influence on the promotion and recruitment actions on the Internet for mobile applications powered by linked data, and therefore, we can confirm previous studies [4, 12, 16]. This result shows that communications made on the social networks of companies in a given sector, including positive metrics such as the number of likes, the number of shares, and the characteristics of the posts and their links, influence promotional actions. The confirmation of this hypothesis also contributes to the positive results from other studies [13, 23, 63]. Therefore, it seems imperative that actions of promotion and recruitment are conditioned by social networks in mobile applications powered by linked data.

However, the results obtained do not confirm that advertising positively influences the recruitment actions in the Internet. This influence does not reach the minimum threshold of significance, confirming the low degree of influence that other authors have found in previous studies [64–66]. This may be due to the fact that advertising is still not widely used in digital marketing strategies and constitutes less than a quarter of the total investment.

These results have also been repeated for the case of the influence of advertising on Internet conversions [67]. It seems obvious that web analytics and, above all, their optimum analysis improve conversions, but not with the direct influence of advertising [68]. The improvement in communication as a result of a correct interpretation of these analyses is not

confirmed in this study. However, we find that the results have been highly positive and confirm interest in these analyses, as in previous studies [27, 69, 70]. Therefore, obtaining better results does not confirm the existence of a causal relationship between advertising and more conversions in mobile applications powered by linked data.

Finally, this research focused on demonstrating that recruitment actions have a positive influence on Internet conversions [71–73]. The existence of measurement models for the different techniques of digital marketing has frequently been seen in the literature over the last few years [14, 74–76], especially as regards the improvement of the investment made in search engines and the optimization of conversions, treating the SEO technique as a way to attract users on the Internet to achieve the objectives or conversions raised by the digital strategy of the company. Other studies studied e-mail marketing to capture customers on the Internet [25, 77–79]. However, the results obtained do not confirm that these recruitment actions have a significant influence on the conversions in mobile applications powered by linked data, which contradicts the results of these authors. Reasons for this could be that incorrect language causes confusion, and above all the design of the user interface of the mobile applications powered by linked data. Other studies explain the data in a similar way [32, 82, 83] and also identify the concern for user privacy as another possibility. These users find a real invasion of their privacy in some recruitment actions [53].

It therefore appears that the quality of the use of these actions is crucial, confirming previous studies [32], although the results have been very unequal depending on the recruitment technique that has been used.

The limitations of this study are linked to the size of the sample that could be expanded in the future to obtain results with different statistical efficiency and representative margins. In addition, the possibility exists for the use of this model in different devices and mobile applications powered by linked data in different areas according to the target market and type of business using A/B testing for the different user interfaces used in different mobile applications powered by linked data.

Authors' Contributions

Pedro R. Palos-Sanchez, Jose Ramon Saura, and Felipe Debasa conceived and designed the review. Jose Ramon Saura performed the methodology. Pedro R. Palos-Sánchez and Felipe Debasa analyzed the results. Jose Ramon Saura, Pedro R. Palos-Sanchez, and Felipe Debasa wrote the paper.

References

[1] L. Pitt and R. Watson, "The World Wide Web as an advertising medium," *Journal of Advertising Research*, vol. 36, no. 1, pp. 432–445, 1996.

[2] J. R. Saura, P. Palos-Sánchez, and L. M. Suárez, "Understanding the digital marketing environment with KPIs and web analytics," *Future Internet*, vol. 9, no. 4, p. 76, 2017.

[3] J. Järvinen and H. Karjaluoto, "The use of Web analytics for digital marketing performance measurement," *Industrial Marketing Management*, vol. 50, pp. 117–127, 2015.

[4] D. Jayaram, A. K. Manrai, and L. A. Manrai, "Effective use of marketing technology in Eastern Europe: web analytics, social media, customer analytics, digital campaigns and mobile applications," *Journal of Economics, Finance and Administrative Science*, vol. 20, no. 39, pp. 118–132, 2015.

[5] J. Järvinen, A. Töllinen, H. Karjaluoto, and C. Jayawardhena, "Digital and social media marketing usage in B2B industrial section," *Marketing Management Journal*, vol. 22, no. 2, 2012.

[6] P. Kannan and H. Li, "Digital marketing: a framework, review and research agenda," *International Journal of Research in Marketing*, vol. 34, no. 1, pp. 22–45, 2017.

[7] R. D. Wilson, "Using web traffic analysis for customer acquisition and retention programs in marketing," *Services Marketing Quarterly*, vol. 26, no. 2, pp. 1–22, 2004.

[8] N. A. Nabout and B. Skiera, "Return on quality improvements in search engine marketing," *Journal of Interactive Marketing*, vol. 26, no. 3, pp. 141–154, 2012.

[9] P. Kireyev, K. Pauwels, and S. Gupta, "Do display ads influence search? Attribution and dynamics in online advertising," *International Journal of Research in Marketing*, vol. 33, no. 3, pp. 475–490, 2016.

[10] S. Mathews, C. Bianchi, K. J. Perks, M. Healy, and R. Wickramasekera, "Internet marketing capabilities and international market growth," *International Business Review*, vol. 25, no. 4, pp. 820–830, 2016.

[11] B. Skiera, J. Eckert, and O. Hinz, "An analysis of the importance of the long tail in search engine marketing," *Electronic Commerce Research and Applications*, vol. 9, no. 6, pp. 488–494, 2010.

[12] M. Roshan, M. Warren, and R. Carr, "Understanding the use of social media by organisations for crisis communication," *Journal of Computers in Human Behavior*, vol. 63, pp. 350–361, 2016.

[13] J. Bernabé-Moreno, A. Tejeda-Lorente, C. Porcel, H. Fujita, and E. Herrera-Viedma, "A system to enrich marketing customers acquisition and retention campaigns using social media information," *Knowledge-Based Systems*, vol. 80, pp. 163–179, 2015.

[14] K. Peters, Y. Chen, A. M. Kaplan, B. Ognibeni, and K. Pauwels, "Social media metrics-a framework and guidelines for managing social media," *Journal of Interactive Marketing*, vol. 27, no. 4, pp. 281–298, 2013.

[15] A. Chunga, P. Andreeva, M. Benyoucef, A. Duane, and P. O'Reilly, "Managing an organisation's social media presence: an empirical stages of growth model," *International Journal of Information Management*, vol. 37, no. 1, pp. 1405–1417, 2017.

[16] R. Wang, J. Kim, A. Xiao, and Y. Jung, "Networked narratives on humans of New York: a content analysis of social media engagement on Facebook," *Computers in Human Behavior*, vol. 66, pp. 149–153, 2017.

[17] R. Lohtia, N. Donthu, and I. Yaveroglu, "Evaluating the efficiency of Internet banner advertisements," *Journal of Business Research*, vol. 60, no. 4, pp. 365–370, 2007.

[18] K. C. Hamborg, M. Bruns, F. Ollermann, and K. Kaspar, "The effect of banner animation on fixation behavior and recall performance in search tasks," *Computers in Human Behavior*, vol. 28, no. 2, pp. 576–582, 2012.

[19] M. T. García-Álvarez, I. Novo-Corti, and L. Varela-Candamio, "The effects of social networks on the assessment of virtual learning environments: a study for social sciences degrees," *Telematics and Informatics*, 2017.

[20] B. Aslam and H. Karjaluoto, "Digital advertising around paid spaces, e-advertising industry's revenue engine: a review and research agenda," *Telematics and Informatics*, vol. 34, no. 8, pp. 1650–1662, 2017.

[21] U. Sumita and J. Zuo, "The impact of mobile access to the Internet on information search completion time and customer conversion," *Electronic Commerce Research and Applications*, vol. 9, no. 5, pp. 410–417, 2010.

[22] E. Crespo-Almendros and S. D. Barrio-García, "Online airline ticket purchasing: influence of online sales promotion type and Internet experience," *Journal of Air Transport Management*, vol. 53, pp. 23–34, 2016.

[23] G. A. Vásquez and E. M. Escamilla, "Best practice in the use of social networks marketing strategy as in SMEs," *Procedia-Social and Behavioral Sciences*, vol. 148, pp. 533–542, 2014.

[24] J. Deane and A. Agarwal, "Scheduling online advertisements to maximize revenue under variable display frequency," *Omega*, vol. 40, no. 5, pp. 562–570, 2012.

[25] A. Marinova, "Permission e-mail marketing: as a means of targeted promotion," *Cornell Hotel and Restaurant Administration Quarterly*, vol. 43, no. 1, pp. 61–69, 2002.

[26] J. Condit, "The suitability of web analytics key performance indicators in the academic library environment," *Journal of Academic Librarianship*, vol. 40, no. 1, pp. 25–34, 2014.

[27] M. L. Kent, B. J. Carr, R. A. Husted, and R. A. Pop, "Learning web analytics: a tool for strategic communication," *Public Relations Review*, vol. 37, no. 5, pp. 536–543, 2011.

[28] G. Lee, "Death of 'last click wins': media attribution and the expanding use of media data," *Journal of Direct, Data and Digital Marketing Practice*, vol. 12, no. 1, pp. 16–26, 2010.

[29] A. Nabout, B. Skiera, T. Stepanchuk, and E. Gerstmeier, "An analysis of the profitability of fee-based compensation

plans for search engine marketing," *International Journal of Research in Marketing*, vol. 29, no. 1, pp. 68–80, 2012.

[30] J. Royle and A. Laing, "The digital marketing skills gap: Developing a Digital Marketer Model for the communication industries," *International Journal of Information Management*, vol. 34, no. 2, pp. 65–73, 2014.

[31] A. A. Ahangar and S. Z. Dastuyi, "Persuasive language in the subgenre of Persian sales e-mails," *Language and Communication*, vol. 53, pp. 69–86, 2017.

[32] K. Kim and E. Tse, "Inferior search engine's optimal choice: knowledge-sharing service versus search quality," *Electronic Commerce Research and Applications*, vol. 13, no. 6, pp. 387–401, 2014.

[33] A. Chong, F. Chan, and O. Keng-Boon, "Predicting consumer decisions to adopt mobile commerce: cross country empirical examination between China and Malaysia," *Decision Support Systems*, vol. 53, no. 1, pp. 34–43, 2012.

[34] T. S. Teo, "Demographic and motivation variables associated with Internet usage activities," *Internet Research*, vol. 11, no. 2, pp. 125–137, 2011.

[35] L. A. Jackson, K. S. Ervin, P. D. Gardner, and N. Schmitt, "Gender and the Internet: women communicating and men searching," *Sex Roles*, vol. 44, no. 5-6, pp. 363–379, 2011.

[36] S. J. Chang, A. van Witteloostuijn, and L. Eden, "From the editors: common method variance in international business research," *Journal of International Business Studies*, vol. 41, no. 2, pp. 178–184, 2010.

[37] P. M. Podsakoff, S. B. MacKenzie, J. Y. Lee, and N. P. Podsakoff, "Common method biases in behavioral research: a critical review of the literature and recommended remedies," *Journal of Applied Psychology*, vol. 88, no. 5, pp. 879–903, 2003.

[38] C. Wang, S. Chow, Q. Wang, K. Ren, and W. Lou, "Privacy-preserving public auditing for secure cloud storage," *IEEE Transactions on Computers*, vol. 62, no. 2, pp. 362–375, 2013.

[39] C. M. Ringle, S. Wende, and J. M. Becker, "SmartPLS 3. Bonningstedt: SmartPLS," 2015, http://www.smartpls.com.

[40] J. Y. Son and I. Benbasat, "Organizational buyers' adoption and use of B2B electronic marketplaces: efficiency- and legitimacy-oriented perspectives," *Journal of Management Information Systems*, vol. 24, no. 1, pp. 55–99, 2007.

[41] W. W. Chin and P. R. Newsted, "Structural equation modeling analysis with small samples using partial least squares," in *Statistical Strategies for Small Sample Research*, R. H. Hoyle, Ed., pp. 307–341, Sage Publications, Thousand Oaks, CA, USA, 1999.

[42] B. Rodríguez Herráez, D. Pérez Bustamante, and J. R. Saura Lacarcel, "Information classification on social networks. Content analysis of e-commerce companies on Twitter. Clasificación de información en redes sociales. Análisis de contenido en Twitter de empresas de comercio electrónico Espacios," *Revista Espacios*, vol. 38, no. 52, 2017.

[43] W. Reinartz, M. Haenlein, and J. Henseler, "An empirical comparison of the efficacy of covariance-based and variance-based SEM," *International Journal of Research in Marketing*, vol. 26, no. 4, pp. 332–344, 2009.

[44] W. W. Chin, "The partial least squares approach to structural equation modeling," in *Modern Methods for Business Research*, G. A. Marcoulides, Ed., pp. 295–336, Lawrence Erlbaum Associates, Publisher, Mahwah, NJ, USA, 1998.

[45] T. Cui, H. Ye, H. H. Teo, and J. Li, "Information technology and open innovation: a strategic alignment perspective," *Information and Management*, vol. 52, no. 3, pp. 348–358, 2015.

[46] D. Sedera, S. Lokuge, V. Grover, S. Sarker, and S. Sarker, "Innovating with enterprise systems and digital platforms: a contingent resource-based theory view," *Information and Management*, vol. 53, no. 3, pp. 366–379, 2016.

[47] K. Wang, "Determinants of mobile value-added service continuance: the mediating role of service experience," *Information and Management*, vol. 52, no. 3, pp. 261–274, 2015.

[48] P. R. Palos-Sanchez, E. Martín Cumbreño, and J. A. Folgado Fernandez, "Factores Condicionantes Del Marketing Móvil: Estudio Empírico De La Expansión de las apps. El caso de la ciudad de Cáceres," *Revista de Estudios Económicos y Empresariales*, vol. 28, pp. 37–72, 2016.

[49] P. R. Palos-Sanchez, F. J. Arenas-Marquez, and M. Aguayo-Camacho, "Cloud Computing (SaaS) adoption as a strategic technology: results of an empirical study," *Mobile Information Systems*, vol. 2017, Article ID 2536040, 20 pages, 2017.

[50] T. Oliveira, M. Thomas, and M. Espadanal, "Assessing the determinants of cloud computing adoption: an analysis of the manufacturing and services sectors," *Information and Management*, vol. 51, no. 5, pp. 497–510, 2014.

[51] C. M. Messerschmidt and O. Hinz, "Explaining the adoption of grid computing: an integrated institutional theory and organizational capability approach," *Journal of Strategic Information Systems*, vol. 22, no. 2, pp. 137–156, 2013.

[52] Z. Yang, Y. Shi, and B. Wang, "Search engine marketing, financing ability and firm performance in e-commerce," *Procedia Computer Science*, vol. 55, pp. 1106–1112, 2015.

[53] P. Palos-Sanchez, J. M. Hernandez-Mogollon, and A. Campon Cerro, "The behavioral response to location based services: an examination of the influence of social and environmental benefits, and privacy," *Sustainability*, vol. 9, no. 11, p. 1988, 2017.

[54] E. G. Carmines and R. A. Zeller, *Reliability and Validity Assessment*, Sage Publications, Beverly Hills, CA, USA, 1979.

[55] D. Barclay, C. Higgins, and R. Thompson, "The partial least squares (PLS) approach to causal modelling: personal computer adoption and use as an illustration," *Technology Studies, Special Issue on Research Methodology*, vol. 2, no. 2, pp. 285–309, 1995.

[56] K. A. Bollen, *Structural Equations with Latent Variables*, John Wiley & Sons, New York, NY, USA, 1989.

[57] O. Götz, K. Liehr-Gobbers, and M. Krafft, "Evaluation of structural equation models using the partial least squares (PLS) approach," in *Handbook of Partial Least Squares*, pp. 691–711, Springer, Heidelberg, Berlin, Germany, 2010.

[58] J. Hair, B. Babin, A. Money, and P. Samouel, *Fundamentos de métodos de pesquisa emadministração*, Bookman Companhia, Sao Paulo, Brazil, 2005.

[59] C. Fornell and D. F. Larcker, "Evaluating structural equation models with unobservable variables and measurement error," *Journal of Marketing Research*, vol. 18, no. 1, pp. 39–50, 1981.

[60] J. Henseler, C. M. Ringle, and R. R. Sinkovics, "The use of partial least squares path modeling in international marketing," *Advances in International Marketing*, vol. 20, no. 1, pp. 277–319, 2009.

[61] R. F. Falk and N. B. Miller, *A Primer for Soft Modeling*, University of Akron Press, Akron, OH, USA, 1992.

[62] R. G. D. Steel and J. H. Torrie, *Principles and Procedures of Statistics with Special Reference to the Biological Sciences*, pp. 187–287, McGraw-Hill, New York, NY, USA, 1960.

[63] T. Mavridis and A. L. Symeonidis, "Identifying valid search engine ranking factors in a Web 2.0 and Web 3.0 context for building efficient SEO mechanisms," *Engineering Applications of Artificial Intelligence*, vol. 41, pp. 75–91, 2015.

[64] D. Qiao, J. Zhang, Q. Wei, and G. Chen, "Finding competitive keywords from query logs to enhance search engine advertising," *Information and Management*, vol. 54, no. 4, pp. 531–543, 2017.

[65] D. Chaffey and M. Patron, "From WA to DM optimization: increasing the commercial value of digital analytics," *Journal of Direct, Data and Digital Marketing Practice*, vol. 14, no. 1, pp. 30–45, 2012.

[66] F. Calisir and D. Karaali, "The impacts of banner location, banner content and navigation style on banner recognition," *Computers in Human Behavior*, vol. 24, no. 2, pp. 535–543, 2008.

[67] M. R. Baye, B. I. Santos, and M. R. Wildenbeest, "What's in a name? Measuring prominence, and its impact on organic traffic from search engines," *SSRN Electronic Journal*, 2012.

[68] K. Choudhari and V. K. Bhalla, "Video search engine optimization using keyword and feature analysis," *Procedia Computer Science*, vol. 58, pp. 691–697, 2015.

[69] R. Welling and L. White, "Web site performance measurement: promise and reality," *Managing Service Quality*, vol. 16, no. 6, pp. 654–670, 2006.

[70] J. P. Dotson, R. R. Fan, E. M. Feit, J. D. Oldham, and Y. Yeh, "Brand attitudes and search engine queries," *Journal of Interactive Marketing*, vol. 37, pp. 105–116, 2017.

[71] P. M. Fiorini and L. R. Lipsky, "Search marketing traffic and performance models," *Computer Standards and Interfaces*, vol. 34, no. 6, pp. 517–526, 2012.

[72] K. Li, G. Huang, and G. Bente, "The impacts of banner format and animation speed on banner effectiveness: evidence from eye movements," *Computers in Human Behavior*, vol. 54, pp. 522–530, 2016.

[73] B. J. Jansen and P. R. Molina, "The effectiveness of Web search engines for retrieving relevant e-commerce links," *Information Processing and Management*, vol. 42, no. 4, pp. 1075–1098, 2006.

[74] S. Huang, "The impact of context on display ad effectiveness: automatic attitude activation and applicability," *Electronic Commerce Research and Applications*, vol. 13, no. 5, pp. 341–354, 2014.

[75] Z. Yang, J. Sun, Y. Zhang, and Y. Wang, "Understanding SaaS adoption from the perspective of organizational users: a tripod readiness model," *Computers in Human Behavior*, vol. 45, pp. 254–264, 2015.

[76] J. H. Kahn, "Factor analysis in counseling psychology research, training, and practice: principles, advances, and applications," *The Counseling Psychologist*, vol. 34, no. 5, pp. 684–718, 2006.

[77] J. Lee, J. H. Ahn, and B. Park, "The effect of repetition in Internet banner ads and the moderating role of animation," *Computers in Human Behavior*, vol. 46, pp. 202–209, 2015.

[78] C. F. Hofacker and J. Murphy, "Clickable World Wide Web banner ads and content sites," *Journal of Interactive Marketing*, vol. 14, no. 1, pp. 49–59, 2000.

[79] M. Hudák, E. Kianičková, and R. Madleňák, "The importance of e-mail marketing in e-commerce," *Procedia Engineering*, vol. 192, pp. 342–347, 2017.

[80] A. Mandelli, "Banners, e-mail, advertainment and sponsored search: proposing a value perspective for online advertising," *International Journal of Internet Marketing and Advertising*, vol. 2, no. 1-2, p. 92, 2005.

[81] R. F. Wilson and J. B. Pettijohn, "Affiliate management software: a premier," *Journal of Website Promotion*, vol. 3, no. 1/2, pp. 118–130, 2008.

[82] B. Plaza, "Google analytics intelligence for information professionals," *Online*, vol. 34, no. 5, pp. 33–37, 2010.

[83] P. R. Palos-Sanchez, "El cambio de las relaciones con el cliente a través de la adopción de APPS: Estudio de las variables de influencia en M-Commerce," *Revista Espacios*, vol. 38, no. 23, 2017.

21

Deep Learning versus Professional Healthcare Equipment: A Fine-Grained Breathing Rate Monitoring Model

Bang Liu⊕, Xili Dai⊕, Haigang Gong, Zihao Guo, Nianbo Liu⊕, Xiaomin Wang, and Ming Liu⊕

Big Data Research Center, Department of Computer Science and Engineering,
University of Electronic Science and Technology of China, Chengdu, China

Correspondence should be addressed to Xili Dai; daixili_cs@163.com

Academic Editor: Pino Caballero-Gil

In mHealth field, accurate breathing rate monitoring technique has benefited a broad array of healthcare-related applications. Many approaches try to use smartphone or wearable device with fine-grained monitoring algorithm to accomplish the task, which can only be done by professional medical equipment before. However, such schemes usually result in bad performance in comparison to professional medical equipment. In this paper, we propose DeepFilter, a deep learning-based fine-grained breathing rate monitoring algorithm that works on smartphone and achieves professional-level accuracy. DeepFilter is a bidirectional recurrent neural network (RNN) stacked with convolutional layers and speeded up by batch normalization. Moreover, we collect 16.17 GB breathing sound recording data of 248 hours from 109 and another 10 volunteers to train and test our model, respectively. The results show a reasonably good accuracy of breathing rate monitoring.

1. Introduction

The emergence of mHealth draws much attention both in industry and academy [1]. Google, Microsoft, and Apple conduct a series of work on mHealth from hardware to software. Google is the first one to get involved in mHealth. In April 2012, Google released Google Glass [2] and applied it to healthcare in July 2013 [3]. Pristine declared to develop medical application for Google Glass. After that, Google accomplished the acquisition of a biotech company Lift Labs, which invented an electronic spoon to help Parkinson patients have food. In 2015, Google X announced that it was working on wearable suits which can exam cancer cell of users. In addition, Microsoft Band, Apple Watch, Fitbit, Jawbone, and more smart wearable devices bloom up everywhere.

There exists a broad array of healthcare-related applications on sleep monitoring by smart wearable devices [4]. They often aim at fine-grained breathing rate monitoring as a kind of nonobtrusive sleep monitoring for the understanding of users' sleep quality. Since inadequate and irregular sleep can lead to serious health problems such as

fatigue, depression, cardiovascular disease, and anxiety [5], breathing rate monitoring is critical to detect early signs of several diseases such as diabetes and heart disease [6]. The breathing rate monitoring can also be applied to the sleep apnea diagnosis and treatment, treatment for asthma [7], and sleep stage detection [8]. Thus, fine-grained breathing rate monitoring is important to facilitate these healthcare-related applications.

Traditionally, one's breathing rate can be captured by professional medical equipment as monitoring machines in hospitals. In most cases, such machines are too expensive, too complex, and too heavy for daily use for ordinary people. A possible solution is to achieve accurate sleep monitoring via smartphone or other devices with recognition algorithm [9], which is more and more popular in current healthcare-related applications. For example, Ren et al. [10] exploit the readily available smartphone earphone placed close to the user to reliably capture the human breathing sound. It cannot work if the earphone is apart from the user. Liu et al. [11] tracks the vital signs of both the breathing rate and the heart rate during sleep, by using off-the-shelf WiFi without any wearable or dedicated devices. However, the wearable devices cannot achieve approximative performance in comparison to professional medical equipment. The latter often has a much lower signal-to-noise ratio (SNR) and can achieve a much higher accuracy in breathing rate monitoring.

In this paper, we aim at developing a fine-grained breathing rate monitoring algorithm that works on smartphone and achieves professional-level accuracy. We propose a deep learning model such as DeepFilter, which can filter the breathing from low SNR data. We empirically exploit the framework of deep learning and apply it to the fine-grained breathing rate monitoring on smartphone. The deep learning model combines several convolutional layers and a bidirectional recurrent layer and is trained in an end-to-end manner using the cross entropy loss function. In addition, batch normalization is adapted to speedup the training. Moreover, we collect 16.17 GB breathing sound recording data of 248 hours from 109 and another 10 volunteers to train and test our model, respectively. The results show a reasonably good accuracy of breathing rate monitoring.

The main contributions of this paper are highlighted as follows:

(i) As to our best knowledge, we are the first to apply deep learning to fine-grained breathing rate monitoring, with low SNR data recognition.

(ii) We run real experiments on smartphone and verify the availability and performance of our model, which directly promotes the sleep monitoring applications in our daily lives.

2. Related Work

Since our scheme involves accurate sleep monitoring and deep learning, we mainly discuss the previous work on the two aspects.

Medical-based sleep-monitoring systems are often developed for clinical usage. In particular, polysomnography [12] is used in medical facilities to perform accurate sleep monitoring by attaching multiple sensors on patients, which requires professional installation and maintenance. It can measure many body functions during sleep, including breathing functions, eye movements, heart rhythm, and muscle activity. Such systems incur high cost and are usually limited to clinical usage. DoppleSleep [13] is a contactless sleep sensing system that continuously and unobtrusively tracks sleep quality, by using commercial off-the-shelf radar modules.

Some smartphone apps, such as Sleep as Android, Sleep Cycle Alarm Clock, and iSleep [14], can perform low-cost sleep monitoring by using the smartphone built-in microphone and motion sensors. These apps, however, only support coarse-grained monitoring, such as the detection of body movements, coughing, and snoring [15], and utilizes the phone usage features such as the duration of phone lock to measure sleep duration. The Respiratory app [16] derives a person's respiratory rate by analyzing the movements of the users' abdomen when placing the phone between the users' rib cage and stomach. ApneaApp [17] is a contactless sleep apnea event detection system that works on smartphone, which does this

by transforming the phone into an active sonar system that emits frequency-modulated sound signals and listens to their reflections to capture the breathing movement. Ren et al. [10] exploit the readily available smartphone earphone placed close to the user to reliably capture the human breathing sound. Liu et al. [11] propose to track the vital signs of both the breathing rate and the heart rate during sleep by using off-the-shelf WiFi without any wearable or dedicated devices. There is still a gap between the performance of professional equipment and that of the approaches above.

Recently, deep neural networks are first used for better phone recognition [18], in which traditional Gaussian mixture models are replaced by deep neural networks that contain many layers of features and a very large number of parameters. Convolutional networks have also been found beneficial for acoustic models. Recurrent neural networks are beginning to be deployed in state-of-the-art recognizers [19] and work well with convolutional layers for the feature extraction [20]. We are inspired by the good performance of the previous work on speech recognition and introduce deep learning algorithm into the problem of fine-grained breathing rate monitoring [21].

3. DeepFilter

In this section, we introduce the whole framework of DeepFilter and investigate the training of the model in detail.

3.1. The Framework. Figure 1 shows the framework of DeepFilter. Our model is a RNN that begins with several convolutional input layers, followed by a fully connected layer and multiple recurrent (uni- or bidirectional) layers, and ends with an output layer. The network is trained end to end and is added batch normalization with cross entropy loss function.

In speech recognition, "end-to-end" is often used to support the training without aligned training labels, which does not involve the frame-level cross entropy loss function. In breathing rate monitoring, we first create frame-aligned training labels and translate them into a classification problem to decide whether the frames belong to inhaling/exhaling or not. Since one inhaling/exhaling event may involve several frames, we exploit recurrent layers to process input sequence, for the recurrent layers can capture the sequence information to improve the performance. Thus, the input/output sequence of our model is similar to that of speech recognition. The only difference is that the input and output sequences of speech recognition have different lengths while that of our model have the same length.

To one sample x^i and label y^i, sequence frames are sampled from training set $\chi = \{X^1, X^2, \ldots, X^N\}$, which generates some voice recordings of size N. We assume that X^i is a sound recording for 136 seconds (the sampling rate is 44100 Hz), and the duration of each frame is 40 ms (which is an empirical value that always used as window size in speech recognition) It can be divided into samples $X^i = \{x^1, x^2, \ldots, x^n\}$, and each sample $x^j = (x_1^j, x_2^j, \ldots, x_T^j)$ combines $T = 50$ frames. And one frame

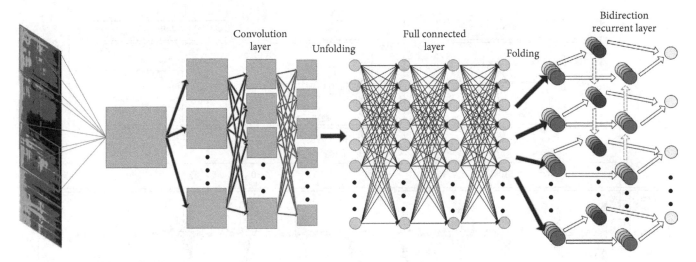

FIGURE 1: The deep learning framework of our model. The model is a bidirectional RNN, which begins with three convolutional layers (the third layer is mean pooling) and is followed by four fully connected layers. The data are translated into spectrogram as input to the network and are trained end to end.

$x_t^j = (x_{t,1}^j, x_{t,2}^j, \ldots, x_{t,f}^j)$ is a $f = 1764$ dimension vector $(44100/(1000/40) = 1764)$. Thus, a voice recording of 136 seconds can be divided into $n = 68$ samples $(136/2 = 68, 40\,\text{ms} * 50 = 2\,\text{s})$. Each sample x^j has a corresponding label sequence $y^j = (y_1^j, y_2^j, \ldots, y_T^j)$, $y_t^j = \{0, 1\}$, in which a frame without breathing is set to 0, and otherwise is set to 1. Generally, the goal of our processing is to convert an input sequence x^j into a 0-1 sequence.

The data described above are suitable as input for a RNN. However, our model is a RNN with several convolutional input layers, which requires the input to be in a two-dimensional structure. Thus, we split one 40 ms frame into 4 frames with 10 ms. Each 10 ms frame is translated from time domain to frequency domain through FFT, which produces a 220-dimension vector. Now, we translate a one-dimensional 40 ms frame into a two-dimensional spectrogram with the size of 220*4.

The main idea of our scheme is to differ the breathing events from the low SNR recordings. It needs to support the high-frequency signals for learning the fine-grained features in deep learning model. Thus, we use the sampling rate of 44100 Hz, which is the highest sampling rate of most smartphones on the market.

3.2. Batch Normalization for Deep Bidirectional RNNs. To efficiently absorb data, we increase the depth of the network by adding more convolution and fully connected layers. However, it becomes more challenging to train the network using gradient descent as the size and the depth increase; even the Adagrad algorithm could achieve limited improvement. We add batch normalization [22] to train the deeper network faster. Recent research has shown that batch normalization can speed convergence, though not always improving generalization error. In contrast, we find that when applied to very deep RNNs, it not only accelerates training but also substantially reduces final generalization error.

In a typical feed-forward layer containing an affine transformation followed by a nonlinearity $f(\cdot)$, we insert a batch normalization transformation by applying $f(Wh + b) \rightarrow f(\mathcal{B}(Wh))$, where

$$\mathcal{B}(x) = \gamma \frac{x - E(x)}{(\text{Var}[x] + \varepsilon)^{1/2}} + \beta, \tag{1}$$

in which the terms E and Var are the empirical mean and variance over a minibatch, respectively. The learnable parameters γ and β allow the layer to scale and shift each hidden unit as desired. The constant ε is small and positive and is included only for numerical stability. In our convolutional layers, the mean and variance are estimated over all the temporal output units for a given convolutional filter on a minibatch. The batch normalization transformation reduces *internal covariate shift* by insulating a given layer from potentially uninteresting changes in the mean and variance of the layers' input.

A recurrent layer is implemented as

$$\overrightarrow{h}_t^l = f\left(W^l h_t^{l-1} + \overrightarrow{U}^l \overrightarrow{h}_{t-1}^l + b^l\right)$$
$$\overleftarrow{h}_t^l = f\left(W^l h_t^{l-1} + \overleftarrow{U}^l \overleftarrow{h}_{t+1}^l + b^l\right), \tag{2}$$

where $\overrightarrow{h}_t^l$ and $\overleftarrow{h}_t^l$ are computed sequentially from $t = 1$ to $t = T$ and from $t = T$ to $t = 1$, respectively. And the $l + 1$ (nonrecurrent) layer takes both the forward and backward units as inputs $h_t^{l+1} = f(W^{l+1} h_t^l + b^{l+1})$, where $h_t^l = \overrightarrow{h}_t^l + \overleftarrow{h}_t^l$, and the activation function $f(x) = \min\{\max\{0, x\}, 20\}$ is the clipped ReLu.

There are two ways of applying batch normalization to recurrent operation:

$$h_t^l = f\left(\mathcal{B}(W^l h_t^{l-1} + U^l h_{t-1}^l)\right)$$
$$h_t^l = f\left(\mathcal{B}(W^l h_t^{l-1}) + U^l h_{t-1}^l\right), \tag{3}$$

where the first one indicates that the mean and variance statistics are accumulated over a single time step of the

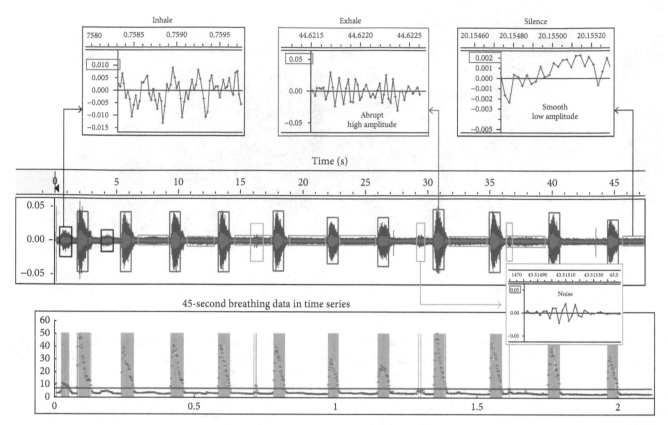

FIGURE 2: A snapshot shows how we label the data semiautomatically, which is motivated from the observation of the frequency and the amplitude of the data.

minibatch, which is ineffective in our study. We find that the second one works well, and Cooijmans et al. [23] have explained the reason.

3.3. Convolutions.
Temporal convolution is commonly used in speech recognition to efficiently model temporal translation invariance for variable length utterances. Convolution in frequency attempts to model spectral variance due to speaker variability more concisely than what is possible with large fully connected networks. We experiment with the use of convolutional layers from one to three. These are both in the time and frequency domains (two-dimensional) and in the time-only domain (one-dimensional).

Some previous works [24] demonstrated that multiple layers of two-dimensional convolution improve results substantially than one-dimensional convolution. And convolution has good performance on noisy data. A key point and necessity of low SNR data recognition is denoise [24]. Thus, the convolution component of the model is the key point for it to work well on low SNR data.

3.4. Bidirectional.
Recurrent model with only forward recurrences routinely performs worse than similar bidirectional ones, so that implying some amount of future context is vital for good performance. However, bidirectional recurrent models are challenging to be deployed in an online, low-latency setting because they cannot stream the

transcription process as the utterance arrives from the user. The DeepSpeech2 of Baidu [24] supports a special layer called lookahead convolution, which is a unidirectional model but without any loss in accuracy comparing to a bidirection one. In our study, we use the bidirectional recurrent model because we do not have the constraint of working in real time.

4. Fine-Grained Breathing Rate Monitoring

4.1. Training Data.
Large-scale deep learning systems require an abundance of labelled data. For our system, we need a lot of labelled low SNR data, but it is difficult to label the low SNR data. To train our large model, we first collect high SNR data (the data collected in a quiet surrounding in which breathing can be heard clearly), which are much easier to be labelled. After that, we combine the labelled data with pink noise to lower the SNR of the data through data synthesis, which has been successfully applied to data extensions of speech recognition.

Figure 2 is one high SNR sound recording of 45 seconds. The 11 red boxes mark 11 expirations, and the black, green, and blue boxes mark 2 inspirations, 8 silences, and 3 noises, respectively. When we enlarge the frames of expiration, inspiration, silence, and noise, it is obvious that the differences between adjacent points in a silence frame is much lower than that in the other three types of frame on average.

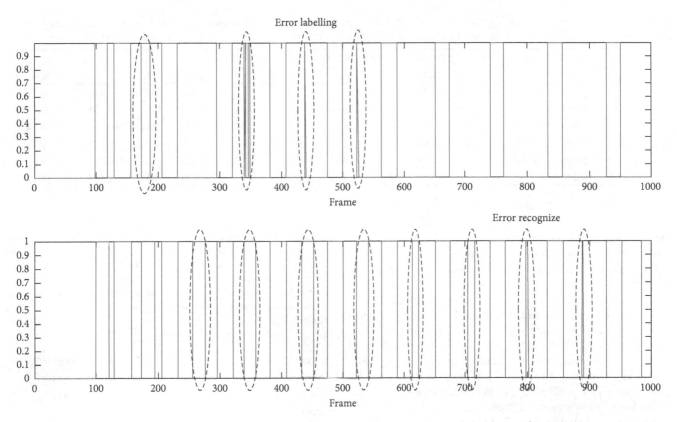

FIGURE 3: Postprocessing. A comparison between truth and test which shows the necessity of postprocessing.

And its amplitudes are also minimum, only 10^{-3}. Then, we give each frame a frame index $l(x^i)$ as follows:

$$l(x^i) = \sum_{t=1}^{n} |x_t^i| + |x_{t+1}^i - x_t^i|, \quad (4)$$

where x^i is the ith frame in data, $n = 1764$. The subfigure on the bottom of Figure 2 shows the label indexes of one sound recording (x-axis is frame and y-axis is the corresponding frame index). To facilitate observation, we add green lines on the frames whose index is larger than the threshold. It makes the label indexes to distinguish the silence frame from the other three types of frame well. For labelling the data, we erased the inspiration and noise manually (since it is a high SNR data, the volunteers are required to keep quiet during recording), and the threshold is also given manually. All the above actions are conducted in a sound processing software *Audacity* [25], and the thresholds and labels are determined on *Matlab*.

It took us 3 weeks for labelling about 7458 sound recordings (one recording is about 2 minutes, and the total recordings from 109 people are about 248 hours). Finally, we use *Audacity* to complete the data synthesis discussed above.

During the labelling, we find that the number of breathing frames is larger than that of nonbreathing frames, which may reduce the classification performance. Thus, we add a weight in loss function as follows:

$$Ł(\hat{y}, y) = \frac{1}{T} \sum_{t=1}^{T} [\eta y^t \ln \hat{y}^t + (1 - y^t) \ln(1 - \hat{y}^t)]. \quad (5)$$

4.2. Postprocessing. Figure 3 is a snapshot of 1000 continuous frames randomly chosen from training data, in which the top figure is the ground truth, while the bottom figure shows the recognition results from our model (the x-axis is the frame and the y-axis is the label value). As shown in the figure, breathing is continual and periodical, while the incorrectly labelled data and false-recognized frames are abrupt and discrete. Thus, we can define postprocessing as follows:

First, we can regard a breathing event as the continuous frames with breathing label. Thus, we delete the breathing events whose frame number is less than a threshold, which is the key point of postprocessing. In this study, we choose a value of 50 because a breathing time less than 0.5 s is abnormal according to our tests. As shown in Figure 3, the postprocessing could remove the green dotted-line cycle. The effect of postprocessing is shown in Table 2, and the values of TTR (Test ground-Truth Rate) can demonstrate its efficiency (TTR is a metric described in Section 5.3).

5. Experiment

5.1. Training. We train our deep RNN on 2 work stations with the configuration as follows: Intel Xeon processor E5-2620, 32 GB memory, standard AnyFabric 4 GB ethernet adapter, and Nvidia GTX Titan GPU with 12 GB memory. We use a PC as *parameter server* and 2 work stations as *workers*. Each individual machine sends gradient updates to the centralized parameter repository, which coordinates

TABLE 1: The results from 6 models: support vector machine (SVM), logistic regression (LR), DRNN (baseline), Model 1, Model 2, and Model 3. All of them are trained and tested on two data sets. The rightmost 4 columns are the average scores over the 4 distances.

	20 cm (0.8 m)		40 cm (0.95 m)		60 cm (1.1 m)		80 cm (1.25 m)					
	TPR	TNR	TPR	TNR	TPR	TNR	TPR	TNR	TPR	TNR	WAR	TTR (bmp)
SVM	0.897	0.923	0.787	0.920	0.402	0.843	0.316	0.820	0.601	0.876	0.807	0.53
LR	0.867	0.913	0.757	0.932	0.413	0.789	0.342	0.829	0.594	0.865	0.798	0.53
Baseline	0.994	**0.988**	0.948	0.916	0.509	0.925	0.461	0.947	0.715	0.944	0.886	0.64
DeepFilter 1	0.996	0.970	0.980	0.986	0.667	**0.932**	0.639	0.921	0.820	**0.952**	0.919	0.71
DeepFilter 2	**0.998**	0.965	0.981	**0.988**	**0.740**	0.910	0.703	0.900	0.855	0.943	0.921	**0.77**
DeepFilter 3	**0.998**	0.976	**0.998**	0.976	0.733	0.900	**0.710**	**0.921**	0.859	0.943	**0.922**	**0.77**

these updates and sends back updated parameters to the individual machines running the model training. We use a public deep learning library Tensorflow[?] to implement our system.

There are four deep learning models trained in our study. The baseline model is a unidirectional RNN with 4 hidden layers, and the last hidden layer is a recurrent layer. The framework is 882-2000-1000-500-100-1, and learning rates $\alpha = 10^{-5}$ without momentum. Training data are described in the previous section, and we take 40 ms as a frame and 50 frames as a group ($T = 50$). Other three models are also RNNs but begin with convolution layers. The detailed model parameters are listed in Table 2. The third line in the table is the number of hidden layers, respectively. The convolution in one dimension and that in two dimensions has different inputs. For the one-dimensional convolution, the input is a 40 ms frame and is translated to a frequency domain with 882 dimensions. The input of the two-dimensional convolution is a 40 ms frame too and is translated into a spectrogram (4×220). Then, one or two convolutional layers are followed with a mean pooling layer, and the mean pooling size is 3×2 (4×4 for one-dimensional mean pooling). All models have three fully connected layers, and each layer has 512 units. They are ended with two unidirectional recurrent layers except DeepFilter 3, which is ended with one bidirectional recurrent layer. All the models are trained through Adagrad with an initial learning rate $\alpha = 1e^{-3}$.

TABLE 2: Model parameters. The convolutional layer parameters are denoted as "⟨convolutional type⟩ conv ⟨receptive field size⟩ – ⟨number of channels⟩." Also, the parameters of recurrent layer are denoted as "⟨uni or bi⟩ – ⟨number of hidden units⟩," where "uni" denoted unidirectional recurrent and "bi" denoted bidirectional recurrent. The ReLU activation function is not shown for brevity.

Model configuration		
DeepFilter 1	DeepFilter 2	DeepFilter 3
6 weight	7 weight	6 weight
Layers	Layers	Layers
Input (882×50 sequence)	Input ($220 \times 4 \times 50$ spectrogram)	
One-dimension-conv9-16	Two-dimension-conv3-16	Two-dimension-conv3-16
	Two-dimension-conv3-32	Two-dimension-conv3-32
	Mean pool	
	FC-512	
	FC-512	
	FC-512	
Uni-128	Uni-128	Bi-128
Uni-128	Uni-128	—
	$\alpha = 1e^{-3}$	
	Output: sigmod	
	Loss: cross-entropy	

5.2. Experimental Data. Figure 4 shows the procedure of data collection. In Figure 4(a), the volunteer sits in front of the desk, and four smartphones are placed on the desk with a distance of 0.2 m, 0.4 m, 0.6 m, and 0.8 m from the margin of the desk, respectively (the distances from the volunteer's nose to smartphones are far enough, which reach 0.6 m, 0.85 m, 1.0 m, and 1.2 m, resp.). The further the distance is, the lower the SNR is, and the more difficult the labelling of data is. We make four smartphones to possess the same label by collecting data in synchronization, while it is easy to label the nearest one. In Figure 4(b), the volunteer sits in front of the desk, with four smartphones on the desk with a distance of 0.4 m from the margin of the desk, with 4 different angles ±30° and ±60°. We collect 10 volunteers' breathing data, each including 2 minutes tests as Figures 4(a) and 4(b), respectively, and label them finally.

We find some differences on the smartphone with different manufacturers. A funny discovery is from iPhone 4s. iPhone 4s has much worse ability to collect sound recording like breathing, since the built-in microphone has a filter function that can filter the low-frequency noise before recording. This function is developed to improve the quality of voice conversations. We test some smartphones from different manufacturers such as OnePlus, Huawei Honor, Mi, Meizu, Oppo, and Vivo and finally find that 4 Mi smartphones can collect more intact data. Consequently, we choose 4 Mi smartphones with the same band, for removing the unexpecting hardware diversities in experiments.

5.3. Results. There are four metrics to measure the performance of an algorithm in Table 1. TPR (true positive rate),

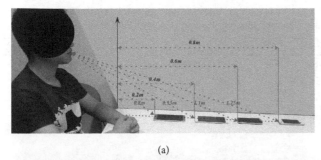

(a)

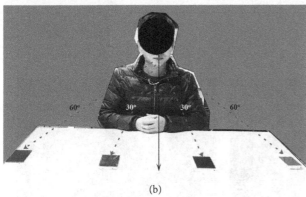

(b)

FIGURE 4: Collecting the test data. (a) Four smartphones in different distances. (b) Four smartphones in different angles.

TNR (true negative rate), WAR (whole accuracy rate), and TTR. There are two classes of samples in our data set: breathing frames (positive samples) and nonbreathing frames (negative samples). TPR is a recognition accuracy on positive samples, while TNR is a recognition accuracy on negative samples. And WAR is the recognition accuracy on the whole data set. After recognizing from deep learning model, breathing frames are calculated into TTR. Here, TTR is a measure of breathing rate, which is defined as a/b, where "a" is the breathing rate calculated by postprocessing and "b" is the ground-truth breathing rate. Table 1 also lists the TPR and TNR of four distances respectively, and it shows that the number of positive samples is quadruple the number of negative ones. That is to say the recognition accuracy of negative samples is much higher than that of positive samples.

We can obtain five results from Table 1 as follows: first, the deep learning models exhibit advantages on precise recognition in comparison to SVM and LR. The superiority increases with the decrease of SNR of the data. Second, the convolution exhibits good performance according to the results of our models and baseline. The two-dimensional convolution is better than the one-dimensional convolution, which demonstrates the ability of feature representation of convolution. And, the frequency domain (two-dimensional) provides more information than the time domain (one-dimensional). It is said that the convolutional layer brings the most improvement on accuracy of recognition. Third, the bidirectional recurrent layer is better than the unidirectional one, according to the results of DeepFilter 2 and DeepFilter 3. It means that not only the history information but also the future information can improve the accuracy of recognition.

In practice, the improvement of the bidirectional recurrent layer is limited, which is not much than that of convolution. Fourth, the results of baseline, DeepFilter 1, DeepFilter 2, and DeepFilter 3 demonstrate that the convolution is performed well in both time and frequency domains. And the performance of negative samples (TNR) is much better than that of positive samples in deep learning models. Finally, DeepFilter 3 obtains the best result in most cases, especially for lower SNR data. And the results from DeepFilter 1 to DeepFilter 3 demonstrate that the convolutional layer and the recurrent layer are not conflicts but boost each other in our problem.

In Table 1, there are significant differences between 40 cm and 60 cm with respect to the recognition accuracy. Since the SNR of breathing recordings decreases exponentially with the increasing of distance, TTR can directly indicate the performance of fine-grained breathing rate monitoring. As we see, the TTR of DeepFilter 3 is close to that of DeepFilter 2, and the TTR values of 6 algorithms are less than other three metric values. It implies that one breathing event is separated by some misclassified frames, in which each part is less than 5 frames. Since such breathing events are removed by postprocessing, the TTR values of 6 algorithms are less than other three metric values.

Table 3 lists four related vital sign monitoring methods, including ApneaAPP [17], FMBS [10], WiFi-RF [11], and DoppleSleep [13]. All the four vital sign monitoring methods belong to contactless sleep monitoring systems, which involve breathing frequency detection. The column "Modalities" lists the method of the system used. "RiP-L" and "RiP-U" are the lower bound and the upper bound of accuracy of the system in the corresponding papers, and "bmp" is the unit which means the difference between the rate detected by the system and the actual rate. "RiO-TTR" is the result that we reproduce in the four methods with our data on the metric "TTR." Different from our work, WiFi-RF and DoppleSleep need extra device to assist breathing monitoring while our system only requires the off-the-shelf smartphone. ApneaAPP uses frequency-modulated continuous wave (FMCW) to capture the breathing frequency. We reproduced the method but obtained poor results (as shown in the first line of the last column of Table 3, < 0.2 means less than 0.2). The reason lies in that FMCW needs the device to transmit ultrasonic, and the higher the frequency of ultrasonic is used, the better the results are found. Most smartphones only support ultrasonic less than 20 kHz, which cannot provide enough accuracy in practical (only 0.2 accuracy can be achieved in our reproduced scheme, which is much lower than the 0.98 listed in paper). FMBS is the only method using voice recording, which is most similar to our work. FMBS uses earphone to reinforce voice recordings of the users during the night and adopts envelope detection to assist the breathing detection. But, it is a coarse-grained breathing detector, which only achieves a low TTR value as 0.53 when it is running on our voice recordings. As so far, there are no any other works using smartphone on fine-grained breathing rate monitoring of voice recordings. WiFi-RF and DoppleSleep use WiFi radio frequency and extra device to capture breathing, respectively, which may

TABLE 3: The comparisons of several breathing rate monitoring techniques. "RiP-L" and "RiP-U" are the lower and upper bounds of accuracy in the papers, respectively. "RiO-TTR" is the result that we obtained by reproducing the methods with our data on metric "TTR."

Related methods	Modalities	RiP-L (bmp)	RiP-U (bmp)	RiO-TTR (bmp)
ApneaAPP [17]	Ultrasonic	<0.98	**>0.996**	>0.2
FMBS [10]	Voice recording	<0.5	>0.95	0.53
WiFi-RF [11]	Radio frequency	<0.6	>0.8	—
DoppleSleep [13]	Radar module	<0.786	>0.893	—

TABLE 4: The results of four angles.

Angles	±30°	−30°	±60°	−60°
Accuracy ratio	95.01%	94.50%	91.67%	92.81%

(a)

(b)

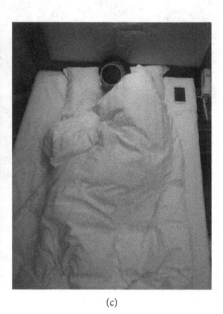
(c)

FIGURE 5: Sleep test.

achieve acceptable accuracy but are not suitable for breathing monitoring based on smartphones.

We can find that the TTR of DeepFilter is 0.77 in Table 1, which is better than 0.53 of FMBS [10]. It means our deep learning algorithm can achieve comparable performance of several professional devices.

We also list the recognition accuracies of four distances in Figure 4(a) and four angles in Figure 4(b). As shown in Table 1, the accuracy is reducing with the raising of distance. An interesting phenomenon of accuracy is dramatically declined on 80 cm, which may be an explanation of critical point of SNR. We will conduct further study on it in our future work. And the results of accuracy ratio affected by different angles are listed in Table 4, which shows a tiny influence on accuracy by different angles.

The precision of polysomnography requires over 99% which is the standard in sleep quality monitoring. In practice, DeepFilter can achieve 90% accuracy in 1 meter but lower than 80% in 2 meters. The 2-meter monitoring distance is sufficient for most fine-grained breathing rate monitoring applications. In most cases, the apps can work well within 1 meter as monitoring distance.

TABLE 5: The results of sleep test.

	TPR	TNR	WAR	TTR
Flat	80.00%	92.10%	90.10%	0.77
Right	94.60%	98.80%	97.20%	0.84
Left	78.70%	87.90%	86.20%	0.69

5.4. Realistic Test. Figure 5 shows the procedure of realistic sleep test, and the results are shown in Table 5. The volunteer lies on the bed, and the smartphone is placed at the side of the pillow. The smartphone records the breathing of the volunteer, and another camera records the procedure. The test lasts for 7 hours, and finally we collect enough dirty data. It includes the snore, the voice of turning, and other unknown voices from outside. We choose three voice clips that include three poses shown in Figure 5 and obtain the relatively clean data (the environment is usually quite during sleep, so that high SNR data are easy to find). The three clips last for 23, 25, and 22 minutes, respectively. We labelled the data by hand and run our model to validate the effectiveness. The results shown in Table 5 prove that our method achieves fine-grained breathing rate monitoring in realistic sleep. And we will conduct more realistic experiments on smartphones and other mobile devices in the near future.

6. Conclusion

In this paper, we try to apply deep learning as fine-grained breathing rate monitoring technique to smartphones for people's daily sleep quality monitoring. We propose DeepFilter, a bidirectional RNN stacked with convolutional layers and speeded up by batch normalization, to perform this task. The desirable results of experiments and realistic sleep test prove that our model achieves professional-level accuracy, and deep learning-based breathing rate monitoring apps on smartphones are promising. Our work also extends the use of deep learning to low SNR data recognition, which is inspiring for more data-processing applications.

In our future work, we will exploit more data to train DeepFilter. It implies that DeepFilter needs to suit more smartphones from different manufacturers. And more robust algorithms of postprocessing should be developed. Then, we will also try more deep learning models to solve our problem. And we will deploy the approaches on smartphones and other mobile devices in the near future.

References

[1] World Health Organization, "mHealth: new horizons for health through mobile technologies," *Social Indicators Research*, vol. 64, no. 7, pp. 471–493, 2011.

[2] T. Arnold, "Google glass," *Alaska Business Monthly*, vol. 56, pp. 1307–1321, 2013.

[3] U. V. Albrecht, U. Von Jan, J. Kuebler et al., "Google glass for documentation of medical findings: evaluation in forensic medicine," *Journal of Medical Internet Research*, vol. 16, no. 2, p. e53, 2014.

[4] M. Tomlinson, M. Jane Rothcramborus, L. Swartz, and A. C. Tsai, "Scaling up mhealth: where is the evidence?," *PLoS Medicine*, vol. 10, no. 2, p. e1001382, 2012.

[5] J. M. Parish, "Sleep-related problems in common medical conditions," *Chest*, vol. 135, no. 2, pp. 563–572, 2009.

[6] J. E. Shaw, N. M. Punjabi, J. P. Wilding, K. G. M. M. Alberti, and P. Z. Zimmet, "Sleep-disordered breathing and type 2 diabetes: a report from the international diabetes federation taskforce on epidemiology and prevention," *Diabetes Research and Clinical Practice*, vol. 81, no. 1, pp. 2–12, 2008.

[7] P. X. Braun, C. F. Gmachl, and R. A. Dweik, "Bridging the collaborative gap: realizing the clinical potential of breath analysis for disease diagnosis and monitoring-ctutorial," *IEEE Sensors Journal*, vol. 12, no. 11, pp. 3258–3270, 2012.

[8] G. S. Chung, B. H. Choi, K. K. Kim et al., "REM sleep classification with respiration rates," in *Proceedings of International Special Topic Conference on Information Technology Applications in Biomedicine*, pp. 194–197, Tokyo, Japan, November 2007.

[9] H. M. S. Hossain, N. Roy, and A. Al Hafiz Khan, "Sleep well: a sound sleep monitoring framework for community scaling," in *Proceedings of IEEE International Conference on Mobile Data Management*, pp. 44–53, Pittsburgh, PA, USA, 2015.

[10] Y. Ren, C. Wang, J. Yang, and Y. Chen, "Fine-grained sleep monitoring: hearing your breathing with smartphones," in *Proceedings of INFOCOM 2015*, pp. 1194–1202, Kowloon, Hong Kong, April 2015.

[11] J. Liu, Y. Wang, Y. Chen, J. Yang, X. Chen, and J. Cheng, "Tracking vital signs during sleep leveraging off-the-shelf wifi," in *Proceedings of the 16th ACM International Symposium on Mobile Ad Hoc Networking and Computing (MobiHoc 15)*, pp. 267–276, New York, NY, USA, 2015.

[12] T. Morgenthaler, C. A. Alessi, D. Bailey, J. Coleman Jr., C. A. Kushida, and M. R. Littner, "Practice parameters for the indications for polysomnography and related procedures: an update for 2005," *Sleep*, vol. 28, no. 4, pp. 499–521, 2005.

[13] T. Rahman, A. T. Adams, R. Vinisha Ravichandran et al., "DoppleSleep: a contactless unobtrusive sleep sensing system using short-range doppler radar," in *Proceedings of ACM International Joint Conference on Pervasive and Ubiquitous Computing*, pp. 39–50, Osaka, Japan, September 2015.

[14] T. Hao, G. Xing, and G. Zhou, "iSleep: unobtrusive sleep quality monitoring using smartphones," in *Proceedings of ACM Conference on Embedded Networked Sensor Systems*, pp. 1–14, Rome, Italy, November 2013.

[15] Z. Chen, M. Lin, F. Chen, and N. D. Lane, "Unobtrusive sleep monitoring using smartphones," in *Proceedings of the ICTs for improving Patients Rehabilitation Research Techniques*, pp. 145–152, Brussels, Belgium, 2013.

[16] AppCrawir, "Respiratory rate," 2014, http://appcrawlr.com/ios/respiratory-rate.

[17] R. Nandakumar, S. Gollakota, and N. Watson, "Contactless sleep apnea detection on smartphones," in *Proceedings of International Conference on Mobile Systems, Applications, and Services*, pp. 45–57, Florence, Italy, May 2015.

[18] A. R. Mohamed, G. E. Dahl, and G. Hinton, "Acoustic modeling using deep belief networks," *IEEE Transactions on Audio Speech and Language Processing*, vol. 20, no. 1, pp. 14–22, 2012.

[19] A. Graves, A.-R. Mohamed, and G. Hinton, "Speech recognition with deep recurrent neural networks," in *Proceedings of IEEE International Conference on Acoustics, Speech and Signal Processing*, pp. 6645–6649, Vancouver, Canada, May 2013.

[20] A. Hannun, C. Case, J. Casper et al., "Deep speech: Scaling up end-to-end speech recognition," *Computer Science*, 2014, in press.

[21] T. N. Sainath, O. Vinyals, A. Senior, and H. Sak, "Convolutional, long short-term memory, fully connected deep neural networks," in *Proceedings of IEEE International Conference on Acoustics*, pp. 4580–4584, Queensland, Australia, 2015.

[22] S. Ioffe and C. Szegedy, "Batch normalization: accelerating deep network training by reducing internal covariate shift," in *International Conference on Machine Learning*, Lille, France, July 2015.

[23] T. Cooijmans, N. Ballas, Laurent, and A. Courville, "Recurrent batch normalization," 2016.

[24] D. Amodei, R. Anubhai, E. Battenberg et al., "Deep speech 2: end-to-end speech recognition in english and mandarin," in *International Conference on Machine Learning*, New York, NY, USA, June 2016.

[25] Audacity, "Audacity," 2015, http://www.audacityteam.org/.

Permissions

List of Contributors

Xavier Ferre, Elena Villalba-Mora, Alberto Sanchez, Williams Aguilera and Francisco del Pozo-Guerrero
Center for Biomedical Technology, Universidad Politécnica de Madrid, Madrid, Spain

Xavier Ferre and Qin Liu
School of Software Engineering, Tongji University, Shanghai, China

Maria-Angeles Caballero-Mora, Nuria Garcia-Grossocordon, Laura Nuñez-Jimenez and Leocadio Rodríguez-Mañas
Servicio de Geriatría, Hospital Universitario de Getafe, Getafe, Madrid, Spain

Francisco del Pozo-Guerrero
Biomedical Research Networking Center in Bioengineering Biomaterials and Nanomedicine (CIBER-BBN), Madrid, Spain

Yi Meng, Chen Qing Kui and Zhang Gang
School of Management, University of Shanghai for Science and Technology, Shanghai, China

Chen Qing Kui
School of Optical Electrical and Computer Engineering, University of Shanghai for Science and Technology, Shanghai, China

Linyuan Xia, Qiumei Huang and Dongjin Wu
School of Geography and Planning, Sun Yat-Sen University, Guangzhou, China

Yea Som Lee and Bong-Soo Sohn
School of Computer Science and Engineering, Chung-Ang University, Seoul, Republic of Korea

Aysun Bozanta and Birgul Kutlu
Department of Management Information Systems, Bogazici University, Istanbul 34342, Turkey

Almudena Ruiz-Iniesta
Universidad Internacional de La Rioja, Logroño, Spain

Luis Melgar
Banco Bilbao Vizcaya Argentaria (BBVA), Bilbao, Spain

Alejandro Baldominos
Smile and Learn Digital Creations, Madrid 28043, Spain

Alejandro Baldominos and David Quintana
Department of Computer Science, Universidad Carlos III de Madrid, Av. de la Universidad 30, Leganés 28911, Spain

Junseop Lee
Department of School of Business, Yonsei University, 50 Yonsei-ro, Seodaemun-gu, Seoul, Republic of Korea

Jungmin Son
College of Economics and Management, Chungnam National University, 99 Daehak-ro, Yuseong-gu, Daejeon, Republic of Korea

H. Luna-Garcia, H. Gamboa-Rosales, J. I. Galván-Tejada, C. E. Galvan-Tejada, J. Arceo-Olague, A. Moreno-Baez, O. Alonso-González, F. E. Lopez-Monteagudo and R. Solis-Robles
Centro de Investigación e Innovación Automotriz de México (CIIAM), Universidad Autónoma de Zacatecas, Jardín Juárez 147, 98000 Centro Histórico, ZAC, Mexico

A. Mendoza-Gonzalez
Instituto de Investigación, Desarrollo e Innovación en Tecnologías Interactivas A.C. (IIDITI), Av. Moscatel 103, Aguascalientes, AGS, Mexico

R. Mendoza-Gonzalez
Depto. de Sistemas y Computación, Tecnologico Nacional de Mexico/Instituto Tecnologico de Aguascalientes, Av. Adolfo López Mateos 1801 Ote. Fracc. Bonagens, 20256 Aguascalientes, AGS, Mexico

J. M. Celaya-Padilla
CONACyT, Centro de Investigación e Innovación Automotriz de México (CIIAM), Universidad Autónoma de Zacatecas, Jardín Juárez 147, 98000 Centro Histórico, ZAC, Mexico

J. Lopez-Veyna
Depto. de Sistemas y Computación, Tecnologico Nacional de Mexico/Instituto Tecnologico de Zacatecas, Carretera Panamericana entronque a Guadalajara s/n, Zacatecas Centro, 98000 Zacatecas, ZAC, Mexico

Sultan Alamri
College of Computing and Informatics, SEU, Riyadh, Saudi Arabia

David Taniar
Clayton School of Information Technology, Monash
University, Melbourne, VIC, Australia

Kinh Nguyen
Department of Computer Science and Computer
Engineering, La Trobe University, Melbourne, VIC,
Australia

**Vladimir S. Kublanov, Mikhail V. Babich and Anton
Yu. Dolganov**
Research Medical and Biological Engineering Centre
of High Technologies, Ural Federal University, Mira
19, 620002 Yekaterinburg, Russia

**Chaoyang He, Nengpan Ju, Qiang Xu and Jianjun
Zhao**
State Key Laboratory of Geohazard Prevention and
Geoenvironment Protection, Chengdu University of
Technology, No. 1 Dongsanlu, Erxianqiao, Chengdu,
Sichuan 610059, China

Yanrong Li
College of Mining Engineering, Taiyuan University of
Technology, Taiyuan, Shanxi 030024, China

**Pablo Pancardo, J. A. Hernández-Nolasco and
Francisco Acosta-Escalante**
Informatics and Information System Academic
Division, Juarez Autonomous University of Tabasco,
Cunduacán, TAB, Mexico

Israr Ullah and DoHyeun Kim
Computer Engineering Department, Jeju National
University, Jeju City, Republic of Korea

Muhammad Sohail Khan
Department of Computer Software Engineering,
University of Engineering and Technology, Mardan,
Pakistan

Ghada Refaat El Said
Department of Management Information Systems,
Future University in Egypt (FUE), 90th Street, Fifth
Settlement, New Cairo, Egypt

Li Wang
College of Information Engineering, Zhejiang
University of Technology, Hangzhou, Zhejiang 310023,
China

Feng Li
School of Electronic Science and Engineering, Nanjing
University, Nanjing, Jiangsu 210023, China

**Moneeb Gohar, Naveed Khan, Awais Ahmad and
Muhammad Najam-Ul-Islam**
Department of Computer Science, Bahria University,
Islamabad, Pakistan

Shahzad Sarwar
College of Information Technology, Punjab University,
Lahore, Pakistan

Seok-Joo Koh
School of Computer Science and Engineering,
Kyungpook National University, Republic of Korea

Kwangtaek Kim
Department of Information and Telecommunication
Engineering, Incheon National University, Incheon,
Republic of Korea

Chunhua Zhu and Jiaojiao Wang
College of Information Science and Engineering,
Henan University of Technology, Zhengzhou, China

Hao Liu
Institute of Industrial Technology, Zhengzhou
University, Zhengzhou, China

Huan Mi
Department of Electronic Engineering, University of
York, York, UK

Seong-Wook Jang, Junho Ko and Yoon Sang Kim
BioComputing Lab, Department of Computer Science
and Engineering, Korea University of Technology
and Education (KOREATECH), Cheonan, Republic of
Korea

Hun Joo Lee
Creative Content Research Laboratory, ETRI, Daejeon,
Republic of Korea

Yoon Sang Kim
Institute for Bioengineering Application Technology,
Korea University of Technology and Education
(KOREATECH), Cheonan, Republic of Korea

Pedro R. Palos-Sanchez
Department of Business Management, University of
Extremadura, Av. Universidad, s/n, 10003 Cáceres,
Spain

Pedro R. Palos-Sanchez
Department of Business Organization, Marketing and
Market Research, International University of La Rioja,
Av. de la Paz 137, 26006 Logroño, Spain

Jose Ramon Saura
Department of Business and Economics, Rey Juan Carlos University, Madrid, Spain

Felipe Debasa
Department of Contemporary History and Actual World, Rey Juan Carlos University, Madrid, Spain

Bang Liu, Xili Dai, Haigang Gong, Zihao Guo, Nianbo Liu, Xiaomin Wang and Ming Liu
Big Data Research Center, Department of Computer Science and Engineering, University of Electronic Science and Technology of China, Chengdu, China

Index

CPSIA information can be obtained
at www.ICGtesting.com
Printed in the USA
BVHW091608160820
586552BV00002B/73